The

WEEKLY TORAH PORTION

EDITED BY

DAVID M. MORGAN, PhD

CHARISMA
HOUSE

Most Charisma House Book Group products are available at special quantity discounts for bulk purchase for sales promotions, premiums, fund-raising, and educational needs. For details, call us at (407) 333-0600 or visit our website at www.charismahouse.com.

THE WEEKLY TORAH PORTION
Edited by David M. Morgan, PhD
Published by Charisma House
Charisma Media / Charisma House Book Group
600 Rinehart Road, Lake Mary, Florida 32746

Library of Congress Cataloging-in-Publication Data

Names: Morgan, David M., editor.
Title: The weekly Torah portion / edited by David M. Morgan, PhD.
Description: Lake Mary : Charisma House, 2019.
Identifiers: LCCN 2019045503 (print) | LCCN 2019045504 (ebook) | ISBN 9781629997667 (hardcover) | ISBN 9781629997650 (ebook)
Subjects: LCSH: Bible. Pentateuch--Commentaries.
Classification: LCC BS1225.53 .W43 2019 (print) | LCC BS1225.53 (ebook) | DDC 296.7/2--dc23
LC record available at https://lccn.loc.gov/2019045503
LC ebook record available at https://lccn.loc.gov/2019045504

19 20 21 22 23 — 987654321

Printed in the United States of America

Table of Contents

Introduction

The secret things belong to the LORD our God, but those things which are revealed belong to us and to our children forever, so that we may keep all the words of this law.

—DEUTERONOMY 29:29

Do not think that I have come to abolish the Law or the Prophets. I have not come to abolish, but to fulfill. For truly I say to you, until heaven and earth pass away, not one dot or one mark will pass from the law until all be fulfilled. Whoever, therefore, breaks one of the least of these commandments and teaches others to do likewise shall be called the least in the kingdom of heaven. But whoever does and teaches them shall be called great in the kingdom of heaven.

—MATTHEW 5:17–19

For Moses has had in every city since early generations those who preach him, being read in the synagogues every Sabbath.

—ACTS 15:21

Shimon the Righteous was among the last surviving members of the Great assembly. He would say: The world stands on three things: Torah, the service of G-d, and deeds of kindness.

—PIRKEI AVOT 1:2

Once there was a gentile who came before Shammai, and said to him: "Convert me on the condition that you teach me the whole Torah while I stand on one foot. Shammai pushed him aside with the measuring stick he was holding. The same fellow came before Hillel, and Hillel converted him, saying: That which is despicable to you, do not do to your fellow [man], this is the whole Torah, and the rest is commentary, go and learn it."

—BABYLONIAN TALMUD, SHABBAT 31A

Throughout the centuries Jewish and Gentile people have been fascinated and transformed by Torah and the Hebrew Bible. The Torah (Law or Instruction) of G-d (YHWH or Hashem) teaches us how to revere and honor the Creator of the universe, even to the detail of how we spell, pronounce, and reference the Divine. The same veneration and awe are rightly given to what G-d speaks, namely His Torah. As noted in the quotes at the beginning of the Introduction, the significance of Torah was endearing and enduring as Jews and later Gentiles cherished Hebrew sacred literature throughout the ages.

Even before the Torah was composed and later copied meticulously by scribes, the importance of Torah was orally learned and disseminated by Jewish communities. This activity increased after the Babylonian captivity and when the Jews resettled in Israel under Ezra during the time of the Persian Empire in the fifth century BC. When synagogues increased during the Hellenistic period and these schools of learning became the epicenter of Jewish communities, on the Sabbath (Friday sunset to an hour after Saturday sunset) the rabbis led their congregations to recite and chant Torah passages. Because the synagogue served both as a house of worship (*beit k'nesset*) and a house of study (*beit midrash*), it was natural for this institution and place to be where the Torah readings, or *parashot*, would be developed. *Parasha* means portion, and the parashot (plural of *parasha*) Torah readings became the centerpiece of synagogue meetings on the Sabbath.

The ancient synagogue service had a structure and procedure that focused on Torah. Parasha readings were done on Monday, Thursday, and twice on Saturday Shabbat (Sabbath). The sixth-century AD Talmud posits that Moses and Ezra had Israel fast and recite Torah three days a week (see also Luke 18:12). The weekly Torah parasha was read at the beginning of the service and divided into seven *aliyot* (ascents) that proclaimed blessings to the congregation with respect to the origin and importance of Torah. This is often done even in modern synagogues by seven readers who lead the congregation in chanting the Shabbat parasha reading in seven sections. The prominence of Torah was not only theological but also geographical. Even in the Diaspora areas, archaeological evidence demonstrates that the Torah shrine was present in ancient synagogues outside the land of Israel. The Torah shrine in ancient synagogues was also constructed in the eastern wall and oriented toward Jerusalem. Both in the synagogue architecture and the religious performance, the Torah had pride of place.

The synagogue service concluded with a *haftarah* (parting) reading from the Prophets. It served as a dismissal of blessing and remembrance to conclude the service. These specific readings were paired with the Torah parasha Shabbat readings by the rabbis and were based largely on thematic coherence. Largely due to sacred attribution, the Torah parashot readings had greater regulation than the concluding haftarah readings. Although the historical origins and development of the haftarah readings in the synagogue largely escape us, there is documented evidence of its practice in Acts 13:15 when "the Law and Prophets" are read. It is probable that attempts at standardization for the Torah parashot and Prophetic *haftarot* (plural of *haftarah*) readings occurred during the Mishnaic or later periods (post–third century AD). Of course, as we will see, vagaries in Judaism are ever present, and the haftarot are no exception.

There are a few differences in the fifty-four Torah parashot readings based on culture, calendar, versification, tradition, and geography. Both Jews and Gentiles preserved Torah readings, but the latter used the Gregorian calendar, and the former the Hebrew calendar. In 1582 Pope Gregory XIII instituted a formal calendar (designed by the astronomer and philosopher Luigi Lilio) that superseded the Julian calendar inaugurated in 46 BC by Julius Caesar. His new Gregorian calendar was more accurate with respect to leap day but continued in the solar tradition of the Julian predecessor. Of course, having a calendar based on the sun is a departure from the lunisolar calendar used by the Jewish people, where both sun and moon cycles were incorporated. In addition the Gregorian calendar has only 365.2425 days in light of leap day, while the Hebrew calendar could have as few as 353 or as many as 385 days. As of this writing, the month on the Gregorian calendar is September 2019, while the Hebrew calendar is Elul 5779 and will be Tishrei 5780 on Rosh Hashanah in just a few days, on September 30. Although it does not affect the Torah parashot readings, there is both a civil Jewish calendar, with the new year in fall on Rosh Hashanah, and a religious calendar, with the new year in spring on Pesach, or Passover. The Hebrew calendar was designed by the twelfth-century Jewish philosopher Maimonides, who set the date of creation at 3761 BC, year 1 of the Hebrew calendar. Maimonides is also credited with the standard designations of the Torah parashot based on his use of the tenth-century Hebrew Aleppo Codex manuscript. These variations provide for quite distinct calendars that both Jews and Gentiles would follow in order to read and live out Torah. Accordingly, the appendixes will provide Torah parashot Sabbath readings that reflect both Gregorian and Hebrew calendrical systems.

The careful reader may note the occasional variance of verses between the Hebrew Bible and the English Bible. As an example, the Psalm titles in the Hebrew Bible are counted as verse 1, while English Bibles have verse 1 starting with the text. This versification distinction, among others that are larger in scope such as whole chapters being combined or separated, is generally attributed to English Bibles preferring the third-century BC Greek Septuagint and fourth-century AD Latin Vulgate versification systems. The Hebrew Bible versification varied less in its various traditions throughout the centuries. In modernity Jewish traditions such as Ashkenazi and Sephardic readings may vary slightly on versification, but the main parasha and haftarah passages are still read in both traditions.

In addition to Jewish and Gentile differences with respect to the calendrical systems and versification, tradition and geography play a role for the Jewish variances in the Torah parashot readings. While Ashkenazi (Eastern European) and Sephardic (Mediterranean) traditions both revere Torah, they differ in reading traditions, as there are some discrepancies in the passages and verses. For example, the haftarah Sabbath readings from the Prophets sometimes differ slightly, with the Ashkenazi readings typically a bit longer than the Sephardic. There are various liturgical and theological reasons for these Jewish traditions to have only slightly different reading lengths for the weekly Sabbath passages. For the calendrical cycles in this book, we have chosen the longer reading, reflecting the Ashkenazi tradition.

The last area of calendrical dissimilarity in Judaism involved whether a synagogue was in Israel or the Diaspora, areas outside the land of Israel or Palestine. In Israel, during Pesach (Passover) and Shavuot (Weeks, or Pentecost), the synagogue parashot are a week ahead. When a Jewish feast falls on a Sabbath, the Torah parasha reading is deferred in Israel until the subsequent Sabbath, but not in the Diaspora. Jews in the Diaspora also celebrate feasts for a second day, so this also alters the Diasporic calendar when compared with the Jewish calendar in Israel, where a feast is only celebrated for one day. It may be complicated to some, but at least we have historical and cultural reasons for why one Torah liturgical calendar may have slightly different parashot passages. The Torah parashot appendixes provided are based on the English versification, longer haftarah readings, and the Diasporic tradition.

There are fifty-four Torah Sabbath readings, but in non–leap years some parashot have to be doubled for a Shabbat service so that the entire Torah can be read during a calendar year. The end of the Torah reading cycle concludes on Simchat Torah (Rejoicing in Torah) with the reading of Parashat Vezot Haberakhah, which ends with Deuteronomy 34, and then the reading cycle begins with Parashat Bereshit (In the beginning) in Genesis 1. Therefore the Torah is read, chanted, and lived out yearly and in perpetuity.

There were specific regulations pertaining to Torah parashot. The medieval Jewish scholar Maimonides stated that any parasha error invalidated a Torah scroll, whether it was missing or simply out of place. He revered not only the actual text but even the space designations of the text. The strictness for how the Torah parashot should be read is not unlike the ancient designations of scribal copying of the Hebrew Bible. Great care and consideration was given to the reading of Torah just as the copying of Torah itself. The preservation and recitation of Torah was of paramount importance. From ancient scribes to Maimonides, Torah was held in the highest regard.

The Torah parashot also served as natural paragraph or reading divisions in Torah. Since Torah was read or chanted in the synagogue, the parashot served as textual breaks or pauses. This allowed for better mnemonic recall and understanding for synagogue communities as they learned Torah. There is a bit of subjectivity since the parashot differ slightly in the various Jewish manuscript and liturgical traditions, but the Dead Sea Scrolls and Masoretic

Text give us some indication that the Torah parashot were a reading strategy for how to interpret Torah in antiquity.

The Torah parashot were divided into open (parasha petuhah) and closed (parasha setumah) portions with paragraph markers. This scribal practice helped to provide thematic and interpretive aids to reading and understanding Torah. An open parasha started on a new line and transitioned into a new theme, while a closed parasha reading continued in the text and introduced a subtopic. Unfortunately, medieval Jewish traditions and manuscripts as well as modern formatted Hebrew Bibles (and even English versions) are inconsistent with these space and paragraph designations and thus obscure the ancient scribal intentions for open and closed parashot readings. Nevertheless these parashot paragraph markings help the rabbi and people to chant and learn Torah through thematic, interpretive, and mnemonic ancient textual divisions.

The smallest, yet quite significant, parasha in Exodus is Parashat Yitro (Jethro), Exodus 18:1–20:26, with the haftarah Isaiah 6:1–7:6; 9:6–7. The Torah portion has a section explaining Jethro's advice to Moses about organizing and judging the tribes of Israel, but it culminates with the Decalogue, or Ten Commandments. Curiously Isaiah 6 and 9 are pivotal prophetic passages regarding G-d's commission of Isaiah to be an emissary and the royal child born as a sign to Isaiah that G-d is indeed keeping His word to the nation of Judah. G-d Himself will fulfill His Decalogue with the promised child of Isaiah 7–9. As we read and study the parasha and haftarah readings, we can glean incredible insight as to how the Torah parashot and Prophetic haftarot play off each other with respect to messianic and kingdom expectations.

Regardless of whether one has tremendous or pedestrian knowledge of the Torah and the annual liturgical reading cycle, the appendixes provide great benefit for the person who wants to understand Torah, Judaism, and the theological trajectory of Jewish liturgy. There is expectation and fulfillment in these Torah readings. Israel was looking for G-d's provisions with respect to the land and covenant. These were ultimately embodied in Messiah Yeshua, who kept Torah and brought both Jew and Gentile into a new humanity (Eph. 2:15; Gal. 3:28). Nevertheless the expectation for fulfillment is still in effect as we are at this writing approaching the Jewish year 5780. Many of the ancient Jewish sources such as the Talmud see year 6000 as the expected age of Messiah.

In the appendix we have meticulously laid out weekly Torah parashot readings for the years 2020 and 2021, with the addition of the reading for Simchat Torah. For each parasha we provide the Gregorian calendar date, the transliterated name of the Hebrew parasha, the translation of the name, the associated Torah passage, and the haftarah, along with the page number for the beginning of the parasha. When a reading for a Jewish festival supersedes the parasha, it is noted in the table in a similar fashion. (To determine the parasha for dates in years other than 2020 and 2021, go to https://www.hebcal.com/sedrot/.) In the appendix there is also a separate table with the Torah and haftarah readings for the Sabbath of selected major Jewish festivals. This book includes all fifty-four Torah readings, using the Modern English Version of the Bible, with chapter and verse numbers removed for ease of reading. To find the parasha reading for the week, look for the appropriate date in the appendix and go to the page number provided.

We hope that you take great pleasure in the weekly Shabbat Torah parashot readings. Recite and meditate on these together with the haftarot so that the Torah and Prophets are read and understood together. Reading Scripture in a manner similar to Jesus and ancient Jewish and Christian communities builds mutual appreciation and respect for all who desire to worship G-d the Creator and Yeshua His Messiah.

BARUCH ATA ADONAI, ELOHEINU MELECH HA-OLAM
(BLESSED ARE YOU, LORD OUR GOD, KING OF THE UNIVERSE)

Bereshit

In the beginning

(Genesis 1:1–6:8)

I n the beginning God created the heavens and the earth. The earth was formless and void, darkness was over the surface of the deep, and the Spirit of God was moving over the surface of the water.

God said, "Let there be light," and there was light. God saw that the light was good, and God separated the light from the darkness. God called the light Day, and the darkness He called Night. So the evening and the morning were the first day.

Then God said, "Let there be an expanse in the midst of the waters, and let it separate the waters from the waters." So God made the expanse and separated the waters which were under the expanse from the waters which were above the expanse. And it was so. God called the expanse Heaven. So the evening and the morning were the second day.

Then God said, "Let the waters under the heavens be gathered together into one place, and let the dry land appear." And it was so. God called the dry land Earth, and the gathering together of the waters He called Seas. Then God saw that it was good.

Then God said, "Let the earth produce vegetation: plants yielding seed and fruit trees on the earth yielding fruit after their kind with seed in them." And it was so. The earth produced vegetation, plants yielding seed after their kind and trees yielding fruit with seed in them after their kind. And God saw that it was good. So the evening and the morning were the third day.

And God said, "Let there be lights in the expanse of the heavens to separate the day from the night, and let them be signs to indicate seasons, and days, and years. Let them be lights in the expanse of the heavens to give light on the earth." And it was so. God made two great lights: the greater light to rule the day and the lesser light to rule the night. He made the stars also. Then God set them in the expanse of the heavens to give light on the earth, to rule over the day and over the night, and to divide the light from the darkness. Then God saw that it was good. So the evening and the morning were the fourth day.

Then God said, "Let the waters swarm with swarms of living creatures and let the birds fly above the earth in the open expanse of the heavens." So God created great sea creatures and every living thing that moves, with which the waters swarmed, according to their kind, and every winged bird according to its kind. And God saw that it was good. Then God blessed them, saying, "Be fruitful and multiply and fill the waters in the seas, and let the birds multiply on the earth." So the evening and the morning were the fifth day.

Then God said, "Let the earth bring forth living creatures according to their kinds: livestock, and creeping things, and beasts of the earth according to their kinds." And it was so. So God made the beasts of the earth according to their kind, and the livestock according to their kind, and everything that creeps on the earth according to its kind. And God saw that it was good.

Then God said, "Let Us make man in Our image, after Our likeness, and let them have dominion over the fish of the sea, and over the birds of the air, and over the livestock, and over all the earth, and over every creeping thing that creeps on the earth."

> So God created man in His own image;
>   in the image of God He created him;
>   male and female He created them.

God blessed them and said to them, "Be fruitful and multiply, and replenish the earth and subdue it. Rule over the fish of the sea and over the birds of the air and over every living thing that moves on the earth." Then God said, "See, I have given you every plant yielding seed which is on the face of all the earth and every tree which has fruit yielding seed. It shall be food for you. To every beast of the earth and to every bird of the air and to everything that creeps on the earth which has the breath of life in it, I have given every green plant for food." And it was so.

God saw everything that He had made, and indeed it was very good. So the evening and the morning were the sixth day.

So the heavens and the earth, and all their hosts, were finished.

On the seventh day God completed His work which He had done, and He rested on the seventh day from all His work which He had done. Then God blessed the seventh day and made it holy, because on it He had rested from all His work which He had created and made.

This is the account of the heavens and the earth when they were created.

In the day that the LORD God made the earth and the heavens, no shrub of the field was yet on the earth, and no plant of the field had yet sprouted, for the LORD God had not caused it to rain on the earth, and there was no man to cultivate the ground. But a mist arose from the earth and watered the whole surface of the ground. Then the LORD God formed man from the dust of the ground and breathed into his nostrils the breath of life, and man became a living being.

The LORD God planted a garden in the east, in Eden, and there He placed the man whom He had formed. Out of the ground the LORD God made to grow every tree that is pleasant to the sight and good for food. The tree of life was also in the midst of the garden, along with the tree of knowledge of good and evil.

A river flowed out of Eden to water the garden, and from there it parted and became four rivers. The name of the first is Pishon; it encompasses the whole land of Havilah, where there is gold. The gold of that land is good; bdellium and the onyx stone are there. The name of the second river is Gihon; it encompasses the whole land of Cush. The name of the third river is Tigris; it goes toward the east of Assyria. The fourth river is the Euphrates.

The LORD God took the man and put him in the garden of Eden to till it and to keep it. And the LORD God commanded the man, saying, "Of every tree of the garden you may freely eat, but of the tree of the knowledge of good and evil you shall not eat, for in the day that you eat from it you will surely die."

Then the LORD God said, "It is not good that the man should be alone. I will make him a helper suitable for him."

Out of the ground the LORD God formed every beast of the field and every bird of the sky, and brought them to the man to see what he would call them. Whatever the man called every living creature, that was its name. The man gave names to all the livestock, to the birds of the sky, and to every beast of the field, but for Adam there was not found a helper suitable for him.

So the LORD God caused a deep sleep to fall on Adam, and he slept. Then He took one of his ribs and closed up the place with flesh. Then the rib which the LORD God had taken from man, He made into a woman, and He brought her to the man.

Then Adam said,

"This is now bone of my bones
    and flesh of my flesh;
she will be called Woman,
    for she was taken out of Man."

Therefore a man will leave his father and his mother and be joined to his wife, and they will become one flesh.

They were both naked, the man and his wife, and were not ashamed.

Now the serpent was more subtle than any beast of the field which the LORD God had made. And he said to the woman, "Has God said, 'You shall not eat of any tree of the garden'?"

And the woman said to the serpent, "We may eat of the fruit from the trees of the garden; but from the fruit of the tree which is in the midst of the garden, God has said, 'You will not eat of it, nor will you touch it, or else you will die.'"

Then the serpent said to the woman, "You surely will not die! For God knows that on the day you eat of it your eyes will be opened and you will be like God, knowing good and evil."

When the woman saw that the tree was good for food, that it was pleasing to the eyes and a tree desirable to make one wise, she took of its fruit and ate; and she gave to her husband with her, and he ate. Then the eyes of both were opened, and they knew that they were naked. So they sewed fig leaves together and made coverings for themselves.

Then they heard the sound of the LORD God walking in the garden in the cool of the day, and the man and his wife hid themselves from the presence of the LORD God among the trees of the garden. The LORD God called to the man and said to him, "Where are you?"

He said, "I heard Your voice in the garden and was afraid because I was naked, so I hid myself."

And He said, "Who told you that you were naked? Have you eaten from the tree of which I commanded you not to eat?"

The man said, "The woman whom You gave to be with me, she gave me *fruit* of the tree, and I ate."

Then the LORD God said to the woman, "What have you done?"

And the woman said, "The serpent deceived me, and I ate."

The LORD God said to the serpent: "Because you have done this,

You are cursed above all livestock,
　　and above every beast of the field;
you will go on your belly,
　　and you will eat dust
　　all the days of your life.
I will put enmity
　　between you and the woman,
　　and between your offspring and her offspring;
he will bruise your head,
　　and you will bruise his heel."

To the woman He said,

"I will greatly multiply your pain in childbirth,
    and in pain you will bring forth children;
your desire will be for your husband,
    and he will rule over you."

And to Adam He said, "Because you have listened to the voice of your wife and have eaten from the tree about which I commanded you, saying, 'You shall not eat of it,'

Cursed is the ground on account of you;
    in hard labor you will eat of it
    all the days of your life.
Thorns and thistles it will bring forth for you,
    and you will eat the plants of the field.
By the sweat of your face
    you will eat bread
until you return to the ground,
    because out of it you were taken;
for you are dust,
    and to dust you will return."

The man called his wife's name Eve because she was the mother of all the living.

The LORD God made garments of skins for both Adam and his wife and clothed them. The LORD God said, "The man has become like one of Us, knowing good and evil. And now, he might reach out his hand, and take also from the tree of life, and eat, and live forever"— therefore the LORD God sent him out from the garden of Eden, to till the ground from which he was taken. He drove the man out, and at the east of the garden of Eden He placed the cherubim and a flaming sword which turned in every direction, to guard the way to the tree of life.

Adam had relations with his wife Eve, and she conceived, gave birth to Cain, and said, "I have gotten a man with the help of the LORD." Then she gave birth again to his brother Abel.

And Abel was a keeper of flocks, but Cain was a tiller of the ground. In the course of time Cain brought an offering to the LORD of the fruit of the ground. Abel also brought the firstborn of his flock and of their fat portions. And the LORD had respect for Abel and for his offering, but for Cain and for his offering, He did not have respect. And Cain was very angry and his countenance fell.

The LORD said to Cain, "Why are you angry? Why is your countenance fallen? If you do well, shall you not be accepted? But if you do not do well, sin is crouching at the door. It desires to dominate you, but you must rule over it."

Cain told Abel his brother. And it came about, when they were in the field, that Cain rose up against his brother Abel and killed him.

The LORD said to Cain, "Where is Abel your brother?"

He said, "I do not know. Am I my brother's keeper?"

And then He said, "What have you done? The voice of your brother's blood is crying out to Me from the ground. Now you are cursed from the ground which opened its mouth to receive your brother's blood from your hand. From now on when you till the ground, it will not yield for you its best. You will be a fugitive and a wanderer on the earth."

Then Cain said to the LORD, "My punishment is more than I can bear. You have driven me out this day from the face of the earth, and from Your face will I be hidden; and I will be a fugitive and a vagabond in the earth, and it will happen that anyone who finds me will kill me."

So the LORD said to him, "Therefore whoever kills Cain, vengeance will be taken on him sevenfold." Then the LORD put a mark upon Cain, so that no one finding him would kill him. Then Cain went out from the presence of the LORD and settled in the land of Nod, east of Eden.

Cain had relations with his wife, and she conceived and gave birth to Enoch. He built a city and called the name of the city after the name of his son, Enoch. To Enoch was born Irad, and Irad was the father of Mehujael, and Mehujael was the father of Methushael, and Methushael was the father of Lamech.

Lamech took two wives. The name of one was Adah, and the name of the other Zillah. Adah gave birth to Jabal. He was the father of those who dwell in tents and have livestock. His brother's name was Jubal. He was the father of all those who play the harp and flute. Zillah gave birth to Tubal-Cain, a forger of every tool of bronze and iron. The sister of Tubal-Cain was Naamah.

Lamech said to his wives:

"Adah and Zillah, hear my voice,
    you wives of Lamech, and listen to my speech.
For I have killed a man for wounding me,
    a young man who hurt me.
If Cain will be avenged sevenfold,
    then truly Lamech seventy-sevenfold."

Adam had relations with his wife again, and she had another son and called his name Seth, for she said, "God has granted me another offspring instead of Abel because Cain killed him." To Seth also was born a son, and he called his name Enosh.

At that time men began to call on the name of the LORD.

This is the book of the generations of Adam.

In the day when God created man, He made him in the likeness of God. He created them male and female. He blessed them and called them Mankind in the day when they were created.

Adam lived one hundred thirty years and became the father of a son in his own likeness, after his own image, and called his name Seth. The days of Adam after he became the father of Seth were eight hundred years, and he had other sons and daughters. So all the days that Adam lived were nine hundred thirty years, and he died.

Seth lived one hundred five years and became the father of Enosh. Seth lived after the birth of Enosh eight hundred seven years and had other sons and daughters. So all the days of Seth were nine hundred twelve years, and he died.

Enosh lived ninety years and became the father of Kenan. Enosh lived after the birth of Kenan eight hundred fifteen years and had other sons and daughters. So all the days of Enosh were nine hundred five years, and he died.

Kenan lived seventy years and became the father of Mahalalel. Kenan lived after the birth of Mahalalel eight hundred forty years and had other sons and daughters. So all the days of Kenan were nine hundred ten years, and he died.

Mahalalel lived sixty-five years and became the father of Jared. Mahalalel lived after the birth of Jared eight hundred thirty years and had other sons and daughters. So all the days of Mahalalel were eight hundred ninety-five years, and he died.

Jared lived one hundred sixty-two years and became the father of Enoch. Jared lived after the birth of Enoch eight hundred years and had other sons and daughters. So all the days of Jared were nine hundred sixty-two years, and he died.

Enoch lived sixty-five years and became the father of Methuselah. Enoch walked with God after the birth of Methuselah for three hundred years and had other sons and daughters. So all the days of Enoch were three hundred sixty-five years. Enoch walked with God, and then he was no more because God took him.

Methuselah lived one hundred eighty-seven years and became the father of Lamech. Methuselah lived after the birth of Lamech seven hundred eighty-two years and had other sons and daughters. So all the days of Methuselah were nine hundred sixty-nine years, and he died.

Lamech lived one hundred eighty-two years and had a son. He named his son Noah, saying, "This one will comfort us concerning our work and the toil of our hands because of the ground which the LORD has cursed." Lamech lived after the birth of Noah five hundred ninety-five years and had other sons and daughters. So all the days of Lamech were seven hundred seventy-seven years, and he died.

Noah was five hundred years old and became the father of Shem, Ham, and Japheth.

When men began to multiply on the face of the earth and daughters were born to them, the sons of God saw that the daughters of men were fair and took as wives any they chose. The LORD said, "My Spirit will not always strive with man, for he is flesh; yet his days will be one hundred twenty years."

The Nephilim were on the earth in those days, and also after that, when the sons of God came in to the daughters of men, and they bore children to them. These were the mighty men who were of old, men of renown.

The LORD saw that the wickedness of man was great on the earth, and that every intent of the thoughts of his heart was continually only evil. The LORD was sorry that He had made man on the earth, and it grieved Him in His heart. So the LORD said, "I will destroy man, whom I have created, from the face of the earth—both man and beast, and the creeping things, and the birds of the sky, for I am sorry that I have made them." But Noah found grace in the eyes of the LORD.

Noach

Noah

(Genesis 6:9–11:32)

These are the generations of Noah.

Noah was a just man and blameless among his contemporaries. Noah walked with God. Noah had three sons: Shem, Ham, and Japheth.

The earth was corrupt before God and filled with violence. God looked on the earth and saw it was corrupt, for all flesh had corrupted their way on the earth. So God said to Noah, "The end of all flesh is come before Me, for the earth is filled with violence because of them. Now I will destroy them with the earth. Make an ark of cypress wood for yourself. Make rooms in the ark, and cover it inside and out with pitch. And this is how you must make it: The length of the ark will be three hundred cubits, the width of it fifty cubits, and the height of it thirty cubits. Make an opening one cubit below the top of the ark all around; and you must set the door of the ark on the side. Make it with a lower, a second, and a third story. I will bring a flood of waters on the earth to destroy all flesh, wherever there is the breath of life under heaven, and everything that is on the earth will die. But I will establish My covenant with you; you must go into the ark—you, and your sons, and your wife, and your sons' wives with you. Bring every living thing of all flesh, two of every kind, into the ark to keep them alive with you. They shall be male and female. Two of every kind of bird, of every kind of animal, and of every kind of creeping thing of the earth will come to you to be kept alive. Also, take with you of every kind of food that is eaten and gather it to yourself, and it will be for food for you and for them."

Noah did this; he did all that God commanded him.

The LORD said to Noah, "You and your entire household go into the ark, for you alone I have seen to be righteous before Me among this generation. Take with you seven each of every clean animal, the male and its female, and two each of every unclean animal, the male and its female, and seven each of birds of the air, the male and female, to keep offspring alive on the face of all the earth. In seven days I will cause it to rain on the earth for forty days and forty nights, and every living thing that I have made I will destroy from the face of the earth."

And Noah did according to all that the LORD commanded him.

Noah was six hundred years old when the floodwaters came upon the earth. And Noah went with his sons and his wife and his sons' wives into the ark because of the floodwaters. Everything that creeps on the land from clean and unclean animals and birds came in two by two, male and female, to Noah into the ark, as God had commanded Noah. After seven days, the waters of the flood were on the earth.

In the six hundredth year of Noah's life, in the second month, on the seventeenth day of the month, the same day, all the fountains of the great deep burst open and the floodgates of the heavens were opened. The rain fell upon the earth for forty days and forty nights.

On the very same day Noah and the sons of Noah, Shem, Ham, and Japheth, and Noah's wife, and the three wives of his sons with them, entered the ark. They and every wild animal according to its kind, and all the live-stock according to their kind, and every creeping thing that creeps on the earth according to its kind, and every bird according to its kind, every bird of every sort, went with Noah into the ark, two by two of all flesh in which was the breath of life. So they went in, male and female of all flesh, just as God had commanded him; then the LORD shut him in.

The flood was on the earth forty days, and the water increased and lifted up the ark, so that it rose up above the earth. The water prevailed and increased greatly upon the earth, and the ark floated on the surface of the water. The water prevailed exceedingly on the earth, and all the high mountains that were under the whole heaven were covered. The waters prevailed upward and the mountains were covered fifteen cubits deep. All flesh that moved on the earth died: birds and livestock and beasts, and every creeping thing that crept on the earth, and every man. All in whose nostrils was the breath of life, all that was on the dry land, died. So He blotted out every living thing which was on the face of the ground, both man and animals and the creeping things and the birds of the heavens. They were blotted out from the earth, and only Noah and those who were with him in the ark remained alive.

The waters prevailed on the earth for one hundred fifty days.

God remembered Noah and every living thing and all the livestock that were with him in the ark. So God made a wind to pass over the earth, and the water receded. Also the fountains of the deep and the floodgates of heaven were closed, and the rain from the heavens was restrained. The water receded steadily from the earth, and after the end of one hundred fifty days the waters decreased. The ark rested in the seventh month, on the seventeenth day of the month, on the mountains of Ararat. The water continually decreased until the tenth month. In the tenth month, on the first day of the month, the tops of the mountains became visible.

Then at the end of forty days, Noah opened the window of the ark which he had made, and he sent forth a raven, which went to and fro until the waters were dried up on the earth. Then he sent out a dove to see if the waters had subsided from the face of the ground. But the dove found no rest for the sole of her foot, so she returned to him into the ark, for the waters were on the surface of all the earth. Then he put forth his hand, and took her, and brought her into the ark to himself. He waited yet another seven days, and again he sent out the dove from the ark. The dove came to him in the evening, and in her mouth there was a freshly plucked olive leaf. So Noah knew that the waters had receded from the earth. He waited another seven days and sent out the dove again, but she did not return to him again.

So in the six hundred first year, in the first month, the first day of the month, the waters were dried up from the earth; and Noah removed the covering of the ark, and looked, and saw the surface of the ground was dry. In the second month, on the twenty-seventh day of the month, the earth was dry.

Then God spoke to Noah, saying, "Go out of the ark, you and your wife, and your sons and your sons' wives with you. Bring out with you every living thing of all flesh that is with you, birds and animals, and every creeping thing that creeps on the earth, so that they may breed abundantly on the earth and be fruitful and multiply on the earth."

So Noah and his sons and his wife and his sons' wives went out. Every beast, every creeping thing, every bird, and everything that moves on the earth, according to their families, went out of the ark.

Then Noah built an altar to the LORD and took of every clean animal and of every clean bird and offered burnt offerings on the altar. The LORD smelled a soothing aroma; and the LORD said in His heart, "I will never again curse the ground because of man, for the inclination of man's heart is evil from his youth, nor will I again destroy every living thing as I have done.

> While the earth remains,
> seedtime and harvest,
> cold and heat,
> summer and winter,
> and day and night
> will not cease."

Then God blessed Noah and his sons and said to them, "Be fruitful and multiply and fill the earth. Every beast of the earth and every bird of the sky and all that moves on the earth and all the fish of the sea will fear you and be terrified of you. They are given into your hand. Every moving thing that lives will be food for you. I give you everything, just as I gave you the green plant.

"Only you shall not eat flesh with its life, *that is*, its blood. But for your own lifeblood I will surely require a reckoning; from every animal will I require it; of man, too, will I require a reckoning for human life, of every man for that of his fellow man.

> Whoever sheds the blood of man,
>   by man shall his blood be shed;
> for God made man
>   in His own image.

And as for you, be fruitful and multiply; increase abundantly in the earth and multiply in it."

Again God spoke to Noah and to his sons with him, saying, "As for Me, I establish My covenant with you, and with your descendants after you; and with every living creature that is with you, the birds, the livestock, and every beast of the earth with you; of all that comes out of the ark, every beast of the earth. I establish My covenant with you. Never again shall all flesh be cut off by the waters of a flood. Never again shall there be a flood to destroy the earth."

Then God said, "This is the sign of the covenant which I am making between Me and you and every living creature that is with you, for all future generations. I have set My rainbow in the cloud, and it shall be a sign of a covenant between Me and the earth. When I bring a cloud over the earth, the rainbow will be seen in the cloud; then I will remember My covenant, which is between Me and you and every living creature of all flesh, and the waters will never again become a flood to destroy all flesh. The rainbow will appear in the cloud, and I will see it and remember the everlasting covenant between God and every living creature of all flesh that is on the earth."

So God said to Noah, "This is the sign of the covenant that I have established between Me and all flesh that is on the earth."

The sons of Noah who went forth from the ark were Shem, Ham, and Japheth. Ham was the father of Canaan. These were the three sons of Noah, and from them the whole earth was populated.

Noah began to be a man of the soil, and he planted a vineyard. Then he drank some of the wine and became drunk, and lay uncovered in his tent. And Ham, the father of Canaan, saw the nakedness of his father, and told his two brothers outside. So Shem and Japheth took a garment, and laid it upon both their shoulders, and went backward, and covered the nakedness of their father. Their faces were turned away, and they did not see their father's nakedness.

When Noah awoke from his wine and knew what his younger son had done to him, he said,

> "Canaan be cursed!
>   He will be a servant of servants
>   to his brothers."

He also said,

"Blessed be the Lord God of Shem,
  and let Canaan be his servant.
May God enlarge Japheth,
  and may he dwell in the tents of Shem,
  and may Canaan be his servant."

Noah lived after the flood three hundred fifty years. All the days of Noah were nine hundred fifty years, and then he died.

Now these are the generations of Shem, Ham, and Japheth, the sons of Noah. And sons were born to them after the flood.

The sons of Japheth were
  Gomer, Magog, Madai, Javan, Tubal, Meshek, and Tiras.
The sons of Gomer were
  Ashkenaz, Riphath, and Togarmah.
The sons of Javan were
  Elishah, Tarshish, the Kittites, and the Rodanites. From these the coast-lands of the nations were divided into their lands, everyone according to his tongue, according to their families, by their nations.

The sons of Ham were
  Cush, Egypt, Put, and Canaan.
The sons of Cush were
  Seba, Havilah, Sabtah, Raamah, and Sabteka;
and the sons of Raamah were
  Sheba and Dedan.

Cush was the father of Nimrod. He became a mighty one on the earth. He was a mighty hunter before the Lord. Therefore it is said, "Even like Nimrod the mighty hunter before the Lord." The beginning of his kingdom was Babel, Uruk, Akkad, and Kalneh in the land of Shinar. From that land he went to Assyria and built Nineveh, the city Rehoboth Ir, and Calah, and Resen between Nineveh and Calah (that is the principal city).

Egypt was the father of
  the Ludites, Anamites, Lehabites, Naphtuhites, Pathrusites, Kasluhites (from whom came the Philistines), and Caphtorites.
Canaan was the father of
  Sidon his firstborn and Heth, and the Jebusites, Amorites, Girgashites, Hivites, Arkites, Sinites, Arvadites, Zemarites, and the Hamathites.

Later the families of the Canaanites spread abroad. The border of the Canaanites was from Sidon toward Gerar to Gaza, and then to Sodom, Gomorrah, Admah, Zeboyim, as far as Lasha.

These are the sons of Ham, according to their families, according to their languages, in their lands and in their nations.

To Shem, who was the father of all the children of Eber, whose older brother was Japheth, were sons born also.

The sons of Shem were
Elam, Ashur, Arphaxad, Lud, and Aram.
The sons of Aram were
Uz, Hul, Gether, and Meshek.
Arphaxad was the father of Shelah,
and Shelah was the father of Eber.
To Eber were born two sons.
The name of one was Peleg, for in his days the earth was divided; his brother's name was Joktan.
Joktan was the father of
Almodad, Sheleph, Hazarmaveth, Jerah, Hadoram, Uzal, Diklah, Obal, Abimael, Sheba, Ophir, Havilah, and Jobab. All these were the sons of Joktan.

Their dwelling place was from Mesha all the way to Sephar, the hill country of the east.

These are the sons of Shem, by their families and their language, in their lands and their nations.

These are the families of the sons of Noah, according to their generations, in their nations. From these were the nations divided in the earth after the flood.

Now the whole earth had one language and the same words. As the people journeyed from the east, they found a plain in the land of Shinar and settled there.

They said to each other, "Let us make bricks and bake them thoroughly." And they had brick for stone and tar for mortar. Then they said, "Come, let us build us a city and a tower, whose top will reach to heaven, and let us make a name for ourselves; otherwise we will be scattered abroad over the face of the whole earth."

But the LORD came down to see the city and the tower that the sons of men built. The LORD said, "The people are one and they have one language, and this is only the beginning of what they will do; now nothing that they propose to do will be impossible for them. Come, let Us go down and there confuse their language, so that they may not understand one another's speech."

So the L ORD scattered them abroad from there over the face of all the earth, and they stopped building the city. Therefore the name of it was called Babel, because there the L ORD confused the language of all the earth. From there the L ORD scattered them abroad over the face of all the earth.

These are the generations of Shem.

Shem was one hundred years old, and two years after the flood he became the father of Arphaxad. Shem lived after the birth of Arphaxad five hundred years, and had other sons and daughters.

Arphaxad lived thirty-five years, and became the father of Shelah. Arphaxad lived after the birth of Shelah four hundred three years, and had other sons and daughters.

Shelah lived thirty years, and became the father of Eber. Shelah lived after the birth of Eber four hundred three years, and had other sons and daughters.

Eber lived thirty-four years, and became the father of Peleg. Eber lived after the birth of Peleg four hundred thirty years, and had other sons and daughters.

Peleg lived thirty years, and became the father of Reu. Peleg lived after the birth of Reu two hundred nine years, and had other sons and daughters.

Reu lived thirty-two years, and became the father of Serug. Reu lived after the birth of Serug two hundred seven years, and had other sons and daughters.

Serug lived thirty years, and became the father of Nahor. Serug lived after the birth of Nahor two hundred years, and had other sons and daughters.

Nahor lived twenty-nine years, and became the father of Terah. Nahor lived after the birth of Terah one hundred nineteen years, and had other sons and daughters.

Now Terah lived seventy years, and became the father of Abram, Nahor, and Haran.

These are the generations of Terah.

Terah became the father of Abram, Nahor, and Haran, and Haran became the father of Lot. Haran died before his father Terah in the land of his birth, in Ur of the Chaldeans. Abram and Nahor took wives. The name of Abram's wife was Sarai, and the name of Nahor's wife, Milkah, the daughter of Haran, the father of Milkah and the father of Iskah. But Sarai was barren; she had no child.

Terah took his son Abram and his grandson Lot, son of Haran, and his daughter-in-law Sarai, his son Abram's wife, and they went out together from Ur of the Chaldeans to go into the land of Canaan; but when they came to Harran, they settled there.

The days of Terah were two hundred five years, and Terah died in Harran.

Lech Lecha

Go forth, yourself!

(Genesis 12:1–17:27)

Now the LORD said to Abram, "Go from your country, your family, and your father's house to the land that I will show you.

I will make of you a great nation;
  I will bless you
and make your name great,
  so that you will be a blessing.
I will bless them who bless you
  and curse him who curses you,
and in you all families of the earth
  will be blessed."

So Abram departed, as the LORD had spoken to him, and Lot went with him. Abram was seventy-five years old when he departed from Harran. Abram took Sarai his wife, Lot his brother's son, and all their possessions that they had accumulated, and the people that they had acquired in Harran, and they set out for the land of Canaan. They came to the land of Canaan.

Then Abram passed through the land to the place of Shechem, to the oak of Moreh. The Canaanites were in the land at that time. The LORD appeared to Abram and said, "To your descendants I will give this land." So he built an altar to the LORD, who had appeared to him.

From there he continued on to a mountain to the east of Bethel and pitched his tent, having Bethel on the west and Ai on the east. There he built an altar to the LORD and called on the name of the LORD. Then Abram continued his journey toward the Negev.

Now there was a famine in the land, so Abram went down to Egypt to live there, for the famine was severe in the land. When he was getting near to Egypt, he said to Sarai his wife, "I know you are a beautiful woman. Therefore, when the Egyptians see you, they will say, 'This is his wife.' They will then kill me, but they will let you live. Say you are my sister so that I may be treated well for your sake. Then my life will be spared because of you."

So when Abram entered Egypt, the Egyptians saw that Sarai was very beautiful. The princes of Pharaoh saw her and commended her to Pharaoh, and she was taken into Pharaoh's house. He treated Abram well for her sake and he had sheep and livestock, male and female donkeys, male and female servants, and camels.

But the LORD afflicted Pharaoh and his house with great plagues because of Abram's wife, Sarai. So Pharaoh called Abram, and said, "What have you done to me? Why did you not tell me that she was your wife? Why did you say, 'She is my sister'? I might have taken her as my wife. Now here is your wife; take her and leave." Pharaoh commanded his men concerning him, and they sent him away with his wife and all that he had.

So Abram went up from Egypt to the Negev, he and his wife and all that he had, and Lot with him. Abram was very wealthy in livestock, in silver, and in gold.

He continued on his journey from the Negev and came to Bethel, to the place where his tent had been at the beginning, between Bethel and Ai, to the place where he first made an altar. There Abram called on the name of the LORD.

Now Lot, who went with Abram, also had flocks and herds and tents. But the land was not able to support them both dwelling together because their possessions were so great. And there was strife between the herdsmen of Abram's livestock and the herdsmen of Lot's livestock. The Canaanites and the Perizzites dwelt in the land at that time.

So Abram said to Lot, "Let there be no strife, I ask you, between me and you, and between my herdsmen and your herdsmen, for we are close relatives. Is not the whole land before you? Please separate from me. If you will go to the left, then I will go to the right, or if you take the right, then I will go to the left."

Lot lifted up his eyes, and looked at all the valley of the Jordan, that it was well watered everywhere like the garden of the LORD, like the land of Egypt as you go to Zoar. This was before the LORD destroyed Sodom and Gomorrah. Then Lot chose for himself the entire valley of the Jordan and journeyed east, and the two of them separated from each other. Abram dwelt in the land of Canaan, and Lot dwelt in the cities of the valley and pitched his tent as far as Sodom. Now the men of Sodom were exceedingly wicked and sinners against the LORD.

After Lot had departed from him, the LORD said to Abram, "Lift up now your eyes, and look from the place where you are, northward and south-ward and eastward and westward. All the land that you see I will give to you and to your descendants forever. I will make your descendants like the dust of the earth, so that if a man could number the dust of the earth, then your descendants could also be numbered. Arise, and walk throughout the land across its length and its width, for I will give it to you."

So Abram moved his tent and came and settled by the oaks of Mamre, which are in Hebron, and built an altar to the LORD there.

In the days that Amraphel was king of Shinar, Arioch king of Ellasar, Kedorlaomer king of Elam, and Tidal king of Goyim, they made war with Bera king of Sodom, Birsha king of Gomorrah, Shinab king of Admah, Shemeber king of Zeboyim, and the king of Bela (that is, Zoar). All these were joined together in the Valley of Siddim (that is, the Dead Sea). For twelve years they had served Kedorlaomer, but in the thirteenth year they rebelled.

In the fourteenth year, Kedorlaomer and the kings who were with him came and defeated the Rephaites in Ashteroth Karnaim, the Zuzites in Ham, and the Emites in Shaveh Kiriathaim, and the Horites in their hill country of Seir, as far as El Paran, which is by the wilderness. Then they turned back and came to En Mishpat (that is, Kadesh) and conquered all the country of the Amalekites and also the Amorites who lived in Hazezon Tamar.

Then the king of Sodom, the king of Gomorrah, the king of Admah, the king of Zeboyim, and the king of Bela (that is, Zoar) came out, and they joined together in battle in the Valley of Siddim against Kedorlaomer, the king of Elam, Tidal king of Goyim, Amraphel king of Shinar, and Arioch king of Ellasar—four kings against five. Now the Valley of Siddim was full of tar pits, and as the kings of Sodom and Gomorrah fled, some fell in them, and the rest fled to the hill country. Then they took all the possessions of Sodom and Gomorrah, and all their provisions, and departed. They also took Lot, Abram's brother's son, who lived in Sodom, and his possessions, and went their way.

Then one who had escaped came and told Abram the Hebrew, who was living near the oaks of Mamre the Amorite, brother of Eshkol and Aner, and these were allies with Abram. When Abram heard that his relative was taken captive, he armed his three hundred eighteen trained servants born in his own house, and pursued them as far as Dan. During the night he divided his men to attack them and defeated them, and pursued them as far as Hobah, which is north of Damascus. He brought back all the possessions, along with his relative Lot and his possessions, and also the women and the people.

After his return from the defeat of Kedorlaomer and the kings who had joined with him, the king of Sodom went out to meet him in the Valley of Shaveh (that is, the King's Valley).

Then Melchizedek king of Salem brought out bread and wine. He was the priest of God Most High. And he blessed him and said,

"Blessed be Abram by God Most High,
    Creator of heaven and earth;
and blessed be God Most High,
    who has delivered your enemies into your hand."

Then Abram gave him one-tenth of everything.

The king of Sodom said to Abram, "Give me the people and take the goods for yourself."

But Abram said to the king of Sodom, "I have lifted up my hand to the LORD, God Most High, the Possessor of heaven and earth, that I will take nothing that is yours, not a thread or a sandal strap; lest you say, 'I have made Abram rich.' I will accept only that which my men have eaten and the portion that belongs to the men who went with me, Aner, Eshkol, and Mamre. Let them take their portion."

After this the word of the LORD came to Abram in a vision, saying,

"Do not fear, Abram.
  I am your shield,
  your exceedingly great reward."

But Abram said, "Lord GOD, what will You give me, seeing I am childless and the heir of my house is Eliezer of Damascus?" Abram said, "Since You have not given me any children, my heir is a servant born in my house."

Then the word of the LORD came to him, saying, "This man will not be your heir, but a son that is from your own body will be your heir." He brought him outside and said, "Look up toward heaven and count the stars, if you are able to count them." And He said to him, "So will your descendants be."

Abram believed the LORD, and He credited it to him as righteousness.

He also said to him, "I am the LORD who brought you out of Ur of the Chaldeans to give you this land to possess it."

But Abram said, "Lord GOD, how may I know that I will possess it?"

So He said to him, "Bring Me a three-year-old heifer, a three-year-old female goat, a three-year-old ram, a turtledove, and a young pigeon."

Then Abram brought all of these to Him and cut them in two and laid each piece opposite the other, but he did not cut the birds in half. When the birds of prey came down on the carcasses, Abram drove them away.

As the sun was going down, a deep sleep fell on Abram, and terror and a great darkness fell on him. Then He said to Abram, "Know for certain that your descendants will live as strangers in a land that is not theirs, and they will be enslaved and mistreated for four hundred years. But I will judge the nation that they serve, and afterward they will come out with great possessions. As for you, you will go to your fathers in peace and you will be buried at a good old age. In the fourth generation, your descendants will return here, for the iniquity of the Amorites is not yet complete."

When the sun went down and it was dark, a smoking fire pot with a flaming torch passed between these pieces. On that same day the LORD made a covenant with Abram, saying, "To your descendants I have given this land, from the river of Egypt to the great Euphrates River— the land of the Kenites, the Kenizzites, the Kadmonites, the Hittites, the Perizzites, the Rephaites, the Amorites, the Canaanites, the Girgashites, and the Jebusites."

Now Sarai, Abram's wife, had borne him no children, and she had a maidservant, an Egyptian, whose name was Hagar. So Sarai said to Abram, "The LORD has prevented me from having children. Please go in to my maid; it may be that I will obtain children through her."

Abram listened to Sarai. So after Abram had been living for ten years in the land of Canaan, Sarai, his wife, took Hagar her maid, the Egyptian, and gave her to her husband Abram to be his wife. He went in to Hagar, and she conceived.

When she saw that she had conceived, she began to despise her mistress. Then Sarai said to Abram, "May the wrong done to me be on you! I gave my maid into your arms; and when she saw that she had conceived, I became despised in her eyes. May the LORD judge between you and me."

But Abram said to Sarai, "Indeed, your maid is in your power; do to her as you please." Then Sarai dealt harshly with her, and she fled from her presence.

The angel of the LORD found her by a spring of water in the wilderness. It was the spring on the way to Shur. And he said, "Hagar, Sarai's maid, where have you come from and where are you going?"

And she said, "I am fleeing from the presence of my mistress Sarai."

Then the angel of the LORD said to her, "Return to your mistress, and submit yourself to her authority." The angel of the LORD also said to her, "I will multiply your descendants exceedingly so that they will be too many to count."

Then the angel of the LORD said to her,

"You are pregnant
   and will bear a son.
You shall call his name Ishmael,
   because the LORD has heard your affliction.
He will be a wild man;
   his hand will be against every man,
   and every man's hand will be against him.
And he will dwell
   in the presence of all his brothers."

Then she called the name of the LORD who spoke to her, "You are the God who sees," for she said, "Have I now looked on Him who sees me?" Therefore the well was called Beer Lahai Roi. It is between Kadesh and Bered.

So Hagar bore Abram a son, and Abram called the son she bore Ishmael. Abram was eighty-six years old when Hagar bore Ishmael to Abram.

When Abram was ninety-nine years old, the LORD appeared to him and said, "I am Almighty God. Walk before Me and be blameless. And I will make My covenant between you and Me and will exceedingly multiply you."

Abram fell on his face and God said to him, "As for Me, My covenant is with you, and you shall be the father of a multitude of nations. No longer will your name be called Abram, but your name will be Abraham, for I have made you the father of a multitude of nations. I will make you exceedingly fruitful; and I will make nations of you, and kings will come from you. I will establish My covenant between Me and you and your descendants after you throughout their generations for an everlasting covenant, to be God to you and your descendants after you. All the land of Canaan, where you now live as strangers, I will give to you and to your descendants for an everlasting possession, and I will be their God."

Then God said to Abraham, "As for you, you shall keep My covenant, you and your descendants after you throughout their generations. This is My covenant, which you shall keep, between Me and you and your descendants after you; every male among you shall be circumcised. You shall circumcise the flesh of your foreskins, and it shall be a sign of the covenant between Me and you. Every male throughout every generation that is eight days old shall be circumcised, whether born in your household or bought with money from a foreigner who is not your descendant. He who is born in your house and he who is bought with your money must be circumcised. My covenant shall be in your flesh as an everlasting covenant. Any uncircumcised male whose flesh of his foreskin is not circumcised shall be cut off from his people. He has broken My covenant."

Then God said to Abraham, "As for Sarai your wife, you will not call her name Sarai, but her name will be Sarah. I will bless her and also give you a son by her. I will bless her, and she will be the mother of nations. Kings of peoples will come from her."

Then Abraham fell on his face and laughed and said in his heart, "Shall a child be born to a man who is one hundred years old? Shall Sarah, who is ninety years old, bear a child?" Abraham said to God, "Oh, that Ishmael might live before You!"

Then God said, "No, but your wife Sarah will bear you a son, and you will call his name Isaac. I will establish My covenant with him as an everlasting covenant and with his descendants after him. And as for Ishmael, I have heard you. I have blessed him, and will make him fruitful and will multiply him exceedingly. He will be the father of twelve princes, and I will make him a great nation. But I will establish My covenant with Isaac, whom Sarah will bear to you at this set time next year." Then He stopped talking with Abraham, and God went up from him.

Then Abraham took Ishmael, his son, and all who were born in his house, and all who were bought with his money, every male among the men of Abraham's household, and circumcised the flesh of their foreskins that very same day as God had said to him. Abraham was ninety-nine years old when he was circumcised in the flesh of his foreskin. His son, Ishmael, was thirteen years old when he was circumcised in the flesh of his foreskin. Abraham and Ishmael were circumcised on the same day. All the men born in Abraham's household or bought from foreigners were circumcised with him.

Vayera

And he appeared

(Genesis 18:1–22:24)

The LORD appeared to Abraham near the great oak trees of Mamre while he sat in the tent door in the heat of the day. Abraham lifted up his eyes and looked and saw three men standing across from him. When he saw them, he ran from the tent door to meet them and bowed himself toward the ground.

He said, "My Lord, if I have found favor in Your sight, do not pass by Your servant. Please let a little water be brought and wash your feet and rest yourselves under the tree. I will bring a piece of bread so that you may refresh yourselves. After that you may pass on, now that you have come to your servant."

And they said, "So do, as you have said."

So Abraham hurried into the tent to Sarah, and said, "Quickly prepare three measures of fine flour, knead it, and make cakes."

Then Abraham ran to the herd and took a choice and tender calf and gave it to a servant, who hurried to prepare it. He then brought butter and milk and the calf that he had prepared and set it before them; and he stood by them under the tree while they ate.

They said to him, "Where is Sarah your wife?"

And he said, "There, in the tent."

One of them said, "I will certainly return to you about this time next year, and Sarah your wife will have a son."

And Sarah heard it in the tent door, which was behind him. Now Abraham and Sarah were old and very advanced in age, and Sarah was well past childbearing. Therefore Sarah laughed to herself, saying, "After I am so old and my lord is old also, shall I have pleasure?"

Then the LORD said to Abraham, "Why did Sarah laugh and say, 'Shall I surely bear a child when I am old?' Is anything too difficult for the LORD? At the appointed time I will return to you, at this time next year, and Sarah will have a son."

Then Sarah denied it, saying, "I did not laugh," because she was afraid.

But He said, "Yes, you did laugh."

Then the men rose up and looked toward Sodom, and Abraham went with them to see them on their way. Then the LORD said, "Should I hide from Abraham what I am doing, since Abraham will surely become a great and mighty nation, and all the nations of the earth will be blessed in him? I chose him, and he will instruct his children and his household after him to keep the way of the Lord by doing righteousness and justice, so that the Lord may bring to Abraham what He promised him."

Then the Lord said, "Because the outcry against Sodom and Gomorrah is great, and because their sin is very grave, I will go down and see if what they have done is as bad as the outcry that has come to Me. If not, I will know."

The men turned away from there and went toward Sodom, but Abraham remained standing before the Lord. Then Abraham drew near and said, "Shall You also destroy the righteous with the wicked? What if there are fifty righteous in the city? Shall You also destroy, and not spare the place, for the fifty righteous who are in it? Far be it from You to do such a thing as this, to slay the righteous with the wicked, so that the righteous should be treated like the wicked; far be it from You. Should not the Judge of all the earth do right?"

So the Lord said, "If I find in Sodom fifty righteous within the city, then I will spare the entire place for their sakes."

Then Abraham answered and said, "I who am but dust and ashes have taken it upon myself to speak to the Lord. Suppose there were five less than the fifty righteous. Will You destroy all the city for lack of five?"

And He said, "If I find forty-five there, I will not destroy it."

And he spoke to Him yet again and said, "Suppose there will be forty found there?"

So He said, "I will not do it for the sake of forty."

Then he said to Him, "Let not the Lord be angry, and I will speak. Suppose there will be thirty found there?"

Again He said, "I will not do it if I find thirty there."

He said, "Behold, I have undertaken to speak to the Lord. Suppose twenty are found there?"

He said, "I will not destroy it for the sake of twenty."

Then he said, "Let not the Lord be angry, and I will speak only once more. Suppose ten will be found there?"

Then He said, "I will not destroy it for the sake of ten."

So the Lord went His way as soon as He had stopped speaking to Abraham, and Abraham returned to his place.

Now the two angels came to Sodom in the evening, and Lot was sitting at the gate of Sodom. When Lot saw them he rose up to meet them, and he bowed himself with his face toward the ground. Then he said, "Here, my lords, please turn in to your servant's house and spend the night and wash your feet; and then you may rise early and go on your way."

They said, "No, we will stay in the open square all night."

But he strongly insisted, so they turned aside with him and entered his house. Then he made them a feast and baked unleavened bread, and they ate. Before they lay down, the men of the city, the men of Sodom, both old and young, all the people from every quarter, surrounded the house. They then called to Lot and said to him, "Where are the men who came to you tonight? Bring them out to us, so that we may have relations with them."

So Lot went out through the door to them and shut the door behind him. Then he said, "Please, my brothers, do not act so wickedly. Look, I have two daughters who have not been with a man. Please, let me bring them out to you, and you may do to them as you wish. Only do nothing to these men, for they have come under the shelter of my roof."

But they replied, "Stand back!" Also, they said, "This man came here as a foreigner, and he keeps acting like a judge. We will deal worse with you than with them." So they pressed hard against Lot, and came close to breaking down the door.

But the men reached out their hands and pulled Lot into the house with them and shut the door. Then they struck the men that were at the door of the house, both small and great, with blindness so that they wore themselves out groping for the door.

Then the men said to Lot, "Have you anyone else here? Sons-in-law, sons, daughters, or anyone you have in the city, take them out of this place! For we are about to destroy this place, because the outcry against its people has grown great before the presence of the LORD, and the LORD has sent us to destroy it."

So Lot went out and spoke to his sons-in-law, who had married his daughters, and said, "Get up, get out of this place, for the LORD will destroy this city!" But to his sons-in-law he seemed to be joking.

When the morning dawned, the angels urged Lot, saying, "Arise, take your wife and your two daughters who are here. Otherwise you will be consumed in the punishment of the city."

And while he lingered, the men took hold of his and his wife's hands, along with the hands of his two daughters, the LORD being merciful to him, and brought him out and set him outside the city. When they had brought them out, one of them said to them, "Escape for your lives! Do not look behind you or stay anywhere in the plain. Escape to the mountain, lest you be destroyed."

Then Lot said to them, "Please, no, my lords! Your servant has found grace in your eyes, and you have shown your mercy, which you have shown to me by saving my life. However, I cannot escape to the mountain. Otherwise some evil will overtake me, and I will die. Look, this city is close enough to flee to, and it is a little one. Please, let me escape there (is it not a little one?), and my life will be saved."

He said to him, "I have granted your request in this matter also. I will not overthrow this city of which you have spoken. Hurry, escape there, for I cannot do anything until you arrive there." Therefore the name of the city was called Zoar.

The sun had risen over the land when Lot entered Zoar. Then the LORD rained brimstone and fire on Sodom and Gomorrah. It was from the LORD out of heaven. So He overthrew those cities, all the valley, all the inhabitants of the cities, and what grew on the ground. But his wife, behind him, looked back, and she became a pillar of salt.

Now Abraham got up early in the morning and went to the place where he stood before the LORD. Then he looked toward Sodom and Gomorrah, and toward all the land of the valley, and he saw the smoke of the land going up like the smoke of a furnace.

So it was that when God destroyed the cities of the valley, God remembered Abraham, and sent Lot out of the middle of the destruction, when He overthrew the cities in which Lot lived.

Then Lot left Zoar, and lived in the mountains, along with his two daughters who were with him, for he was afraid to dwell in Zoar. He and his two daughters lived in a cave. And the firstborn said to the younger, "Our father is old, and there is no man on the earth to have relations with us after the manner of all the earth. Let us make our father drink wine and let us lie with him, so that we may preserve the lineage of our father."

So they made their father drink wine that night, and the firstborn went in and had relations with her father. He did not know when she lay down or when she arose.

On the next day the firstborn said to the younger, "Indeed, last night I had relations with my father. Let us make him drink wine tonight also, so that you may go in and have relations with him, so that we may preserve the lineage of our father." So they made their father drink wine that night also. Then the younger arose and lay down with him, and he did not know when she lay down or when she arose.

Therefore both the daughters of Lot were pregnant by their father. The firstborn bore a son and called his name Moab. He is the father of the Moabites to this day. The younger also gave birth to a son and called his name Ben-Ammi. He is the father of the Ammonites to this day.

Abraham journeyed from there toward the Negev, settled between Kadesh and Shur, and then he sojourned in Gerar. Then Abraham said about Sarah his wife, "She is my sister." So Abimelek, king of Gerar, sent for her and took Sarah.

But God came to Abimelek in a dream by night and said to him, "You are a dead man because of the woman whom you have taken, for she is a man's wife."

Abimelek had not gone near her, and he said, "Lord, will You slay a righteous nation? Did he not say to me, 'She is my sister,' and did not even she herself say, 'He is my brother'? In the integrity of my heart and innocence of my hands I have done this."

And God said to him in a dream, "Yes, I know that you did this in the integrity of your heart. For I also kept you from sinning against Me. Therefore, I did not let you touch her. Therefore return the man's wife, for he is a prophet and he will pray for you. Moreover, you will live. However, if you do not return her, know that you will surely die, you and all who are yours."

So Abimelek rose early in the morning, and called all his servants and told them all these things, and the men were very afraid. Then Abimelek called Abraham and said to him, "What have you done to us? How have I offended you that you would bring on me and on my kingdom a great sin? You have done things to me that should not have been done." Then Abimelek said to Abraham, "What were you thinking of, that you did this thing?"

Abraham said, "Because I thought, surely there is no fear of God in this place, and they will slay me because of my wife. Still, indeed, she is my sister. She is the daughter of my father, but not the daughter of my mother. She became my wife. When God caused me to travel from my father's house, I said to her, 'This is your kindness which you must show me: Every place where we go, say concerning me, He is my brother.'"

Then Abimelek took sheep, oxen, and male and female servants, and gave them to Abraham, and returned his wife Sarah to him. Abimelek said, "My land is before you; settle wherever it pleases you."

To Sarah he said, "I have given your brother one thousand shekels of silver. It is a sign of your innocence in the eyes of all who are with you, and before everyone you are vindicated."

So Abraham prayed to God, and God healed Abimelek, his wife, and his female servants. Then they bore children. For the LORD had closed up all the wombs of the house of Abimelek because of Sarah, Abraham's wife.

The LORD visited Sarah as He had said, and the LORD did for Sarah as He had spoken. For Sarah conceived and bore Abraham a son in his old age, at the set time that God had spoken to him. Abraham called the name of his son who was born to him, whom Sarah bore to him, Isaac. Then Abraham circumcised his son Isaac when he was eight days old, as God had commanded him. Now Abraham was one hundred years old when his son Isaac was born to him.

And Sarah said, "God has made me laugh. All who hear will laugh with me." Also she said, "Who would have said to Abraham that Sarah would nurse children? Yet I have borne him a son in his old age."

So the child grew and was weaned. Then Abraham made a great feast the same day that Isaac was weaned. Sarah saw the son of Hagar the Egyptian, whom she had borne to Abraham, mocking. Therefore she said to Abraham, "Throw out this slave woman and her son, for the son of this slave woman shall not be heir with my son, Isaac."

This matter was very displeasing in Abraham's sight because of his son. But God said to Abraham, "Do not be upset concerning the boy and your slave wife. Whatever Sarah has said to you, listen to what she says, for in Isaac your descendants will be called. Yet I will also make a nation of the son of the slave woman, because he is your offspring."

So Abraham rose up early in the morning, and took bread and a skin of water and gave it to Hagar, putting it on her shoulder, and sent her away with the child. So she departed and wandered in the Wilderness of Beersheba.

When the water in the skin was gone, she placed the child under one of the shrubs. Then she went and sat down across from him at a distance of about a bowshot, for she said to herself, "Let me not see the death of the child." She sat across from him, and lifted up her voice and wept.

And God heard the boy's voice. Then the angel of God called to Hagar out of heaven and said to her, "What is the matter with you, Hagar? Do not be afraid, for God has heard the voice of the boy where he is. Arise, pick up the boy and hold him in your hands, for I will make him a great nation."

Then God opened her eyes, and she saw a well of water. And she went and filled the skin with water and gave the boy a drink.

God was with the boy; and he grew and lived in the wilderness and became an archer. He lived in the Wilderness of Paran, and his mother found a wife for him out of the land of Egypt.

Now it came to pass at that time that Abimelek and Phicol, the commander of his army, spoke to Abraham, saying, "God is with you in all that you do. Now therefore, swear to me by God that you will not deal deceitfully with me, or with my children, or with my descendants. Instead, according to the kindness that I have shown to you, you will show to me and to the land where you have lived."

Abraham said, "I will swear."

Then Abraham complained to Abimelek about a well of water that Abimelek's servants had violently seized. And Abimelek said, "I do not know who has done this. You did not tell me, and I have not heard of it until today."

So Abraham took sheep and oxen and gave them to Abimelek, and the two of them made a covenant. Then Abraham set seven ewe lambs of the flock by themselves. And Abimelek said to Abraham, "What is the meaning of these seven ewe lambs that you have set by themselves?"

And he said, "You shall take these seven ewe lambs from my hand so that they may be a witness that I have dug this well."

Therefore he called that place Beersheba, because the two of them swore an oath there.

Thus they made a covenant at Beersheba. Then Abimelek rose with Phicol, the commander of his army, and they returned to the land of the Philistines. Abraham planted a tamarisk tree in Beersheba, and there he called on the name of the Lord, the Everlasting God. Abraham stayed in the land of the Philistines many days.

After these things God tested Abraham and said to him, "Abraham!"

And he said, "Here I am."

Then He said, "Take your son, your only son Isaac, whom you love, and go to the land of Moriah, and offer him there as a burnt offering on one of the mountains of which I will tell you."

So Abraham rose up early in the morning and saddled his donkey, and took two of his young men with him and Isaac his son; and he split the wood for the burnt offering, and arose and went to the place that God had told him. Then on the third day Abraham lifted up his eyes and saw the place from a distance. Abraham said to his young men, "Stay here with the donkey. The boy and I will go over there and worship and then return to you."

So Abraham took the wood of the burnt offering and laid it on Isaac his son; and he took the fire in his hand and the knife. So the two of them walked on together. But Isaac spoke to Abraham his father and said, "My father!"

And he said, "Here I am, my son."

Then he said, "Here is the fire and the wood, but where is the lamb for the burnt offering?"

Abraham said, "My son, God will provide for Himself the lamb for a burnt offering." So the two of them went together.

Then they came to the place that God had told him. So Abraham built an altar there and arranged the wood; and he bound Isaac his son and laid him on the altar, on the wood. Then Abraham stretched out his hand and took the knife to slay his son. But the angel of the LORD called to him out of heaven and said, "Abraham, Abraham!"

And he said, "Here I am."

Then He said, "Do not lay your hands on the boy or do anything to him, because now I know that you fear God, seeing you have not withheld your only son from Me."

Then Abraham lifted up his eyes and looked, and behind him was a ram caught in a thicket by his horns. So Abraham went and took the ram and offered him up as a burnt offering in the place of his son. Abraham called the name of that place The LORD Will Provide, as it is said to this day, "In the mount of the LORD it will be provided."

Then the angel of the LORD called to Abraham out of heaven a second time, and said, "By Myself I have sworn, says the LORD, because you have done this thing, and have not withheld your son, your only son, I will indeed bless you and I will indeed multiply your descendants as the stars of the heavens and as the sand that is on the seashore. Your descendants will possess the gate of their enemies. Through your offspring all the nations of the earth will be blessed, because you have obeyed My voice."

So Abraham returned to his young men, and they arose and went together to Beersheba. Then Abraham lived at Beersheba.

After these things Abraham was told, "Milkah has also borne children to your brother Nahor: Uz his firstborn, Buz his brother, Kemuel the father of Aram, Kesed, Hazo, Pildash, Jidlaph, and Bethuel." Bethuel became the father of Rebekah. Milkah gave birth to these eight to Nahor, Abraham's brother. His concubine, whose name was Reumah, also bore Tebah, Gaham, Tahash, and Maakah.

Chayei Sara
Life of Sarah
(Genesis 23:1–25:18)

S arah lived one hundred twenty-seven years. These were the years of the life of Sarah. Then Sarah died in Kiriath Arba (that is, Hebron) in the land of Canaan, and Abraham went in to mourn for Sarah and to weep for her.

Then Abraham stood up from before his dead and spoke to the Hittites, saying, "I am a stranger and a foreigner among you. Give me property for a burying place among you, that I may bury my dead out of my sight."

So the Hittites answered Abraham, "Hear us, my lord. You are a mighty prince among us. Bury your dead in the choicest of our burial places. None of us will withhold from you his burial place that you may bury your dead."

Then Abraham stood up and bowed himself to the people of the land, the Hittites. He spoke with them, saying, "If it be your wish that I bury my dead out of my sight, hear me and entreat Ephron the son of Zohar for me, that he may give me the cave of Machpelah, which he owns, at the end of his field. Let him give it to me in your presence for the full price for a burial site."

Now Ephron was sitting among the Hittites; and Ephron the Hittite answered Abraham in the presence of all the Hittites, all who went in at the gate of his city, saying, "No, my lord. Hear me: I give you the field and the cave that is in it. I give it to you in the presence of the sons of my people. Bury your dead."

Then Abraham bowed before the people of the land. Then he spoke to Ephron in the hearing of the people of the land, saying, "Indeed, if you will give it, please hear me. I will give you money for the field; take it from me and I will bury my dead there."

Then Ephron answered Abraham, saying to him, "My lord, listen to me. The land is worth four hundred shekels of silver. What is that between me and you? So bury your dead."

Abraham listened to Ephron; and Abraham weighed out for Ephron four hundred shekels of silver, the price that he had named in the hearing of the Hittites, according to the standard commercial measure.

So the field of Ephron, which was in Machpelah, which was before Mamre, the field and the cave that was in it, and all the trees that were in the field that were within all the surrounding borders were deeded to Abraham as a possession in the presence of the Hittites, before all who went in at the gate of his city. After this, Abraham buried Sarah his wife in the cave of the field of Machpelah before Mamre (that is, Hebron) in the land of Canaan. So the field and the cave that was in it were deeded to Abraham by the Hittites as property for a burial place.

Now Abraham was old, well advanced in age; and the LORD had blessed Abraham in all things. So Abraham said to his servant, the oldest of his household, who was in charge over all that he had, "Please, place your hand under my thigh, and I will make you swear by the LORD, the God of heaven and the God of the earth, that you will not take a wife for my son from the daughters of the Canaanites, among whom I live. But you shall go to my country and to my family, and take a wife for my son Isaac."

Then the servant said to him, "Perhaps the woman will not be willing to follow me to this land. Must I take your son back to the land from which you came?"

Abraham said to him, "See to it that you do not take my son back there. The LORD God of heaven, who took me from my father's family and from the land of my relatives, and who spoke to me and swore to me, saying, 'To your descendants I will give this land,' He shall send His angel before you and you shall take a wife for my son from there. If the woman is not willing to follow you, then you will be free from my oath. Only do not take my son back there." So the servant put his hand under the thigh of Abraham his master and swore to him concerning this matter.

Then the servant took ten of his master's camels and departed, for all the goods of his master were in his hand. And he arose and went to the city of Nahor in Aram Naharaim. He made his camels kneel down outside the city by a well of water in the evening when the women came out to draw water.

Then he said, "O LORD, the God of my master Abraham, please let me have success this day and show kindness to my master Abraham. See, here I stand by the well of water, and the daughters of the men of the city are coming out to draw water. Let it be that the young woman to whom I shall say, 'Please lower your pitcher, that I may drink,' and she shall say, 'Drink, and I will give your camels water also'—let her be the one that You have appointed for Your servant Isaac. Then I will know that You have shown kindness to my master."

Before he had finished speaking, Rebekah, who was born to Bethuel, son of Milkah, the wife of Nahor, Abraham's brother, came out with a pitcher on her shoulder. The young woman was very beautiful to look at, a virgin, and no man had ever been with her. She went down to the well and filled her pitcher and came up.

Then the servant ran to meet her and said, "Please let me drink a little water from your pitcher."

So she said, "Drink, my lord." Then she quickly let down her pitcher to her hand and gave him a drink.

When she had finished giving him a drink, she said, "I will draw water for your camels also, until they have finished drinking." Then she quickly emptied her pitcher into the trough and ran to the well to draw water and drew for all his camels. The man, gazing at her, remained silent, trying to discern whether the LORD had made his journey a success or not.

When the camels had finished drinking, the man took a gold nose ring of half a shekel weight and two bracelets for her wrists of ten shekels weight in gold, and said, "Whose daughter are you? Please tell me, is there room in your father's house for us to lodge?"

She said to him, "I am the daughter of Bethuel the son of Milkah, whom she bore to Nahor." Again she said to him, "We have both straw and provision enough, and room in which to lodge."

Then the man bowed down his head and worshipped the LORD. And he said, "Blessed be the LORD God of my master Abraham, who has not forsaken His mercy and His truth toward my master. As for me, the LORD led me to the house of my master's relatives."

So the young woman ran and told her mother's household of these things. Now Rebekah had a brother whose name was Laban, and Laban ran out to the man at the well. When he saw the nose ring and bracelets on his sister's hands and when he heard the words of Rebekah his sister, saying, "This is what the man said to me," he went to the man who stood by the camels at the well. And he said, "Come in, blessed of the LORD. Why do you stand outside? I have prepared the house and a place for the camels."

So the man came to the house. Then he unloaded his camels and gave straw and provision to the camels and water to wash his feet and the feet of the men who were with him. He then set food before him to eat, but he said, "I will not eat until I have told about my errand."

And he said, "Speak on."

So he said, "I am Abraham's servant. The LORD has greatly blessed my master, and he has become wealthy. He has given him flocks and herds, and silver and gold, and male and female servants, and camels and donkeys. Sarah my master's wife bore a son to my master when she was old, and he has given to him all that he has. My master made me swear, saying, 'You must not take a wife for my son from the daughters of the Canaanites, in whose land I live. But you shall go to my father's house, and to my relatives, and take a wife for my son.'

"So I said to my master, 'Perhaps the woman will not follow me.'

"Then he said to me, 'The LORD, before whom I walk, will send His angel with you and prosper your way, and you will take a wife for my son from my relatives and from my father's house. You will be free from my oath, when you come to my family, if they will not give her to you; then you will be released from my oath.'

"So today I came to the well and said, 'O LORD, the God of my master Abraham, if You will now give me success in my task; I am standing by the well of water, and let it be that when the virgin comes forth to draw water, and I say to her, "Please give me a little water from your pitcher to drink," and she says to me, "Drink, and I will also draw for your camels," let her be the woman whom the LORD has appointed for my master's son.'

"Before I had finished speaking in my heart, there was Rebekah coming out with her pitcher on her shoulder; and she went down to the well and drew water. Then I said to her, 'Please let me drink.'

"She then quickly let down her pitcher from her shoulder and said, 'Drink, and I will give your camels a drink also.' So I drank, and she gave the camels a drink also.

"Then I asked her, 'Whose daughter are you?'

"And she said, 'The daughter of Bethuel, Nahor's son, whom Milkah bore for him.'

"So I put the nose ring on her nose and the bracelets on her wrists. And I bowed down my head and worshipped the LORD, and blessed the LORD God of my master Abraham, who had led me in the right way to take the daughter of my master's brother for his son. And now if you will deal kindly and truly with my master, tell me; and if not, tell me, so that I may turn to the right hand or to the left."

Then Laban and Bethuel answered and said, "This thing comes from the LORD; we cannot speak to you bad or good. Here is Rebekah before you; take her and go, and let her be the wife of your master's son, as the LORD has spoken."

When Abraham's servant heard their words, he worshipped the LORD, bowing himself to the earth. Then the servant brought out jewels of silver and gold, and clothing and gave them to Rebekah. He also gave precious things to her brother and to her mother. Then they ate and drank, he and the men who were with him, and stayed all night.

The next morning they arose, and he said, "Send me away to my master."

But her brother and her mother said, "Let the young woman remain with us a few days, at least ten; after that she may go."

So he said to them, "Do not delay me, seeing the LORD has given me success. Let me go that I may go to my master."

They said, "We will call the girl and ask her." Then they called Rebekah and said to her, "Will you go with this man?"

And she said, "I will go."

So they sent away Rebekah their sister and her nurse, and Abraham's servant and his men. They blessed Rebekah and said to her,

"May you, our sister, become the mother
    of thousands of ten thousands;
and may your descendants possess
    the gate of those who hate them."

Then Rebekah and her maids arose and they rode on the camels and followed the man. So the servant took Rebekah and went his way.

Now Isaac came from the way of Beer Lahai Roi, for he lived in the Negev. Isaac went out in the evening to meditate in the field; and he lifted up his eyes and looked, and surely the camels were coming. And Rebekah lifted up her eyes, and when she saw Isaac, she dismounted from her camel and said to the servant, "Who is this man walking in the field to meet us?"

The servant said, "It is my master." Therefore she took a veil and covered herself.

Then the servant told Isaac all the things he had done. So Isaac brought her into the tent of his mother Sarah; and he took Rebekah and she became his wife and he loved her. So Isaac was comforted after his mother's death.

Then Abraham took another wife, whose name was Keturah. And she bore to him Zimran, Jokshan, Medan, Midian, Ishbak, and Shuah. Jokshan was the father of Sheba and Dedan. The descendants of Dedan were the Ashurites, the Letushites, and the Leummites. The sons of Midian were Ephah, Epher, Hanok, Abida, and Eldaah. All these were the children of Keturah.

Abraham gave all that he had to Isaac. But to the sons of his concubines Abraham gave gifts, and while he was still living, he sent them away from his son Isaac eastward to the east country.

These are the years of Abraham's life that he lived: one hundred seventy-five years. Then Abraham breathed his last and died at a good old age, an old man and full of years; and he was gathered to his people. His sons Isaac and Ishmael buried him in the cave of Machpelah, in the field of Ephron the son of Zohar the Hittite, east of Mamre, the field that Abraham purchased from the sons of Heth. There Abraham was buried with his wife Sarah. After the death of Abraham, God blessed his son Isaac. Isaac lived at Beer Lahai Roi.

These are the generations of Ishmael, Abraham's son, whom Hagar the Egyptian, Sarah's maidservant, bore to Abraham.

These are the names of the sons of Ishmael, by their names, according to their generations: the firstborn of Ishmael, Nebaioth, and then Kedar, Adbeel, Mibsam, Mishma, Dumah, Massa, Hadad, Tema, Jetur, Naphish, and Kedemah. These were the sons of Ishmael, and these were their names, by their towns and their settlements, twelve princes according to their peoples. These were the years of the life of Ishmael: one hundred thirty-seven years. He breathed his last and died; and he was gathered to his people. They lived from Havilah as far as Shur, which is east of Egypt, as you go toward Assyria. He died in the presence of all his relatives.

Toldot

Generations

(Genesis 25:19–28:9)

These are the generations of Isaac, Abraham's son.

Abraham was the father of Isaac. Isaac was forty years old when he took Rebekah as his wife, the daughter of Bethuel the Syrian of Paddan Aram, the sister to Laban the Syrian.

Now Isaac pleaded with the LORD for his wife, because she was barren; and the LORD granted his plea, and Rebekah his wife conceived. But the children struggled together within her, and she said, "If all is well, why am I like this?" So she went to inquire of the LORD.

Then the LORD said to her,

"Two nations are in your womb,
  and two peoples will be separated from your body;
one people will be stronger than the other,
  and the older will serve the younger."

Now when the time of her delivery came, there were twins in her womb. The first came out red all over, like a hairy garment, and they called his name Esau. After that his brother came out, and his hand took hold of Esau's heel, so he was named Jacob. Isaac was sixty years old when she bore them.

So the boys grew. Esau was a cunning hunter, a man of the field, while Jacob was a calm man, living in tents. Isaac loved Esau, because he ate of his game, but Rebekah loved Jacob.

Now Jacob cooked a stew; and Esau came in from the field and he was famished. So Esau said to Jacob, "Please feed me some of that red stew, for I am famished." Therefore his name was called Edom.

Then Jacob said, "First sell me your birthright."

Esau said, "Look, I am about to die; of what use is the birthright to me?"

Then Jacob said, "Swear to me this day." So he swore to him, and he sold his birthright to Jacob.

Then Jacob gave Esau bread and lentil stew. Then he ate and drank, arose, and went his way.

Thus Esau despised his birthright.

There was a famine in the land, in addition to the first famine that was during the days of Abraham. Isaac went to Abimelek king of the Philistines in Gerar. The LORD appeared to him and said, "Do not go down to Egypt. Live in the land of which I will tell you. Sojourn in this land, and I will be with you and will bless you; for I will give to you and all your descendants all these lands, and I will fulfill the oath which I swore to Abraham your father. I will make your descendants multiply as the stars of the heavens and will give your descendants all these lands. By your descendants all the nations of the earth will be blessed, because Abraham obeyed Me and kept My charge, My commandments, My statutes, and My laws." So Isaac lived in Gerar.

The men of the place asked him about his wife. And he said, "She is my sister," for he was afraid to say, "She is my wife," *thinking,* "The men of the place might kill me on account of Rebekah, because she is beautiful in appearance."

When he had been there a long time, Abimelek the king of the Philistines looked out of a window and saw Isaac caressing Rebekah his wife. Abimelek summoned Isaac and said, "She is surely your wife, so how is it you said, 'She is my sister'?"

Then Isaac said to him, "Because I said, 'I might die on account of her.'"

Abimelek said, "What is this you have done to us? One of the people might have easily lain with your wife, and you might have brought guilt upon us!"

Abimelek charged all his people, saying, "He who touches this man or his wife will surely be put to death."

Then Isaac sowed in that land and reaped in the same year a hundredfold; the LORD blessed him. The man became rich and continued to prosper until he became very wealthy. For he had possessions of flocks and herds and a great number of servants so that the Philistines envied him. For the Philistines had stopped up all the wells which his father's servants had dug in the days of Abraham his father by filling them with dirt.

Abimelek said to Isaac, "Go away from us, for you are much more powerful than we are."

So Isaac departed from there and pitched his tent in the Valley of Gerar and settled there. Isaac dug again the wells of water, which they had dug in the days of Abraham his father, for the Philistines had stopped them up after the death of Abraham. He called their names after the names his father had called them.

But when Isaac's servants dug in the valley and found a well of running water there, the herdsmen of Gerar contended with Isaac's herdsmen, saying, "The water is ours." So he called the name of the well Esek, because they contended with him. They dug another well and quarreled over that also. So he called the name of it Sitnah. Then he moved away from there and dug another well, and they did not quarrel over it. So he called the name of it Rehoboth, for he said, "For now the LORD has made room for us, and we will be fruitful in the land."

He went up from there to Beersheba. The LORD appeared to him that same night and said, "I am the God of Abraham your father. Do not fear, for I am with you. I will bless you and multiply your descendants for the sake of My servant Abraham."

He built an altar there, called on the name of the LORD, and pitched his tent there. And there Isaac's servants dug a well.

Then Abimelek went to him from Gerar, along with Ahuzzath, one of his friends, and Phicol the commander of his army. Isaac said to them, "Why have you come to me, since you hate me and have sent me away from you?"

And they said, "We saw plainly that the LORD was with you. So we said, 'Let there now be an oath between us, between you and us, and let us make a covenant with you, so that you will do us no harm, just as we have not touched you, and have done you nothing but good and have sent you away in peace. You are now the blessed of the LORD.'"

Then he made them a feast, and they ate and drank. They rose up early in the morning and swore an oath with one another. Isaac sent them away, and they departed from him in peace.

That same day Isaac's servants came and told him about the well that they had dug and said to him, "We have found water." And he called it Shibah. Therefore, the name of the city is Beersheba to this day.

Esau was forty years old when he took as wives Judith the daughter of Beeri the Hittite, and Basemath the daughter of Elon the Hittite, and they brought grief to Isaac and to Rebekah.

When Isaac was old and his eyes were so weak that he could not see, he called Esau his oldest son and said to him, "My son."

And he answered him, "Here I am."

He said, "I am old. I do not know the day of my death. Therefore, please take your weapons, your quiver and your bow, and go out to the field and hunt game for me. And prepare for me savory food, such as I love, and bring it to me that I may eat, so that my soul may bless you before I die."

Rebekah was listening when Isaac spoke to Esau his son. So when Esau went to the field to hunt for wild game and bring it back, Rebekah said to her son Jacob, "I heard your father speak to your brother Esau, saying, 'Bring me wild game, and prepare for me savory food, that I may eat and bless you in the presence of the LORD before my death.' Now therefore, my son, listen to me as I command you. Go now to the flock, and get me two choice young goats, so that I may prepare from them savory food for your father, such as he loves. Then you will take it to your father, so that he may eat and so that he may bless you before his death."

But Jacob said to his mother Rebekah, "Look, my brother Esau is a hairy man, and I am a man of smooth *skin*. Perhaps my father will feel me, and

I will seem to him as a deceiver, and I will bring a curse on myself and not a blessing."

His mother said to him, "Let your curse be upon me, my son. Only listen to me and go get them for me."

He went and got them and brought them to his mother. Then his mother prepared savory food such as his father loved. Then Rebekah took the best clothes belonging to her older son Esau, which were with her in the house, and put them on Jacob her younger son. Then she put the skins of the young goats on his hands and on the smooth part of his neck. She put the savory food and the bread, which she had prepared, into the hands of her son Jacob.

He came to his father and said, "My father."

And he said, "Here I am. Who are you, my son?"

And Jacob said to his father, "I am Esau your firstborn. I have done just as you asked me. Please arise, sit and eat of my wild game, so that your soul may bless me."

Isaac said to his son, "How is it that you have found it so quickly, my son?"

And he said, "Because the LORD your God brought it to me."

Isaac said to Jacob, "Please come near, so that I may feel you, my son, whether you are really my son Esau or not."

Jacob went near to his father Isaac, and he felt him and said, "The voice is the voice of Jacob, but the hands are the hands of Esau." He did not recognize him because his hands were hairy, just like his brother Esau's hands; so he blessed him. He asked, "Are you really my son Esau?"

And he said, "I am."

He said, "Bring it near to me, and I will eat of my son's wild game, so that my soul may bless you."

And he brought it near to him, and he ate. He also brought him wine, and he drank. His father Isaac said to him, "Come near now and kiss me, my son."

He came near and kissed him; and he smelled the smell of his clothing and blessed him and said,

> "See, the smell of my son
>   is like the smell of the field
>   which the LORD has blessed.
> Therefore, may God give you of the dew of heaven
>   and the fatness of the earth,
>   and plenty of grain and new wine.
> Let peoples serve you,
>   and nations bow down to you.
> Be master over your brothers,
>   and let your mother's sons bow down to you.
> Cursed be everyone who curses you,
>   and blessed be those who bless you!"

As soon as Isaac had finished blessing Jacob, and Jacob had barely gone out from the presence of his father Isaac, Esau his brother came in from his hunting. He also had prepared savory food and brought it to his father, and said to his father, "Let my father arise and eat of his son's wild game, so that your soul may bless me."

Isaac his father said to him, "Who are you?"

And he said, "I am your son, your firstborn, Esau."

Then Isaac trembled violently, and said, "Who? Where then is he who hunted game and brought it to me? I ate all of it before you came, and I have blessed him. Yes, and he shall be blessed."

When Esau heard the words of his father, he cried with a great and exceedingly bitter cry, and said to his father, "Bless me, even me also, O my father!"

He said, "Your brother came deceitfully and has taken away your blessing."

Esau said, "Is he not rightly named Jacob? For he has supplanted me these two times. He took away my birthright, and now he has taken away my blessing." And he said, "Have you not reserved a blessing for me?"

Then Isaac answered and said to Esau, "I have made him your lord, and I have given to him all his brothers as servants; and I have sustained him with grain and new wine. What can I now do for you, my son?"

And Esau said to his father, "Do you have only one blessing, my father? Bless me, even me also, O my father!" Then Esau lifted up his voice and wept.

Isaac his father answered and said to him,

"Your dwelling shall be
   away from the fatness of the earth
   and away from the dew of heaven from above.
You will live by your sword
   and will serve your brother.
When you become restless,
   you will break his yoke
   from your neck."

So Esau hated Jacob because of the blessing with which his father blessed him. And Esau said in his heart, "The days of mourning for my father are at hand; then I will kill my brother Jacob."

These words of Esau her older son were told to Rebekah; and she sent and called Jacob her younger son, and said to him, "Your brother Esau consoles himself regarding you by planning to kill you. Now therefore, my son, listen to me and get up and flee to Laban, my brother in Harran. Stay with him a few days until your brother's fury subsides, until your brother's anger

against you turns away, and he forgets what you have done to him. Then I
will send and get you from there. Why should I lose both of you in one day?"

Then Rebekah said to Isaac, "I am tired of my life because of the daughters of Heth. If Jacob takes a wife from the daughters of Heth, such as these
who are of the daughters of the land, what good will my life be to me?"

Then Isaac called Jacob and blessed him. Then he charged him and said
to him, "You must not take a wife of the daughters of Canaan. Arise, go to
Paddan Aram to the house of Bethuel your mother's father, and take for
yourself a wife from there, from the daughters of Laban your mother's
brother. May God Almighty bless you and make you fruitful and multiply
you, so that you may become a multitude of people. May He give you the
blessing of Abraham, to you and your descendants with you, that you may
inherit the land where you are a stranger, which God gave to Abraham."
Then Isaac sent Jacob away, and he went to Paddan Aram to Laban, the son
of Bethuel the Syrian, the brother of Rebekah, Jacob's and Esau's mother.

Esau saw that Isaac had blessed Jacob and sent him away to Paddan Aram
to take for himself a wife from there, and that as he blessed him he gave him
a charge, saying, "You must not take a wife of the daughters of Canaan,"
and that Jacob obeyed his father and his mother and had gone to Paddan
Aram. Esau saw that the daughters of Canaan did not please Isaac his father.
So Esau went to Ishmael and took as his wife Mahalath the daughter of Ishmael, Abraham's son, the sister of Nebaioth, in addition to the wives he had.

Vayetzei

And he went out

(Genesis 28:10–32:2)

Then Jacob went out from Beersheba and went toward Harran. He came to a certain place and stayed there all night, because the sun had set. He took one of the stones of that place and put it under his head, and lay down in that place to sleep. He dreamed and saw a ladder set up on the earth with the top of it reaching to heaven. The angels of God were ascending and descending on it. The LORD stood above it and said, "I am the LORD God of Abraham your father and the God of Isaac. The land on which you lie, to you will I give it and to your descendants. Your descendants will be like the dust of the earth, and you will spread abroad to the west and to the east and to the north and to the south, and in you and in your descendants all the families of the earth will be blessed. Remember, I am with you, and I will protect you wherever you go, and I will bring you back to this land. For I will not leave you until I have done what I promised you."

Jacob awoke out of his sleep, and he said, "Surely the LORD is in this place, and I did not know it." He was afraid and said, "How awesome is this place! This is none other but the house of God, and this is the gate of heaven."

So Jacob rose up early in the morning and took the stone that he had put under his head, set it up as a pillar, and poured oil on top of it. He called the name of that place Bethel, but previously the name of the city was called Luz.

Jacob vowed a vow, saying, "If God will be with me and will protect me in this way that I go, and will give me bread to eat and clothing to put on, so that I return to my father's house in peace, then the LORD will be my God. Then this stone, which I have set for a pillar, will be the house of God, and from all that You give me I will surely give one-tenth to You."

Then Jacob went on his journey and came into the land of the people of the east. As he looked, he saw a well in the field and three flocks of sheep lying by it, for out of that well the flocks were watered. A large stone was on the well's opening. When all the flocks were gathered there, the shepherds rolled the stone from the well's opening, watered the sheep, then put the stone back on the well's opening in its place.

Jacob said to them, "My brothers, where are you from?"

And they said, "We are from Harran."

Then he said to them, "Do you know Laban the son of Nahor?"

And they said, "We know him."

He said to them, "Is he well?"

And they said, "He is well, and here is Rachel his daughter coming with the sheep."

He said, "Since it is yet midday, it is not the time that the livestock should be gathered together. Water the sheep, and go and feed them."

They said, "We cannot until all the flocks are gathered together and the stone is rolled from the well's opening. Then we may water the sheep."

While he was still speaking with them, Rachel came with her father's sheep, for she kept them. When Jacob saw Rachel the daughter of Laban his mother's brother and the sheep of Laban his mother's brother, Jacob went near and rolled the stone from the well's opening and watered the flock of Laban his mother's brother. Jacob kissed Rachel and wept aloud. Jacob told Rachel that he was her father's relative and that he was Rebekah's son. Then she ran and told her father.

When Laban heard the news of Jacob his sister's son, he ran to meet him and embraced him and kissed him and brought him to his house. Then Jacob told Laban all these things. Laban said to him, "Surely you are my bone and my flesh."

And he stayed with him for a month. Laban said to Jacob, "Since you are my relative, should you therefore serve me for nothing? Tell me, what shall your wages be?"

Now Laban had two daughters. The name of the older was Leah, and the name of the younger was Rachel. Leah's eyes were tender, but Rachel was beautiful in form and appearance. Jacob loved Rachel, so he said, "I will serve you seven years for Rachel your younger daughter."

Laban said, "It is better that I give her to you than that I should give her to another man. Stay with me." So Jacob served seven years for Rachel, and they seemed to him but a few days because of the love he had for her.

Then Jacob said to Laban, "Give me my wife, for my days are fulfilled, so that I may have relations with her."

Laban gathered together all the men of the place and prepared a feast. But in the evening he took Leah his daughter and brought her to Jacob, and Jacob had relations with her. Laban gave Zilpah his maid to his daughter Leah for a maidservant.

In the morning Jacob discovered it was Leah, and he said to Laban, "What is this you have done to me? Did I not serve you for Rachel? Why then have you tricked me?"

Then Laban said, "It is not the custom in our country to marry off the younger before the firstborn. Fulfill the period of seven days for this one, and we will give you the other also in return for serving me another seven years."

Jacob did so and completed her week. Then Laban gave him Rachel his daughter as his wife also. Laban gave Bilhah his maidservant to Rachel his daughter to be her maid. So Jacob also had relations with Rachel, and he loved Rachel more than Leah and served Laban another seven years.

When the LORD saw that Leah was unloved, He opened her womb, but Rachel was barren. Leah conceived and gave birth to a son, and she called his name Reuben, for she said, "Surely the LORD has looked upon my affliction. Now therefore my husband will love me."

She conceived again and gave birth to a son and said, "Because the LORD has heard that I was unloved, He has therefore given me this son also." Then she called his name Simeon.

She conceived again and gave birth to a son and said, "Now this time my husband will be joined to me, because I have borne him three sons." Therefore his name was called Levi.

She conceived again and gave birth to a son, and she said, "Now I will praise the LORD!" Therefore she called his name Judah. Then she stopped giving birth.

When Rachel saw that she could not give Jacob children, she became jealous of her sister. She said to Jacob, "Give me children, or I will die."

Jacob became angry with Rachel and said, "Am I in the place of God, who has withheld from you the fruit of the womb?"

Then she said, "Here is my maid Bilhah. Have relations with her so that she may bear *a child* on my knees, so that I may also have children through her."

So she gave him Bilhah her maidservant as a wife, and Jacob had relations with her. Bilhah conceived and gave Jacob a son. Rachel said, "God has vindicated me, and He has also heard my voice and has given me a son." Therefore she called his name Dan.

Bilhah, Rachel's maid, conceived again and gave Jacob a second son. Then Rachel said, "With great wrestling have I wrestled with my sister, and I have prevailed." So she called his name Naphtali.

When Leah saw that she had stopped having children, she took Zilpah her maid and gave her to Jacob as a wife. Zilpah, Leah's maid, gave Jacob a son. Then Leah said, "How fortunate!" So she called his name Gad.

Zilpah, Leah's maid, gave Jacob a second son. Then Leah said, "Happy am I, for women will call me happy." So she called his name Asher.

At the time of the wheat harvest, Reuben went and found mandrakes in the field and brought them to his mother Leah. Then Rachel said to Leah, "Please give me some of your son's mandrakes."

Leah said to her, "Is it a small matter that you have taken my husband? Would you take away my son's mandrakes also?"

So Rachel said, "All right, he may lie with you tonight in exchange for your son's mandrakes."

When Jacob came out of the field in the evening, Leah went out to meet him and said, "You must sleep with me, because I have paid for you with my son's mandrakes." And he slept with her that night.

God listened to Leah, and she conceived and gave Jacob a fifth son. Leah said, "God has given me my reward because I have given my maid to my husband." So she called his name Issachar.

Leah conceived again and gave Jacob a sixth son. Leah said, "God has given me a good gift. Now my husband will dwell with me, because I have given him six sons." So she called his name Zebulun.

Afterwards she gave birth to a daughter and called her name Dinah.

Then God remembered Rachel, and God listened to her and opened her womb. She conceived and gave birth to a son and said, "God has taken away my reproach." And she called his name Joseph, saying, "The LORD will add to me another son."

When Rachel had given birth to Joseph, Jacob said to Laban, "Send me away, so that I may go to my own place, to my country. Give me my wives and my children, for whom I have served you, and let me go. For you know the service that I have given you."

Laban said to him, "If I have found favor in your eyes, please stay. For I have learned by divination that the LORD has blessed me on account of you." He said, "Name me your wages, and I will give it."

Jacob said to him, "You know how I have served you, and how your livestock have fared with me. For you had little before I came, and it is now increased to a multitude. The LORD has blessed you since I came, and now when may I also provide for my own house?"

Laban said, "What may I give you?"

And Jacob said, "You may not give me anything, but if you will do this *one* thing for me, I will continue to feed and keep your flock. I will pass through all your flock today, removing from it all the speckled and spotted sheep, and every brown sheep from among the lambs, and the spotted and speckled among the goats. These shall be my wages. So my integrity will answer for me in time to come. When you come to examine my wages, every one that is not speckled and spotted among the goats, and brown among the sheep that are with me will be considered stolen."

Laban said, "Agreed. Let it be according to your word." He removed that day the male goats that were striped and spotted and all the female goats that were speckled and spotted, every one that had some white in it, and all the brown ones among the sheep, and gave them into the care of his sons. He put three days' journey between himself and Jacob, and Jacob fed the rest of Laban's flocks.

Then Jacob took rods of fresh-cut poplar, almond, and plane trees, and peeled white streaks in them, exposing the white which was in the rods. He set the rods which he had peeled before the flocks in the troughs, that is, the watering places, where the flocks came to drink, so that they would mate when they came to drink. The flocks mated before the rods and gave birth to *young* that were striped, speckled, and spotted. Jacob separated the lambs and made the flocks face toward the striped and all the brown in the flock of Laban. He put his own flocks by themselves and did not put them with Laban's sheep. Whenever the stronger sheep mated, Jacob laid the rods before the eyes of the sheep in the troughs, so that they might mate among the rods. But when the livestock were feeble, he did not put them in. So the weaker were Laban's and the stronger Jacob's. The man became exceedingly prosperous and had many sheep and female servants and male servants and camels and donkeys.

Now *Jacob* heard the words of Laban's sons, saying, "Jacob has taken away all that was our father's, and he has gotten all his wealth from what was our father's." Jacob saw the look of Laban and saw he was not congenial toward him as before.

Then the LORD said to Jacob, "Return to the land of your fathers, to your family, and I will be with you."

So Jacob sent and called Rachel and Leah to the field where his flock was, and said to them, "I see your father's demeanor, that it is not congenial toward me as before; but the God of my father has been with me. You know that with all my strength I have served your father. Your father has deceived me and changed my wages ten times, but God did not allow him to hurt me. If he said, 'The speckled will be your wages,' then all the flock produced speckled. If he said, 'The striped will be your pay,' then all the flock produced striped. In this way God has taken away your father's flock and given them to me.

"When the livestock conceived, I lifted up my eyes and saw in a dream that the male goats mating with the flock were striped, speckled, and spotted. The angel of God spoke to me in a dream, saying, 'Jacob.' And I said, 'Here I am.' He said, 'Now lift up your eyes and see all the male goats which mate with the flock are striped, speckled, and spotted, for I have seen all that Laban has done to you. I am the God of Bethel, where you anointed the pillar, where you vowed a vow to Me. Now arise, and get out of this land, and return to the land of your family.'"

Rachel and Leah answered him, "Is there any portion or inheritance left for us in our father's house? Are we not seen by him as foreigners? For he has sold us and has completely spent our money also. For all the riches which God has taken from our father are ours and our children's. Now then, whatever God has said to you, do it."

Then Jacob rose up and set his sons and his wives on camels. Then he carried away all his livestock and all his goods which he had obtained, his acquired livestock which he had gotten in Paddan Aram, in order to go to Isaac his father in the land of Canaan.

When Laban went to shear his sheep, Rachel stole the household idols that were her father's. Jacob also deceived Laban the Syrian by not telling him that he was fleeing. So Jacob fled with all that he had, and he rose up and passed over the river and headed toward the mountains of Gilead.

Laban was told on the third day that Jacob had fled. He took his kinsmen with him and pursued him for seven days until he caught up with him in the mountains of Gilead. But God came to Laban the Syrian in a dream by night and said to him, "Take care that you speak to Jacob neither good nor bad."

Then Laban overtook Jacob. Now Jacob had pitched his tent on the mountain, and Laban with his kinsmen pitched in the mountains of Gilead. Laban said to Jacob, "What have you done that you have stolen away without my knowing and carried away my daughters like captives taken with the sword? Why did you flee away secretly and sneak away from me and not tell me? I would have sent you away with joy and with songs, with the tambourine and harp. And why did you not permit me to kiss my sons and my daughters farewell? You have acted foolishly in so doing. It is in my power to do you harm, but the God of your father spoke to me last night, saying, 'Take care that you not speak to Jacob either good or bad.' Now you surely have gone away because you longed desperately after your father's house, yet why have you stolen my gods?"

Then Jacob answered and said to Laban, "Because I was afraid, for I thought that you would take your daughters from me by force. But anyone with whom you find your gods, let him not live. In the presence of our kinsmen, point out what I have that is yours and take it." For Jacob did not know that Rachel had stolen them.

So Laban went into Jacob's tent and into Leah's tent and into the two female servants' tents, but he did not find them. Then he went out of Leah's tent and entered into Rachel's tent. Now Rachel had taken the household idols and put them in the camel's saddle and sat on them. Laban searched the entire tent, but could not find them.

She said to her father, "Let not my lord be displeased that I cannot rise before you, for the manner of women is on me." So he searched, but he did not find the household idols.

Then Jacob became angry and berated Laban. And Jacob asked Laban, "What is my offense? What is my sin that you have so hotly pursued after me? You have searched all my things, and yet what have you found of all your household things? Set it here before my kinsmen and your kinsmen, so that they may judge between us both.

"This twenty years I have been with you. Your ewes and your female goats have not miscarried their young, and the male goats of your flock I have not eaten. That which was torn by beasts I did not bring to you. I bore the loss of it. You required it from my hand *whether it* was stolen by day or stolen by night. It was like this with me: In the day the heat consumed me and the frost by night, and my sleep fled from my eyes. I have been twenty years in your house. I served you fourteen years for your two daughters and six years for your flock, and you have changed my wages ten times. If the God of my father, the God of Abraham and the Fear of Isaac, had not been with me, surely you would have sent me away empty now. God has seen my affliction and the labor of my hands and rebuked you last night."

Laban answered and said to Jacob, "These daughters are my daughters, and these children are my children, and the flocks are my flocks, and all that you see is mine. But what can I do this day to my daughters or to their children whom they have borne? Now therefore come, let us make a covenant, you and I, and let it be as a witness between you and me."

So Jacob took a stone and set it up for a pillar. Jacob said to his kinsmen, "Gather stones." So they took stones and made a pile, and they ate there on the pile. And Laban called it Jegar Sahadutha, but Jacob called it Galeed.

Laban said, "This pile is a witness between me and you this day." Therefore its name was called Galeed, and Mizpah, for he said, "May the LORD watch between you and me, when we are apart from one another. If you mistreat my daughters, or if you take other wives beside my daughters, although no one else is with us, remember that God is witness between you and me."

Then Laban said to Jacob, "See this pile and see this pillar which I have thrown between you and me. This heap is a witness, and this pillar is a witness, so that I will not cross over this pile to you and so that you will not pass over this pile and this pillar to me for harm. The God of Abraham, the God of Nahor, and the God of their father, judge between us."

Then Jacob vowed by the Fear of his father Isaac. Then Jacob offered a sacrifice on the mountain and called his kinsmen to eat bread. And they ate bread and stayed all night on the mountain.

Early in the morning Laban rose up, kissed his grandchildren and his daughters, and blessed them. Then Laban departed and returned to his place.

Jacob went on his way, and the angels of God met him. When Jacob saw them, he said, "This is God's camp." So he called the name of that place Mahanaim.

Vayishlach

And he sent

(Genesis 32:3–36:43)

Jacob sent messengers before him to his brother Esau in the land of Seir, the country of Edom. He commanded them, saying, "This is what you must say to my lord Esau: This is what your servant Jacob says, 'I have sojourned with Laban and stayed there until now. I have oxen and donkeys, flocks, and male servants and female servants, and I am sending *this message* to tell my lord, so that I may find favor in your sight.'"

The messengers returned to Jacob, saying, "We went to your brother Esau. He is coming to meet you, and what is more, four hundred men are with him."

Then Jacob was very afraid and distressed, and he divided the people that were with him, along with the flocks and herds and the camels, into two groups. He said, "If Esau comes to the one camp and attacks it, then the other camp which is left may escape."

And Jacob said, "O God of my father Abraham and God of my father Isaac, the LORD who said to me, 'Return to your country and to your relatives, and I will prosper you,' I am not worthy of all the lovingkindness and of all the faithfulness which You have shown to Your servant. For with my staff I crossed over this Jordan, and now I have become two encampments. Deliver me, I pray, from the hand of my brother, from the hand of Esau. For I fear him, that he will come and attack me and the mothers with the children. You said, 'I will surely prosper you and make your descendants as the sand of the sea, which is too many to be counted.'"

So he spent the night there. Then he selected from what he had with him a gift for his brother Esau: two hundred female goats and twenty male goats, two hundred ewes and twenty rams, thirty female camels with their colts, forty cows and ten bulls, twenty female donkeys and ten male donkeys. He gave them to his servants, every drove by itself, and said to his servants, "Pass over before me, and keep a distance between each drove."

He commanded the one leading, saying, "When my brother Esau meets you and asks you, saying, 'To whom do you belong, and where are you going, and to whom do these *animals* belong?' then you are to say, 'They belong to your servant Jacob. They are a gift sent to my lord Esau, and he is also behind us.'"

Likewise he commanded the second and the third and all that followed the droves, saying, "This is what you are to say to Esau when you find him. Moreover, say, 'Your servant Jacob is behind us.' " For he said, "I will appease him with the gift that goes before me, and then I will see his face. Perhaps he will accept me." So the gift went before him, but he lodged that night in the encampment.

The same night he arose and took his two wives, his two female servants, and his eleven sons, and crossed over the ford of the Jabbok. He took them and sent them across the stream along with all that he had. Jacob was left alone, and a man wrestled with him there until daybreak. When the man saw that He did not prevail against Jacob, He touched the socket of his thigh, so the socket of Jacob's thigh was dislocated, as he wrestled with Him. Then He said, "Let Me go, for the day breaks."

But Jacob said, "I will not let You go, unless You bless me."

So He said to him, "What is your name?"

And he said, "Jacob."

Then the man said, "Your name will no more be called Jacob, but Israel. For you have fought with God and with men, and have prevailed."

Then Jacob asked Him, "Tell me, I pray You, Your name."

But He said, "Why do you ask Me My name?" Then He blessed him there.

Jacob called the name of the place Peniel, saying, "I have seen God face to face, and my life has been preserved."

As he crossed over Peniel, the sun rose over him, and he was limping on his thigh. Therefore to this day the children of Israel do not eat the sinew which is attached to the socket of the thigh, because He touched the socket of Jacob's thigh in the sinew of the hip.

Then Jacob looked up and saw Esau coming and four hundred men with him. So he divided the children among Leah, Rachel, and the two female servants. He put the female servants and their children in front, then Leah and her children next, and then Rachel and Joseph last. He went on before them, bowing himself to the ground seven times, until he came near to his brother.

But Esau ran to meet him and embraced him and fell on his neck and kissed him, and they wept. When Esau looked up and saw the women and the children, he said, "Who are those with you?"

Jacob said, "The children whom God has graciously given your servant."

Then the female servants came near, they and their children, and they bowed down. Leah also with her children came near and bowed themselves. Afterward Joseph and Rachel came near, and they bowed themselves.

Esau said, "What do you mean by all this company that I met?"

Jacob answered, "These are to find favor in the sight of my lord."

Esau said, "I have enough, my brother. Keep what you have for yourself."

Jacob said, "No, I pray you, if I have now found favor in your sight, then receive my gift from my hand. For I have seen your face, and it is as though I have seen the face of God, with you having received me favorably. Please take my blessing that has been brought to you, because God has dealt graciously with me and because I have plenty." So he urged him, and he took it.

Then Esau said, "Let us journey on our way, and I will go ahead of you."

But Jacob said to him, "My lord knows that the children are weak, and the flocks and herds with young are with me. If they are driven too hard one day, all the flock will die. Please let my lord pass over before his servant, and I will lead on slowly, according to the pace of the livestock that goes before me and the pace the children will be able to endure, until I come to my lord at Seir."

So Esau said, "Let me leave some of the people that are with me with you."

But Jacob said, "What need is there? Let me find favor in the sight of my lord."

So Esau returned that day making his way back to Seir. But Jacob journeyed to Sukkoth and built himself a house and made booths for his livestock. Therefore the name of the place is called Sukkoth.

Jacob came peacefully to the city of Shechem, which is in the land of Canaan, on his way from Paddan Aram, and camped before the city. He bought a parcel of a field, where he had pitched his tent, from the children of Hamor, Shechem's father, for one hundred pieces of silver. He erected an altar there and called it El Elohe Israel.

Now Dinah, the daughter of Leah, whom she bore to Jacob, went out to see the daughters of the land. When Shechem, the son of Hamor the Hivite, prince of the land, saw her, he took her and lay with her and defiled her. He was very smitten by Dinah the daughter of Jacob, and he loved the girl and spoke kindly to her. Shechem spoke to his father Hamor, saying, "Get me this girl for *my* wife."

Now Jacob heard that Shechem had violated his daughter Dinah, but his sons were with his livestock in the field, so Jacob held his peace until they came.

Hamor the father of Shechem went out to Jacob to commune with him. The sons of Jacob came out of the field when they heard it, and the men were grieved and were very disturbed, because Shechem had disgraced Israel by lying with Jacob's daughter, a thing that should not be done.

Hamor spoke with them, saying, "The soul of my son Shechem longs for your daughter. I pray that you will give her to him to marry. Make marriages with us, and give your daughters to us, and take our daughters for yourselves. You may dwell with us, and the land will be before you. Dwell and trade in it and get possessions in it."

Shechem said to her father and to her brothers, "Let me find favor in your eyes, and whatever you say to me I will give. You can make the dowry and gift I must bring high, and I will give according to what you say to me. Just give me the girl to marry."

The sons of Jacob answered Shechem and Hamor his father deceitfully, because he had defiled Dinah their sister. They said to them, "We cannot do this. To give our sister to one who is uncircumcised would be a disgrace to us. But we will consent to you in this: If you will become as we are, that is, every one of your males be circumcised, then we will give our daughters to you, and we will take your daughters to us, and we will dwell with you, and we will become one people. But if you will not listen to us and be circumcised, then we will take our daughter, and we will leave."

Their words pleased Hamor and Shechem, Hamor's son. The young man did not delay to do the thing, because he wanted Jacob's daughter. Now he was more respected than all the household of his father. So Hamor and Shechem his son came to the gate of their city, and they spoke with the men of their city, saying, "These men are at peace with us. Therefore let them dwell in the land and trade in it. For the land is large enough for them. Let us take their daughters as our wives, and let us give them our daughters. Only on this condition will the men consent to dwell with us and be one people: if every male among us will be circumcised as they are circumcised. Will not their livestock and their possessions and every animal of theirs be ours? Only, let us agree with them, and they will dwell with us."

All who went out of the gate of his city listened to Hamor and Shechem his son, and every male was circumcised, all who went out of the gate of his city.

On the third day, when they were in pain, two of Jacob's sons, Simeon and Levi, Dinah's brothers, took their swords and went to the unsuspecting city and killed all the males. They killed Hamor and Shechem his son with the edge of the sword and took Dinah out of the house of Shechem and departed. The sons of Jacob came upon the slain and looted the city, because they had defiled their sister. They took their flocks and their herds, their donkeys and whatever was in the city and in the fields. They took captive and looted all their wealth, all their little ones, and their wives, even all that was in each house.

Then Jacob said to Simeon and Levi, "You have brought trouble on me by making me revolting among the inhabitants of the land, among the Canaanites and the Perizzites. Our being few in number, they will gather themselves together against me and slay me, and I will be destroyed, both I and my household."

But they said, "Should he treat our sister like a prostitute?"

Then God said to Jacob, "Arise, go up to Bethel, dwell there, and there make an altar to God, who appeared to you when you fled from the face of Esau your brother."

So Jacob said to his household and to all who were with him, "Put away the foreign gods that are among you. Purify yourselves and change your clothes. Let us arise and go up to Bethel, and there I will make an altar to God, who answered me in the day of my distress and has been with me wherever I have gone." So they gave Jacob all the foreign gods which were in their possession and all their earrings which were in their ears, and Jacob hid them under the oak which was near Shechem. As they traveled, the terror of God was on the cities that were around them, and they did not pursue the sons of Jacob.

So Jacob came to Luz (that is, Bethel), which is in the land of Canaan, he and all the people who were with him. There he built an altar and called the place El Bethel, because God had appeared to him there when he fled from his brother.

Now Deborah, Rebekah's nurse, died and was buried beneath Bethel under the oak. So it was called Allon Bakuth.

God appeared to Jacob again when he came out of Paddan Aram and blessed him. God said to him, "Your name is Jacob. Your name shall not be called Jacob any more, but Israel shall be your name." So He called his name Israel.

God said to him, "I am God Almighty. Be fruitful and multiply. A nation and a company of nations will come from you, and kings shall come forth from you. The land that I gave Abraham and Isaac, I will give to you, and to your descendants after you I will give the land." Then God went up from him in the place where He had spoken with him.

Jacob set up a pillar in the place where He had spoken with him, a pillar of stone, and he poured out a drink offering on it, and he poured oil on it *too*. So Jacob called the name of the place where God had spoken with him Bethel.

They journeyed from Bethel, and when they were still some distance from Ephrath, Rachel went into labor, and she had a difficult labor. When she was in hard labor, the midwife said to her, "Do not fear. You will have this son also." As her soul was departing (for she died), she called his name Ben-Oni, but his father called him Benjamin.

Rachel died and was buried on the way to Ephrath, which is Bethlehem. Jacob set a pillar on her grave. It is the pillar of Rachel's grave to this day.

Israel journeyed and pitched his tent beyond the tower of Eder. When Israel lived in that land, Reuben went and lay with Bilhah, his father's concubine, and Israel heard about it.

Now the sons of Jacob were twelve:
The sons of Leah were
   Reuben, Jacob's firstborn, and Simeon and Levi and Judah and Issachar and Zebulun.
The sons of Rachel were
   Joseph and Benjamin.

And the sons of Bilhah, Rachel's maidservant, were
    Dan and Naphtali.
And the sons of Zilpah, Leah's maidservant, were
    Gad and Asher.
These are the sons of Jacob, which were born to him in Paddan Aram.

Jacob came back to Isaac his father in Mamre of Kiriath Arba (which is
Hebron), where Abraham and Isaac had sojourned. Now the days of Isaac
were one hundred eighty years. And Isaac breathed his last and died and
was gathered to his people, being old and full of days, and his sons Esau
and Jacob buried him.
Now these are the generations of Esau, who is Edom.

Esau took his wives from the daughters of Canaan: Adah the daughter
of Elon the Hittite, and Oholibamah the daughter of Anah the daughter of Zibeon the Hivite, and Basemath, Ishmael's daughter, sister of
Nebaioth.
Adah bore to Esau Eliphaz, and Basemath bore Reuel, and Oholibamah
bore Jeush, Jalam, and Korah. These are the sons of Esau, who were born
to him in the land of Canaan.
Then Esau took his wives, his sons, his daughters, and all the people
of his house, his livestock, all his animals, and all his property that he had
acquired in the land of Canaan, and he moved to a land some distance from
his brother Jacob. For their possessions were too great for them to dwell
together, and the land where they were foreigners could not sustain them
because of their livestock. So Esau settled in the hill country of Seir. Esau
is Edom.

These are the generations of Esau the father of the Edomites in the hill
country of Seir.

These are the names of Esau's sons:
    Eliphaz the son of Adah the wife of Esau, and Reuel the son of Basemath
    the wife of Esau.
The sons of Eliphaz were
    Teman, Omar, Zepho, Gatam, and Kenaz.
    Timna was a concubine to Eliphaz, Esau's son, and she bore to Eliphaz
    Amalek. These were the sons of Adah, Esau's wife.
These are the sons of Reuel:
    Nahath, Zerah, Shammah, and Mizzah. These were the sons of Base-
    math, Esau's wife.
These were the sons of Oholibamah, the daughter of Anah the daughter of
    Zibeon, Esau's wife: she bore to Esau Jeush, Jalam, and Korah.

These were chiefs of the sons of Esau.
The sons of Eliphaz the firstborn son of Esau were
Chief Teman, Chief Omar, Chief Zepho, Chief Kenaz, Chief Korah, Chief Gatam, and Chief Amalek. These are the chiefs who came from Eliphaz in the land of Edom. These were the sons of Adah.
These were the sons of Reuel Esau's son:
Chief Nahath, Chief Zerah, Chief Shammah, and Chief Mizzah. These are the chiefs who came from Reuel in the land of Edom. These were the sons of Basemath, Esau's wife.
These were the sons of Oholibamah, Esau's wife:
Chief Jeush, Chief Jalam, and Chief Korah. These were the chiefs who came from Oholibamah, the daughter of Anah, Esau's wife.
These were the sons of Esau, who is Edom, and these were their chiefs.
These were the sons of Seir the Horite, who inhabited the land:
Lotan, Shobal, Zibeon, Anah, Dishon, Ezer, and Dishan. These were the chiefs of the Horites, the children of Seir in the land of Edom.
The children of Lotan were
Hori and Homam, and Lotan's sister was Timna.
The children of Shobal were these:
Alvan, Manahath, Ebal, Shepho, and Onam.
These were the children of Zibeon:
Aiah and Anah. This was the Anah who found the water in the wilderness as he fed the donkeys of Zibeon, his father.
The children of Anah were these:
Dishon and Oholibamah, the daughter of Anah.
These are the children of Dishon:
Hemdan, Eshban, Ithran, and Keran.
The children of Ezer were these:
Bilhan, Zaavan, and Akan.
The children of Dishan were these:
Uz and Aran.
These were the chiefs that came from the Horites:
Chief Lotan, Chief Shobal, Chief Zibeon, Chief Anah, Chief Dishon, Chief Ezer, and Chief Dishan. These are the chiefs who came from Hori, among their chiefs in the land of Seir.

These were the kings who reigned in the land of Edom before there reigned any king over the children of Israel.
Bela the son of Beor reigned in Edom, and the name of his city was Dinhabah.
Bela died, and Jobab the son of Zerah of Bozrah reigned in his stead.
Jobab died, and Husham of the land of Temani reigned in his stead.
Husham died, and Hadad the son of Bedad, who defeated Midian in the field of Moab, reigned in his stead, and the name of his city was Avith.

Hadad died, and Samlah of Masrekah reigned in his stead.

Samlah died, and Shaul of Rehoboth by the river reigned in his stead.

Shaul died, and Baal-Hanan the son of Akbor reigned in his stead.

Baal-Hanan the son of Akbor died, and Hadad reigned in his stead, and the name of his city was Pau. His wife's name was Mehetabel, the daughter of Matred, the daughter of Me-Zahab.

These are the names of the chiefs who came from Esau, according to their families, according to their places, by their names:

Chief Timnah, Chief Alvah, Chief Jetheth, Chief Oholibamah, Chief Elah, Chief Pinon, Chief Kenaz, Chief Teman, Chief Mibzar, Chief Magdiel, and Chief Iram. These were the chiefs of Edom, according to their settlements in the land of their possession.

Esau *was* the father of the Edomites.

Vayeshev

And he settled

(Genesis 37:1–40:23)

N ow Jacob lived in the land where his father was a foreigner, in the land of Canaan.

These are the generations of Jacob.

Joseph, being seventeen years old, was feeding the flock with his brothers, and the boy was with the sons of Bilhah and with the sons of Zilpah, his father's wives. Joseph brought back a bad report about them to their father.

Now Israel loved Joseph more than all his sons, because he was the son of his old age, and he made him a coat of many colors. But when his brothers saw that their father loved him more than all his brothers, they hated him and could not speak peaceably to him.

Now Joseph dreamed a dream, and when he told it to his brothers, they hated him even more. He said to them, "Please listen to this dream which I have dreamed. We were binding sheaves in the field. All of a sudden my sheaf rose up and stood upright, and your sheaves stood around it and bowed down to my sheaf."

His brothers said to him, "Will you really reign over us, or will you really have dominion over us?" So they hated him even more because of his dreams and his words.

Then he dreamed another dream and told it to his brothers and said, "I have dreamed another dream. The sun and the moon and eleven stars were bowing to me."

But when he told it to his father and his brothers, his father rebuked him and said to him, "What is this dream that you have dreamed? Will I and your mother and your brothers really come to bow down ourselves to you to the ground?" So his brothers were jealous of him, but his father kept the matter *in mind*.

Now his brothers went to feed their father's flock in Shechem. Israel said to Joseph, "Are not your brothers feeding the flock in Shechem? Come, and I will send you to them."

He answered, "Here I am."

Israel said to him, "Please go and see if it is well with your brothers and well with the flocks, and bring back word to me." So he sent him out of the Valley of Hebron, and he came to Shechem.

A certain man found him wandering in the field. The man asked him, "What are you looking for?"

And he said, "I am looking for my brothers. Please tell me where they are feeding their flocks."

The man said, "They have departed from here. I heard them say, 'Let us go to Dothan.'"

So Joseph went after his brothers and found them in Dothan.

When they saw him some distance away, before he came near to them, they conspired against him to kill him.

They said one to another, "The master of dreams comes! Come now, let us kill him and throw him into some pit, and we will say, 'Some evil beast has devoured him.' Then we will see what will become of his dreams."

But when Reuben heard it, he rescued him out of their hands, saying, "Let us not kill him." Reuben said to them, "Shed no blood, but throw him into this pit here in the wilderness, but lay no hand on him," so that he might rescue him out of their hands and deliver him to his father again.

When Joseph came to his brothers, they stripped Joseph of his coat—his coat of many colors that he had on. And they took him and threw him into a pit. The pit was empty, and there was no water in it.

Then they sat down to eat. And looking up, they saw a caravan of Ishmaelites coming from Gilead, with their camels bearing spices, balm, and myrrh, carrying it down to Egypt.

Then Judah said to his brothers, "What profit is it if we kill our brother and cover up his blood? Come, let us sell him to the Ishmaelites, and let us not lay our hand on him, for he is our brother and our own flesh." So his brothers agreed.

Then when the Midianite merchants passed by, they drew Joseph up and lifted him out of the pit and sold Joseph to the Ishmaelites for twenty shekels of silver. They took Joseph to Egypt.

When Reuben returned to the pit and saw that Joseph was not in the pit, he tore his clothes. He returned to his brothers, and said, "The boy is not *there*, and I, where can I go?"

They took Joseph's coat and killed a young goat and dipped the coat in the blood. Then they took the coat of many colors and brought it to their father and said, "This we have found. Do you know whether it is your son's robe or not?"

He knew it and said, "It is my son's coat. A wild beast has devoured him. Joseph has without a doubt been torn into pieces."

Jacob tore his clothes and put sackcloth on his waist and mourned for his son many days. All his sons and all his daughters rose up to comfort him, but he refused to be comforted. And he said, "For I will go down into the grave mourning for my son." So his father wept for him.

Meanwhile the Midianites sold him in Egypt to Potiphar, an officer of Pharaoh and captain of the guard.

At that time Judah left his brothers and visited a certain Adullamite, whose name was Hirah. There Judah saw the daughter of a certain Canaanite, whose name was Shua, and he took her and had relations with her. She conceived and bore a son, and he called his name Er. She conceived again and bore a son, and she called his name Onan. She again conceived and bore a son and called his name Shelah. He was at Kezib when she bore him.

Judah took a wife for Er his firstborn, whose name was Tamar. But Er, Judah's firstborn, was wicked in the sight of the LORD, so the LORD killed him.

Then Judah said to Onan, "Go have relations with your brother's wife, and marry her, and raise up descendants for your brother." But Onan knew that the descendant would not be his, so when he had relations with his brother's wife, he let his semen go on the ground, so that he would not give a descendant to his brother. What he did displeased the LORD; therefore He killed him also.

Then Judah said to Tamar, his daughter-in-law, "Remain a widow at your father's house until Shelah my son grows up." For he thought, "He may die also, just as his brothers did." So Tamar went and lived in her father's house.

As time went on, the daughter of Shua, Judah's wife, died. After Judah was consoled, he went up to his sheepshearers in Timnah, he and his friend Hirah the Adullamite.

It was told to Tamar, "Your father-in-law is going up to Timnah to shear his sheep." She took off her widow's clothing, covered herself with a veil, wrapped herself up, and sat in an open place, which is by the road to Timnah. For she saw that Shelah was grown, and she was not given to him as *his* wife.

When Judah saw her, he thought she was a prostitute, because she had covered her face. He turned to her by the road and said, "Come now, let me have relations with you" (for he did not know that she was his daughter-in-law).

And she said, "What will you give me, so that you may have relations with me?"

And he said, "I will send you a young goat from the flock."

And she said, "Will you give me a pledge, until you send it?"

And he said, "What pledge should I give you?"

And she said, "Your signet, your bracelets, and your staff that is in your hand." So he gave them to her and had relations with her, and she conceived by him. She arose and went away, and taking off her veil, she put on her widow's clothing.

Judah sent the young goat by his friend the Adullamite to receive his pledge from the woman's hand, but he could not find her. Then he asked the men of the place, "Where is the cult prostitute who was at Enaim by the road?"

And they said, "There was no prostitute in this place."

So he returned to Judah and said, "I cannot find her. Also, the men of the place said there was no cult prostitute in this place."

Judah replied, "Let her keep them for herself, or we shall be laughed at. I sent this young goat, and you did not find her."

After about three months, it was told Judah, "Tamar your daughter-in-law has turned to prostitution, and what is more, as a result of prostitution she is pregnant."

Then Judah said, "Bring her forth, and let her be burned!"

When she was brought forth, she sent *word* to her father-in-law, saying, "By the man to whom these belong am I with child." And she said, "Please identify whose these are—the signet and bracelet and staff."

Judah recognized them and said, "She has been more righteous than I, because I did not give her to Shelah my son." He did not have relations with her again.

When it was time for her to give birth, there were twins in her womb. While she was giving birth, one put out his hand, and the midwife took and tied on his hand a scarlet thread, saying, "This one came out first." But as he drew back his hand, his brother came out. Then she said, "How have you made a breach for yourself?" Therefore his name was called Perez. Afterward his brother came out, the one that had the scarlet thread on his hand, and his name was called Zerah.

Now Joseph was brought down to Egypt, and Potiphar, an officer of Pharaoh, captain of the guard, an Egyptian, bought him from the Ishmaelites who had brought him down there.

The LORD was with Joseph, so that he became a prosperous man. He was in the house of his master, the Egyptian. His master saw that the LORD was with him and that the LORD made all that he did to prosper. Joseph found favor in his sight and served him. So he made him overseer over his house, and all that he had he put under his charge. From the time that he had made him overseer in his house and over all that he had, the LORD blessed the Egyptian's house on account of Joseph. So the blessing of the LORD was on all that he had in the house and in the field. So he left all that he had in Joseph's charge, and he had no concerns regarding anything except the food he ate.

Now Joseph was handsome and well-built. After a time, his master's wife took notice of Joseph and said, "Lie with me."

But he refused and said to his master's wife, "My master does not concern himself with *anything* regarding me in the house, and he has committed all that he has to my charge. There is none greater in this house than I. He has kept nothing back from me but you, because you are his wife. How then can I do this great wickedness and sin against God?" She spoke to Joseph every day, but he did not listen to her about lying with her or being with her.

But it happened one day that Joseph went into the house to do his work, and none of the men of the house was there. She caught him by his clothing, saying, "Lie with me." But he left his clothing in her hand and fled and got outside.

When she saw that he had left his clothing in her hand and had fled outside, she called to the men of her house and spoke to them, saying, "See, he has brought in a Hebrew among us to humiliate us. He came in to me to lie with me, and I cried out with a loud voice. When he heard that I lifted up my voice and cried out, he left his clothing with me, fled, and got outside."

She laid up his clothing next to her until his master came home. She spoke to him using these words, saying, "The Hebrew servant, whom you have brought to us, came in to me to mock me. When I lifted up my voice and cried out, he left his clothing with me and fled outside."

When his master heard the words of his wife, which she spoke to him, saying, "This is what your servant did to me," he became enraged. Joseph's master took him and put him into the prison, a place where the king's prisoners were confined.

So he was there in the prison. But the LORD was with Joseph and showed him mercy and gave him favor in the sight of the keeper of the prison. The keeper of the prison committed all the prisoners that were in the prison to the charge of Joseph. So whatever they did there, he was the one responsible for it. The keeper of the prison did not concern himself with anything that was under Joseph's charge because the LORD was with him. And whatever he did, the LORD made it to prosper.

Sometime after this, the cupbearer of the king of Egypt and his baker offended their lord, the king of Egypt. Pharaoh was angry with his two officials, with the chief of the cupbearers and with the chief of the bakers. So he put them in confinement in the house of the captain of the guard, in the prison, the place where Joseph was confined. The captain of the guard charged Joseph with them, and he attended to them.

They continued to be in confinement for some time. Then the cupbearer and the baker for the king of Egypt, who were confined in the prison, both had a dream the same night, each man with his own dream and each dream with its *own* interpretation.

Joseph came in to them in the morning and looked at them and realized they were sad. So he asked Pharaoh's officials who were with him in the care of his lord's house, saying, "Why do you look so sad today?"

And they said to him, "We have dreamed a dream, and there is no interpreter for it."

Then Joseph said to them, "Do not interpretations belong to God? Please tell them to me."

The chief cupbearer told his dream to Joseph and said to him, "In my dream, a vine was in front of me. And in the vine there were three branches. As it budded, its blossoms shot forth and its clusters brought forth ripe grapes. Pharaoh's cup was in my hand, and I took the grapes, and pressed them into Pharaoh's cup, and I put the cup into Pharaoh's hand."

Joseph said to him, "This is the interpretation of it. The three branches are three days. Within three days Pharaoh will lift up your head and restore you to your place, and you will deliver Pharaoh's cup into his hand in the same way you did before when you were his cupbearer. But remember me when it is well with you, and show kindness, I pray you, to me, and make mention of me to Pharaoh, and get me out of this house. For I was indeed kidnapped out of the land of the Hebrews, and I have done nothing that they should put me in the dungeon."

When the chief baker saw that the interpretation was good, he said to Joseph, "I also was in my dream, and I had three white baskets on my head. In the uppermost basket there was all manner of baked goods for Pharaoh, and the birds ate them out of the basket on my head."

Joseph answered and said, "This is the interpretation: The three baskets are three days. Within three days Pharaoh will lift your head from off you and will hang you on a tree, and the birds will eat your flesh from you."

It happened on the third day, which was Pharaoh's birthday, that he made a feast for all his servants. He lifted up the heads of the chief cupbearer and the chief baker among his servants. He restored the chief cupbearer to his position again, and he put the cup into Pharaoh's hand. However, he hanged the chief baker, just as Joseph had interpreted to them.

Yet, the chief cupbearer did not remember Joseph, but forgot him.

Miketz

At the end of

(Genesis 41:1–44:17)

After two whole years, Pharaoh had a dream that he was standing by the Nile. Seven fine-looking and fattened cows suddenly came up out of the river, and they grazed in the meadow. Then seven other cows came up after them out of the river, ugly and gaunt, and stood by the other cows on the riverbank. The ugly and gaunt cows ate up the seven fine-looking and fattened cows. Then Pharaoh awoke.

He slept and dreamed a second time. Seven ears of grain suddenly came up on one stalk, plump and good. Then seven thin ears, scorched by the east wind, sprang up after them. The seven thin ears devoured the seven plump and full ears. Then Pharaoh awoke and realized it was a dream.

In the morning his spirit was troubled, and he sent and called for all the magicians of Egypt and all its wise men. Pharaoh told them his dreams, but there was no one who could interpret them to Pharaoh.

Then the chief cupbearer spoke to Pharaoh, saying, "Today I remember my offenses. Pharaoh was angry with his servants and put me in confinement in the captain of the guard's house, both me and the chief baker. And we had a dream in the same night, he and I. We, each of us, dreamed according to the interpretation of his *own* dream. A young Hebrew man was with us there, a servant to the captain of the guard. We told him and he interpreted our dreams for us. To each man he interpreted according to his *own* dream. It happened just as he interpreted. He restored me to my position, and the baker was hanged."

So Pharaoh sent and called for Joseph, and they brought him hastily out of the dungeon. He shaved himself, changed his clothes, and came to Pharaoh.

Pharaoh said to Joseph, "I have dreamed a dream, and there is no one who can interpret it. I have heard it said of you that you can understand a dream to interpret it."

Joseph answered Pharaoh, saying, "It is not in me. God will give Pharaoh a favorable answer."

Then Pharaoh said to Joseph, "In my dream, I stood on the bank of the Nile. And suddenly there came up out of the river seven cows, fattened and fine-looking, and they grazed in the reeds. Then seven other cows came up after them, poor and very ugly and gaunt. I have never seen such ugliness in all the land of Egypt. And the gaunt and ugly cows ate up the first seven fat cows. And when they had eaten them up, no one would have known that they had eaten them, for they were still as ugly as before. Then I awoke.

"I also saw in my dreams seven ears *of grain*, full and good, suddenly come up on one stalk. Then seven ears, thin and scorched by the east wind, sprang up after them. And the thin ears swallowed the seven good ears. So I told this to the magicians, but there was no one who could explain it to me."

Then Joseph said to Pharaoh, "The dreams of Pharaoh are *one and the same*. God has shown Pharaoh what He is about to do. The seven good cows are seven years, and the seven good ears are seven years. The dreams are one. The seven gaunt and ugly cows that came up after them are seven years, and the seven empty ears scorched by the east wind will be seven years of famine.

"It is as I have spoken to Pharaoh. God has shown Pharaoh what He is about to do. Seven years of great abundance will come throughout all the land of Egypt. However, there will arise after them seven years of famine. All the abundance will be forgotten in the land of Egypt, and the famine will consume the land. The abundance will be unknown in the land because of the famine following, for it will be very severe. The reason the dream was repeated to Pharaoh twice is because the matter is established by God, and God will soon bring it to pass.

"Now, therefore, let Pharaoh seek out a man *who is* discerning and wise and set him over the land of Egypt. Let Pharaoh do this, and let him appoint officials over the land and collect one-fifth of the produce of the land of Egypt in the seven abundant years. Let them gather all the food from those good years that come and lay up grain under the authority of Pharaoh, and let them keep food in the cities. This food will be for a reserve for the land for the seven years of famine which will be in the land of Egypt, so that the land does not perish during the famine."

The counsel seemed good to Pharaoh and to all of his servants. Pharaoh said to his servants, "Can we find anyone like this man, in whom is the Spirit of God?"

And Pharaoh said to Joseph, "Since God has shown you all this, there is no one as discerning and wise as you. You will be over my house, and according to your word all my people will be ruled. Only in regard to the throne will I be greater than you."

Then Pharaoh said to Joseph, "See, I have set you over all the land of Egypt." Pharaoh took off his ring from his hand and put it on Joseph's hand and arrayed him in clothes of fine linen and put a gold chain around his neck. Then he had him ride in the second chariot which was his, and they cried out before him, "Bow the knee!" So he set him over all the land of Egypt.

Pharaoh said to Joseph, "I am Pharaoh, and without your consent no man will lift up his hand or foot in all the land of Egypt." Pharaoh called

Joseph's name Zaphenath-Paneah, and he gave him a wife, Asenath the daughter of Potiphera priest of On. And Joseph went out over all the land of Egypt.

Joseph was thirty years old when he stood before Pharaoh, the king of Egypt. And Joseph went out from the presence of Pharaoh and went throughout all the land of Egypt. In the seven abundant years the earth brought forth plentifully. So he gathered up all the food of the seven years which was in the land of Egypt and laid up the food in the cities. He put in every city the food of the fields which surrounded the city. Joseph gathered great quantities of grain as the sand of the sea until he stopped measuring it, for it was beyond measure.

Before the years of famine came, two sons were born to Joseph, whom Asenath, the daughter of Potiphera priest of On, bore to him. Joseph called the name of the firstborn Manasseh, "For God," he said, "has made me forget all my trouble and all my father's house." The name of the second he called Ephraim, *saying*, "For God has caused me to be fruitful in the land of my affliction."

The seven years of abundance that were in the land of Egypt ended. The seven years of famine began to come, just as Joseph had said. The famine was in all lands, but there was food in all the land of Egypt. When all the land of Egypt was hungry, the people cried to Pharaoh for food, and Pharaoh said to all the Egyptians, "Go to Joseph. Do whatever he says to you."

The famine was over all the face of the earth, so Joseph opened all the storehouses and sold to the Egyptians, and the famine was severe throughout the land of Egypt. Moreover, all countries came to Egypt to Joseph to buy grain, because the famine was so severe in all the lands.

Now when Jacob saw that there was grain in Egypt, Jacob said to his sons, "Why do you look at one another?" And he said, "I have heard that there is grain in Egypt. Go down there and buy *some* for us, so that we may live and not die."

Joseph's ten brothers went down to buy grain in Egypt. But Jacob did not send Benjamin, Joseph's brother, with his brothers for he said, "Perhaps some harm might happen to him." Thus the sons of Israel came to buy grain among those who came, for the famine was in the land of Canaan.

Now Joseph was the governor over the land, and it was he who sold to all the people of the land. So Joseph's brothers came and bowed themselves down before him with their faces to the ground. Joseph saw his brothers, and he recognized them, but he pretended to be a stranger to them and spoke harshly to them. He said to them, "From where do you come?"

And they said, "From the land of Canaan to buy food."

Joseph knew his brothers, but they did not know him. Joseph also remembered the dreams that he had dreamed of them. He said to them, "You are spies! You came to see the nakedness of the land!"

They said to him, "No, my lord, your servants have come only to buy food. We are all one man's sons. We are honest men. Your servants are not spies."

But he said to them, "No, you have come to see the nakedness of the land!"

They said, "Your servants are twelve brothers, the sons of one man in the land of Canaan. The youngest is with our father today, and one is no longer living."

Joseph said to them, "It is as I said to you, 'You are spies!' Here is how you will be tested. By the life of Pharaoh, you will not leave here unless your youngest brother comes here. Send one of you, and let him get your brother, and you will be kept in prison, so that your words may be tested, whether there be any truth in you. Or else, by the life of Pharaoh, you are surely spies." He put them all together in custody for three days.

Joseph said to them the third day, "Do this and live, for I fear God. If you are honest men, let one of your brothers be confined in your prison house. The rest of you go and carry grain for the famine of your households. Nevertheless, bring your youngest brother to me so that your words may be verified and you shall not die." And they did so.

Then they said one to another, "We are guilty concerning our brother, because we saw the anguish of his soul when he pleaded with us, but we would not listen. Therefore, this distress has come upon us."

Reuben answered them, saying, "Did I not speak to you, saying, 'Do not sin against the boy'; and you would not listen? Therefore, his blood is now required of us." They did not know that Joseph understood them, for he spoke to them through an interpreter.

He turned himself away from them and wept, but then turned back to them again and spoke with them. Then he took Simeon from them and bound him before their eyes.

Joseph then gave the command to fill their sacks with grain and to restore every man's money to his sack and to give them provisions for the way. And it was done for them.

They loaded their donkeys with the grain and departed from there.

As one of them opened his sack to give his donkey feed in the lodging place, he saw his money. It was in the mouth of his sack. And he said to his brothers, "My money has been returned. Here it is in my sack!"

Then their hearts sank, and they were afraid, saying to one another, "What is this that God has done to us?"

They came to Jacob their father in the land of Canaan and told him all that had happened to them, saying, "The man, the lord of the land, spoke harshly to us and took us for spies of the country. And we said to him, 'We are honest men. We are not spies. We are twelve brothers, *all* sons of our father. One is no longer living, and the youngest is with our father today in the land of Canaan.'

"The man, the lord of the country, said to us, 'Here is how I may know that you are honest men. Leave one of your brothers here with me, take food for the famine of your households, and be gone. But bring your youngest brother back to me. Then I will know that you are not spies, but that you are honest men. Then I will deliver your brother to you, and you may trade in the land.'"

As they emptied their sacks, every man's bundle of money was in his sack. When both they and their father saw the bundles of money, they were afraid. Then Jacob their father said to them, "You have bereaved me of my children! Joseph is no more, Simeon is no more, and you will take Benjamin away. All these things are against me."

Reuben spoke to his father, saying, "Kill my two sons if I fail to bring him to you. Put him in my hands, and I will bring him back to you."

But Jacob said, "My son must not go down with you, for his brother is dead, and he alone is left. If harm should happen to him on the journey you are to make, then you will bring down my gray hairs with sorrow to the grave."

Now the famine was severe in the land. When they had eaten up the grain which they had brought out of Egypt, their father said to them, "Go back and buy us a little food."

Judah spoke to him, saying, "The man solemnly warned us, saying, 'You will not see my face unless your brother is with you.' If you will send our brother with us, we will go down and buy food for you. But if you will not send him, we will not go down. For the man said to us, 'You will not see my face unless your brother is with you.'"

Israel said, "Why did you treat me so badly as to tell the man that you had *another* brother?"

And they said, "The man asked us directly about ourselves and our family, saying, 'Is your father still alive? Do you have another brother?' So we answered his questions. How could we even know that he would say, 'Bring your brother down'?"

And Judah said to Israel his father, "Send the boy with me, and we will arise and go, so that we may live and not die, both we and you, and also our little ones. I will be a surety for him. You may hold me personally responsible for him. If I fail to bring him back to you and set him before you, then let me bear the blame forever. For if we had not delayed, we could have returned twice."

Their father Israel said to them, "If it must be so, do this. Take some of the best fruits in the land in your bags, and carry down a present for the man: a little balm and a little honey, spices, and myrrh, pistachio nuts and almonds. Take double the money with you, along with the money that was brought back in the mouths of your sacks. Carry it with you again. Perhaps it was a mistake. Also, take your brother and arise, return to the man. And may God Almighty give you mercy before the man, so that he may send away your other brother, along with Benjamin. As for me, if I am bereaved, I am bereaved."

The men took the gift, and they took double the money with them, along with Benjamin. Then they went on their way down to Egypt and stood before Joseph. When Joseph saw Benjamin with them, he said to the house steward, "Bring these men home, slaughter an animal and prepare it, for these men will dine with me at noon."

The man did as Joseph ordered, so the man brought the men into Joseph's house. The men were afraid because they were brought into Joseph's house. They said, "We have been brought in because of the money that was returned in our sacks the first time, so that he may seek occasion against us and fall upon us and take us for slaves with our donkeys."

They approached the steward of Joseph's house, and they spoke with him at the entrance of the house. They said, "My lord, we indeed came down the first time to buy food. When we came to the lodging place, we opened our sacks and realized every man's money was in the mouth of his sack, our money in full weight. So we have brought it again with us. We have also brought additional money with us to buy food. We cannot tell who put our money in our sacks."

He said, "Be at peace; do not be afraid. Your God and the God of your father has given you treasure in your sacks. I had your money." Then he brought Simeon out to them.

The man brought the men into Joseph's house and gave them water to wash their feet and gave feed to their donkeys. Then they made ready the gift for Joseph's coming at noon, for they heard that they would be eating a meal there.

When Joseph came home, they brought into the house to him the present that they had with them and bowed themselves to him to the ground. He asked them about their well-being and said, "Is your father well, the old man of whom you spoke? Is he still alive?"

And they answered, "Your servant our father is in good health. He is still alive." And they bowed down their heads and prostrated themselves.

He lifted up his eyes and saw his brother Benjamin, his mother's son, and said, "Is this your younger brother of whom you spoke to me?" And he said, "God be gracious to you, my son." Joseph hurried *out*, for he was deeply moved over his brother and sought a place to weep. So he entered into his chamber and wept there.

Then he washed his face and came out. Controlling himself, he said, "Serve the food."

They served him by himself and them by themselves and the Egyptians who ate with him by themselves, because the Egyptians could not eat a meal with the Hebrews, for that is an abomination to the Egyptians. They sat before him, the firstborn according to his birthright and the youngest according to his youth, and the men looked at one another in astonishment. He gave them portions from his own table, but Benjamin's serving was five times more than any of theirs. So they drank and feasted with him.

Then he commanded the steward of his house, saying, "Fill the men's sacks with food, as much as they can carry, and put every man's money in the mouth of his sack. Put my cup, the silver cup, in the mouth of the sack of the youngest, along with his grain money." And he did according to what Joseph had spoken.

As soon as the morning was light, the men were sent away, they and their donkeys. When they were gone out of the city, but not yet far off, Joseph said to his steward, "Get up, follow after the men. When you overtake them, say to them, 'Why have you rewarded evil for good? Is this not the one from which my lord drinks and uses as he practices divination? You have done evil in doing this.'"

So he overtook them, and he spoke to them these same words. They said to him, "Why does my lord say these words? Far be it from your servants that they should do such a thing. Look, we brought back to you from the land of Canaan the money that we found in the top of our sacks. Why then would we steal silver or gold from your lord's house? Whichever of your servants is found with it shall die, and the rest of us will become my lord's slaves."

He said, "Now let it also be according to your words. He with whom it is found shall be my slave, and you will be blameless."

Then every man hurriedly took down his sack to the ground, and every man opened his sack. He searched, beginning with the oldest and ending with the youngest. The cup was found in Benjamin's sack. Then they tore their clothes, and every man loaded his donkey and returned to the city.

When Judah and his brothers came to Joseph's house, he was still there; and they fell to the ground before him. Joseph said to them, "What deed is this that you have done? Did you not know that such a man as I can certainly practice divination?"

And Judah said, "What shall we say to my lord? What shall we speak? Or how shall we clear ourselves? God has found out the iniquity of your servants. Here we are, my lord's servants, both we and he also in whose possession the cup was found."

But he said, "Far be it from me that I should do so. The man in whose possession the cup was found shall be my slave; but as for you, go up in peace to your father."

Vayigash

And he drew near

(Genesis 44:18–47:27)

Then Judah approached him and said, "O my lord, please let your servant speak a word in my lord's ears, and do not be angry with your servant, for you are equal to Pharaoh. My lord asked his servants, saying, 'Have you a father or a brother?' And we said to my lord, 'We have a father, an old man, and a young brother, the child of his old age. His brother is dead, and he alone is left of his mother, and his father loves him.'

"You said to your servants, 'Bring him down to me, so that I may set my eyes on him.' We said to my lord, 'The boy cannot leave his father, for if he should leave his father, his father would die.' You said to your servants, 'Unless your youngest brother comes down with you, you will not see my face again.' When we went back to your servant, my father, we told him the words of my lord.

"Our father said, 'Go again and buy us a little food.' We said, 'We cannot go down. If our youngest brother is with us, then we will go down, for we may not see the man's face, unless our youngest brother is with us.'

"Your servant, my father, said to us, 'You know that my wife bore me two sons. And the one went out from me, and I said, "Surely he was torn in pieces," and I have not seen him since. And if you take this one also from me and he is harmed, you will bring down my gray hairs with sorrow to the grave.'

"Now therefore when I come to your servant, my father, and the boy is not with us, as his life is bound up in the boy's life, when he sees that the boy is not with us, he will die, and your servants will bring down the gray hairs of your servant, our father, with sorrow to the grave. For your servant became surety for the boy to my father, saying, 'If I fail to bring him to you, then I shall bear the blame to my father forever.'

"Now therefore, please let your servant stay as a slave to my lord instead of the boy, and let the boy go up with his brothers. For how can I go up to my father if the boy is not with me, lest perhaps I see the evil that would find my father?"

Then Joseph could not restrain himself before all who stood by him, and he cried out, "Make every man go out from me." So no man stood with him when Joseph made himself known to his brothers. He wept so loudly that the Egyptians and the house of Pharaoh heard about it.

Joseph said to his brothers, "I am Joseph. Is my father still alive?" But his brothers could not answer him, for they were dismayed in his presence.

Joseph said to his brothers, "Please come near to me," and they came near. Then he said, "I am your brother, Joseph, whom you sold into Egypt. Now do not be upset or angry with yourselves because you sold me here, for God sent me before you to preserve life. For these two years the famine has been in the land, and there are still five years in which there will be neither plowing nor harvesting. God sent me ahead of you to preserve you *as* a remnant on the earth and to save your lives by a great deliverance.

"So now it was not you who sent me here, but God. He has made me a father to Pharaoh and lord of his entire household and a ruler throughout all the land of Egypt. Hurry and go up to my father and say to him, 'This is what your son Joseph says, "God has made me lord of all Egypt. Come down to me; do not delay. And you will dwell in the land of Goshen, and you will be near me, you and your children and your children's children, along with your flocks, your herds, and all that you have. I will provide for you there, for there are still five years of famine *to come, lest* you and your household, and all that you have, come to poverty."'

"Your eyes and the eyes of my brother Benjamin see that it is my mouth that is speaking to you. You must tell my father of all my glory in Egypt and of all that you have seen, and you must hurry and bring my father down here."

Then he fell on his brother Benjamin's neck and wept, and Benjamin wept on his neck. Moreover he kissed all his brothers and wept on them. After that his brothers talked with him.

When the news reached Pharaoh's palace that Joseph's brothers had come, it pleased Pharaoh and his servants. Pharaoh said to Joseph, "Say to your brothers, 'Do this. Load your animals and go to the land of Canaan. Get your father and your households and come to me, and I will give you the best of the land of Egypt, and you shall eat the fat of the land.'

"You are also commanded to say, 'Do this: Take your wagons out of the land of Egypt for your little ones and for your wives, and get your father and come. Also do not concern yourself with your goods, for the best of all the land of Egypt is yours.'"

So the sons of Israel did so, and Joseph gave them wagons, according to the commandment of Pharaoh, and gave them provisions for the journey. To each of them he gave a change of clothes, but he gave to Benjamin three hundred shekels of silver and five changes of clothes. To his father he sent the following: ten donkeys loaded with the best things of Egypt and ten female donkeys loaded with grain and bread and provisions for his father on the journey. So he sent his brothers away, and they departed. He said to them, "Do not quarrel on the way."

They went up out of Egypt and came to the land of Canaan to Jacob their father. They told him, "Joseph is still alive, and he is governor over all the land of Egypt." And Jacob's heart stood still because he could not believe them. They told him all the words of Joseph, which he had said to them, and when he saw the wagons that Joseph had sent to carry him, the spirit of their father Jacob revived. Then Israel said, "Enough! Joseph my son is still alive. I will go and see him before I die."

So Israel set out with all that he had and came to Beersheba and offered sacrifices to the God of his father Isaac.

God spoke to Israel in visions of the night and said, "Jacob, Jacob."

And he said, "Here I am."

Then He said, "I am God, the God of your father. Do not be afraid to go down to Egypt, for I will make you into a great nation there. I will go down with you to Egypt, and I will also surely bring you back again. And Joseph's own hand shall close your eyes."

Jacob arose from Beersheba, and the sons of Israel carried Jacob their father and their little ones and their wives in the wagons that Pharaoh had sent to carry him. They took their livestock and their possessions that they had acquired in the land of Canaan, and came to Egypt, Jacob and all his descendants with him. He brought with him to Egypt his sons and his sons' sons, his daughters and his sons' daughters, and all his descendants.

These were the names of the sons of Israel, Jacob and his sons, who came to Egypt:

Reuben, Jacob's firstborn.
The sons of Reuben were
    Hanok, Pallu, Hezron, and Karmi.
The sons of Simeon were
    Jemuel, Jamin, Ohad, Jakin, Zohar, and Shaul the son of a Canaanite woman.
The sons of Levi were
    Gershon, Kohath, and Merari.
The sons of Judah were
    Er, Onan, Shelah, Perez, and Zerah (but Er and Onan died in the land of Canaan).
        The sons of Perez were
        Hezron and Hamul.
The sons of Issachar were
    Tola, Puah, Job, and Shimron.
The sons of Zebulun were
    Sered, Elon, and Jahleel.

These were the sons of Leah, whom she bore to Jacob in Paddan Aram, with his daughter Dinah. All his sons and his daughters *numbered* thirty-three.

And the sons of Gad were
Zephon, Haggi, Shuni, Ezbon, Eri, Arodi, and Areli.
The sons of Asher were
Imnah, Ishvah, Ishvi, Beriah, and Serah their sister.
The sons of Beriah:
Heber and Malkiel.
These were the sons of Zilpah, whom Laban gave to Leah his daughter; and these she bore to Jacob, sixteen in all.

The sons of Rachel, Jacob's wife, were
Joseph and Benjamin. To Joseph in the land of Egypt were born Manasseh and Ephraim, whom Asenath the daughter of Potiphera, the priest of On, bore to him.
The sons of Benjamin were
Bela, Beker, Ashbel, Gera, Naaman, Ehi, Rosh, Muppim, Huppim, and Ard.
These were the sons of Rachel who were born to Jacob, fourteen in all.

The son of Dan was
Hushim.
The sons of Naphtali:
Jahziel, Guni, Jezer, and Shillem.
These were the sons of Bilhah, whom Laban gave to Rachel his daughter, and she bore these to Jacob, seven in all.

All those who came with Jacob to Egypt, who were direct descendants, besides the wives of Jacob's sons, were sixty-six in all. And the sons of Joseph, who were born to him in Egypt, were two. All those of the house of Jacob who came to Egypt were seventy.

Now he sent Judah ahead of him to Joseph to get directions to Goshen. And they came into the land of Goshen. Joseph readied his chariot and went up to Goshen to meet Israel his father. As soon as he appeared to him, he fell on his neck and wept on his neck a long time.

Israel said to Joseph, "Now let me die, since I have seen your face, because you are still alive."

Joseph said to his brothers and to his father's household, "I will go up and tell Pharaoh and say to him, 'My brothers and my father's household, who were in the land of Canaan, have come to me. The men are shepherds; their work has been to feed livestock, and they have brought their flocks and their herds and all that they have.' When Pharaoh calls you and asks,

'What is your occupation?' you shall say, 'Your servants have been keepers of livestock from our youth even until now, both we and our fathers,' so that you may dwell in the land of Goshen, because every shepherd is an abomination to the Egyptians."

Then Joseph went and told Pharaoh, "My father and my brothers and their flocks and their herds and all that they possess have come from the land of Canaan and are *now* in the land of Goshen." He took five men from among his brothers and presented them before Pharaoh.

Pharaoh asked his brothers, "What is your occupation?"

And they said to Pharaoh, "Your servants are shepherds, both we and also our fathers." They said to Pharaoh, "We have come to sojourn in the land, for your servants have no pasture for their flocks, because the famine is severe in the land of Canaan. Now therefore, please allow your servants to dwell in the land of Goshen."

Pharaoh spoke to Joseph, saying, "Your father and your brothers have come to you. The land of Egypt is before you. Have your father and your brothers dwell in the best of the land. Have them dwell in the land of Goshen, and if you know any capable men among them, then put them in charge over my livestock."

Then Joseph brought in Jacob his father and presented him to Pharaoh, and Jacob blessed Pharaoh. Pharaoh said to Jacob, "How old are you?"

And Jacob said to Pharaoh, "The days of the years of my pilgrimage are one hundred thirty years. My days of the years of my life have been few and evil, and they have not attained to the days of the years of the lives of my fathers in the days of their pilgrimage." And Jacob blessed Pharaoh and went out from his presence.

So Joseph settled his father and his brothers and gave them a possession in the land of Egypt, in the best *part* of the land, in the land of Rameses, as Pharaoh had commanded. Joseph provided food for his father, his brothers, and his father's entire household, according to the number *of their* children.

There was no food in all the land, for the famine was very severe, so that the land of Egypt and all the land of Canaan languished because of the famine. Joseph gathered up all the money that was found in the land of Egypt and in the land of Canaan for the grain that they bought, and Joseph brought the money into Pharaoh's house. When the money was all spent in the land of Egypt and in the land of Canaan, all the Egyptians came to Joseph and said, "Give us food, for why should we die in your presence? For our money is gone."

Joseph said, "Give your livestock, and I will give you *food* for your livestock, if *your* money is gone." They brought their livestock to Joseph, and Joseph gave them food in exchange for the horses, the flocks, the herds, and the donkeys; and he fed them with food in exchange for all their livestock for that year.

When that year was ended, they came to him the second year and said to him, "We will not hide it from our lord, that our money is all spent. Our lord also has our herds of livestock. There is nothing left in the sight of my lord but our bodies and our lands. Why should we die before your eyes, both we and our land? Buy us and our land for food, and we and our land will be slaves to Pharaoh. Also give us seed, so that we may live and not die, so that the land will not be desolate."

So Joseph bought all the land of Egypt for Pharaoh, for every Egyptian man sold his field because the famine was severe on them. So the land became Pharaoh's. As for the people, he removed them to cities from one end of the borders of Egypt to the other end. Only the land of the priests he did not buy; for the priests had an allotment from Pharaoh, and they lived off their allotment that Pharaoh gave them. Therefore they did not sell their lands.

Then Joseph said to the people, "I have bought you and your land today for Pharaoh; here is seed for you so you may sow the land. At the harvest, you must give one-fifth to Pharaoh and four parts will be your own, as seed for the field and for your food and for those of your households and for food for your little ones."

They said, "You have saved our lives. Let us find grace in the sight of my lord, and we will be Pharaoh's slaves."

So Joseph made it a law over the land of Egypt to this day, that Pharaoh should have one-fifth, except from the land of the priests, which did not become Pharaoh's.

Israel lived in the land of Egypt, in the land of Goshen, and they had possessions there and grew and became very numerous.

Vayechi

And he lived

(Genesis 47:28–50:26)

And Jacob lived in the land of Egypt seventeen years, so the years of Jacob's life were one hundred forty-seven years. When the time drew near when Israel would die, he called his son Joseph and said to him, "If now I have found grace in your sight, please put your hand under my thigh and deal kindly and truly with me. Please do not bury me in Egypt, but let me lie with my fathers. Carry me out of Egypt and bury me in their burial place."

And he said, "I will do as you have said."

And he said, "Swear to me," and he swore to him. Then Israel bowed himself at the head of his bed.

After these things, Joseph was told, "Your father is sick." So he took his two sons Manasseh and Ephraim with him. When Jacob was told, "Your son Joseph is coming to you," Israel strengthened himself and sat up in the bed.

Jacob said to Joseph, "God Almighty appeared to me at Luz in the land of Canaan, and blessed me. And He said to me, 'I will make you fruitful and multiply you, and I will make you into a multitude of people and will give this land to your descendants after you for an everlasting possession.'

"Now your two sons, Ephraim and Manasseh, who were born to you in the land of Egypt before I came to you in Egypt, are mine; as Reuben and Simeon, they shall be mine. Any children you have after them will be yours and will be called by the names of their brothers in their inheritance. As for me, when I came from Paddan, Rachel died beside me in the land of Canaan on the way, when there was still some distance to get to Ephrath, and I buried her there on the way to Ephrath (that is, Bethlehem)."

Then Israel saw Joseph's sons and said, "Whose are these?"

And Joseph said to his father, "They are my sons, whom God has given me in this place."

And he said, "Please bring them to me, and I will bless them."

Now the eyes of Israel were dim with age, so that he could not see. So Joseph brought them near to him, and he kissed them and embraced them.

Israel said to Joseph, "I never thought I would see your face, but here God has also shown me your children."

So Joseph took them from beside his knees, and he bowed down with his face to the ground. Joseph took them both, Ephraim in his right hand toward Israel's left hand, and Manasseh in his left hand toward Israel's right hand, and brought them near him. Israel stretched out his right hand and laid it on Ephraim's head, who was the younger, and his left hand on Manasseh's head, crossing his hands, for Manasseh was the firstborn.

He blessed Joseph and said,

"God, before whom my fathers
    Abraham and Isaac walked,
the God who fed me
    all my life long to this day,
the angel who redeemed me from all evil,
    bless the boys;
let them be called by my name,
    and the name of my fathers, Abraham and Isaac;
and let them grow into a multitude
    in the midst of the earth."

When Joseph saw that his father laid his right hand on the head of Ephraim, it displeased him, and he took hold of his father's hand to remove it from Ephraim's head to Manasseh's head. Joseph said to his father, "Not so, my father, for this one is the firstborn. Put your right hand on his head."

His father refused and said, "I know it, my son, I know it. He will also become a people, and he will also be great, but truly his younger brother will be greater than he, and his descendants will become a multitude of nations." He blessed them that day, saying,

"By you Israel will bless, saying,
    'May God make you like Ephraim and Manasseh.' "

So he set Ephraim before Manasseh.

Israel said to Joseph, "I am about to die, but God will be with you and return you again to the land of your fathers. Moreover, I have given to you one portion more than your brothers, which I took out of the hand of the Amorites with my sword and my bow."

Jacob called to his sons and said, "Gather yourselves together, so that I may tell you what will befall you in the last days.

Gather yourselves together and hear, sons of Jacob,
    and listen to your father Israel.

Reuben, you are my firstborn,
  my might and the beginning of my strength,
  the excellency of dignity, and the excellency of
    power.
Unstable as water, you shall not excel,
  because you went up to your father's bed;
  then you defiled it—he went up to my couch.

Simeon and Levi are brothers;
  weapons of violence are their swords.
Let my soul not enter into their council;
  let my glory not be united with their assembly;
for in their anger they killed men
  and in their self-will they hamstrung oxen.
Cursed be their anger, for it is fierce;
  and their wrath, for it is cruel!
I will divide them in Jacob
  and scatter them in Israel.

Judah, your brothers shall praise you;
  your hand shall be on the neck of your enemies;
  your father's sons will bow down before you.
Judah is a lion's cub;
  from the prey, my son, you have gone up.
He crouches and lies down like a lion;
  and as a lion, who dares rouse him?
The scepter shall not depart from Judah,
  nor a lawgiver from between his feet,
until Shiloh comes;
  and to him will be the obedience of the people.
He tethers his foal to the vine,
  and his colt to the choicest vine;
he washes his garments in wine,
  his clothes in the blood of grapes.
His eyes are darker than wine,
  and his teeth whiter than milk.

Zebulun shall dwell at the haven of the sea;
  and he shall be a haven of ships.
  His border shall be at Sidon.

Issachar is a strong donkey,
  lying down between two burdens;

he saw that a resting place was good,
    and that the land was pleasant;
so he bowed his shoulder to bear the burden
    and became a slave to forced labor.

Dan shall judge his people
    as one of the tribes of Israel.
Dan shall be a serpent by the road,
    a viper on the path,
that bites the horse's heels
    so that its rider will fall backward.

I wait for Your salvation, O Lord!

Gad shall be attacked by raiding bands,
    but he shall raid at their heels.

Asher's food shall be rich,
    and he shall yield royal delicacies.

Naphtali is a doe set loose;
    he gives beautiful words.

Joseph is a fruitful bough,
    a fruitful bough by a spring,
    whose branches run over the wall.
The archers bitterly attacked him,
    they shot at him and hated him.
But his bow remained firm.
    His arms were agile
because of the hands of the Mighty One of Jacob,
    because of the Shepherd, the rock of Israel,
because of the God of your father who will help you,
    and by the Almighty who will bless you
with blessings from heaven above,
    blessings from the deep that lies beneath,
    the blessings of the breasts and the womb.
The blessings of your father have surpassed
    the blessings of my fathers,
    up to the utmost bound of the everlasting hills.
They will be on the head of Joseph,
    and on the crown of the head of him who was set apart from his
      brothers.

Benjamin is a ravenous wolf;
in the morning he devours the prey,
and at night he divides the spoil."

These are all the twelve tribes of Israel, and this is what their father said to them when he blessed them. He blessed them, each with the blessing appropriate to him.

Then he charged them and said to them, "I am about to be gathered to my people. Bury me with my fathers in the cave that is in the field of Ephron the Hittite, in the cave that is in the field of Machpelah, which is before Mamre in the land of Canaan, which Abraham bought along with the field from Ephron the Hittite as a burial place. They buried Abraham and Sarah his wife there. They buried Isaac and Rebekah his wife there, and I buried Leah there. The field and the cave that is there were purchased from the children of Heth."

When Jacob finished instructing his sons, he drew his feet into the bed, breathed his last, and was gathered to his people.

Then Joseph fell on his father's face and wept over him and kissed him. Joseph commanded his servants the physicians to embalm his father. So the physicians embalmed Israel. Forty days were required for him, for such is the time required for those who are embalmed. Then the Egyptians mourned for him seventy days.

When the days of his mourning were past, Joseph spoke to the household of Pharaoh, saying, "If now I have found favor in your eyes, speak to Pharaoh, saying, 'My father made me swear, saying, "I am about to die. Bury me in my tomb which I dug for myself in the land of Canaan." Now therefore please let me go up and bury my father, and then I will return.'"

Pharaoh said, "Go up and bury your father, as he made you swear to do."

Joseph went up to bury his father, and all the servants of Pharaoh went up with him too, the elders of his household and all the elders of the land of Egypt, all the house of Joseph and his brothers and his father's household. They left only their little ones and their flocks and their herds in the land of Goshen. Both the chariots and horsemen also went up with him. It was a very great company.

When they came to the threshing floor of Atad, which is beyond the Jordan, they mourned with a great and very sorrowful lamentation. He observed seven days of mourning for his father. When the inhabitants of the land, the Canaanites, saw the mourning at the threshing floor of Atad, they said, "This is a grievous mourning for the Egyptians." Therefore the place was called Abel Mizraim, which is beyond the Jordan.

So his sons did with him just as he had commanded them. For his sons carried him into the land of Canaan and buried him in the cave of the field of Machpelah, near Mamre, which Abraham bought with the field as a burial site from Ephron the Hittite. After he had buried his father, Joseph returned to Egypt, he and his brothers and all who went up with him to bury his father.

When Joseph's brothers saw that their father was dead, they said, "Perhaps Joseph will hate us and will certainly pay us back for all the wrong we did to him." So they sent a message to Joseph, saying, "Your father gave this command before he died: 'Say to Joseph, "I beg you, forgive the transgressions of your brothers and their sin. For they did evil to you." ' Now, please forgive the transgressions of the servants of the God of your father." And Joseph wept when they spoke to him.

Then his brothers also went and fell down before his face and said, "We are your servants."

Joseph said to them, "Do not be afraid, for am I in the place of God? But as for you, you intended to harm me, but God intended it for good, in order to bring it about as it is this day, to save many lives. So now, do not fear. I will provide for you and your little ones." So he comforted them and spoke kindly to them.

Joseph stayed in Egypt, he and his father's household, and Joseph lived one hundred ten years. Joseph saw Ephraim's children to the third generation. Also, the children of Makir, the son of Manasseh, were brought up on Joseph's knees.

Joseph said to his brothers, "I am about to die. God will surely come to you and bring you out of this land to the land of which He swore to Abraham, to Isaac, and to Jacob." Then Joseph made the sons of Israel swear, saying, "God will surely visit you, and you shall carry up my bones from here."

So Joseph died at the age of one hundred ten years old, and they embalmed him, and he was put in a coffin in Egypt.

Shemot

Names

(*Exodus 1:1–6:1*)

Now these are the names of the sons of Israel, which came into Egypt (each man and his household came with Jacob): Reuben, Simeon, Levi, and Judah; Issachar, Zebulun, and Benjamin; Dan, Naphtali, Gad, and Asher. All the people who came from the seed of Jacob were seventy people, but Joseph was in Egypt *already*.

Joseph died, as did all his brothers, and all that generation. Nevertheless, the sons of Israel were fruitful, and increased abundantly, and multiplied, and became exceedingly mighty, so that the land was filled with them.

Now there rose up a new king over Egypt, who did not know Joseph. He said to his people, "Surely, the people of the sons of Israel are more numerous and powerful than we. Come, let us deal wisely with them, lest they multiply, and it come to pass that when any war breaks out, they also join our enemies, and fight against us, and escape from the land."

Therefore they set taskmasters over them to afflict them with their labor. They built for Pharaoh storage cities: Pithom and Rameses. But the more they afflicted them, the more they multiplied and grew so that as a result they abhorred the sons of Israel. The Egyptians made the children of Israel to serve with rigor, and they made their lives bitter with hard service—in mortar and in brick, and in all manner of service in the field, all their service in which they made them serve was with rigor.

The king of Egypt spoke to the Hebrew midwives, of which the name of one was Shiphrah, and the name of the other Puah, and he said, "When you perform the office of a midwife to the Hebrew women and see them on the stools, if it is a son, then you must kill him, but if it is a daughter, then she may live." However, the midwives feared God, and did not do as the king of Egypt commanded them, but kept the male children alive. The king of Egypt called for the midwives and said to them, "Why have you done this thing and preserved the male children's lives?"

The midwives said to Pharaoh, "Because the Hebrew women are not like the Egyptian women, for they are vigorous and give birth before the midwives come to them."

Therefore God dealt well with the midwives, and the people multiplied and grew very mighty. So it happened that because the midwives feared God, He gave them families.

Pharaoh charged all his people, saying, "You must cast every son that is born into the river, and you must preserve every daughter's life."

Now a man of the house of Levi went and married a daughter of Levi. And the woman conceived and bore a son, and when she saw him, that he was a beautiful child, she hid him three months. When she could no longer hide him, she got a papyrus basket for him, and daubed it with tar and pitch. She then put the child in it and set it in the reeds by the river's bank. Then his sister stood afar off so that she might know what would happen to him.

The daughter of Pharaoh came down to wash herself at the river while her maidens walked along by the river's side, and when she saw the container among the reeds, she sent her maid, and she retrieved it. When she opened it, she saw the child. He was crying. She had compassion on him and said, "This is one of the Hebrews' children."

Then his sister said to Pharaoh's daughter, "Shall I go and call for you a nursing woman of the Hebrew women so that she may nurse the child for you?"

And Pharaoh's daughter said to her, "Go." So the young girl went and called the child's mother. Pharaoh's daughter said to her, "Take this child away, and nurse him for me, and I will give you your wages." So the woman took the child and nursed him. Now the child grew, and she brought him to Pharaoh's daughter, and he became her son. And she called his name Moses and said, "Because I drew him out of the water."

In those days, when Moses was grown, he went out to his brothers and looked on their burdens; and he saw an Egyptian striking a Hebrew, one of his brothers. He looked this way and that way, and when he saw no one, he killed the Egyptian and hid him in the sand. When he went out the next day, two men of the Hebrews struggled with each other; and he said to him that did the wrong, "Why do you strike your companion?"

He said, "Who made you a prince and a judge over us? Do you intend to kill me as you killed the Egyptian?" Moses feared and said, "Surely this thing is known."

Now when Pharaoh heard this thing, he sought to slay Moses. But Moses fled from the presence of Pharaoh and settled in the land of Midian, and he dwelt by a well. Now the priest of Midian had seven daughters, and they came and drew water, and filled the troughs to water their father's flock. Then shepherds came and drove them away, but Moses stood up and helped them, and watered their flock.

When they came to Reuel their father, he said, "Why is it you have come *back* so soon today?"

And they said, "An Egyptian delivered us out of the hand of the shepherds and also drew water for us and watered the flock."

He said to his daughters, "So where is he? Why is it that you have left the man? Call him so that he may eat bread."

Moses was content to dwell with the man, and he gave Zipporah, his daughter, to Moses. Then she gave birth to a son, and he called his name Gershom, for he said, "I have been a sojourner in a foreign land."

In the passing of time the king of Egypt died. And the children of Israel sighed because of the bondage, and they cried out, and their cry came up to God on account of the bondage. God heard their groaning, and God remembered His covenant with Abraham, Isaac, and Jacob. God looked on the children of Israel, and God had concern for them.

Now Moses kept the flock of Jethro his father-in-law, the priest of Midian, and he led the flock to the far side of the desert and came to the mountain of God, to Horeb. The angel of the LORD appeared to him in a flame of fire from the midst of a bush, and he looked, and the bush burned with fire, but the bush was not consumed. So Moses said, "I will now turn aside and see this great sight, why the bush is not burnt."

When the LORD saw that he turned aside to see, God called to him from out of the midst of the bush and said, "Moses, Moses."

And he said, "Here am I."

He said, "Do not approach here. Remove your sandals from off your feet, for the place on which you are standing is holy ground." Moreover He said, "I am the God of your father, the God of Abraham, the God of Isaac, and the God of Jacob." And Moses hid his face, for he was afraid to look upon God.

The LORD said, "I have surely seen the affliction of My people who are in Egypt and have heard their cry on account of their taskmasters, for I know their sorrows. Therefore, I have come down to deliver them out of the hand of the Egyptians, and to bring them up out of that land to a good and spacious land, to a land flowing with milk and honey, to the place of the Canaanites, the Hittites, the Amorites, the Perizzites, the Hivites, and the Jebusites. Now therefore, the cry of the children of Israel has come to Me. Moreover, I have also seen the oppression with which the Egyptians are oppressing them. Come now therefore, and I will send you to Pharaoh so that you may bring forth My people, the children of Israel, out of Egypt."

Moses said to God, "Who am I that I should go to Pharaoh and that I should bring forth the children of Israel out of Egypt?"

And He said, "Certainly I will be with you, and this will be a sign to you, that I have sent you: When you have brought forth the people out of Egypt, all of you shall serve God on this mountain."

Moses said to God, "I am going to the children of Israel and will say to them, 'The God of your fathers has sent me to you.' When they say to me, 'What is His name?' what shall I say to them?"

And God said to Moses, "I AM WHO I AM," and He said, "You will say this to the children of Israel, 'I AM has sent me to you.'"

God, moreover, said to Moses, "Thus you will say to the children of Israel, 'The LORD, the God of your fathers, the God of Abraham, the God of Isaac, and the God of Jacob, has sent me to you. This is My name forever, and this is My memorial to all generations.'

"Go, and gather the elders of Israel together, and say to them, 'The LORD, the God of your fathers, the God of Abraham, of Isaac, and of Jacob, appeared to me, saying, "I am indeed concerned about you and what has been done to you in Egypt. Therefore, I said, I will bring you up out of the affliction of Egypt to the land of the Canaanites, the Hittites, the Amorites, the Perizzites, the Hivites, and the Jebusites, to a land flowing with milk and honey."'

"They shall listen to your voice, and you shall come, you and the elders of Israel, to the king of Egypt, and you must say to him, 'The LORD, the God of the Hebrews has met with us. Therefore, now, let us go, we ask you, three days' journey into the wilderness so that we may sacrifice to the LORD our God.' However, I know that the king of Egypt will not let you go, no, not even under a forceful hand. So I will stretch out My hand and strike Egypt with all My wonders which I will perform in its midst, and after that he will let you go.

"I will give this people favor in the sight of the Egyptians, and it will come to pass, that, when you go, you will not go empty-handed. But every woman will borrow of her neighbor, and of her that sojourns in her house, articles of silver, and articles of gold, and clothing, and you will put them on your sons, and on your daughters—in this way you will plunder the Egyptians."

And Moses answered and said, "But they will not believe me, nor listen to my voice. For they will say, 'The LORD has not appeared to you.'"

The LORD said to him, "What is that in your hand?"

And he said, "A rod."

He said, "Throw it on the ground."

And he threw it on the ground, and it became a serpent. Then Moses fled from it. Then the LORD said to Moses, "Put forth your hand and take it by the tail." And he put forth his hand, and caught it, and it became a rod in his hand. "*This is so* that they may believe that the LORD, the God of their fathers, the God of Abraham, the God of Isaac, and the God of Jacob, has appeared to you."

The LORD said furthermore to him, "Now put your hand into your bosom." He put his hand into his bosom, and when he took it out, his hand was as leprous as snow.

He said, "Put your hand into your bosom again." So he put his hand into his bosom again and brought it out of his bosom, and it was restored like his other flesh.

"If they will not believe you, nor listen to the voice of the first sign, then they may believe the voice of the latter sign. But if they will not believe also these two signs or listen to your voice, then you shall take water from the river and pour it on the dry land, and the water which you take out of the river will become blood on the dry land."

Then Moses said to the LORD, "O my Lord, I am not eloquent, neither before nor since You have spoken to Your servant. But I am slow of speech, and of a slow tongue."

The LORD said to him, "Who has made man's mouth? Or who made the dumb, or deaf, or the seeing, or the blind? Have not I, the LORD? Now therefore go, and I will be with your mouth and teach you what you must say."

He said, "O my Lord, send, I pray, by the hand of whomever else You will send."

The anger of the LORD was inflamed against Moses, and He said, "Is not Aaron the Levite your brother? I know that he can speak well. And also, he comes out to meet you, and when he sees you, he will be glad in his heart. You shall speak to him and put the words in his mouth, and I will be with your mouth, and with his mouth, and will teach you what you must do. What's more, he will be your spokesman to the people, and he will be as a mouth for you, and you will be as God to him. You must take this rod in your hand, with which you will perform the signs."

Moses went and returned to Jethro his father-in-law and said to him, "Please let me go and return to my brothers who are in Egypt, and see whether they be yet alive."

And Jethro said to Moses, "Go in peace."

The LORD said to Moses in Midian, "Go, return to Egypt, for all the men are dead who sought your life." Moses took his wife and his sons and set them on a donkey, and he returned to the land of Egypt. And Moses took the rod of God in his hand.

The LORD said to Moses, "When you go to return into Egypt, see that you do all those wonders before Pharaoh, which I have put in your hand, but I will harden his heart, so that he shall not let the people go. You shall say to Pharaoh, 'Thus says the LORD: Israel is My son, even My firstborn. So I say to you, "Let My son go, that he may serve Me. And if you refuse to let him go, I will slay your son, even your firstborn."'"

At a lodging place on the way, the LORD met him and sought to kill him. Then Zipporah took a sharp stone, and cut off the foreskin of her son, and threw it at his feet, and said, "Surely a bloody husband are you to me." So He let him go. Then she said, "A bloody husband *you are*, because of the circumcision."

Now the LORD said to Aaron, "Go into the wilderness to meet Moses." So he went, and met him at the mount of God, and kissed him. Moses told Aaron all the words of the LORD who had sent him, and all the signs which He had commanded him.

Moses and Aaron went and gathered together all the elders of the children of Israel. And Aaron spoke all the words which the LORD had spoken to

Moses and did the signs in the sight of the people. And the people believed. And when they heard that the LORD had visited the children of Israel and that He had looked on their affliction, they bowed down and worshipped.

And afterward Moses and Aaron went in and said to Pharaoh, "Thus says the LORD, the God of Israel, 'Let My people go, that they may hold a feast to Me in the wilderness.'"

And Pharaoh said, "Who is the LORD that I should obey His voice to let Israel go? I do not know the LORD, nor will I let Israel go."

They said, "The God of the Hebrews has met with us. Let us go, we pray you, three days' journey into the wilderness, and sacrifice to the LORD our God, lest He fall upon us with pestilence or with the sword."

But the king of Egypt said to them, "Why do you, Moses and Aaron, take the people from their work? Get back to your labor." Pharaoh said, "Look, the people of the land now are numerous, and you make them rest from their labor."

Pharaoh commanded the same day the taskmasters of the people and their officers, saying, "You shall no more give the people straw to make brick, as before. Let them go and gather straw for themselves. However, the quota of the bricks, which they were making previously, you shall lay upon them. You shall not diminish any of it. For they are idle. Therefore they cry out, saying, 'Let us go and sacrifice to our God.' Let there be more work laid upon the men so that they may labor therein, and let them not regard deceptive words."

The taskmasters of the people and their officers went out, and they spoke to the people, saying, "Thus says Pharaoh, 'I will not give you straw. Go, get straw where you can find it, yet nothing of your work shall be diminished.'" So the people scattered abroad throughout all the land of Egypt to gather stubble for straw. The taskmasters pushed them, saying, "Fulfill your works, your daily tasks, just as when there was straw." The officers of the children of Israel, which Pharaoh's taskmasters had set over them, were beaten and were asked, and demanded, "Why have you not fulfilled your task in making brick both yesterday and today, as previously?"

Then the officers of the children of Israel came and cried to Pharaoh, saying, "Why do you deal this way with your servants? There is no straw being given to your servants, and they say to us, 'Make brick.' And indeed, your servants are beaten, but the fault is in your *own* people."

But he said, "You are slackers! Slackers! Therefore you say, 'Let us go and do sacrifice to the LORD.' Go therefore now and work, for there shall no straw be given you, yet shall you deliver the quota of bricks."

The officers of the children of Israel saw that they were in trouble, after it was said, "You shall not diminish anything from your bricks of your daily task." Then they met Moses and Aaron, who stood in the way, as they came forth from Pharaoh. And they said to them, "May the LORD look on you and judge, because you have made our scent stink in the estimation of Pharaoh and in the estimation of his servants, to put a sword in their hand to slay us."

Moses returned to the LORD, and said, "Lord, why have You caused trouble for this people? Why is it that You have sent me? For since I came to Pharaoh to speak in Your name, he has done evil to this people; neither have You delivered Your people at all."

Then the LORD said to Moses, "Now you shall see what I will do to Pharaoh, for with a strong hand shall he let them go, and with a strong hand shall he drive them out of his land."

Vaera

Appeared

(Exodus 6:2–9:35)

Then God spoke to Moses, and said to him, "I am the LORD, and I appeared to Abraham, to Isaac, and to Jacob, by the name of God Almighty, but by My name, The LORD, I was not known to them. I have also established My covenant with them, to give them the land of Canaan, the land of their pilgrimage, wherein they sojourned. I have also heard the groaning of the children of Israel, whom the Egyptians keep in bondage, and I have remembered My covenant.

"Therefore say to the children of Israel: 'I am the LORD, and I will bring you out from under the burdens of the Egyptians, and I will rid you out of their bondage, and I will redeem you with an outstretched arm and with great judgments. And I will take you to Me for a people, and I will be to you a God. And you shall know that I am the LORD your God, who brings you out from under the burdens of the Egyptians. I will bring you into the land, which I swore to give to Abraham, to Isaac, and to Jacob, and I will give it to you for an inheritance. I am the LORD.'"

Moses spoke so to the children of Israel, but they did not listen to Moses on account of *their* anguish of spirit and for cruel bondage.

The LORD spoke to Moses, saying, "Go in, tell Pharaoh king of Egypt to let the children of Israel go out of his land."

Moses spoke before the LORD, saying, "The children of Israel have not listened to me. How then shall Pharaoh listen to me, as I am of uncircumcised lips?"

And the LORD spoke to Moses and to Aaron, and gave them a command for the children of Israel, and for Pharaoh, king of Egypt, to bring the children of Israel out of the land of Egypt.

These are the heads of their fathers' houses:

The sons of Reuben the firstborn of Israel: Hanok, Pallu, Hezron, and Karmi. These are the families of Reuben.

The sons of Simeon: Jemuel, Jamin, Ohad, Jakin, Zohar, and Shaul the son of a Canaanite woman. These are the families of Simeon.

These are the names of the sons of Levi according to their generations: Gershon, Kohath, and Merari, and the years of the life of Levi were one hundred thirty-seven years.

The sons of Gershon: Libni, and Shimei, according to their families.

The sons of Kohath: Amram, Izhar, Hebron, and Uzziel, and the years of the life of Kohath were one hundred thirty-three years.

The sons of Merari: Mahli and Mushi.

These are the families of Levi according to their generations.

Now Amram married Jochebed his father's sister, and she bore him Aaron and Moses. And the years of the life of Amram were one hundred thirty-seven years.

The sons of Izhar: Korah, Nepheg, and Zikri.

The sons of Uzziel: Mishael, Elzaphan, and Sithri.

Aaron took to himself Elisheba, daughter of Amminadab, sister of Nahshon, to wife; and she bore him Nadab, Abihu, Eleazar, and Ithamar.

The sons of Korah: Assir, Elkanah, and Abiasaph. These are the families of the Korahites.

Eleazar, Aaron's son, married one of the daughters of Putiel, and she bore him Phinehas.

These are the heads of the fathers of the Levites according to their families.

It was that Aaron and Moses to whom the LORD said, "Bring out the children of Israel from the land of Egypt according to their armies." They are the ones who spoke to Pharaoh king of Egypt to bring out the children of Israel from Egypt. It was that Moses and Aaron.

On the day when the LORD spoke to Moses in the land of Egypt, the LORD spoke to Moses, saying, "I am the LORD. Speak to Pharaoh the king of Egypt all that I say to you."

However, Moses said before the LORD, "Listen! I am unskilled in speech, so how will Pharaoh listen to me?"

So the LORD said to Moses, "See, I have made you a god to Pharaoh, and Aaron your brother will be your prophet. You shall speak all that I command you, and Aaron your brother shall tell Pharaoh to send the children of Israel out of his land. But I will harden Pharaoh's heart and multiply My signs and My wonders in the land of Egypt. Nevertheless, Pharaoh will not listen to you, so that I may lay My hand upon Egypt and bring forth My armies and My people, the children of Israel, out of the land of Egypt by great judgments. And the Egyptians shall know that I am the LORD when I stretch forth My hand upon Egypt and bring out the children of Israel from among them."

So Moses and Aaron did it. Just as the LORD commanded them, so they did. Moses was eighty years old, and Aaron was eighty-three years old when they spoke to Pharaoh.

Now the LORD spoke to Moses and to Aaron, saying, "When Pharaoh shall speak to you, saying, 'Show a miracle,' then you shall say to Aaron, 'Take your rod, and throw it before Pharaoh,' and it shall become a serpent."

So Moses and Aaron went to Pharaoh, and they did what the LORD had commanded. And Aaron threw down his rod before Pharaoh and before his servants, and it became a serpent. Then Pharaoh also called the wise men and the sorcerers. Then the magicians of Egypt likewise performed with their secret arts. For every man threw down his rod, and they became serpents. But Aaron's rod swallowed up their rods. Nonetheless, Pharaoh's heart hardened so that he would not listen to them, just as the LORD had said.

The LORD said to Moses, "Pharaoh's heart is hardened. He refuses to let the people go. Go to Pharaoh in the morning as he goes out to the water, and you shall stand by the river's bank to meet him. You must take the rod which was turned to a serpent in your hand. Then you are to say to him, 'The LORD, the God of the Hebrews, has sent me to you, saying, "Let My people go, so that they may serve Me in the wilderness." But up to this point you have not listened! Thus says the LORD, "In this you shall know that I am the LORD: Indeed, I will strike the waters of the Nile with the rod that is in my hand, and they shall be turned to blood. And the fish that are in the river shall die, and the river shall stink so that the Egyptians shall be weary of drinking the river's water." ' "

Then the LORD spoke to Moses, "Say to Aaron, 'Take your rod, and stretch out your hand over the waters of Egypt, over their rivers, over their canals, over their ponds, and over all their pools of water, so that they may become blood. And there will be blood throughout all the land of Egypt, both in *vessels* of wood, and in *vessels* of stone.' "

Moses and Aaron did so, just as the LORD commanded. And he lifted up the rod and struck the waters that were in the river, in the sight of Pharaoh, and in the sight of his servants, and all the waters that were in the river were turned to blood. The fish that were in the river died, the river stank, and the Egyptians could not drink of the water of the river. Blood was everywhere throughout the land of Egypt.

Nevertheless, the magicians of Egypt did the same with their secret arts, and Pharaoh's heart was hardened, and he did not listen to them, as the LORD had said. Then Pharaoh turned and went into his house, and he did not concern himself with this either. So all the Egyptians dug around about the river for water to drink, because they could not drink of the water of the river.

Seven days passed after the LORD had struck the river.

Then the LORD said to Moses, "Go to Pharaoh and say to him, 'Thus says the LORD: Let My people go, so that they may serve Me. But if you refuse to let them go, then I will plague all your borders with frogs. And the river will swarm with frogs, which shall go up and come into your house, and into your bedchamber, and on your bed, and into the houses of your servants, and on your people, and into your ovens, and into your kneading troughs. So the frogs shall come upon you, upon your people, and upon all your servants.'"

Then the LORD said to Moses, "Say to Aaron, 'Stretch forth your hand with your rod over the streams, over the rivers, and over the ponds, and cause frogs to come up on the land of Egypt.'"

Aaron stretched out his hand over the waters of Egypt, and the frogs came up, and covered the land of Egypt. The magicians did the same with their secret arts and brought up frogs upon the land of Egypt.

Then Pharaoh called for Moses and Aaron, and said, "Entreat the LORD, that He may take away the frogs from me, and from my people, and I will let the people go, so that they may sacrifice to the LORD."

Moses said to Pharaoh, "Glory yourself over me: When shall I entreat for you, your servants, and your people, to destroy the frogs from you and your houses, that they may remain in the river only?"

And he said, "Tomorrow."

Then he said, "Be it according to your word, in order that you may know that there is no one like the LORD our God. The frogs shall depart from you, and from your houses, from your servants, and from your people. They shall remain in the river only."

Moses and Aaron went out from Pharaoh, and Moses cried out to the LORD concerning the frogs which he had brought against Pharaoh. Then the LORD did according to the word of Moses. And the frogs died out of the houses, the villages, and the fields. So they gathered them together in heaps, and the land stank. But when Pharaoh saw that there was relief, he hardened his heart and did not listen to them, as the LORD had said.

Then the LORD said to Moses, "Say to Aaron, 'Stretch out your rod, and strike the dust of the land, so that it may become gnats throughout all the land of Egypt.'" They did so, for Aaron stretched out his hand with his rod and smote the dust of the earth, and it became gnats on man and on beast. All the dust of the land became gnats throughout all the land of Egypt. Then the magicians tried with their secret arts to bring forth gnats, but they could not, so there were gnats upon man and beast.

Then the magicians said to Pharaoh, "This is the finger of God." Nevertheless, Pharaoh's heart was hardened, and he did not listen to them, just as the LORD had said.

So the LORD said to Moses, "Rise up early in the morning and stand before Pharaoh as he comes forth to the water and say to him, 'Thus says the LORD: Let My people go, so that they may serve Me. Otherwise, if you will not let My people go, indeed I will send swarms *of flies* on you, and on your servants, and on your people, and into your houses. And the houses of the Egyptians shall be full of swarms *of flies* and also the ground wherever they are.

"'I will in that day set apart the land of Goshen, in which My people dwell, so that no swarms of flies shall be there, in order that you may know that I am the LORD in the midst of the earth. I will put a division between My people and your people. Tomorrow this sign will happen.'"

The LORD did so, and great swarms *of flies* came into the house of Pharaoh, and into his servants' houses, and into all the land of Egypt. The land was corrupted because of the swarms *of flies*.

Pharaoh called for Moses and Aaron, and said, "Go, sacrifice to your God in the land."

Moses said, "It is not right to do so, for what we shall sacrifice to the LORD our God would be an abomination to the Egyptians. If we shall sacrifice what is an abomination of the Egyptians before their eyes, will they not stone us? We will go three days' journey into the wilderness, and then we will sacrifice to the LORD our God, as He shall command us."

Pharaoh said, "I will let you go, that you may sacrifice to the LORD your God in the wilderness. Only you shall not go very far away. Make entreaty for me."

Moses said, "Indeed, I am leaving you, and I will plead with the LORD that the swarms *of flies* may depart from Pharaoh, from his servants, and from his people tomorrow. But let not Pharaoh deal deceitfully any more by not letting the people go to sacrifice to the LORD."

Moses went away from Pharaoh and entreated the LORD. Then the LORD did according to the word of Moses, and He removed the swarms *of flies* from Pharaoh, from his servants, and from his people. Not one remained. Nevertheless, Pharaoh hardened his heart at this time also, nor would he let the people go.

Then the LORD said to Moses, "Go to Pharaoh, and speak to him, 'Thus says the LORD, the God of the Hebrews: Let My people go, so that they may serve Me. For if you refuse to let *them* go and continue holding them, indeed, the hand of the LORD will be upon your livestock which are in the field, upon the horses, upon the donkeys, upon the camels, upon the oxen, and upon the sheep. There shall be a very grievous pestilence. The LORD shall separate between the livestock of Israel and the livestock of Egypt, and nothing shall die of all that belongs to the children of Israel.'"

So the LORD appointed a set time, saying, "Tomorrow the LORD shall do this thing in the land." Then the LORD did this thing the next day, so that all the livestock of Egypt died, but not one of the livestock of the children of Israel died. Pharaoh sent, and there was not one of the livestock of the children of Israel dead. And the heart of Pharaoh was hardened, so that he did not let the people go.

Then the LORD said to Moses and to Aaron, "Take for yourselves handfuls of ashes from a kiln, and let Moses toss it toward the heavens in the sight of Pharaoh. It shall become fine dust over all the land of Egypt and shall be a boil breaking forth with blisters upon man and beast, throughout all the land of Egypt."

So they took the ashes from a kiln and stood before Pharaoh. Then Moses tossed it up toward the heavens, and it became a boil breaking forth with blisters upon man and beast. The magicians could not stand before Moses because of the boils, for the boils were upon the magicians and upon all the Egyptians. Moreover, the LORD hardened the heart of Pharaoh, so that he did not listen to them, just as the LORD had spoken to Moses.

Then the LORD said to Moses, "Rise up early in the morning, and stand before Pharaoh, and say to him, 'Thus says the LORD, the God of the Hebrews: Let My people go, so that they may serve Me. For I will at this time send all My plagues upon you and your servants and your people, so that you may know that there is none like Me in all the earth. For by now I could have stretched out My hand, so that I might strike you and your people with pestilence, and you would be cut off from the earth. But, indeed, for this cause I have raised you up, in order to show in you My power and so that My name may be declared throughout all the earth. Still, you exalt yourself against My people by forbidding them to go. Certainly, tomorrow about this time I will cause it to rain a very severe hail, such as has not happened in Egypt since it was founded until now. Send therefore now and bring your livestock and all that you have in the field to safety. Every man and beast which shall be found in the field and not brought home when the hail comes down upon them will die.'"

He that feared the word of the LORD among the servants of Pharaoh made his servants and his livestock flee into the houses. But he that failed to regard the word of the LORD left his servants and his livestock in the field.

So the LORD said to Moses, "Stretch forth your hand toward the heavens, so that there may be hail in all the land of Egypt, upon man and beast, and upon every herb of the field, throughout the land of Egypt." Moses stretched forth his rod toward the heavens, and the LORD sent thunder and hail, and fire ran along upon the ground. So the LORD rained hail upon the land of Egypt. So there was hail, and fire mingled with the hail. It was so severe that there had been none like it in all the land of Egypt since it became a nation. The hail struck all the land of Egypt, all that was in the field, both man and beast, and the hail struck every herb of the field and broke every tree of the field. Only in the land of Goshen, where the children of Israel *were*, was there no hail.

Then Pharaoh sent and called for Moses and Aaron, and said to them, "I have sinned this time. The LORD is righteous, and I and my people are wicked. Entreat the LORD, for there has been enough of God's mighty thunder and hail, and I will let you go, and you shall stay no longer."

Moses said to him, "As soon as I am gone out of the city, I will spread out my hands to the LORD. The thunder shall cease, and there shall no longer be any more hail, so that you may know that the earth is the LORD's. But as for you and your servants, I know that you will not yet fear the LORD God."

Now the flax and the barley were struck, for the barley was in the ear, and the flax was in bud. But the wheat and the spelt were not struck, for they grow up later.

So Moses went out of the city from Pharaoh and spread out his hands to the LORD, and the thunders and hail ceased, and the rain was no longer poured upon the earth. However, when Pharaoh saw that the rain and the hail and the thunders were ceased, he sinned yet more, and hardened his heart, he and his servants. The heart of Pharaoh hardened, and he would not let the children of Israel go, just as the LORD had spoken by Moses.

Bo

Come!

(Exodus 10:1–13:16)

Then the LORD said to Moses, "Go to Pharaoh, for I have hardened his heart and the heart of his servants, that I might show these signs of Mine before him, in order that you may tell in the hearing of your son, and of your son's son, what things I have done in Egypt, and My signs which I have done among them, that you may know that I am the LORD."

Moses and Aaron came to Pharaoh and said to him, "Thus says the LORD, the God of the Hebrews, 'How long will you refuse to humble yourself before Me? Let My people go, that they may serve Me. For if you refuse to let My people go, indeed, tomorrow I will bring locusts into your territory. And they shall cover the face of the earth, such that no one will be able to see the earth. What's more, they shall eat the remainder of that which has escaped—that which remains to you from the hail—and shall eat every tree which grows for you out of the field. And they shall fill your houses, and the houses of all your servants, and the houses of all the Egyptians—which neither your fathers, nor your fathers' fathers have seen since the day that they were on the earth until this day.'" And he turned and went out from Pharaoh.

Then Pharaoh's servants said to him, "How long shall this man be a snare to us? Let the men go, so that they may serve the LORD their God. Do you not yet know that Egypt is destroyed?"

So Moses and Aaron were brought back to Pharaoh, and he said to them, "Go, serve the LORD your God! But who are the ones that shall go?"

And Moses said, "We will go with our young and our old, with our sons and our daughters, with our flocks and our herds will we go, for *we must hold* a feast to the LORD."

Then he said to them, "The LORD indeed be with you when I let you and your little ones go. Beware, for evil is before you. Not so! Go now, you that are men, and serve the LORD, for that is what you desire." Then they were driven out from Pharaoh's presence.

Then the LORD said to Moses, "Stretch out your hand over the land of Egypt for the locusts, so that they may come up upon the land of Egypt and eat every herb of the land, even all that the hail has left."

So Moses stretched forth his rod over the land of Egypt; then the LORD brought an east wind upon the land all that day and all that night. And when it was morning, the east wind brought the locusts. The locusts went up over all the land of Egypt and settled down in all the territory of Egypt. They were very grievous. Never before had there been such locusts as they, nor would there be such ever again. For they covered the face of the whole earth, so that the land was darkened, and they ate every herb of the land, and all the fruit of the trees which the hail had left. As a result, nothing green remained there in the trees or herbs of the field, through all the land of Egypt.

Then Pharaoh called for Moses and Aaron in haste and said, "I have sinned against the LORD, your God, and against you. Now therefore please forgive my sin only this once, and entreat the LORD your God, so that He may take away from me this death only."

So he went out from Pharaoh and prayed to the LORD. Then the LORD turned a mighty strong west wind, which took away the locusts and threw them into the Red Sea. Not one locust remained in all the territory of Egypt. But the LORD hardened Pharaoh's heart, so that he would not let the children of Israel go.

Then the LORD said to Moses, "Stretch out your hand toward the heavens, so that there may be darkness over the land of Egypt, a darkness which may be felt." So Moses stretched forth his hand toward the heavens, and there was a thick darkness in all the land of Egypt for three days. They did not see one another; nor did anyone rise from his place for three days. But all the children of Israel had light in their dwellings.

Then Pharaoh called to Moses and said, "Go, serve the LORD. Only let your flocks and your herds be detained. Even let your little ones also go with you."

But Moses said, "You must also give us sacrifices and burnt offerings, so that we may sacrifice to the LORD our God. Our livestock will go with us also. Not a hoof will be left behind, for we must take of them to serve the LORD our God. And we do not know with what we must serve the LORD, until we get there."

But the LORD hardened Pharaoh's heart, and he would not let them go. So Pharaoh said to him, "Get away from me! Watch yourself, do not see my face anymore; for in the day you see my face you shall die."

Then Moses said, "As you wish. I will never see your face again."

Now the LORD said to Moses, "I will still bring one plague more upon Pharaoh, and upon Egypt. Afterwards he will let you go from here. When he lets you go, he shall surely thrust you out from here altogether. Speak now in the hearing of the people, and let every man borrow of his neighbor and every woman of her neighbor, articles of silver and articles of gold." Then the LORD gave the people favor in the sight of the Egyptians. Moreover, the man Moses was very great in the land of Egypt, in the sight of Pharaoh's servants, and in the sight of the people.

Moses said, "Thus says the LORD, 'About midnight I will go out into the midst of Egypt, and all the firstborn in the land of Egypt shall die, from the first-born of Pharaoh who sits on his throne, even to the firstborn of the maidservant that is behind the mill, as well as all the firstborn of beasts. Then there shall be a great cry throughout all the land of Egypt, such as there has never been, nor shall ever be again. But against any of the children of Israel a dog will not even move his tongue, against man or beast, in order that you may know how that the LORD distinguishes between Egypt and Israel.' Then all these your servants shall come down to me and bow themselves to me, saying, 'Get out, and all the people who follow you!' After that I will go out." And he went out from Pharaoh in great anger.

Then the LORD said to Moses, "Pharaoh shall not listen to you so that My wonders may be multiplied in the land of Egypt." So Moses and Aaron did all these wonders before Pharaoh, and the LORD hardened Pharaoh's heart, and he would not let the children of Israel go out of his land.

Now the LORD spoke to Moses and Aaron in the land of Egypt, saying: This month shall be the beginning of months to you. It shall be the first month of the year to you. Speak to all the congregation of Israel, saying: On the tenth day of this month every man shall take a lamb, according to the house of their fathers, a lamb for a household. And if the household be too little for the lamb, let him and his neighbor next to his house take it according to the number of the persons; according to what each man shall eat, divide the lamb. Your lamb shall be without blemish, a male of the first year. You shall take it out from the sheep, or from the goats. You shall keep it up until the fourteenth day of the same month, and then the whole assembly of the congregation of Israel shall kill it in the evening. They shall take some of the blood and put it on the two side posts and on the upper doorpost of the houses in which they shall eat it. They shall eat the flesh on that night, roasted with fire, and they shall eat it with unleavened bread and bitter herbs. Do not eat it raw, nor boiled at all with water, but roasted with fire, its head with its legs and its entrails. And you shall let nothing of it remain until the morning, but that of it which remains until the morn-ing you shall burn with fire. In this way shall you eat it: with your waist girded, your sandals on your feet, and your staff in your hand. So you shall eat it in haste. It is the LORD's Passover.

For I will pass through the land of Egypt this night and will smite all the firstborn in the land of Egypt, both man and beast, and against all the gods of Egypt I will execute judgment. I am the LORD. The blood shall be to you for a sign on the houses where you are. And when I see the blood, I will pass over you, and the plague shall not be upon you to destroy *you* when I smite the land of Egypt.

This day shall be a memorial to you, and you shall keep it as a feast to the LORD. Throughout your generations you shall keep it a feast by an eternal ordinance. Seven days you shall eat unleavened bread. On the first day you shall put away leaven out of your houses, for whoever eats leavened bread from the first day until the seventh day, that person shall be cut off from Israel. On the first day there shall be a holy convocation, and on the seventh day there shall be a holy convocation for you. No manner of work shall be done on them; but that which every man must eat—that only may be prepared for you.

You shall observe the Feast of Unleavened Bread. For on this very day I brought your armies out of the land of Egypt. Therefore you shall observe this day throughout your generations as an ordinance forever. In the first *month*, on the fourteenth day of the month at evening, you shall eat unleavened bread until the twenty-first day of the month at evening. Seven days shall there be no leaven found in your houses, for whoever eats that which is leavened, that person shall be cut off from the congregation of Israel, whether he be a stranger or born in the land. You shall eat nothing leavened. In all your dwellings you shall eat unleavened bread.

Then Moses called for all the elders of Israel and said to them, "Draw out and take for yourselves a lamb according to your families and kill the Passover *lamb*. You shall take a bunch of hyssop, and dip it in the blood that is in the basin, and apply the lintel and the two side posts with the blood that is in the basin, and none of you shall go out from the door of his house until the morning. For the LORD will pass through to kill the Egyptians. And when He sees the blood upon the lintel and on the two side posts, the LORD will pass over the door and will not permit the destroyer to come to your houses to kill *you*.

"And you shall observe this thing as an ordinance to you and to your sons forever. When you enter the land which the LORD will give you, according as He has promised, that you shall observe this service. And when your children shall say to you, 'What does this service mean to you?' that you shall say, 'It is the sacrifice of the LORD's Passover, who passed over the houses of the children of Israel in Egypt, when He smote the Egyptians, and delivered our households.'" And the people bowed down and worshipped. Then the children of Israel went and did *so*. Just as the LORD had commanded Moses and Aaron, so they did.

At midnight the LORD smote all the firstborn in the land of Egypt, from the firstborn of Pharaoh that sat on his throne to the firstborn of the captive who was in the dungeon and all the firstborn of livestock. Pharaoh rose up in the night, he and all his servants and all the Egyptians, and there was a great cry in Egypt, for there was not a house where there was not someone dead.

Then he called for Moses and Aaron at night and said, "Rise up, and get out from among my people, both you and the children of Israel, and go, serve the LORD, as you have said. Also take your flocks and your herds, as you have said, and be gone, and bless me also."

The Egyptians urged the people, so that they might send them out of the land in haste, for they said, "We all will be dead." So the people took their dough before it was leavened, *with* their kneading troughs being bound up in their clothes on their shoulders. Now the children of Israel did according to the word of Moses, and they requested of the Egyptians articles of silver and articles of gold, and clothing. And the LORD gave the people favor in the sight of the Egyptians, so that they gave them *what they requested*. Thus they plundered the Egyptians.

Then the children of Israel journeyed from Rameses to Sukkoth, about six hundred thousand men on foot, besides children. A mixed multitude also went up with them along with flocks and herds, a large amount of livestock. They baked unleavened cakes of the dough which they brought forth out of Egypt, for it was not leavened because they were driven out of Egypt and could not linger, nor had they prepared for themselves any food.

Now the sojourning of the children of Israel who lived in Egypt was four hundred thirty years. And at the end of the four hundred thirty years, on the very day, all the hosts of the LORD went out from the land of Egypt. It is a night to be observed to the LORD for bringing them out from the land of Egypt. This is that night for the LORD to be observed by all the children of Israel in their generations.

So the LORD said to Moses and Aaron: This is the ordinance of the Passover:

No foreigner may eat of it. But every man's servant bought with money, when you have circumcised him, may eat it. A foreigner or a hired servant shall not eat it.

In one house shall it be eaten. You shall not carry any of the flesh outside of the house, nor shall you break a bone of it. All the congregation of Israel shall keep it.

Now when a stranger sojourns with you and keeps the Passover to the LORD, let all his males be circumcised, and then let him come near and keep it. And he shall be as one that is born in the land. However, no uncircumcised person shall eat of it. The same law shall apply to him that is a native and to the stranger who sojourns among you.

So all the children of Israel did it. They did just as the LORD commanded Moses and Aaron. And that same day the LORD brought the children of Israel out of the land of Egypt by their hosts.

Then the LORD spoke to Moses, saying: Sanctify unto Me all the firstborn, the firstborn of every womb among the children of Israel, both of man and of beast. It is Mine.

Moses said to the people, "Remember this day, in which you came out from Egypt, out of the house of bondage, for by strength of hand the LORD brought you out from this place. Nothing leavened shall be eaten. On this day, you are going out, in the month of Aviv. It shall be when the LORD brings you into the land of the Canaanites and the Hittites and the Amorites and the Hivites and the Jebusites, which He swore to your fathers to give you, a land flowing with milk and honey, that you shall keep this ceremony in this month. Seven days you shall eat unleavened bread, and on the seventh day shall be a feast to the LORD. Unleavened bread shall be eaten seven days. And there shall be no leavened bread seen among you, nor shall there be leaven seen among you in all your borders. You shall declare to your son on that day, saying, 'This is done because of that which the LORD did for me when I came forth out of Egypt.' It shall be as a sign to you on your hand and as a memorial on your forehead, in order that the LORD's law may be in your mouth. For with a strong hand the LORD brought you out of Egypt. You shall, therefore, keep this ordinance at its appointed time from year to year.

"It shall be when the LORD brings you into the land of the Canaanites, just as He swore to you and to your fathers, and shall give it you, that you shall set apart to the LORD the first offspring of every womb and the first offspring of every beast which you have. The males shall be the LORD's. But every first offspring of a donkey you shall redeem with a lamb. And if you do not redeem it, then you shall break its neck, and all the firstborn of man among your sons you shall redeem.

"It shall be when your son asks you in time to come, saying, 'What is this?' that you shall say to him, 'With a strong hand the LORD brought us out from Egypt, from the house of bondage. And when Pharaoh stubbornly refused to let us go, that the LORD killed all the firstborn in the land of Egypt, both the firstborn of man, and the firstborn of beast. Therefore, I sacrifice to the LORD the first male offspring of every womb, but all the first-born of my sons I redeem.' It shall be as a sign on your hand and as frontlets on your forehead, for with a strong hand the LORD brought us out of Egypt."

Beshalach

When he sent out

(Exodus 13:17–17:16)

N ow when Pharaoh had let the people go, God did not lead them through the way of the land of the Philistines, although it was nearby. For God said, "Lest the people change their minds when they see war, and they return to Egypt." Therefore, God led the people around, *through* the way of the wilderness to the Red Sea, and the children of Israel went up prepared for war out of the land of Egypt.

Moses took the bones of Joseph with him, for he had made the children of Israel solemnly swear, saying, "God will surely attend to you, and you shall carry my bones away from here with you."

They took their journey from Sukkoth and camped in Etham, on the edge of the wilderness. The LORD went before them by day in a pillar of cloud to lead them *along* the way, and by night in a pillar of fire, to give them light, so that they might travel by day and by night. He did not remove the pillar of cloud by day or the pillar of fire by night from before the people.

Now the LORD spoke to Moses, saying: Speak to the children of Israel, so that they turn and camp before Pi Hahiroth, between Migdol and the sea, before Baal Zephon. Opposite it you shall camp by the sea. For Pharaoh will say of the children of Israel, "They are confused in the land. The wilderness has shut them in." So I will harden Pharaoh's heart, so that he shall pursue them. And I will be honored because of Pharaoh and because of all his army, so that the Egyptians may know that I am the LORD. And they did so.

When it was told the king of Egypt that the people fled, the heart of Pharaoh and of his servants was turned against the people, and they said, "Why have we done this, that we have let Israel go from serving us?" So he made ready his chariot and took his people with him. And he took six hundred select chariots, and all the chariots of Egypt, and officers over every one of them. The LORD hardened the heart of Pharaoh king of Egypt, and he pursued after the children of Israel. However, the children of Israel went out with confidence. But the Egyptians pursued after them, all the horses and chariots of Pharaoh, and his horsemen, and his army, and overtook them camping by the sea, beside Pi Hahiroth, before Baal Zephon.

When Pharaoh drew near, the children of Israel lifted up their eyes, and indeed, the Egyptians were marching after them, and they were extremely terrified, so the children of Israel cried out to the LORD. Then they said to Moses, "Is it because there were no graves in Egypt that you have taken us away to die in the wilderness? Why have you dealt with us in this way, bringing us out of Egypt? Is not this the word that we spoke to you in Egypt, saying, 'Let us alone, that we may serve the Egyptians'? For it would have been better for us to serve the Egyptians than to die in the wilderness."

But Moses said to the people, "Fear not! Stand firm! And see the salvation of the LORD, which He will show you today. For the Egyptians whom you have seen today, you shall never see again. The LORD shall fight for you, while you hold your peace."

The LORD said to Moses, "Why do you cry out to Me? Speak to the children of Israel, so that they go forward. And as for you, lift up your rod, and stretch out your hand over the sea, and divide it; then the children of Israel shall go on dry ground through the midst of the sea. As for Me, surely, I will harden the hearts of the Egyptians, so that they shall follow them, and I will be honored through Pharaoh, through all his army, his chariots, and his horsemen. Then the Egyptians shall know that I am the LORD when I am honored through Pharaoh, his chariots, and his horsemen."

Then the angel of God, which went before the camp of Israel, moved and went behind them, and the pillar of the cloud moved before them and stood behind them. So it came between the camp of the Egyptians and the camp of Israel, and there was a cloud and darkness to them, but it gave light by night. Therefore, the one did not come near the other the entire night.

Then Moses stretched out his hand over the sea, and the LORD caused the sea to go back by a strong east wind all that night, and made the sea dry land, so that the waters were divided. The children of Israel went into the midst of the sea on the dry ground, and the waters were a wall unto them on their right hand, and on their left.

Then the Egyptians pursued and went in after them into the midst of the sea, even all Pharaoh's horses, his chariots, and his horsemen. And in the morning watch the LORD looked down on the army of the Egyptians through the pillar of fire and of the cloud and threw the camp of the Egyptians into confusion. He removed their chariot wheels, so that they drove them with difficulty, and the Egyptians said, "Let us flee from the face of Israel, for the LORD is fighting for them against Egypt."

Then the LORD said to Moses, "Stretch out your hand over the sea, so that the waters may come back upon the Egyptians, upon their chariots, and their horsemen." So Moses stretched forth his hand over the sea, and the sea returned to its normal place when the morning appeared, while the Egyptians fled against it, so the LORD overthrew the Egyptians in the midst of the sea. The waters returned and covered the chariots, and the horsemen, and all the host of Pharaoh that came into the sea after them. There remained not so much as one of them.

But the children of Israel walked on dry land in the midst of the sea. And the waters were a wall to them on their right hand and on their left. Thus the LORD saved Israel that day from the hand of the Egyptians, and Israel saw the Egyptians dead upon the seashore. When Israel saw the great power which the LORD used upon the Egyptians, the people feared the LORD, and they believed in the LORD and in His servant Moses.

Then Moses and the children of Israel sang this song to the LORD and spoke, saying:

"I will sing to the LORD,
  for He has triumphed gloriously!
He has thrown the horse and his rider
  into the sea!
The LORD is my strength and song,
  and He has become my salvation.
He is my God, and I will praise Him;
  my father's God, and I will exalt Him.
The LORD is a man of war;
  the LORD is His name.
Pharaoh's chariots and his army
  He has thrown into the sea;
his chosen captains also
  are drowned in the Red Sea.
The depths have covered them;
  they sank to the bottom like a stone.

"Your right hand, O LORD,
  is glorious in power.
Your right hand, O LORD,
  shatters the enemy.
In the greatness of Your excellence,
  You overthrow those who rise up against You.
You send out Your wrath;
  it consumes them like stubble.
With the blast of Your nostrils
  the waters were gathered together.
The flowing waters stood upright as a heap;
  and the depths were congealed in the heart of the sea.

"The enemy said,
  'I will pursue. I will overtake.

I will divide the spoil;
    my lust shall be satisfied upon them.
I will draw my sword,
    my hand shall destroy them.'
You blew with Your wind,
    and the sea covered them;
they sank like lead
    in the mighty waters.

"Who is like You, O Lord, among the gods?
    Who is like You,
        glorious in holiness,
        fearful in praises,
        doing wonders?
You stretched out Your right hand,
    and the earth swallowed them.

"In Your mercy You have led
    the people whom You have redeemed;
You have guided them by Your strength
    to Your holy dwelling.
The peoples have heard and are afraid;
    sorrow has taken hold on the inhabitants of Philistia.
Then the chiefs of Edom were amazed;
    the mighty men of Moab, trembling takes hold of them;
all the inhabitants of Canaan are melted away.
    Fear and dread fall upon them;
by the greatness of Your arm
    they are as still as a stone,
until Your people pass over, O Lord,
    until the people whom You have purchased pass over.
You shall bring them in, and plant them
    on the mountain of Your inheritance,
in the place, O Lord, which You have made for Your dwelling,
    in the sanctuary, O Lord, which Your hands have
        established.
The Lord will reign
    forever and ever."

For the horses of Pharaoh went in with his chariots and with his horse-men into the sea, and the Lord brought back the waters of the sea upon them, but the children of Israel walked on dry land in the midst of the sea.

Miriam the prophetess, the sister of Aaron, took a timbrel in her hand, and all the women went out after her with timbrels and with dancing. Miriam answered them,

"Sing to the LORD,
    for He triumphed gloriously!
The horse and his rider
    He has hurled into the sea."

Then Moses led Israel from the Red Sea, and they went out into the Wilderness of Shur, and they went three days in the wilderness and found no water. When they came to Marah, they could not drink of the waters of Marah, for they were bitter. Therefore, the name of it was called Marah. So the people murmured against Moses, saying, "What shall we drink?"

And he cried to the LORD, and the LORD showed him a tree. When he had thrown it into the waters, the waters were made sweet.

There He made for them a statute and an ordinance, and there He tested them. He said, "If you diligently listen to the voice of the LORD your God, and do what is right in His sight, and give ear to His commandments, and keep all His statutes, I will not afflict you with any of the diseases with which I have afflicted the Egyptians. For I am the LORD who heals you."

Then they came to Elim, where there were twelve wells of water and seventy palm trees, and they camped there by the waters.

Then they set out from Elim, and all the congregation of the children of Israel came to the Wilderness of Sin, which is between Elim and Sinai, on the fifteenth day of the second month after their departing out of the land of Egypt. The whole congregation of the children of Israel murmured against Moses and Aaron in the wilderness. Now the children of Israel said to them, "Would to God we had died by the hand of the LORD in the land of Egypt, when we sat by the pots of meat, when we ate bread to the full, for you have brought us forth into this wilderness to kill this whole assembly with hunger."

Then the LORD said to Moses, "Indeed, I will rain bread from heaven for you. And the people shall go out and gather a certain amount every day, that I may test them, whether they will walk in My law or not. And it shall come to pass that on the sixth day they shall prepare that which they bring in, and it will be twice as much as they gather daily."

So Moses and Aaron said to all the children of Israel, "At evening, you shall know that the LORD has brought you out from the land of Egypt. And in the morning you shall see the glory of the LORD, because He hears your murmurings against the LORD. And what are we that you murmur against us?" Then Moses said, "This will happen when the LORD gives you meat to eat in the evening and bread in the morning to satisfy, for the LORD hears your murmurings which you murmur against Him. And what are we? Your murmurings are not against us, but against the LORD."

Then Moses said to Aaron, "Say to all the congregation of the children of Israel, 'Come near before the LORD, for He has heard your murmurings.'"

So as Aaron spoke to the whole congregation of the children of Israel, they looked toward the wilderness, and indeed, the glory of the LORD appeared in the cloud.

Then the LORD spoke to Moses, saying, "I have heard the murmurings of the children of Israel. Speak to them, saying, 'In the evening you shall eat meat, and in the morning you shall be filled with bread. And you shall know that I am the LORD your God.'"

So in the evening the quail came up and covered the camp, and in the morning a layer of dew was surrounding the camp. When the layer of dew evaporated, on the surface of the wilderness there lay a small flaky thing, as fine as the frost on the ground. When the children of Israel saw it, they said one to another, "What is it?" For they did not know what it was.

And Moses said to them, "This is the bread which the LORD has given you to eat. This is what the LORD has commanded, 'Every man is to gather of it according to what he will eat, one omer for every man, according to the number of your people. Every man should take for them for whoever lives in his tent.'"

The children of Israel did so, and gathered, some more, some less. When they measured it with an omer, he that gathered much had nothing left over, and he that gathered little had no lack. They gathered every man according what he could eat.

Moses said to them, "Let no man leave any of it until the morning."

However, they did not listen to Moses, and some of them left part of it until the morning, and it bred worms, and stank, and Moses was angry with them.

So they gathered it every morning, every man according to what he could eat. And when the sun got hot, it melted. Now on the sixth day they gathered twice as much bread, two omers per man, and then all the leaders of the congregation came and told Moses. He said to them, "This is what the LORD has said, 'Tomorrow is the Sabbath, a holy Sabbath to the LORD. Bake that which you will bake today, and boil that you will boil, and all that which remains over lay up for yourselves to be kept until the morning.'"

So they laid it up until the morning, just as Moses commanded, and it did not stink, nor was there any worm in it. Moses said, "Eat it today, for today is a Sabbath to the LORD. Today you will not find it in the field. Six days you shall gather it, but on the seventh day, the Sabbath, there will be none."

It happened that some of the people went out on the seventh day to gather, but they found nothing. Then the LORD said to Moses, "How long will you refuse to keep My commandments and My instructions? See, the

LORD has given you the Sabbath; therefore He gives you bread for two days on the sixth day. Every man remain in his place. Let no man go out of his place on the seventh day." So the people rested on the seventh day.

The house of Israel named it manna, and it was like coriander seed and was white, and its taste was like wafers made with honey. Then Moses said, "This is what the LORD has commanded, 'Fill an omer of it to be kept for your generations *to come,* so that they may see the bread that I fed you in the wilderness, when I brought you forth from the land of Egypt.'"

Moses said to Aaron, "Take a pot and put an omer full of manna in it, and place it before the LORD, to be kept for generations *to come.*"

As the LORD commanded Moses, so Aaron placed it before the testimony, to be kept. The children of Israel ate manna forty years, until they came to an inhabited land. They ate the manna until they came to the border of the land of Canaan.

Now an omer is one-tenth of an ephah.

All the congregation of the children of Israel journeyed from the Wilderness of Sin, from place to place, according to the commandment of the LORD, and pitched in Rephidim, but there was no water for the people to drink. Therefore the people contended with Moses and said, "Give us water so that we may drink."

And Moses said to them, "Why do you contend with me? Why do you test the LORD?"

But the people thirsted there for water, and the people murmured against Moses, and said, "Why is it that you have brought us up out of Egypt, to kill us and our children and our livestock with thirst?"

Then Moses cried out to the LORD, saying, "What shall I do to this people? They are almost ready to stone me."

The LORD said to Moses, "Pass over before the people, and take with you some of the elders of Israel. And take in your hand your rod with which you struck the Nile, and go. Indeed, I will stand before you there on the rock in Horeb, and you shall strike the rock, and there water shall come out of it, so that the people may drink." Then Moses did so in the sight of the elders of Israel. He called the name of the place Massah, and Meribah, because of the contending of the children of Israel, and because they tested the LORD, saying, "Is the LORD among us, or not?"

Then Amalek came and fought with Israel in Rephidim. So Moses said to Joshua, "Choose men for us and go out, fight against Amalek. Tomorrow I will stand on the top of the hill with the rod of God in my hand."

So Joshua did as Moses had said to him and fought against Amalek. And Moses, Aaron, and Hur went up to the top of the hill. Now when Moses held up his hand, Israel prevailed, but when he let down his hand, Amalek prevailed. But Moses' hands became heavy. So they took a stone, and put it under him, and he sat on it. And Aaron and Hur supported his hands, one on one side, and the other on the other side. And his hands were steady until the going down of the sun. So Joshua laid low Amalek and his people with the edge of the sword.

Then the LORD said to Moses, "Write this as a memorial in a book and rehearse it to Joshua, for I will utterly wipe out the remembrance of Amalek from under heaven."

Then Moses built an altar and called the name of it, The LORD Is My Banner; for he said, "For the LORD has sworn that the LORD will have war with Amalek from generation to generation."

Yitro

Jethro

(Exodus 18:1–20:26)

Jethro, the priest of Midian, Moses' father-in-law, heard of all that God had done for Moses, and for Israel His people, and that the LORD had brought Israel out of Egypt.

Then Jethro, Moses' father-in-law, took Zipporah, Moses' wife, after he had sent her back, and her two sons, one of whom was named Gershom; for he said, "I have been a sojourner in a foreign land." And the name of the other was Eliezer, for *he said*, "The God of my father was my help, and He delivered me from the sword of Pharaoh."

Then Jethro, Moses' father-in-law, came with his sons and his wife to Moses in the wilderness, where he camped at the mountain of God. And he said to Moses, "I, your father-in-law, Jethro, am coming to you, and your wife, and her two sons with her."

Then Moses went out to meet his father-in-law, and bowed down and kissed him; and they asked each other of the other's welfare, and then they went into the tent. Moses told his father-in-law all that the LORD had done to Pharaoh and to the Egyptians for Israel's sake, and all the hardships that had come on them along the way, and how the LORD delivered them.

Jethro rejoiced because of all the goodness which the LORD had done for Israel, whom He had delivered out of the hand of the Egyptians. Jethro said, "The LORD be blessed, who has delivered you out of the hand of the Egyptians, and out of the hand of Pharaoh, who has delivered the people from under the hand of the Egyptians. Now I know that the LORD is greater than all gods, for in the matter in which they treated the *people* insolently, *He was* above them." Then Jethro, Moses' father-in-law, took a burnt offering and sacrifices for God, and Aaron and all the elders of Israel came to eat bread with Moses' father-in-law before God.

On the next day, Moses sat to judge the people, and the people stood around Moses from the morning until the evening. When Moses' father-in-law saw all that he was doing for the people, he said, "What is this thing that you are doing for the people? Why are you sitting by yourself while all the people stand around you from morning until evening?"

Then Moses said to his father-in-law, "Because the people come to me to inquire of God. When they have a dispute, it comes to me, and I judge between a man and his neighbor, and I make known the statutes of God and His laws."

Moses' father-in-law said to him, "What you are doing is not good. You will surely wear yourself out, both you, and these people who are with you, for this thing is too heavy for you. You are not able to do it by yourself. Now listen to me, I will advise you, and may God be with you: You be a representative for the people to God so that you may bring *their* disputes to God. And you shall teach them the statutes and laws and shall show them the way in which they must walk and the work that they must do. Moreover, you shall choose out of all the people capable men who fear God, men of truth, hating dishonest gain, and place *these men* over them, to be rulers of thousands, rulers of hundreds, rulers of fifties, and rulers of tens. Let them judge the people at all times, and let it be that every difficult matter they shall bring to you, but every small matter they shall judge, so that it will be easier for you, and they will bear *the burden* with you. If you shall do this thing and God commands you *so*, then you will be able to endure, and all these people also will go to their place in peace."

So Moses listened to his father-in-law and did everything that he had said. Moses chose capable men out of all Israel and made them heads over the people, rulers of thousands, rulers of hundreds, rulers of fifties, and rulers of tens. They judged the people at all times. They brought the difficult cases to Moses, but they judged every small matter themselves.

Moses sent out his father-in-law, and he went his way to his own land.

In the third month after the children of Israel had gone forth out of the land of Egypt, on the same day they came into the Wilderness of Sinai. When they set out from Rephidim, they came to the Wilderness of Sinai and camped in the wilderness. Israel camped there before the mountain.

Moses went up to God, and the LORD called to him from the mountain, saying, "Thus you shall say to the house of Jacob and tell the children of Israel: 'You have seen what I did to the Egyptians, and how I lifted you up on eagles' wings, and brought you to Myself. Now therefore, if you will faithfully obey My voice and keep My covenant, then you shall be My special possession out of all the nations, for all the earth is Mine. And you will be to Me a kingdom of priests and a holy nation.' These are the words which you shall speak to the children of Israel."

So Moses came and called for the elders of the people and laid before them all these words which the LORD commanded him. Then all the people answered together and said, "All that the LORD has spoken we will do." And Moses brought back the words of the people to the LORD.

The LORD said to Moses, "Indeed, I am going to come to you in a thick cloud, so that the people may hear when I speak with you and always believe in you." Then Moses told the words of the people to the LORD.

The LORD said to Moses, "Go to the people and sanctify them today and tomorrow, and have them wash their clothes, and be ready for the third day, for on the third day the LORD will come down in the sight of all the people on Mount Sinai. You shall set boundaries for the people all around, saying, 'Take heed to yourselves so that you not go up onto the mountain or touch its border. Whoever touches the mountain will surely be put to death. No hand will touch him, but he shall surely be stoned or shot through, whether it be beast or man. He shall not live.' When the trumpet sounds a long *blast*, they shall come up to the mountain."

So Moses went down from the mountain to the people and sanctified the people, and they washed their clothes. He said to the people, "Be ready for the third day. Do not go near *your* wives."

So on the third day, in the morning, there was thunder and lightning, and a thick cloud on the mountain, and the sound of an exceedingly loud trumpet. All the people who were in the camp trembled. Then Moses brought the people out of the camp to meet with God, and they stood at the foot of the mountain. Now Mount Sinai was completely covered in smoke because the LORD had descended upon it in fire, and the smoke ascended like the smoke of a furnace, and the whole mountain shook violently. When the sound of the trumpet grew louder and louder, Moses spoke, and God answered him with a voice.

The LORD came down on Mount Sinai, on the top of the mountain. And the LORD called Moses up to the top of the mountain, and Moses went up. Then the LORD said to Moses, "Go down, warn the people, lest they force their way to the LORD to look, and many of them perish. Let the priests also, which come near to the LORD, sanctify themselves, lest the LORD break through against them."

Moses said to the LORD, "The people cannot come up to Mount Sinai, for You warned us, saying, 'Set boundaries around the mountain, and sanctify it.'"

Then the LORD said to him, "Go, get down, and come up, you and Aaron with you, but do not let the priests and the people force their way through to come up to the LORD, lest He break through against them."

So Moses went down to the people and spoke to them.

Now God spoke all these words, saying:

I am the LORD your God, who brought you out of the land of Egypt, out of the house of bondage.

You shall have no other gods before Me.

You shall not make for yourself any graven idol, or any likeness of anything that is in heaven above, or that is in the earth beneath, or that is in the water below the earth. You shall not bow down to them or serve them; for I, the LORD your God, am a jealous God, visiting the iniquity of the fathers on the children to the third and fourth generation of them who hate Me, and showing mercy to thousands of them who love Me and keep My commandments.

You shall not take the name of the LORD your God in vain, for the LORD will not hold guiltless anyone who takes His name in vain.

Remember the Sabbath day and keep it holy. Six days you shall labor and do all your work, but the seventh day is a Sabbath to the LORD your God. On it you shall not do any work, you, or your son, or your daughter, or your male servant, or your female servant, or your livestock, or your sojourner who is within your gates. For in six days the LORD made heaven and earth, the sea, and all that is in them, and rested on the seventh day. Therefore the LORD blessed the Sabbath day and made it holy.

Honor your father and your mother, that your days may be long in the land which the LORD your God is giving you.

You shall not murder.

You shall not commit adultery.

You shall not steal.

You shall not bear false witness against your neighbor.

You shall not covet your neighbor's house; you shall not covet your neighbor's wife, or his manservant, or his maidservant, or his ox, or his donkey, or anything that is your neighbor's.

All the people witnessed the thunder and the lightning and the sound of the trumpet and the mountain smoking; and when the people saw it, they trembled and stood at a distance. They said to Moses, "You speak to us, and we will listen, but do not let God speak to us, lest we die."

Moses said to the people, "Do not fear, for God has come to test you, so that the fear of Him may be before you so that you do not sin."

The people stood a distance away as Moses drew near to the thick darkness where God was.

Then the LORD said to Moses: Thus you shall say to the children of Israel, "You yourselves have seen that I have spoken to you from heaven. You shall not make gods of silver alongside Me or make gods of gold for yourselves.

"You shall make an altar of earth for Me and on it you shall sacrifice your burnt offerings and your peace offerings, your sheep, and your oxen. In every place where I cause My name to be honored, I will come to you and bless you. If you will make Me an altar of stone, you shall not build it of cut stones, for if you use your tool on it, you will have polluted it. And you shall not go up by steps to My altar, so that your nakedness will not be exposed on it."

Mishpatim

Laws

(Exodus 21:1–24:18)

Now these are the judgments which you will set before them.
If you buy a Hebrew servant, he will serve for six years, but in the seventh he shall go out free without paying anything. If he came in by himself, he shall go out by himself. If he is married, then his wife will go out with him. If his master gives him a wife, and she bears him sons or daughters, the wife and her children shall belong to her master, and he will go out by himself.

However, if the servant plainly says, "I love my master, my wife, and my children. I will not go out free," then his master will bring him to the judges, then he shall also bring him to the door or to the doorpost, and his master shall bore his ear through with an awl, and he shall serve him forever.

If a man sells his daughter to be a female servant, she shall not go out as the male servants do. If she does not please her master, who has betrothed her to himself, then he shall let her be redeemed. He has no authority to sell her to a foreign nation, because he has dealt deceitfully with her. If he has designated her for his son, then he shall deal with her according to the customary rights of daughters. If he marries another wife, then he must not diminish the first one's food, her clothing, or her marital rights. If he does not provide these three for her, then she shall go out free, without paying money.

He that strikes a man so that he dies shall surely be put to death. However, if it was not premeditated, but God let him fall into his hand, then I will appoint you a place where he may flee. But if a man willfully comes upon his neighbor in order to kill him cunningly, then you must take him from My altar, that he may die.

He who strikes his father or his mother shall surely be put to death.

He who kidnaps a man and sells him, or if he is found in his possession, shall surely be put to death.

He who curses his father or his mother shall surely be put to death.

If men fight and one strikes the other with a stone or with his fist, and he does not die, but must remain in bed, and then if he gets up and walks around on his staff, then he who struck him shall go unpunished. Only he must pay for his loss of time and shall see to it that he is thoroughly healed.

If a man strikes his male or female servant with a rod and the servant dies at his hand, then he shall surely be punished. But if he survives for a day or two, then he shall not be punished, for it is his money.

If men fight and hurt a pregnant woman so that her child is born prematurely, yet there is no serious injury, then he shall be surely punished in accordance with what the woman's husband demands of him, and he shall pay as the judges determine. But if there is any serious injury, then you shall give life for life, eye for eye, tooth for tooth, hand for hand, foot for foot, burn for burn, wound for wound, bruise for bruise.

If a man strikes the eye of his male or female servant, and destroys it, then he must let him go free on account of his eye. If he knocks out the tooth of his male or female servant, then he shall let him go free on account of the tooth.

If an ox gores a man or a woman to death, then the ox must surely be stoned and its flesh must not be eaten, but the owner of the ox will be acquitted. But if the ox has had the habit of goring, and the owner has been made aware of it, and he has not kept it in, and it has killed a man or a woman, then the ox shall be stoned and its owner also shall be put to death. If a ransom is set for him, then he shall give for the ransom of his life whatever is demanded of him. Whether it gored a son or gored a daughter, it will be done to him according to this rule. If the ox gores a male servant or a female servant, then its owner shall give thirty shekels of silver to their master, and the ox must be stoned.

If a man opens a pit or if a man digs a pit and does not cover it, and an ox or a donkey falls into it, the owner of the pit must make restitution. He must give money to their owner, and the dead animal will be his.

If one man's ox hurts another's so that it dies, then they shall sell the live ox and divide its proceeds and divide the dead ox also. Or if it be known that the ox has had the habit of goring and its owner has not kept it in, then he shall surely pay ox for ox and the dead *animal* will become his own.

If a man steals an ox or a sheep and kills it or sells it, then he shall repay five oxen for an ox, and four sheep for a sheep.

If a thief is caught breaking in and is struck so that he dies, then there will be no blood guilt for him. If the sun has risen on him, then there is blood guilt for him.

He must make full restitution. If he has nothing, then he will be sold for his theft. If the stolen item is in fact found alive in his possession, whether it be an ox, or donkey, or sheep, then he shall repay double.

If a man causes a field or vineyard to be eaten and puts out his beast so that it feeds in another man's field, he must make restitution of the best of his own field and of the best of his own vineyard.

If fire breaks out and catches in thorn bushes, so that stacked grain or the standing grain or the field are consumed, then he who started the fire must surely make restitution.

If a man gives his neighbor money or items to be kept *for him*, and it is stolen from the man's house, if the thief is caught, he must repay double. If the thief is not caught, then the owner of the house will be brought before the judges to determine if he has laid his hand on his neighbor's goods. For any kind of trespass, whether it be for an ox, for a donkey, for a sheep, for clothing, or for any type of lost thing, where another says it is his, the case of both parties shall come before the judges. And whoever the judges find guilty will pay double to his neighbor.

If a man gives his neighbor a donkey, or an ox, or a sheep, or any beast to keep *for him*, and it dies, or is injured, or is driven away while no one sees it, then there will be an oath before the LORD between both of them that he has not laid his hand upon his neighbor's property. And its owner must accept this, and he will not have to make restitution. However, if it was stolen from him, he shall make restitution to its owner. If it is torn in pieces, then let him bring it as evidence, and he will not have to repay for that which was torn.

If a man borrows anything from his neighbor, and it is hurt or dies when the owner was not with it, then he shall surely make restitution. But if the owner was with it, he shall not make restitution. If it was a hired thing, it came with his hire.

If a man seduces a virgin who is not engaged and has relations with her, he must surely endow her to be his wife. If her father absolutely refuses to give her to him, he must pay money according to the dowry of virgins.

You must not allow a sorceress to live.

Whoever has relations with a beast must surely be put to death.

He who sacrifices to any god other than the LORD alone shall be utterly destroyed.

You must neither wrong a foreigner nor oppress him, for you were foreigners in the land of Egypt.

You shall not afflict any widow or orphan. If you afflict them in any way and they cry at all to Me, I will surely hear their cry. And My anger will burn, and I will kill you with the sword, and your wives will become widows, and your children fatherless.

If you lend money to any of My people who is poor among you, do not be a creditor to him, and do not charge him interest. If you take your neighbor's garment as a pledge, you shall return it to him before the sun goes down, for that is his only covering; it is his garment for his body. In what else will he sleep? And when he cries out to Me, I will hear, for I am gracious.

You shall not curse God or curse the ruler of your people.

You must not delay to offer the first of your harvest and of your vats.

You must give to Me the firstborn of your sons. Likewise you must do the same with your oxen and with your sheep. Seven days it shall remain with its mother, but on the eighth day you must give it to Me.

You will be holy men to Me; therefore you must not eat any flesh that is torn by beasts in the field. You must throw it to the dogs.

You must not give a false report. Do not join your hand with the wicked to be a malicious witness.

You must not follow the masses to do evil, and do not testify in a dispute that agrees with the crowd to pervert *justice*. You must not show partiality to a poor man in his dispute.

If you meet your enemy's ox or his donkey going astray, you shall surely return it to him. If you see the donkey of someone who hates you lying under its burden, you must not ignore it; you must surely help with him.

You shall not turn justice away from your poor in his dispute. Keep far away from a false charge, and do not kill the innocent and the righteous, for I will not justify the wicked.

You shall not take a bribe, for a bribe blinds those who see and subverts the words of the righteous.

Also you shall not oppress a foreigner, for you know the life of a foreigner, seeing you were foreigners in the land of Egypt.

You shall sow your land for six years and shall gather in its produce, but in the seventh year you shall let it rest and lie fallow, so that the poor of your people may eat, and what they leave the beasts of the field may eat. You shall do likewise with your vineyard and with your olive grove.

For six days you are to do your work, but on the seventh day you must cease, so that your ox and your donkey may rest, and the son of your female servant and the foreigner may refresh themselves.

In all things that I have said to you, watch yourselves, and do not mention the name of other gods, nor let *them* be heard from your mouth.

Three times in the year you must celebrate a feast to Me.

You shall observe the Feast of Unleavened Bread. For seven days you shall eat unleavened bread, as I commanded you, in the appointed time of the month Aviv, for in it you came out from Egypt.

No one shall appear before Me empty-handed.

You shall observe the Feast of Harvest, the first fruits of your labors, which you have sown in the field.

You shall observe the Feast of Ingathering at the end of the year, when you have gathered in the fruit of your labors from the field.

Three times in the year all your males shall appear before the Lord GOD.

You shall not offer the blood of My sacrifice with leavened bread, nor shall the fat of My sacrifice remain until the morning.

The first of the first fruits of your land you shall bring into the house of the LORD your God.

You shall not boil a young goat in its mother's milk.

Indeed, I am going to send an angel before you to guard you along the way and to bring you into the place which I have prepared. Be on guard before him and obey his voice. Do not provoke him, for he will not pardon your transgressions, for My name is in him. But if you diligently obey his voice and do all that I say, then I will be an enemy to your enemies and an adversary to your adversaries. For My angel will go before you and bring you to the Amorites, and the Hittites, and the Perizzites, and the Canaanites, the Hivites, and the Jebusites, and I will completely destroy them. You must not bow down to their gods, or serve them, or do according to their practices, but you shall utterly overthrow them and break down their images in pieces. You shall serve the LORD your God, and He shall bless your bread and your water, and I will remove sickness from your midst. No one shall be miscarrying or be barren in your land. I will fulfill the number of your days.

I will send My fear before you, and I will throw into panic all the people to whom you shall come. I will make all your enemies turn their backs to you. I will send hornets before you which shall drive out the Hivite, the Canaanite, and the Hittite from before you. I will not drive them out before you in one year, lest the land become desolate and the beasts of the field multiply against you. Little by little I will drive them out before you, until you become fruitful and inherit the land.

I will set your boundaries from the Red Sea to the sea of the Philistines, and from the desert to the Euphrates River; for I will deliver the inhabitants of the land into your hand, and you will drive them out before you. You must not make a covenant with them or with their gods. They shall not live in your land, lest they cause you to sin against Me, for if you serve their gods, it will surely be a snare to you.

Then He said to Moses, "Come up to the LORD, you, and Aaron, Nadab, and Abihu, and seventy of the elders of Israel, and you shall worship from a distance. Moses alone shall come near the LORD, but they shall not come near, nor may the people go up with him."

Moses came and told the people all the words of the LORD and all the ordinances. Then all the people answered with one voice and said, "All the words which the LORD has said we will do." Moses wrote all the words of the LORD, and rose up early in the morning, and built an altar at the foot of the mountain with twelve pillars for the twelve tribes of Israel. He sent young Israelite men who offered burnt offerings and sacrificed peace offerings of young bulls to the LORD. Moses took half of the blood and put it in basins, and half of the blood he sprinkled on the altar. He took the Book of the Covenant and read in the hearing of the people, and they said, "All that the LORD has said we will do, and we will be obedient."

So Moses took the blood, and sprinkled it on the people, and said, "This is the blood of the covenant, which the LORD has made with you in accordance with all these words."

Then Moses went up with Aaron, Nadab, and Abihu, and seventy of the elders of Israel, and they saw the God of Israel, and under His feet there was something like a paved work of sapphire stone as clear as the sky itself. He did not lay His hand upon the nobles of the children of Israel. Also they saw God, and they ate and they drank.

The LORD said to Moses, "Come up to Me to the mountain and stay there, and I will give you the stone tablets with law and the commandments which I have written, so that you may teach them."

Moses rose up with Joshua his attendant, and Moses went up to the mountain of God. He said to the elders, "Wait for us in this place until we return to you. Aaron and Hur are with you. Whoever has any matters of dispute let him come to them."

Moses went up to the mountain, and the cloud covered the mountain. The glory of the LORD rested on Mount Sinai, and the cloud covered it for six days. And on the seventh day He called to Moses from the midst of the cloud. Now the appearance of the glory of the LORD was like a consuming fire on the top of the mountain to the eyes of the children of Israel. Moses went into the midst of the cloud and went up to the mountain. And Moses was on the mountain for forty days and forty nights.

Terumah

Offering

(Exodus 25:1–27:19)

T he Lord said to Moses: Tell the children of Israel to bring Me an offering. From every man who gives willingly with his heart you shall receive My offering. This is the offering which you shall take from them: gold, silver, and bronze, blue, purple, scarlet, fine linen, goats' hair, rams' skins dyed red, fine leather, acacia wood, oil for the light, spices for anointing oil and for fragrant incense, onyx stones, and stones to be set in the ephod and in the breastplate.

Let them make Me a sanctuary that I may dwell among them. According to all that I show you—the pattern of the tabernacle and the pattern of all its furniture—you shall make it just so.

They shall make an ark of acacia wood two and a half cubits long, and one and a half cubits wide, and one and a half cubits high. You shall overlay it with pure gold, inside and out shall you overlay it, and you shall make a gold border around it. You shall cast four gold rings for it and put them on the four feet with two rings on the one side of it and two rings on the other side of it. You shall make poles of acacia wood and overlay them with gold. You shall put the poles into the rings on the sides of the ark in order to carry the ark with them. The poles must remain in the rings of the ark. They must not be removed from it. You shall put into the ark the testimony which I shall give you.

You shall make a mercy seat of pure gold, two and a half cubits long and one and a half cubits wide. You shall make two cherubim of gold, make them of hammered work at the two ends of the mercy seat. Make one cherub on the one end and the other cherub on the other end. From the mercy seat you shall make the cherubim on its two ends. The cherubim shall stretch forth their wings upward, covering the mercy seat with their wings and facing one another. The faces of the cherubim are to face toward the mercy seat. You shall put the mercy seat above upon the ark, and in the ark you shall put the testimony that I will give you. I will meet with you there, and I will meet with you from above the mercy seat, from between the two cherubim which are upon the ark of the testimony. I will speak with you all that I will command you for the children of Israel.

You shall also make a table of acacia wood, two cubits long, one cubit wide, and half a cubit high. You shall overlay it with pure gold and make a gold border around it. You shall make a border around it of one handbreadth, and you shall make a gold molding for the frame all around. You shall make four gold rings for it and put the rings on the four corners that are on its four feet. The rings shall be close to the frame to provide places for the poles to carry the table. You shall make the poles of acacia wood and overlay them with gold, so that the table may be carried with them. You shall make the dishes, its spoons, its pitchers, and its bowls with which to pour drink offerings. You shall make them of pure gold. You shall set the showbread on the table before Me always.

You shall make a lampstand of pure gold. The lampstand and its base and its shaft are to be made of hammered metal. Its cups, its buds, and its flowers shall be of one piece. Six branches shall go out from its sides, three branches of the lampstand from its one side and three branches of the lampstand from its other side. Three cups shall be made shaped like almond *flowers* with buds and blossoms on one branch, and three cups made like almond *flowers* in the other branch, with buds and blossoms, and the same for the six branches that come out of the lampstand. On the lampstand shall be four cups shaped like almond *flowers*, with their buds and their blossoms. There shall be a bud under two branches of the same, and a bud under two branches of the same, and a bud under *the next* two branches of the same, according to the six branches that proceed out of the lampstand. Their buds and their branches shall be of the same *piece*, all of it shall be one hammered work of pure gold.

You shall make its seven lamps, and they shall light its lamps so that they may give light to the area in front of it. Its snuffers and their snuff dishes shall be of pure gold. It shall be made from a talent of pure gold along with all these utensils. See that you make them according to their pattern which was shown to you on the mountain.

Moreover you shall make the tabernacle with ten curtains of fine twisted linen, and blue, and purple, and scarlet. Make them with cherubim, the work of a skilled workman. The length of each curtain shall be twenty-eight cubits, and the width of each curtain four cubits. All of the curtains shall have the same measurements. Five curtains shall be joined together, one to another. And the other five curtains are to be joined, one to another. You shall make loops of blue on the edge of the end curtain in one set, and likewise you shall make *loops* in the outermost edge of the end curtain in the second set. You shall make fifty loops in the one curtain, and you shall make fifty loops in the edge of the curtain that is in the second set. The loops are to be opposite to one another. You shall make fifty clasps of gold and join the curtains together with the clasps so that the tabernacle shall be one unit.

You shall make curtains of goats' hair to be a covering upon the tabernacle. You shall make eleven curtains. The length of each curtain shall be thirty cubits, and the width of each curtain four cubits, and the eleven curtains shall all have the same measure. You shall join five curtains by themselves, and six curtains by themselves. You shall double over the sixth curtain at the front of the tabernacle. You shall make fifty loops on the edge of the end curtain in one set and fifty loops on the edge of the curtain that joins the second set. You shall make fifty bronze clasps, and put the clasps into the loops, and join the tent together so that it may be one unit. The part that remains of the curtains of the tent, the half curtain that remains, shall hang over the back of the tabernacle. One cubit on the one side and one cubit on the other side of that which remains in the length of the curtains of the tent shall hang over the sides of the tabernacle on this side and on that side to cover it. You shall make a covering for the tent out of rams' skins dyed red and a covering above of fine leather.

You shall make boards for the tabernacle of acacia wood, standing upright. Ten cubits shall be the length of each board, and one cubit and a half shall be the width of each board. There shall be two tenons for each board, fitted to one another. You shall make all the boards of the tabernacle in this way. You shall make the boards for the tabernacle, twenty boards for the south side. You shall make forty sockets of silver under the twenty boards, two sockets under one board for its two tenons and two sockets under another board for its two tenons. For the second side of the tabernacle, on the north side, there shall be twenty boards, and their forty sockets of silver, two sockets under one board, and two sockets under another board. For the back of the tabernacle, to the west, you shall make six boards. You shall make two boards for the corners of the tabernacle at the back. They shall be doubled together beneath and finished together at the top of it into one ring. So it shall be for both of them. They shall form the two corners. There shall be eight boards with their sockets of silver, sixteen sockets, two sockets under one board and two sockets under another board.

You shall make bars of acacia wood, five for the boards of the one side of the tabernacle, and five bars for the boards of the other side of the tabernacle, and five bars for the boards of the side of the tabernacle for the back to the west. The middle bar in the center of the boards shall reach from end to end. You shall overlay the boards with gold and make their rings of gold to provide places for the bars, and you shall overlay the bars with gold.

You shall set up the tabernacle according to the plan which you have been shown on the mountain.

You shall make a veil of blue, and purple, and scarlet, and fine twined linen. It shall be made with cherubim, the skillful work of a workman. You shall hang it on four pillars of acacia wood overlaid with gold. Their hooks *also* shall be of gold on four sockets of silver. You shall hang up the veil under the clasps, so that you may bring in the ark of the testimony within the veil; and the veil shall serve for you as a partition between the holy place and the Most Holy. You shall put the mercy seat on the ark of the testimony in the Most Holy. You shall set the table outside the veil, and the lampstand opposite the table on the side of the tabernacle toward the south, and you shall put the table on the north side.

You shall make a screen for the doorway of the tent of blue, and purple, and scarlet, and fine twined linen, the work of an embroiderer. You shall make five pillars of acacia wood for the screen and overlay them with gold, with their hooks also made of gold, and you shall cast five sockets of bronze for them.

You shall make an altar of acacia wood, five cubits long and five cubits wide. The altar shall be square, and its height shall be three cubits. You shall make its horns on its four corners. Its horns shall be part of it, and you shall overlay it with bronze. You shall make its pots for its ashes, and its shovels, and its basins, and its meat hooks, and its fire pans. You shall make all of its vessels out of bronze. You shall make a grating for it, a latticework of bronze, and on the net you shall make four bronze rings at its four corners. You shall put it under the ledge of the altar beneath, so that the net will reach halfway up the altar. You shall make poles for the altar, poles of acacia wood, and overlay them with bronze. The poles shall be put into the rings, so that the poles shall be on the two sides of the altar when carrying it. You shall make it hollow with boards. Just as it was shown you on the mountain, so shall they make it.

You shall make the court of the tabernacle. On the south side there shall be curtains for the court of fine twined linen one hundred cubits long for one side; and it *shall have* twenty pillars with twenty bronze sockets. The hooks of the pillars and their bands shall be of silver. Likewise for the north side in length there shall be curtains one hundred cubits long, and its twenty pillars and their twenty sockets of bronze. The hooks of the pillars and their bands *shall be* of silver.

For the width of the court on the west side shall be curtains of fifty cubits with their ten pillars and their ten sockets. The width of the court on the east side shall be fifty cubits. The curtains on one side of the gate shall be fifteen cubits with their three pillars and their three sockets. On the other side shall be curtains fifteen cubits with their three pillars and their three sockets.

For the gate of the court there shall be a curtain of twenty cubits, of blue, and purple, and scarlet, and fine twined linen, the work of an embroiderer, with their four pillars and their four sockets. All the pillars around about the court shall be furnished with silver bands. Their hooks shall be of silver, and their sockets of bronze. The length of the court shall be one hundred cubits, and the width fifty throughout, and the height five cubits of fine twisted linen, and their sockets of bronze. All the utensils of the tabernacle used in all its service, and all its tent pegs, and all the tent pegs of the court shall be of bronze.

Tetzaveh

You shall command

(Exodus 27:20–30:10)

You shall command the children of Israel that they bring you pure oil of olive pressed for the light, to cause the lamp to burn continually. In the tent of meeting, outside the veil which is before the testimony, Aaron and his sons shall arrange it from evening to morning before the Lord. It shall be a perpetual statute for the children of Israel for generations to come.

And bring near to yourself Aaron, your brother, and his sons with him from among the children of Israel, so that they may minister to Me as priests—Aaron, Nadab and Abihu, Eleazar and Ithamar, Aaron's sons. You shall make holy garments for your brother Aaron, for glory and for beauty. You shall speak to all who are specially skilled, whom I have filled with the spirit of wisdom, that they may make Aaron's garments to consecrate him, that he may minister to Me as a priest. These are the garments which they shall make: a breastplate, and an ephod, and a robe, and an embroidered coat, a turban, and a sash. They shall make holy garments for Aaron your brother and his sons, that he may minister to Me as priest. They shall take the gold, the blue, the purple, and the scarlet, and fine linen.

They shall make the ephod of gold, of blue, and of purple, of scarlet, and fine twined linen, the work of a skilled workman. It shall have the two shoulder pieces attached to its two corners, so it shall be joined together. The skillfully woven waistband of the ephod, which is on it, shall be of the same workmanship, of the same material: of gold, of blue and purple, and scarlet, and fine twisted linen.

You shall take two onyx stones and engrave on them the names of the children of Israel, six of their names on one stone, and the other six names of the rest on the other stone, according to their birth. With the work of an engraver in stone, like the engravings of a signet, you shall engrave the two stones with the names of the children of Israel. You shall set them in filigree of gold. You shall put the two stones on the shoulders of the ephod as stones of memorial for the children of Israel, and Aaron shall bear their names before the Lord on his two shoulders as a memorial. You shall make filigree settings of gold, and two chains of pure gold. You shall make them of twisted cord and fasten the braided chains to the filigree settings.

You shall make the breastplate of judgment, the work of a skillful work-man. You shall make it in the same manner as the ephod. Of gold, of blue, and of purple, and of scarlet, and of fine twisted linen you shall make it. It is to be square when doubled: one span in length and one span in width. You shall set in it four rows of stones. The first row shall be a sardius, a topaz, and a car-buncle; the second row an emerald, a sapphire, and a diamond; the third row a jacinth, an agate, and an amethyst; and the fourth row a beryl, an onyx, and a jasper. They shall be set in gold filigree. The stones shall be according to the names of the children of Israel, twelve, according to their names, each like the engravings of a signet, every one according to his name for the twelve tribes.

You shall make for the breastplate braided chains of pure gold. You shall make on the breastplate two rings of gold and shall put the two rings on the two ends of the breastplate. You shall put the two braided chains of gold on the two rings which are on the ends of the breastplate. You shall fasten the other two ends of the two braided chains in the two filigree settings and put them on the front of the shoulder pieces of the ephod. You shall make two rings of gold and shall put them on the two ends of the breastplate, on the edge of it which is toward the inner side of the ephod. You shall make two other rings of gold and shall put them on the two shoulder pieces of the ephod underneath toward the front, close to the place where it is joined above the skillfully woven waistband of the ephod. They shall bind the breastplate by its rings to the rings of the ephod with a blue cord, so that it may be above the skillfully woven waistband of the ephod, and so that the breastplate will not come loose from the ephod.

Aaron shall bear the names of the children of Israel on the breastplate of judgment over his heart when he goes into the holy place, as a memorial before the Lord continually. You shall put the Urim and the Thummim in the breastplate of judgment, and they shall be over Aaron's heart when he goes in before the Lord. And Aaron shall bear the judgment of the children of Israel over his heart before the Lord continually.

You shall make the robe of the ephod completely blue. There shall be a hole at the top of it, in the middle of it. Around its opening it shall have a binding of woven work, like the opening of a coat of mail, so that it will not be torn. You shall make on its hem pomegranates of blue, and of pur-ple, and of scarlet, all around its hem, and bells of gold between them all around: a golden bell and a pomegranate, a golden bell and a pomegranate, all around on the hem of the robe. It shall be on Aaron when he ministers. And its sound shall be heard when he goes into the holy place before the Lord, and when he comes out, so that he does not die.

You shall make a plate of pure gold and engrave on it, like the engravings of a signet,

HOLINESS TO THE LORD.

You shall put it on a blue cord, so that it may be upon the turban. It is to be on the front of the turban. It shall be on Aaron's forehead, so that Aaron may bear the iniquity of the holy things which the children of Israel shall consecrate in regard to all their holy gifts. And it shall always be on his forehead, so that they may be accepted before the LORD.

You shall embroider the tunic of fine linen, and you shall make the turban of fine linen, and you shall make the sash, the work of an embroiderer. For Aaron's sons you shall make tunics. You shall make sashes for them, and you shall make caps for them, for glory and for beauty. You shall put them on Aaron your brother, and on his sons with him, and shall anoint them, and consecrate them, and sanctify them, that they may minister to Me as priests.

You shall make linen undergarments for them to cover their naked skin. They shall reach from the waist to the thighs. They shall be on Aaron and on his sons when they come into the tent of meeting or when they come near to the altar to minister in the holy place, so that they may not bear iniquity and die.

It shall be a perpetual statute to him and his descendants after him.

Now this is the thing that you shall do to them to consecrate them, to minister as priests to Me: Take one young bull and two rams without blemish, and unleavened bread, and unleavened cakes mixed with oil, and unleavened wafers anointed with oil—you shall make them of wheat flour. You shall put them into one basket and bring them in the basket with the bull and the two rams. Then you shall bring Aaron and his sons to the door of the tent of meeting and wash them with water. You shall take the garments and clothe Aaron *with* the tunic and the robe of the ephod and the ephod and the breastplate, and gird him with the skillfully woven band of the ephod. And you shall put the turban on his head and put the holy crown on the turban. Then shall you take the anointing oil and pour it on his head and anoint him. You shall bring his sons and put tunics on them. You shall gird them with sashes, Aaron and his sons, and put the headbands on them, and the priest's office shall be theirs for a perpetual statute.

Thus you shall consecrate Aaron and his sons.

Then you shall bring a bull before the tent of meeting, and Aaron and his sons shall put their hands on the head of the bull. You shall kill the bull before the LORD by the door of the tent of meeting. You shall take of the blood of the bull, and put it on the horns of the altar with your finger, and pour all the blood beside the bottom of the altar. You shall take all the fat that covers the entrails, and the lobe that is above the liver, and the two kidneys, and the fat that is on them, and burn them on the altar. But the flesh of the bull, its skin, and its dung, you shall burn with fire outside the camp. It is a sin offering.

You shall also take one ram, and Aaron and his sons shall put their hands on the head of the ram. You shall slay the ram, and you shall take its blood and sprinkle it around on the altar. Then you shall cut the ram in pieces, and wash its entrails and its legs, and put *them* with its pieces and its head. You shall burn the whole ram on the altar. It is a burnt offering to the LORD. It is a soothing aroma, an offering made by fire to the LORD.

Then you shall take the other ram, and Aaron and his sons shall put their hands on the head of the ram. You shall kill the ram and take some of its blood and put it on the tip of the right ear of Aaron, and on the tip of the right ear of his sons, and on the thumb of their right hand, and on the great toe of their right foot, and sprinkle the blood around on the altar. You shall take some of the blood that is on the altar and some of the anointing oil and sprinkle it on Aaron and on his garments, and on his sons, and on the garments of his sons with him. So he and his garments shall be consecrated, along with his sons and his sons' garments with him.

Also you shall take the fat and the rump of the ram, and the fat that covers the entrails and the lobe above the liver, and the two kidneys, and the fat that is on them and the right shoulder (for it is a ram of consecration), and one loaf of bread, and one cake of oiled bread, and one wafer out of the basket of the unleavened bread that is before the LORD. And you shall put all of these in the hands of Aaron and in the hands of his sons, and shall wave them for a wave offering before the LORD. Then you shall take them from their hands and burn them on the altar for a burnt offering, for a soothing aroma before the LORD. It is an offering made by fire to the LORD. You shall take the breast of Aaron's ram of consecration, and wave it as a wave offering before the LORD, and it shall be your portion.

You shall consecrate the breast of the wave offering that is waved and the thigh of the priest's portion that is contributed from the ram of the consecration, from that which was for Aaron and from that which was for his sons. It shall be for Aaron and his sons by a statute forever, for it is a contribution. It shall be a contribution from the children of Israel from their peace offerings, their contributions to the LORD.

The holy garments belonging to Aaron are to belong to his sons after him, so that they may be anointed in them and be consecrated in them. The son that is priest in his stead shall put them on seven days when he comes into the tent of meeting to minister in the holy place.

You shall take the ram of the consecration and boil its flesh in a holy place. Aaron and his sons shall eat the flesh of the ram and the bread that is in the basket by the door of the tent of meeting. They shall eat those things by which the atonement was made in order to consecrate and sanctify them, but no one else shall eat *them*, because they are holy. If any of the flesh from the consecrations or from the bread remain until the morning, then you shall burn the remainder with fire. It shall not be eaten, because it is holy.

Thus shall you do to Aaron and his sons according to all that I have commanded you. You shall consecrate them for seven days. Every day you must offer a bull as a sin offering for atonement, and you must cleanse the altar when you make atonement for it. You must anoint it to consecrate it. For seven days you must make atonement for the altar and consecrate it, and then the altar will be most holy, and whatever touches the altar will be holy.

Now this is what you are to offer on the altar: two one-year-old lambs every day, continually. The one lamb you must offer in the morning, and the other lamb you must offer at sundown. And with the first lamb *will be* one-tenth *of an ephah* of flour mingled with one-fourth of a hin of beaten oil, and one-fourth of a hin of wine for a drink offering. The other lamb you must offer at sundown and must offer with it the same grain offering and the same drink offering as in the morning, for a soothing aroma, an offering made by fire to the LORD.

This will be a continual burnt offering throughout your generations at the door of the tent of meeting before the LORD, where I will meet with you, to speak to you there. I will meet there with the children of Israel, and it will be consecrated by My glory.

I will sanctify the tent of meeting and the altar. I will also sanctify both Aaron and his sons to minister as priests to Me. I will dwell among the children of Israel and will be their God. Then they will know that I am the LORD their God who brought them out of the land of Egypt, so that I may dwell among them. I am the LORD their God.

Also, you must make an altar for burning incense. You must make it of acacia wood. It must be one cubit in length, and its width one cubit. It will be square. Its height will be two cubits; the horns shall be of one piece with it. You must overlay it with pure gold, its top, its sides all around, and its horns; and you must make a molding of gold all around it. You must make two golden rings for it under its molding. You must make *them* on its two sides, on opposite sides of it, and they will be holders for the poles with which to carry it. Then you must make the poles of acacia wood and overlay them with gold. You must put it before the veil that is by the ark of the testimony, in front of the mercy seat that is over the testimony, where I will meet with you.

Aaron must burn sweet incense on it. Every morning, when he trims the lamps, he must burn incense. When Aaron lights the lamps at sundown, he must burn incense on it. It is to be a perpetual incense before the LORD throughout your generations. You must offer no strange incense on it, nor burnt sacrifice, nor grain offering, and you must not pour out a drink offering on it. Aaron must make atonement on its horns once a year with the blood of the sin offering of atonement. Once a year he must make atonement on it throughout your generations. It is most holy to the LORD.

Ki Tisa

When you elevate

(Exodus 30:11–34:35)

T he LORD spoke to Moses, saying: When you take the census of the children of Israel according to their number, then each man is to pay a ransom for his life to the LORD when you count them, so that there be no plague among them when you number them. This is what everyone who is counted must give: half a shekel according to the shekel of the sanctuary (one shekel is twenty gerahs). The half shekel will be the offering to the LORD. Everyone who is counted, from twenty years old and above, must give an offering to the LORD. The rich must not give more and the poor must not give less than half a shekel when they give the offering to the LORD, to make atonement for your lives. You must take the atonement money of the children of Israel and give it for the service of the tent of meeting, so that it may be a memorial to the children of Israel before the LORD, to make atonement for your lives.

The LORD spoke to Moses, saying: You must also make a basin of bronze, with its base also of bronze, for washing, and you must put it between the tent of meeting and the altar, and you must put water in it. For Aaron and his sons must wash their hands and their feet from it. When they go into the tent of meeting, or when they come near the altar to minister by burning incense as an offering made by fire to the LORD, they must wash with water so that they will not die. So they must wash their hands and their feet, so that they will not die. And it will be a perpetual statute for them, even to him and to his seed throughout their generations.

Moreover the LORD spoke to Moses, saying: Take for yourself choice spices: five hundred shekels of pure myrrh, half as much sweet-smelling cinnamon (two hundred fifty shekels), two hundred fifty shekels of sweet-smelling cane, five hundred shekels of cassia, according to the shekel of the sanctuary, and one hin of olive oil. And you must make with it a holy anointing oil, a perfumed compound, the work of a perfumer. It will be a holy anointing oil. And you must anoint the tent of meeting with it, along with the ark of the testimony, and the table and all its utensils, and the lampstand and its utensils, and the altar of incense, and the altar of burnt offering with all its utensils, and the basin and its stand. You must consecrate them, so that they may be most holy. Whatever touches them must be holy.

You must anoint Aaron and his sons and consecrate them, so that they may minister as priests to Me. You must speak to the children of Israel, saying, "This will be a holy anointing oil to Me throughout your generations. It must not be poured out on anyone's body, nor shall you make any other like it in composition. It is holy, and it will be holy to you. Whoever makes anything like it or whoever puts any of it on a layman will be cut off from his people."

Then the LORD said to Moses: Take for yourself sweet spices, stacte and onycha and galbanum, sweet spices with pure frankincense of equal amounts. You shall make of these an incense, a compound expertly blended, mingled with salt, pure and holy. You must beat some of it very fine and put part of it before the testimony in the tent of meeting where I will meet with you. It will be most holy to you. As for the perfume which you will make, you may not make *it* for yourselves using the same recipe. It must be holy for the LORD to you. Whoever makes anything like it in order to use it as perfume must be cut off from his people.

Now the LORD spoke to Moses, saying: See, I have called by name Bezalel the son of Uri, the son of Hur, of the tribe of Judah. I have filled him with the Spirit of God in wisdom, in understanding, in knowledge, and in all manner of craftsmanship to devise artistic works for work with gold, with silver, and with bronze, and in the cutting of stones for settings, and in carving of wood, to work in all manner of craftsmanship. I, indeed, I have given him Oholiab, the son of Ahisamak, of the tribe of Dan, and I have given skill to all who are specially skilled, that they may make everything that I have commanded you: the tent of meeting, the ark of the testimony, and the mercy seat that is on it, and all the furniture of the tent, the table and its utensils, and the pure lampstand with all its utensils, and the altar of incense, the altar of burnt offering with all its utensils, and the basin and its stand, the woven garments, the holy garments for Aaron the priest and the garments of his sons, to minister as priests, the anointing oil and sweet incense for the holy place. They must make *them* according to all that I have commanded you.

The LORD spoke to Moses, saying: Speak also to the children of Israel, saying, "You must surely keep My Sabbaths, for it is a sign between Me and you throughout your generations, that you may know that I am the LORD who sanctifies you.

"You shall keep the Sabbath, for it is holy to you. Everyone who defiles it will surely be put to death. For whoever does any work on it, that person will be cut off from among his people. Six days may work be done, but on the seventh is the Sabbath of complete rest, holy to the LORD. Whoever does any work on the Sabbath day will surely be put to death. Therefore the children of Israel must keep the Sabbath, to observe the Sabbath throughout their generations, for a perpetual covenant. It is a sign between Me and the children of Israel forever, for in six days the LORD made heaven and earth, but on the seventh day He rested and was refreshed."

When He had made an end of communing with him on Mount Sinai, He gave Moses the two tablets of testimony, tablets of stone, written with the finger of God.

Now when the people saw that Moses delayed coming down from the mountain, the people gathered themselves together around Aaron and said to him, "Come, make us gods which will go before us. As for this Moses, the man who brought us up out of the land of Egypt, we do not know what has become of him."

Aaron said to them, "Break off the gold earrings that are in the ears of your wives, your sons, and your daughters, and bring *them* to me." So all the people broke off the gold earrings that were in their ears and brought *them* to Aaron. He received *them* from their hand, and fashioned it with an engraving tool, and made it into a molded calf. Then they said, "This is your god, O Israel, who brought you up from the land of Egypt."

When Aaron saw *it*, he built an altar before it. And Aaron made a proclamation and said, "Tomorrow will be a feast to the LORD." So they rose up early on the next day, and offered burnt offerings, and brought peace offerings. And the people sat down to eat and to drink, and rose up to play.

The LORD spoke to Moses, "Go, and get down, for your people, whom you brought out of the land of Egypt, have corrupted *themselves*. They have quickly turned aside from the way which I commanded them. They have made for themselves a molded calf, and have worshipped it, and have sacrificed to it, and said, 'This is your god, O Israel, which has brought you up from the land of Egypt.'"

Then the LORD said to Moses, "I have seen this people, and certainly, it is a stiff-necked people. Now therefore let Me alone, so that My wrath may burn against them and I may destroy them. And I will make of you a great nation."

But Moses sought the favor of the LORD his God, and said, "LORD, why does Your wrath burn against Your people, whom You have brought forth from the land of Egypt with great power and with a mighty hand? Why should the Egyptians speak, saying, 'With evil *intent* He brought them out, to kill them in the mountains and to destroy them from the face of the earth'? Turn from Your fierce wrath and relent of this harm against Your people. Remember Abraham, Isaac, and Israel, Your servants, to whom You swore by Yourself, and said to them, 'I will multiply your descendants as the stars of the heavens, and all this land that I have spoken of will I give to your descendants, and they will inherit *it* forever.'" Then the LORD relented of the harm which He said He would do to His people.

Moses turned and went down from the mountain with the two tablets of testimony in his hand. The tablets were written on both their sides. They were written on one side and on the other. The tablets were God's work, and the writing was God's writing, engraved on the tablets.

When Joshua heard the noise of the people as they shouted, he said to Moses, "There is a sound of war in the camp."

But he said:

"It is not the sound of those who shout for victory,
   nor is it the sound of those who cry because of being overcome,
   but I hear the sound of singing."

As soon as he came near the camp, he saw the calf and the dancing, and Moses' anger burned, so he threw the tablets from his hands and shattered them at the bottom of the mountain. Then he took the calf which they had made and burned it in the fire, ground it to powder, and scattered it on the water, and made the children of Israel drink it.

Moses said to Aaron, "What did this people do to you, that you have brought so great a sin upon them?"

Aaron said, "Do not let the anger of my lord burn. You know that the people are set on evil. For they said to me, 'Make a god for us which will go before us, for this Moses, the man that brought us up from the land of Egypt, we do not know what has become of him.' I said to them, 'Whoever has any gold, let them break it off.' So they gave it to me, and then I threw it into the fire, and this calf came out."

Now when Moses saw the people were in a frenzy, for Aaron had let them get completely out of control, causing derision from their enemies, then Moses stood in the gate of the camp and said, "Whoever is on the LORD's side, come to me." And all the Levites gathered themselves together around him.

He said to them, "Thus says the LORD, the God of Israel, 'Every man fasten his sword on his side, and go back and forth from gate to gate throughout the camp, and let every man kill his brother, and every man his friend, and every man his neighbor.'" The Levites did according to the word of Moses, and about three thousand men of the people died that day. For Moses had said, "Consecrate yourselves today to the LORD, that He may bestow a blessing on you this day, for every man opposes his son and his brother."

On the next day Moses said to the people, "You have committed a great sin, and now I will go up to the LORD. Perhaps I can make atonement for your sin."

Then Moses returned to the LORD and said, "Oh, this people has committed a great sin and have made a god of gold for themselves. Yet now, if You will, forgive their sin, but if not, I pray, blot me out of Your book which You have written."

Then the LORD said to Moses, "Whoever has sinned against Me, I will blot him out of My book. So go now, lead the people to the place of which I have spoken to you. Indeed, My angel will go before you. Nevertheless in the day when I punish, I will indeed punish them for their sin."

And the LORD plagued the people because they had made the calf, the one that Aaron made.

Then the LORD said to Moses, "Depart, go up from here, you and the people whom you have brought up from the land of Egypt, to the land which I swore to Abraham, Isaac, and Jacob, saying, 'To your descendants I will give it.' I will send an angel before you, and I will drive out the Canaanite, the Amorite, the Hittite, the Perizzite, the Hivite, and the Jebusite. *Go up* to a land flowing with milk and honey. However, I will not go up in your midst, for you are a stiff-necked people, and I might destroy you on the way."

When the people heard this disturbing word, they mourned. And no one put on his ornaments. For the LORD had said to Moses, "Say to the children of Israel, 'You are a stiff-necked people. If I went up among you for one moment, I might destroy you. Now therefore, take off your ornaments, so that I may know what I will do to you.'" The children of Israel stripped themselves of their ornaments by Mount Horeb.

Moses took the tent and pitched it outside the camp, a good distance from the camp, and called it the tent of meeting. And anyone who sought the LORD would go out to the tent of meeting which was outside the camp. So whenever Moses went out to the tent, all the people would rise up and stand, every man at the entrance of his tent, and gaze after Moses until he entered the tent. And whenever Moses entered the tent, the pillar of cloud descended and stood at the entrance of the tent, and the LORD spoke with Moses. When all the people saw the pillar of cloud standing at the entrance of the tent, all the people rose up and worshipped, every man at the entrance of his tent. The LORD spoke to Moses face to face, just as a man speaks to his friend. When he returned to the camp, his servant Joshua, the son of Nun, a young man, did not depart from the tent.

Moses said to the LORD, "See, You say to me, 'Bring up this people,' but You have not let me know whom You will send with me. Yet You have said, 'I know you by name, and you have also found grace in My sight.' Now therefore, I pray You, if I have found favor in Your sight, show me now Your way, that I may know You, and that I may find favor in Your sight. Consider too that this nation is Your people."

And He said, "My Presence will go with you, and I will give you rest."

Then he said to Him, "If Your Presence does not go with us, do not bring us up from here. For how will it be known that I have found favor in Your sight, I and Your people? Is it not by Your going with us, so that we will be distinguished, I and Your people, from all the people who are on the face of the earth?"

The LORD said to Moses, "I will do this thing of which you have spoken, for you have found favor in My sight, and I know you by name."

Then Moses said, "I pray, show me Your glory."

Then He said, "I will make all My goodness pass before you, and I will proclaim the name of the LORD before you. I will be gracious to whom I will be gracious and will show mercy on whom I will show mercy." He said, "You cannot see My face, for no man can see Me and live."

Then the LORD said, "Indeed, there is a place by Me. You must stand on the rock. While My glory passes by, I will put you in a cleft of the rock and will cover you with My hand while I pass by. Then I will take away My hand, and you will see My back, but My face may not be seen."

Now the LORD said to Moses, "Cut out for yourself two tablets of stone like the first, and I will write on these tablets the words that were on the first tablets, which you broke. Be ready in the morning, and come up in the morning to Mount Sinai, and present yourself there to Me on the top of the mountain. No one is to come up with you. Do not let anyone be seen anywhere on the mountain, and the flocks or herds may not graze in front of the mountain."

So he cut out two tablets of stone like the first, and Moses rose up early in the morning and went up to Mount Sinai, just as the LORD had commanded him, and took in his hand the two tablets of stone. Then the LORD descended in the cloud, and stood with him there, and proclaimed the name of the LORD. The LORD passed by before him, and proclaimed, "The LORD, the LORD God, merciful and gracious, slow to anger, and abounding in goodness and truth, keeping mercy for thousands, forgiving iniquity and transgression and sin, but who will by no means clear *the guilty*, visiting the iniquity of fathers on the children and on the children's children, to the third and the fourth generation."

Moses made haste and bowed to the ground and worshipped. He said, "If now I have found favor in Your sight, O Lord, let my Lord, I pray, go among us, for we are a stiff-necked people. Pardon our iniquity and our sin, and take us for your inheritance."

Then He said: Indeed, I am going to make a covenant before all your people. I will do wonders such as have not been done in all the earth nor in any nation. And all the people among whom you live will see the work of the LORD, for it is a fearful thing that I will do with you. Obey what I command you this day. Indeed, I am going to drive out before you the Amorite, the Canaanite, the Hittite, the Perizzite, the Hivite, and the Jebusite. Watch yourself so that you make no covenant with the inhabitants of the land where you are going, lest it become a snare in your midst. But you shall destroy their altars, break their *sacred* pillars, and cut down their Asherah poles (for you shall not worship any other god, for the LORD, whose name is Jealous, is a jealous God), lest you make a covenant with the inhabitants of the land, and they prostitute themselves with their gods, and sacrifice to their gods, and someone invites you to eat of his sacrifice. And then you take of their daughters for your sons, and their daughters prostitute themselves after their gods. They will make your sons prostitute themselves after their gods.

You shall make no molded gods for yourselves.

You shall keep the Feast of Unleavened Bread. For seven days you are to eat unleavened bread, as I commanded you, in the month of Aviv, for in the month of Aviv you came out of Egypt.

Every firstborn of the womb belongs to Me, and every firstborn male among your livestock, whether ox or sheep. But you must redeem with a lamb the firstborn of a donkey, and if you fail to redeem him, then you must break his neck. You must redeem all the firstborn of your sons.

No one may appear before Me empty-handed.

You shall work six days, but on the seventh day you must rest. Even at the time of plowing and harvest you must rest.

You must observe the Feast of Weeks, the first fruits of the wheat harvest, and the Feast of Ingathering at the end of the year. Three times in the year all your males must appear before the Lord GOD, the God of Israel. For I will drive out the nations before you and enlarge your borders. No man will covet your land when you go up to appear before the LORD your God three times in the year.

You must not offer the blood of My sacrifice with leaven, nor is the sacrifice of the Feast of the Passover to be left until the following morning.

The first of the first fruits of your land you must bring to the house of the LORD your God.

You must not boil a young goat in its mother's milk.

Then the LORD said to Moses: Write down these words, for in accordance with these words I have made a covenant with you and with Israel. So he was there with the LORD forty days and forty nights. He did not eat bread or drink water. And He wrote on the tablets the words of the covenant, the Ten Commandments.

When Moses came down from Mount Sinai with the two tablets of testimony in the hands of Moses, when he came down from the mountain, Moses did not know that the skin of his face shone while he talked with Him. So when Aaron and all the children of Israel saw Moses, amazingly, the skin of his face shone, and they were afraid to come near him. But Moses called to them, and Aaron and all the rulers of the congregation returned to him, and Moses spoke to them. Afterward all the children of Israel drew near, and he commanded them all that the LORD had spoken to him on Mount Sinai.

When Moses finished speaking with them, he put a veil over his face. But whenever Moses went in before the LORD to speak with Him, he took the veil off until he came out. Then he came out and spoke to the children of Israel what he had been commanded. The children of Israel saw the face of Moses, that the skin of Moses' face shone, and then Moses put the veil over his face again until he went in to speak with Him.

Vayakhel

And he assembled

(Exodus 35:1–38:20)

Moses gathered all the congregation of the children of Israel together, and said to them: These are the things the LORD has commanded you to do. Six days shall work be done, but on the seventh day you shall have a holy day, a Sabbath of rest to the LORD. Whoever does any work on it must be put to death. You must not kindle fire in any of your dwellings on the Sabbath day.

Moses said to all the congregation of the children of Israel: This is the thing which the LORD commanded, saying: Take from among you an offering to the LORD. Whoever is of a willing heart, let him bring it as an offering to the LORD: gold, silver, and bronze, and blue, purple, and scarlet, fine linen, goats' hair, rams' skins dyed red, and porpoise skins, and acacia wood, oil for the light, and spices for anointing oil, and for the fragrant incense, onyx stones, and gemstones to be set for the ephod and for the breastplate.

Every skilled craftsman among you shall come and make all that the LORD has commanded: the tabernacle with its tent and its covering, its hooks and its boards, its bars, its pillars, and its sockets; the ark with its poles, the mercy seat, and the veil that conceals it; the table with its poles, and all its utensils, and the showbread; the lampstand also for the light and its utensils and its lamps, and the oil for the light; and the incense altar with its poles, and the anointing oil and the fragrant incense, and the hanging for the door at the entrance of the tabernacle; the altar of burnt offering with its bronze grating, its poles, and all its utensils, the basin and its stand; the hangings of the court, its pillars and their sockets, and the curtain for the gate of the court; the pegs of the tabernacle and the pegs of the court and their cords; the woven garments for serving in the holy place, the holy garments for Aaron the priest and the garments of his sons, to minister as priests.

Then all the congregation of the children of Israel departed from the presence of Moses. Everyone whose heart stirred him and everyone whose spirit was willing came and brought the LORD's offering for the work of the tent of meeting and for all its service and for the holy garments. They came, both men and women, as many as had willing hearts, and brought brooches, earrings, rings and bracelets, all kinds of gold jewelry, and everyone that offered an offering of gold to the LORD. Everyone who had blue, purple, and scarlet, and fine linen, and goats' hair, and red skins of rams, and porpoise skins, brought them. Everyone who was making a contribution of silver and bronze brought the LORD's offering, and everyone who had acacia wood for any work of the service brought it. All the women that were skilled spun with their hands and brought what they had spun, both of blue, purple, and scarlet, and of fine linen. All the women whose hearts stirred them to action and were skilled spun goats' hair. The leaders brought onyx stones and gemstones to be set for the ephod and for the breastplate, and spice and oil for the light, and for the anointing oil, and for the fragrant incense. The children of Israel brought a willing offering to the LORD, every man and woman whose heart was willing to bring *material* for all the work which the LORD had commanded through Moses to be made.

Moses said to the children of Israel: See, the LORD has called by name Bezalel the son of Uri, the son of Hur, of the tribe of Judah. And He has filled him with the Spirit of God, in wisdom, in understanding, and in knowledge, and in all manner of craftsmanship, to design artistic works, to work in gold, in silver, and in bronze, and in the cutting of stones for settings and in the carving of wood in order to make every manner of artistic work. He also has put in his heart to teach, both he and Oholiab, the son of Ahisamak, of the tribe of Dan. He has filled them with skill to do all manner of work as craftsmen; as designers; as embroiderers in blue, in purple, in scarlet, and in fine linen; and as weavers: as craftsmen of every work and artistic designers.

So Bezalel and Oholiab, and every skilled person, in whom the LORD has put skill and understanding to know how to do all manner of work for the service of the sanctuary, are to do the work according to all that the LORD has commanded.

Moses called Bezalel and Oholiab and every skilled person in whom the LORD had put wisdom, everyone whose heart stirred him to come to the work to do it. They received from Moses all the offerings which the children of Israel had brought to do the work of the service of the sanctuary, and they *continued* to bring to him freewill offerings every morning. And all the skilled men who were doing all the work of the sanctuary came from the work they were doing, and they said to Moses, "The people are bringing much more than is needed for the service of the work which the LORD commanded *us* to do."

So Moses issued a command, and they circulated a proclamation throughout the camp, saying, "Let no man or woman do any more work for the offering of the sanctuary." So the people were restrained from bringing *any more*. For the material they had was sufficient for all the work and more than enough to do it.

Every skilled man among those who were doing the work made the tabernacle with ten curtains of fine twisted linen, and blue, and purple, and scarlet, with cherubim that were the work of skillful workmen. The length of each curtain was twenty-eight cubits, and the width of each curtain four cubits. All of the curtains were the same size. He joined the five curtains to one another, and the other five curtains he joined to one to another. He made loops of blue on the edge of the outermost curtain in the first set. He did likewise along the edge of the outermost curtain in the second set. He made fifty loops in the one curtain and made fifty loops on the edge of the curtain which was in the second set. The loops were opposite one another. He made fifty gold clasps and joined the curtains to one another with the clasps, so that the tabernacle was a unit.

He made curtains of goats' hair for a tent over the tabernacle. He made eleven curtains in all. The length of each curtain was thirty cubits, and the width of each curtain was four cubits. The eleven curtains were all the same size. He joined five curtains by themselves and six curtains by themselves. He made fifty loops on the outermost edge of the curtain in the *first* set, and he made fifty loops on the edge of the curtain which joined the second set. He made fifty bronze clasps to join the tent together, so that it would be one unit. He made a covering for the tent out of rams' skins dyed red and a covering of porpoise skins above.

Then he made boards for the tabernacle out of acacia wood, standing upright. The length of each board was ten cubits, and the width of each board was one and a half cubits. Each board had two tenons, equally distant from each other. He did this for all the boards of the tabernacle. He made boards for the tabernacle: twenty boards for the south side. He made forty sockets of silver under the twenty boards; two sockets under one board for its two tenons and two sockets under another board for its two tenons. For the other side of the tabernacle, which is toward the north corner, he made twenty boards, and their forty sockets of silver: two sockets under one board, and two sockets under another board. For the back of the tabernacle westward he made six boards. He made two boards for the corners of the tabernacle at the back. They were doubled beneath and joined together at the top in one ring. He did this with both of them in both the corners. There were eight boards with their sockets of silver, sixteen sockets, two under every board.

He made bars of acacia wood, five for the boards of one side of the tabernacle, and five bars for the boards of the other side of the tabernacle, and five bars for the boards of the tabernacle for the back to the west. He made the middle bar to pass through the boards from the one end to the other. He overlaid the boards with gold, and made their rings of gold to be places for the bars, and overlaid the bars with gold.

He made a veil of blue, and purple, and scarlet, and fine twined linen. He made cherubim, the work of a skillful designer. He made four pillars of acacia wood and overlaid them with gold with their hooks of gold, and he cast four sockets of silver for them. He made a hanging for the tabernacle entrance of blue, purple, scarlet, and fine twisted linen, the work of an embroiderer. And he made its five pillars with their hooks, and he overlaid their tops and their bands with gold, but their five sockets were of bronze.

Now Bezalel made the ark of acacia wood. Its length was two and a half cubits, and its width one cubit and a half, and its height one cubit and a half. He overlaid it with pure gold, inside and out, and made a gold molding for it all around. He cast four rings of gold for it on its four feet, with two rings on one side and two rings on the other side of it. He made poles of acacia wood and overlaid them with gold. He put the poles into the rings on the sides of the ark to carry the ark.

He made the mercy seat of pure gold, two and a half cubits long and one and a half cubits wide. He made two cherubim of gold. He made them of hammered metal on the two ends of the mercy seat: one cherub on one end, and one cherub on the other end. Of one piece with the mercy seat he made the cherubim on its two ends. The cherubim spread out their wings upward, covering the mercy seat with their wings, with their faces toward each other. The faces of the cherubim were looking toward the mercy seat.

He made the table of acacia wood, two cubits long and one cubit wide and one cubit and a half high. And he overlaid it with pure gold and made a gold molding for it all around. Also he made a rim for it of one handbreadth all around, and he made a gold molding for the rim all around. He cast four rings of gold for it and put the rings on the four corners that were on its four feet. Close by the rim were the rings, the holders for the poles to carry the table. He made the poles of acacia wood and overlaid them with gold, to carry the table. He made the utensils which were on the table, its dishes and its pans and its bowls and its jars, to be used in pouring out offerings, of pure gold.

Then he made the lampstand of pure gold. He made it of hammered work, its base and its shaft. Its cups, its buds, and its blossoms were of the same *piece*. Six branches were extending from its sides, three branches of the lampstand from one side of it, and three branches of the lampstand from the other side of it. Three cups shaped like almond flowers, a bulb and a flower were on the first branch, and three cups shaped like almond flowers, a bulb and a flower were on the next branch, and the same for the six branches going out of the lampstand. In the lampstand there were four cups made like almond flowers, its bulbs and its flowers. And a bulb was under the first two branches from it, and a bulb under the next two branches from it, and a bulb under the third two branches from it, according to the six branches coming out of it. Their bulbs and their branches were of the same *piece*. All of it was one hammered work of pure gold.

He made its seven lamps with its snuffers and its trays of pure gold. He made it and all of its utensils from a talent of pure gold.

He made the incense altar of acacia wood. Its length was one cubit, and the width one cubit, a square, and two cubits high. Its horns were of the same *piece*. He overlaid it with pure gold, its top, its sides all around, and its horns. He also made a gold molding for it all around. He also made two rings of gold for it under its molding, on its two sides, on opposite sides, to be places for the poles to carry it. He made the poles of acacia wood and overlaid them with gold.

He made the holy anointing oil and the pure incense of sweet spices, according to the work of a perfumer.

He made the altar of burnt offering of acacia wood. It was five cubits long and five cubits wide. It was square, and it was three cubits high. He made its horns on its four corners. The horns were part of the same *piece*, and he overlaid it with bronze. He made all the utensils of the altar, the pots, and the shovels, and the basins, the flesh hooks, and the fire pans. He made all its utensils of bronze. He made for the altar a bronze grating, a latticework beneath, under its ledge, reaching halfway up. He cast four rings for the four ends of the bronze grating to provide places for the poles. He made the poles of acacia wood and overlaid them with bronze. He put the poles into the rings on the sides of the altar with which to carry it. He made *the altar* hollow, out of boards.

He made the basin of bronze with its base of bronze from the mirrors of the women who served at the entrance of the tent of meeting.

He made the courtyard: On the south side southward the hangings of the courtyard were of fine twisted linen, one hundred cubits; their twenty pillars and their twenty bases were of bronze. The hooks of the pillars and their bands *were* of silver. For the north side the hangings were one hundred cubits; their twenty pillars and their twenty sockets *were* of bronze. The hooks of the pillars and their bands *were* of silver.

For the west side the hangings were fifty cubits *with* their ten pillars and their ten sockets. The hooks of the pillars and their bands *were* of silver. For the east side eastward, fifty cubits. The hangings of one side of the gate were fifteen cubits *with* their three pillars and their three sockets, and also for the other side of the court gate. On both sides of the gate of the court-yard the hangings *were* fifteen cubits *with* their three pillars and their three sockets. All the hangings of the courtyard all around were of fine twisted linen. The sockets for the pillars were of bronze, the hooks of the pillars and their bands *were* of silver, and the overlaying of their tops of silver, and all the pillars of the courtyard were furnished with silver bands.

The screen for the gate of the courtyard was embroidered of blue, and purple, and scarlet, and fine twisted linen. Its length was twenty cubits, and its height was five cubits, corresponding to the hangings of the courtyard. Their four pillars and their four sockets *were* of bronze. Their hooks and their bands *were* of silver, and the overlaying of their tops and their bands *were* of silver. All the tent pegs of the tabernacle and of the courtyard all around were bronze.

Pekudei

Accountings

(Exodus 38:21–40:38)

This is the inventory of the tabernacle, the tabernacle of testimony, as it was counted according to the commandment of Moses for the service of the Levites by the hand of Ithamar, son of Aaron the priest. Bezalel, the son of Uri the son of Hur of the tribe of Judah, made all that the LORD commanded Moses. With him was Oholiab the son of Ahisamak, of the tribe of Dan, an engraver and designer, an embroiderer in blue and purple and scarlet yarns, and fine linen. All the gold that was used for the work, in all the work of the sanctuary, even the gold of the wave offering, was twenty-nine talents, and seven hundred thirty shekels, according to the shekel of the sanctuary.

The silver of those who were numbered of the congregation was one hundred talents, and one thousand seven hundred seventy-five shekels, according to the shekel of the sanctuary; one bekah for every man, that is, half a shekel, according to the shekel of the sanctuary, for everyone who was numbered, from twenty years old and upward, for six hundred three thousand five hundred fifty men. The hundred talents of silver were for casting the sockets of the sanctuary and the sockets of the veil—one hundred sockets of the hundred talents, one talent for a socket. Of the one thousand seven hundred seventy-five shekels, he made hooks for the pillars and overlaid their tops and made bands for them.

The bronze of the wave offering was seventy talents and two thousand four hundred shekels. With it he made the sockets for the door of the tent of meeting, and the bronze altar and its bronze grating, and all the utensils of the altar, and the sockets of the courtyard all around, and the sockets of the courtyard gate, and all the tent pegs of the tabernacle, and all the tent pegs of the courtyard all around.

Now from the blue, purple, and scarlet they made woven garments for serving in the holy place and made the holy garments for Aaron, just as the LORD commanded Moses.

He made the ephod of gold, blue, purple, and scarlet, and fine twisted linen. Then they hammered the gold into thin sheets and cut it into threads to work them into the blue, the purple, the scarlet, and the fine linen, with skillful work. They made shoulder pieces for it, in order to attach it together. It was joined by the two edges together. The skillfully woven waistband of his ephod that was on it was like it, of the same material, of gold, blue, purple, and scarlet, and fine twisted linen, just as the LORD commanded Moses.

They set the onyx stones enclosed in gold filigree settings; they were engraved like the engravings of a signet, according to the names of the children of Israel. And he put them on the shoulder pieces of the ephod, to be stones for a memorial to the children of Israel, just as the LORD commanded Moses.

He made the breastplate, the work of a skillful workman, like the workmanship of the ephod: of gold, blue, purple, and scarlet, and fine twisted linen. It was square. They made the breastplate folded double, one span long and one span wide when doubled. They set in it four rows of stones. A row of sardius, topaz, and carbuncle was the first row; the second row, an emerald, a sapphire, and a diamond; the third row, a jacinth, an agate, and an amethyst; and the fourth row, a beryl, an onyx, and a jasper. They were enclosed in settings of gold filigree. The stones were corresponding to the names of the children of Israel, twelve, corresponding to their names, like the engravings of a signet, each with its name, corresponding to the twelve tribes.

They made on the breastplate braided chains like cords of pure gold. They made two gold filigree settings and two gold rings and put the two rings in the two ends of the breastplate. They put the two braided chains of gold in the two rings on the ends of the breastplate. The other two ends of the two braided chains they fastened in the two filigree settings and put them on the shoulder pieces of the ephod at the front of it. They made two rings of gold and put them on the two ends of the breastplate, on the edge of it which was on the inner side of the ephod. They made two other golden rings and put them on the two sides of the ephod underneath, toward the front of it, over against where it joined, above the waistband of the ephod. They bound the breastplate by its rings to the rings of the ephod with a blue cord, so that it might be above the waistband of the ephod, and that the breastplate might not come loose from the ephod, just as the LORD commanded Moses.

Then he made the robe of the ephod of woven work, all of blue. There was an opening in the middle of the robe, like the opening of a coat of mail, with a band all around the opening so that it should not be torn. They made on the hems of the robe pomegranates of blue, purple, and scarlet, and twisted linen. They made bells of pure gold and put the bells between the pomegranates all around on the hem of the robe. There was a bell and a pomegranate, a bell and a pomegranate, all around about the hem of the robe to be used in service, just as the LORD commanded Moses.

They made tunics of finely woven linen for Aaron and his sons, and the turban of fine linen, and the decorated caps of fine linen, and linen breeches of fine twisted linen. The sash was of fine twisted linen and blue, purple, and scarlet, the work of an embroiderer, just as the LORD commanded Moses.

They made the plate of the holy crown of pure gold and wrote on it an inscription, like the engravings of a signet:

HOLINESS TO THE LORD.

They attached to it a blue cord, to fasten it to the turban above, just as the LORD commanded Moses.

Thus all the work of the tabernacle of the tent of meeting was finished, and the children of Israel did according to all that the LORD commanded Moses—so they did. They brought the tabernacle to Moses, the tent and all its furnishings: its clasps, its boards, its bars, and its pillars, and its sockets; and the covering of rams' skins dyed red, and the covering of porpoise skins, and the screening veil; the ark of the testimony and its poles and the mercy seat; the table, and all its utensils, and the showbread; the pure gold lampstand, with its arrangement of lamps, and all its utensils, and the oil for the light; and the gold altar, and the anointing oil, and the fragrant incense, and the curtain for the entrance to the tent; the bronze altar, and its bronze grating, its poles and all its utensils, the basin and its stand; the hangings of the courtyard, its pillars, and its sockets, and the curtain for the courtyard gate, its cords, and its pegs, and all the utensils for the service of the tabernacle, for the tent of meeting; the woven garments of service to do service in the holy place, and the holy garments for Aaron the priest and his sons' garments, to minister as priests.

The children of Israel did all the work according to all that the LORD commanded Moses. Moses looked over all the work, and indeed they had done it; as the LORD had commanded, so they had done. Then Moses blessed them.

Now the LORD spoke to Moses, saying: On the first day of the first month you shall set up the tabernacle of the tent of meeting. You shall put the ark of the testimony in it and screen the ark with the veil. You shall bring in the table and arrange the things that are to be arranged on it, and you shall bring in the lampstand and set up its lamps. You shall set the gold altar of incense before the ark of the testimony and put the curtain for the entrance to the tabernacle.

You shall set the altar of the burnt offering in front of the entrance of the tabernacle of the tent of meeting. You shall set the basin between the tent of meeting and the altar and put water in it. You shall set up the courtyard around it and hang up the curtain at the courtyard gate.

You shall take the anointing oil and anoint the tabernacle and all that is in it and shall consecrate it and all its furnishings, and it shall be holy. Then you shall anoint the altar of the burnt offering and all its utensils, and consecrate the altar, and the altar shall be most holy. You shall anoint the basin and its stand, and consecrate it.

Then you shall bring Aaron and his sons to the entrance of the tent of meeting and wash them with water. You shall put the holy garments on Aaron and anoint him and consecrate him, so that he may minister to Me as a priest. You shall bring his sons and clothe them with tunics. Then you shall anoint them just as you anointed their father, so that they may minister to Me as priests, for their anointing will surely be an everlasting priesthood throughout their generations. Thus Moses did. According to all that the LORD commanded him, so he did.

In the first month of the second year, on the first day of the month, the tabernacle was erected. Moses erected the tabernacle and fastened its sockets, and set up its boards, and inserted its bars, and erected its pillars. Then he spread the tent over the tabernacle and put the covering of the tent on top of it, just as the LORD commanded Moses.

He took the testimony and put it into the ark, attached the poles to the ark, and put the mercy seat on top of the ark. And he brought the ark into the tabernacle, and set up the veil of the screening, and screened the ark of the testimony, just as the LORD commanded Moses.

Then he put the table in the tent of meeting on the north side of the tabernacle outside the veil. He set the bread in order on it before the LORD, just as the LORD had commanded Moses.

And he put the lampstand in the tent of meeting, opposite the table, on the south side of the tabernacle. He lighted the lamps before the LORD, just as the LORD commanded Moses.

Then he put the gold altar in the tent of meeting before the veil. And he burned fragrant incense on it, just as the LORD commanded Moses. Then he set up the curtain at the entrance of the tabernacle.

He put the altar of burnt offering by the entrance of the tabernacle of the tent of meeting and offered on it the burnt offering and the grain offering, just as the LORD commanded Moses.

Then he set the basin between the tent of meeting and the altar and put water in it for washing. It was there Moses and Aaron and his sons washed their hands and their feet. Whenever they went into the tent of meeting, and whenever they came near the altar, they washed, just as the LORD commanded Moses.

He erected the courtyard all around the tabernacle and the altar, and set up the curtain of the courtyard gate. So Moses finished the work.

Then the cloud covered the tent of meeting, and the glory of the LORD filled the tabernacle. Moses was not able to enter into the tent of meeting because the cloud settled on it, and the glory of the LORD filled the tabernacle.

When the cloud was lifted up from over the tabernacle, the children of Israel would set out in all their journeys. But if the cloud was not lifted up, then they did not set out until the day that it was lifted. For the cloud of the LORD was on the tabernacle by day, and fire was on it by night, in the sight of all the house of Israel, throughout all their journeys.

Vayikra

And he called

(Leviticus 1:1–6:7)

A nd the LORD called Moses and spoke to him from the tent of meeting, saying: Speak to the children of Israel and say to them: When an individual among you brings an offering to the LORD, you shall bring your offering from the livestock, either from the herd or from the flock.

If his offering is a burnt sacrifice, and it is from the herd, he shall offer a male without blemish. At the door of the tent of meeting, he shall offer it of his own free will before the LORD. Then he shall lay his hand on the head of the burnt offering, and it shall be accepted for him to make atonement for him. And he shall slaughter the bull before the LORD, and the sons of Aaron, the priests, shall bring the blood and sprinkle the blood on all the sides of the altar that is at the door of the tent of meeting. Then he shall skin the burnt offering and cut it up into parts. The sons of Aaron the priest shall put fire on the altar and arrange the wood on the fire. Then the priests, the sons of Aaron, shall arrange the parts, with the head and the fat, on the wood that is on the fire that is on the altar. But he shall wash its entrails and its legs in water, and the priest shall burn everything on the altar. It is a burnt sacrifice, a food offering made by fire, which is a pleasing aroma for the LORD.

If his gift for a burnt offering is from the flocks, whether from the sheep or from the goats, he shall bring a male without blemish. He shall slaughter it at the north side of the altar before the LORD. And the sons of Aaron, the priests, shall sprinkle its blood on all the sides of the altar. He shall cut it up into parts, with its head and its fat, and the priest shall arrange them on the wood that is on the fire that is on the altar. But he shall wash the entrails and the legs with water. The priest shall bring it all and burn it on the altar. It is a burnt sacrifice, a food offering made by fire, which is a pleasing aroma for the LORD.

If his offering to the LORD is a burnt sacrifice of birds, then he shall bring his offering from turtledoves or from young pigeons. The priest shall bring it to the altar, wring off its head, and burn it on the altar. Its blood shall be drained out on the side of the altar. He shall remove its entrails with its feathers and throw it to the east side of the altar to the place of the ashes.

And he shall split it open by its wings, but not tear it in two. The priest shall burn it on the altar on the wood that is on the fire. It is a burnt sacrifice, a food offering made by fire, which is a pleasing aroma for the LORD.

When a person offers a grain offering to the LORD, his offering shall be of wheat flour. He shall pour olive oil on it and put frankincense on it. And he shall bring it to the sons of Aaron, the priests, and he shall scoop out a handful of the flour and its oil, along with all its frankincense. And the priest shall burn this memorial portion on the altar, a food offering made by fire, which is a pleasing aroma for the LORD. And the remainder of the grain offering shall belong to Aaron and to his sons, which is a most holy part of the food offerings to the LORD made by fire.

When you bring an oven-baked grain offering, it shall be unleavened cakes of fine flour mixed with oil or unleavened wafers spread with oil. If your offering is grain on a griddle, it shall be of unleavened wheat flour mixed with olive oil. Break it into pieces and pour oil on it. It is a grain offering. If your offering is grain in a skillet, it shall be made of wheat flour in olive oil. You shall bring the grain offering that is made of these things to the LORD, and when it is presented to the priest, he shall take it to the altar. The priest shall remove a memorial portion from the grain offering and burn it on the altar, a food offering made by fire, which is a pleasing aroma for the LORD. The remainder of the grain offering shall belong to Aaron and to his sons, which is a most holy part of the food offerings to the LORD made by fire.

No grain offering that you bring to the LORD shall be made with leaven, for you shall not burn leaven nor any honey as a food offering by fire to the LORD. As an offering of first fruits, you may offer them to the LORD, but they shall not be offered on the altar for a pleasing aroma. You shall season all your grain offerings with salt. You shall not fail to use the salt of the covenant of your God on your grain offering. With all your offerings you shall offer salt.

If you offer a grain offering of your first fruits to the LORD, you shall offer for the grain offering of your first fruits fresh ripe grain roasted by fire, coarsely ground new grain. You shall put olive oil on it and frankincense on it. It is a grain offering. The priest shall burn its memorial portion and some of its coarsely ground new grain and oil, along with all its frankincense as a food offering made by fire to the LORD.

If his offering is a peace sacrifice, and if he is offering from the herd, whether male or female, then he shall offer it without blemish before the LORD. He shall lay his hand on the head of his offering and slaughter it at the door of the tent of meeting, and the sons of Aaron, the priests, shall sprinkle the blood on the sides of the altar. He shall offer from the peace sacrifice, as a food offering made by fire to the LORD, the fat that covers the entrails and all the fat that is on the entrails, and the two kidneys with the fat that is above them, which is on the loins, and the appendage on the liver which he shall remove with the kidneys. Then the sons of Aaron shall burn it on the altar on the burnt sacrifice that is on the wood that is on the fire, as a food offering made by fire, which is a pleasing aroma for the LORD.

If his offering for a peace sacrifice to the LORD is from the flock, male or female, he shall offer it without blemish. If he is offering a sheep for his offering, he shall offer it before the LORD. He shall lay his hand upon the head of his offering and slaughter it before the tent of meeting, and the sons of Aaron shall sprinkle its blood on the sides of the altar. He shall offer from the peace sacrifice, a food offering made by fire for the LORD, its fat, and the whole fatty tail which he shall remove close to the backbone, and the fat that covers the entrails, and all the fat that is on the entrails, and the two kidneys with the fat that is above them, which is on the loins, and the appendage on the liver which he shall remove with the kidneys. The priest shall burn it on the altar as a food offering made by fire for the LORD.

If his offering is a goat, he shall offer it before the LORD. He shall lay his hand on its head and slaughter it before the tent of meeting, and the sons of Aaron shall sprinkle its blood on the sides of the altar. He shall offer from it as his offering, an offering made by fire for the LORD, the fat that covers the entrails and all the fat that is on the entrails, and the two kidneys with the fat that is above them, which is on the loins, and the appendage on the liver which he shall remove with the kidneys. The priest shall burn them on the altar as a food offering made by fire for a pleasing aroma. All the fat belongs to the LORD.

As a continual statute for your generations in all your settlements, you shall not eat any fat or any blood.

And the LORD spoke to Moses, saying: Speak to the children of Israel, saying: When a person sins unintentionally against any of the commandments of the LORD that should not be done, and he violates one of them, if the anointed priest sins, so as to bring guilt on the people, he shall bring for his sin that he has committed a bull without blemish to the LORD for a sin offering. He shall bring the bull to the opening of the tent of meeting before the LORD, and he shall lay his hand on the bull's head and slaughter the bull before the LORD. The anointed priest shall take some of the bull's blood and bring it into the tent of meeting. The priest shall dip his finger in the blood and sprinkle some of the blood seven times before the LORD in front of the veil of the sanctuary. Then the priest shall put some of the blood on the horns of the altar of fragrant incense before the LORD which is in the tent of meeting, and shall pour *the rest of* the blood of the bull at the base of the altar of the burnt offering which is at the door of the tent of meeting. Then he shall remove all the fat of the bull that is for the sin offering—the fat that covers the entrails—and all the fat that is on the entrails, and the two kidneys with the fat that is above them, which is on the loins, and the appendage on the liver which he shall remove with the kidneys, just as these are removed from the bull of the peace sacrifice, and the priest shall burn them on the altar of the burnt offering. The skin of the bull, and all its flesh, with its head, its legs, its entrails, and its dung, all *the rest of* the bull, he shall bring outside the camp to a *ritually* clean place at the ash pile and burn it on wood with fire. It shall be burned on the ash heap.

If the whole congregation of Israel commits an unintentional sin, and the matter is hidden from the eyes of the assembly, and they do any one of the things that by the commandments of the LORD should not be done, and they are *found* guilty, and the sin that they committed against *the commandment* becomes known, the congregation shall offer a bull for a sin offering, and they will bring it before the tent of meeting. The elders of the congregation shall lay their hands on the head of the bull before the LORD, and the bull will be slaughtered before the LORD. The anointed priest shall bring some of the bull's blood to the tent of meeting. And the priest shall dip his finger in some of the blood and sprinkle it seven times before the LORD in front of the veil. He shall put some of the blood on the horns of the altar that is before the LORD, which is in the tent of meeting, and he shall pour all *the rest* of the blood at the base of the altar of the burnt offering that is at the opening of the tent of meeting. He shall remove all the fat from it and burn it on the altar. He shall do to this bull just as he did to the bull of the sin offering; this is what he will do to it. And the priest shall make atonement for them, and they shall be forgiven. He shall bring the bull outside the camp, and he shall burn it just as he burned the first bull. It is the sin offering of the congregation.

Whenever a leader sins, and he does unintentionally any one of the things that by the commandments of the LORD his God should not be done and is *found* guilty, or his sin that he committed was made known to him, he shall bring as his offering a male goat without blemish, and he shall lay his hand on the head of the goat, and he shall slaughter it in the place where they slaughter the burnt offering before the LORD. It is a sin offering. The priest shall take some of the blood of the sin offering on his finger and put it on the horns of the altar of the burnt offering, and he shall pour out its blood at the base of the altar of the burnt offering. And he shall burn all its fat on the altar, like the fat of the peace sacrifice, and the priest shall make atonement for him for his sin, and he shall be forgiven.

If any one of the common people should sin unintentionally by doing one of the things that by the commandments of the LORD should not be done, and is *found* guilty, or his sin that he committed was made known to him, he shall bring as his offering a female goat without blemish, for his sin that he committed. He shall lay his hand on the head of the sin offering, and he shall slaughter the sin offering in the place of the burnt offering. The priest shall take some of its blood on his finger and put it on the horns of the altar of the burnt offering, and he shall pour out *the rest of* its blood at the base of the altar. And he shall remove all its fat, just as the fat is removed from the peace sacrifice, and the priest shall burn it on the altar for a pleasing aroma to the LORD, and the priest shall make atonement for him, and he shall be forgiven.

And if he brings a sheep for a sin offering, he shall bring a female without blemish, and lay his hand on the head of the sin offering, and he shall slaughter it for a sin offering in the place where they slaughter the burnt offering. The priest shall take some of the blood of the sin offering on his finger and put it on the horns of the altar of the burnt offering, and all the *rest of* its blood he shall pour out at the base of the altar. And he shall remove all the fat, just as the fat of the sheep is removed from the peace sacrifice, and the priest shall burn it on the altar as a food offering to the LORD made by fire. And the priest shall make atonement for his sin that he committed, and he shall be forgiven.

When a person sins in hearing the spoken oath, and he is a witness, whether he saw or knew *about the incident*, if he does not report it, he bears guilt.

Or *when* a person touches any *ceremonially* unclean thing, whether it is a carcass of unclean wildlife, or a carcass of an unclean domesticated animal, or the carcass of an unclean crawling thing, and he did not realize it, then he has become unclean and guilty.

Or when he touches human uncleanness, any uncleanness by which he may become *ceremonially* unclean, and he did not realize it, when he realizes it, then he shall be guilty.

Or when a person swears by speaking rashly with his lips to do evil or to do good, anything that a man may speak rashly by oath, and he did not realize it, but when he realizes it, then he has become guilty of any of these things.

When he becomes guilty of one of these things, he shall confess that he has sinned in that thing. And he shall bring his guilt offering to the LORD for his sin which he has committed, a female from the flock, a lamb or goat, for a sin offering. And the priest shall make atonement for him concerning his sin.

If he cannot afford an animal, then he shall bring for his guilt offering, on account of the sin that he committed, two turtledoves or two pigeons to the LORD, one for a sin offering and one for a burnt offering. He shall bring them to the priest who shall offer the one for the sin offering first. He will wring off its head at its neck, but he shall not sever it. Then he shall sprinkle some of the blood of the sin offering on the side of the altar, and the rest of the blood shall be poured out at the base of the altar. It is a sin offering.

But the second he shall treat as a burnt offering according to the regulation. The priest shall make atonement for him for his sin that he committed, and he shall be forgiven.

But if he cannot afford to bring two turtledoves or two pigeons, he shall bring for his offering *for the sin* that he committed one-tenth of an ephah of wheat flour for a sin offering. He shall not place olive oil on it, nor shall he put frankincense on it, for it is a sin offering. Then he shall bring it to the priest, and *the priest* shall scoop out a handful from it as a memorial portion and burn it on the altar as a food offering to the LORD made by fire. It is a sin offering. The priest shall make atonement for him concerning his sin that he committed from any of these *offenses*, and he shall be forgiven. The *remainder* will belong to the priest, like the grain offering.

The LORD spoke to Moses, saying: When a person acts unfaithfully and sins unintentionally in regard to the holy things of the LORD, then for his restitution offering to the LORD he shall bring a ram without blemish from the flock—or *its equivalent, in* your estimation, *in* silver shekels (using the sanctuary shekel)—for a guilt offering. And he shall repay *the sin* that he committed with regard to the holy thing and shall add one-fifth to it and give it to the priest. The priest shall make atonement for him with the ram of the guilt offering, and he shall be forgiven.

If a person sins unintentionally and does any one of the things that by commandments of the LORD should not be done and he is *found* guilty, he shall bear his iniquity. He shall bring to the priest a ram without blemish from the flock—or its equivalent value—for a guilt offering. The priest shall make atonement for him concerning his error that he made unintentionally, and he shall be forgiven. It is a guilt offering: He has indeed incurred guilt before the LORD.

And the LORD spoke to Moses, saying: When a person sins and acts unfaithfully against the LORD by lying to another concerning *something left in* storage, or entrusted *to him*, or theft, or by extorting his neighbor, or by finding a lost item and lying about it, and he swears falsely concerning one of all the things that a man may do to sin in these things, when he sins and he is *found* guilty, he shall return whatever he stole, or whatever he extorted, or whatever was left in storage with him, or the lost item which he found, or about which he swore falsely, then he shall repay it in full and shall add one-fifth to it. He shall give it to whom it belongs on the day that he is found guilty. And he shall bring his guilt offering to the LORD, a ram without blemish from the flock—or its equivalent value—for a guilt offering to the priest. And the priest shall make atonement for him before the LORD, and he shall be forgiven for anything he may have done to incur guilt.

Tzav

Command!

(Leviticus 6:8–8:36)

The LORD spoke to Moses, saying: Command Aaron and his sons, saying: This is the law for the burnt offering. The burnt offering shall be on the hearth upon the altar all night until the morning, and the fire of the altar shall be kept burning on it. The priest shall put on his linen robe, and his linen undergarments on his body. Then he shall remove the ashes from the fire of the burnt offering on the altar, and he shall put them beside the altar. Then he shall take off his garments and put on other garments, and he shall bring the ashes outside the camp to a clean place. The fire on the altar shall be kept burning on it. It shall not go out. The priest shall feed it with wood every morning. He will arrange the burnt offering on it, and he shall burn the fat of the peace offerings on it. A perpetual fire shall be kept burning on the altar. It shall never go out.

This is the law of the grain offering. The sons of Aaron shall offer it before the LORD on the altar. He shall take from it a handful of the flour of the grain offering, and of the oil and all the frankincense which is on the grain offering, and shall burn it on the altar for a pleasing aroma as a memorial to the LORD. Aaron and his sons shall eat the remainder of it; it shall be eaten without leaven in a holy place. They shall eat it in the court of the tent of meeting. It shall not be baked with leaven. I have given it to them for their portion of My food offerings made by fire. It is most holy, as is the sin offering and as is the guilt offering. All the males among the children of Aaron shall eat of it. It shall be a perpetual statute in your generations concerning the food offerings of the LORD made by fire. Everyone who touches them shall become holy.

The LORD spoke to Moses, saying: This is the offering of Aaron and of his sons which they shall offer to the LORD in the day when he is anointed: one-tenth of an ephah of wheat flour for a regular grain offering, half of it in the morning and half at night. It shall be made on a griddle with olive oil. When it is well mixed, you shall bring it; and the baked pieces of the grain offering you shall offer as a pleasing aroma to the LORD. The priest from among the sons of Aaron who is anointed to succeed him shall offer it. It is a perpetual statute to the LORD. It shall be completely burned up. For every grain offering for the priest shall be completely burned up. It shall not be eaten.

The LORD spoke to Moses, saying: Speak to Aaron and to his sons, saying: This is the law of the sin offering: In the place where the burnt offering is killed shall the sin offering also be killed before the LORD. It is most holy. The priest who offers it for sin shall eat it. In a holy place it shall be eaten in the court of the tent of meeting. Whatever touches its flesh shall be holy, and when blood is sprinkled on any garment, you shall wash it in a holy place. And the clay vessel where it is boiled shall be broken, and if it is boiled in a bronze pot, it shall be both scoured and rinsed in water. All the males among the priests shall eat *from this offering*. It is most holy. Any sin offering where blood is brought into the tent of meeting to make atonement in the holy place shall not be eaten. It shall be burned up in the fire.

Likewise this is the law of the guilt offering. It is most holy. In the place where they kill the burnt offering they shall kill the guilt offering, and its blood shall he sprinkle on the sides of the altar. He shall offer all the fat. The fatty tail and the fat that covers the entrails, and the two kidneys and the fat that is on them, which is on the loins, and the appendage that is above the liver, along with the kidneys, he shall take away. And the priest shall burn them on the altar for a food offering made by fire to the LORD. It is a guilt offering. Every male among the priests shall eat from it. It shall be eaten in a holy place. It is most holy.

As the sin offering, so is the guilt offering; there is one law for them: the priest who makes atonement shall have it. The priest who offers anyone's burnt offering shall have for himself the skin of the burnt offering that he has offered. Every grain offering that is baked in the oven and all that is prepared in a pan or griddle shall be for the priest who offers it. And every grain offering, *whether* mixed with oil or dry, shall be equally shared among all the sons of Aaron.

This is the law of the sacrifice of peace offerings that a person shall offer to the LORD.

If he gives it as a thanksgiving *offering*, then he shall offer with the thanksgiving sacrifice unleavened cakes mixed with oil, and unleavened wafers smeared with oil, and cakes of wheat flour mixed with olive oil. Besides the cakes, he shall offer for his offering leavened bread with the sacrifice of his thanksgiving peace offerings. From this he shall offer one loaf from each offering, as a gift to the LORD. It shall be for the priest who sprinkles the blood of the peace offerings. The flesh of the sacrifice of his peace offerings for thanksgiving shall be eaten the same day that it is offered; he shall not leave any of it until the morning.

But if the sacrifice of his offering is a vow or a voluntary offering, it shall be eaten the same day that he offers his sacrifice, and on the next day also the remainder of it can be eaten. But the remainder of the flesh of the sacrifice on the third day shall be burned up with fire. If any of the flesh of the sacrifice of his peace offerings is eaten at all on the third day, the one eating shall not be accepted, nor shall it be imputed to him who offers it. It shall be contaminated, and the one who eats of it shall bear his iniquity.

The flesh that touches any unclean thing shall not be eaten. It shall be burned up with fire. And as for the *other* flesh, all who are *ritually* clean can eat of it. But the person who eats of the flesh of the sacrifice of peace offerings that belong to the LORD, and who has any uncleanness on him, that individual shall be cut off from his people. Moreover the person who shall touch any unclean thing, whether the uncleanness of man or any unclean beast or any detestable unclean creature, and then eats of the flesh of the sacrifice of the peace offering that belongs to the LORD, that individual shall be cut off from his people.

The LORD spoke to Moses, saying: Speak to the children of Israel, saying: You shall not eat any fat of an ox, a sheep, or a goat. The fat of an animal that dies of itself and the fat of that which is torn by beasts may be used in any other way, but you shall certainly not eat of it. For whoever eats the fat of an animal that is a food offering made by fire to the LORD, that individual shall be cut off from his people. Moreover you shall not eat any manner of blood, whether from a fowl or animal, in any of your dwellings. Whoever eats any manner of blood, that individual shall be cut off from his people.

The LORD spoke to Moses, saying: Speak to the children of Israel, saying: He who offers the sacrifice of his peace offerings to the LORD shall bring his sacrifice to the LORD from his peace offerings. His own hands shall bring the food offerings of the LORD made by fire, the fat with the breast that the breast may be waved for a wave offering before the LORD. The priest shall burn the fat on the altar, but the breast shall be for Aaron and his sons. The right thigh you shall give to the priest for a contribution offering for the sacrifice of your peace offerings. The one among the sons of Aaron who offers the blood of the peace offerings and the fat shall have the right thigh for his portion. For the breast that is waved and the thigh that is contributed I have taken from the children of Israel, from the sacrifices of their peace offerings, and have given them to Aaron the priest and to his sons as a perpetual portion from the children of Israel.

This is the consecrated portion for Aaron and his sons, from the food offerings of the LORD made by fire, in the day when *Moses* presented them to minister as priests before the LORD, which the LORD commanded that they be given this, in the day that he anointed them, from the children of Israel as a perpetual portion throughout their generations.

This is the law of the burnt offering, of the grain offering, and of the sin offering, and of the guilt offering, and of the ordinations, and of the sacrifice of the peace offerings, which the LORD commanded Moses on Mount Sinai, in the day that He commanded the children of Israel to offer their offerings to the LORD in the Wilderness of Sinai.

And the LORD spoke to Moses, saying: Take Aaron and his sons with him, and the garments, and the anointing oil, and a bull for the sin offering, and two rams, and a basket of unleavened bread, and gather all the congregation together at the entrance of the tent of meeting. And Moses did as the LORD commanded him, and the assembly was gathered together at the entrance of the tent of meeting.

Moses said to the congregation, "This is the thing which the LORD commanded to be done." Moses brought Aaron and his sons and washed them with water. Then he put the tunic on him, and tied the sash around him, and clothed him with the robe, and put the ephod upon him, and he girded him with the decorative band of the ephod and bound the ephod to him. He put the breastplate on him. He also put the Urim and the Thummim in the breastplate. Then he put the turban upon his head. Also on the turban at the front he put the golden plate, the holy crown, as the LORD commanded Moses.

Moses took the anointing oil, and anointed the tabernacle and all that was in it, and sanctified them. He sprinkled oil on the altar seven times and anointed the altar and all its vessels, both the laver and its stand, to sanctify them. Then he poured some of the anointing oil on the head of Aaron and anointed him to sanctify him. Moses brought the sons of Aaron and put tunics on them, and girded them with sashes, and put headbands on them, as the LORD commanded Moses.

He brought the bull for the sin offering, and Aaron and his sons laid their hands on the head of the bull for the sin offering. He slaughtered it, and Moses took the blood, and put it on the horns of the altar around it with his finger, and purified the altar, and poured the blood at the base of the altar, and sanctified it to make reconciliation on it. He took all the fat that was on the entrails, and the appendage above the liver, and the two kidneys with their fat, and Moses burned them on the altar. But the bull, and its hide, its flesh, and its refuse he burned with fire outside the camp, as the LORD commanded Moses.

Then he brought the ram for the burnt offering, and Aaron and his sons laid their hands on the head of the ram. He killed it, and Moses sprinkled the blood on the sides of the altar. He cut the ram into pieces, and Moses burned the head, the pieces, and the fat. He washed the entrails and the legs in water, and Moses burned the whole ram on the altar. It was a burnt offering for a pleasing aroma, and a food offering made by fire to the LORD, as the LORD commanded Moses.

Next he brought the other ram, the ram of consecration, and Aaron and his sons laid their hands on the head of the ram. He slaughtered it, and Moses took some of its blood and put it on the tip of the right ear of Aaron, and on the thumb of his right hand, and on the big toe of his right foot. He brought the sons of Aaron, and Moses put some of the blood on the tips of their right ears, and on the thumbs of their right hands, and on the big toes of their right feet. Then Moses sprinkled the blood on the sides of the altar. He took the fat, and the fatty tail, and all the fat that was on the entrails, and the appendage above the liver, and the two kidneys, and their fat, and the right thigh, and out of the basket of unleavened bread that was before the LORD he took one unleavened cake, and a cake of oiled bread, and one wafer and put them on the fat and on the right thigh. And he put all *these* on the hands of Aaron and on the hands of his sons and waved them for a wave offering before the LORD. Then Moses took them from off their hands and burned them on the altar with the burnt offering. This was a consecration for a pleasing aroma, an offering made by fire to the LORD. Moses took the breast and waved it for a wave offering before the LORD. This part of the ram of consecration was for Moses, as the LORD commanded Moses.

Then Moses took some of the anointing oil and some of the blood which was on the altar and sprinkled it on Aaron, and on his garments, and on his sons, and on the garments of his sons with him and sanctified Aaron, and his garments, and his sons, and the garments of his sons with him.

Moses said to Aaron and to his sons, "Boil the flesh at the entrance of the tent of meeting and eat it there with the bread that is in the basket of consecrations just as I commanded, saying, 'Aaron and his sons shall eat it.' That which remains of the flesh and of the bread you shall burn up. You shall not go out of the door of the tent of meeting for seven days, until the days of your consecration are at an end, for your consecration will take seven days. As he has done this day, so the LORD has commanded what is to be done to make atonement for you. Therefore you shall abide at the entrance of the tent of meeting day and night for seven days and keep the charge of the LORD that you do not die, for so I have been commanded."

So Aaron and his sons did all things which the LORD commanded by the hand of Moses.

Shmini

Eighth

(Leviticus 9:1–11:47)

A nd it came to pass on the eighth day that Moses called Aaron and his sons and the elders of Israel. Then he said to Aaron, "Take a young calf for a sin offering and a ram for a burnt offering, without blemish, and offer them before the LORD. To the children of Israel you shall speak, saying, 'Take a male goat for a sin offering, and a calf and a lamb—both one year old without blemish—for a burnt offering, also an ox and a ram for peace offerings to sacrifice before the LORD, and a grain offering mixed with oil. For today the LORD will appear to you.'"

They brought that which Moses commanded before the tent of meeting, and the entire congregation drew near and stood before the LORD. Moses said, "This is the thing which the LORD commanded that you should do; then the glory of the LORD shall appear to you."

Then Moses said to Aaron, "Go to the altar, and offer your sin offering and your burnt offering, and make atonement for yourself and for the people, and offer the sacrifice of the people, and make atonement for them, as the LORD commanded."

Aaron therefore went to the altar and slaughtered the calf of the sin offering which was for himself. The sons of Aaron brought the blood to him, and he dipped his finger in the blood, and put it on the horns of the altar, and poured out the blood at the base of the altar. But the fat, the kidneys, and the appendage above the liver of the sin offering he burned on the altar, as the LORD commanded Moses. The flesh and the hide he burned with fire outside the camp.

He slaughtered the burnt offering, and the sons of Aaron presented the blood to him, which he sprinkled on the sides of the altar. They presented the burnt offering to him, with its pieces, and the head, and he burned them on the altar. He then washed the entrails and the legs and burned them with the burnt offering on the altar.

He brought the people's offering, and took the goat which was the sin offering for the people, and slaughtered it, and offered it for sin as the first offering.

And he brought the burnt offering and offered it according to its regulation. Then he brought the grain offering, took a handful of it, and burned it on the altar, besides the burnt sacrifice of the morning.

He slaughtered the ox and the ram as a sacrifice of peace offerings for the people, and the sons of Aaron presented the blood to him, which he sprinkled on the sides of the altar, and the fat of the ox and of the ram, the fatty tail, and that which covers the entrails, and the kidneys, and the appendage above the liver. They put the fat pieces on the breasts, and he burned the fat on the altar. But the breasts and the right thigh Aaron waved for a wave offering before the LORD just as Moses commanded.

Aaron lifted up his hand toward the people, and blessed them, and came down from offering the sin offering, the burnt offering, and peace offerings.

Moses and Aaron went into the tent of meeting, and when they came out they blessed the people, and the glory of the LORD appeared to all the people. A fire came out from before the LORD, and it consumed the burnt offering and the fat that were on the altar. When all the people saw this, they shouted and fell on their faces.

Now Nadab and Abihu, the sons of Aaron, each took his censer and put fire in it, and put incense on it, and offered strange fire before the LORD, which He did not command them *to do*. Then a fire came out from the LORD and devoured them, and they died before the LORD. Then Moses said to Aaron, "This is what the LORD spoke, saying:

'I will be sanctified
    by those who come near Me;
and before all the people
    I will be glorified.' "

And Aaron held his peace.

Moses called Mishael and Elzaphan, the sons of Uzziel the uncle of Aaron, and said to them, "Come near, and carry your brothers from before the sanctuary out of the camp." So they went near, and carried them in their tunics out of the camp as Moses had said.

Moses said to Aaron, and to Eleazar and Ithamar his sons, "Do not let your hair be loosely disheveled, nor rend your clothes, lest you die, and lest wrath come upon all the people. Instead, let your brothers, the whole house of Israel, mourn the burning which the LORD has caused. You shall not go out from the entrance of the tent of meeting, lest you die, for the anointing oil of the LORD is upon you." And they did according to the word of Moses.

The LORD spoke to Aaron, saying: Do not drink wine nor strong drink, you or your sons with you, when you go into the tent of meeting, lest you die. It shall be a perpetual statute throughout your generations, so that you may differentiate between what is holy and common and between what is unclean and clean. And so you may teach the children of Israel all the statutes that the LORD has spoken to them by the hand of Moses.

Moses spoke to Aaron, and to Eleazar and Ithamar, his sons who were left: Take the grain offering that remains of the food offerings of the LORD made by fire and eat it without leaven beside the altar. For it is most holy. And you shall eat it in a holy place, because it is your due and your sons' due from the food sacrifices of the LORD made by fire. For so I have been commanded. The breast that is waved and the thigh that is contributed you shall eat in a clean place, you, and your sons, and your daughters with you, for they are your due and your sons' due which are given out of the sacrifices of peace offerings of the children of Israel. The thigh that is contributed and the breast that is waved they shall bring with the fat pieces of the food offerings made by fire to wave them as a wave offering before the LORD, and it shall be yours and your sons' with you as a perpetual statute, as the LORD has commanded.

Moses diligently sought the goat of the sin offering and saw it was burned up. And he was angry with Eleazar and Ithamar, the sons of Aaron who were left alive, saying, "Why have you not eaten the sin offering in the sacred area, knowing that it is most holy and God has given it to you to bear the iniquity of the congregation to make atonement for them before the LORD? Its blood was not brought into the inner part of the sanctuary. Indeed you should have eaten it in the sanctuary as I commanded."

Aaron said to Moses, "Today they have offered their sin offering and their burnt offering before the LORD, and such things have happened to me! If I had eaten the sin offering today, should it have been accepted in the sight of the LORD?" And when Moses heard that, he approved.

The LORD spoke to Moses and Aaron, saying to them: Speak to the children of Israel, saying: These are the living things which you shall eat among all the animals that are on the earth. Whatever animal has a parted hoof (that is, split-hoofed), and chews the cud among the animals, that one you shall eat.

Nevertheless these you shall not eat of those that chew the cud or of those that have a divided hoof: The camel, because it chews the cud but does not have a divided hoof, is unclean to you; the rock badger, because it chews the cud but does not have a divided hoof, is unclean to you; the hare, because it chews the cud but does not have a divided hoof, is unclean to you; the pig, though it does have a divided hoof (that is, split-hoofed), yet it does not chew the cud, is unclean to you; you shall not eat of their flesh, and their carcasses you must not touch; they are unclean to you.

These you shall eat of all that are in the waters: Whatever has fins and scales in the waters, in the seas and in the rivers, these you shall eat; all that do not have fins and scales in the seas and in the rivers, from all that move in the waters and from any living thing that is in the waters, they are detestable to you; they shall be detestable to you. You shall not eat of their flesh, and you shall detest their carcasses. Whatever has no fins or scales in the waters is detestable to you.

These you shall detest among the birds; they shall not be eaten; they are detestable: the griffon vulture, the bearded vulture, and the black vulture, the kite, and buzzard of any kind, the raven of any kind, and the eagle owl, the short-eared and long-eared owls, and the hawk of any kind, and the little owl, the cormorant, and the screech owl, and the white owl, the scops owl, and the osprey, and the stork, the heron of any kind, the hoopoe, and the bat.

All flying insects that walk, moving on all fours, shall be detestable to you. Yet these you may eat of every flying insect that creeps on all fours: those that have jointed legs above their feet with which to hop on the ground. Even of these you may eat: the locust of any kind, the bald locust of any kind, the cricket of any kind, and the grasshopper of any kind. But all other flying insects that have four feet shall be detestable to you.

And by these you shall be unclean. Whoever touches the carcass of these shall be unclean until the evening.

Whoever carries any of the carcasses of these shall wash his clothes and be unclean until the evening. The carcass of every animal that divides the hoof but is not completely split-hoofed nor chews the cud is unclean to you. Everyone who touches them shall be unclean. Whatever animal that walks on its paws, among all manner of animals that go on all fours, those are unclean to you. Whoever touches their carcass shall be unclean until the evening. He who carries the carcass of these shall wash his clothes and be unclean until the evening; they are unclean to you.

These also shall be unclean to you among the crawling things that move on the ground: the mole rat, the mouse, and the great lizard of any kind, and the gecko, the lizard, the wall gecko, the sand lizard, and the chameleon. These are unclean to you among all that crawl. Whoever touches them when they are dead shall be unclean until the evening. And anything on which any of them falls when they are dead shall be unclean, whether it be an article of wood or clothing or a skin or a sack, any article that is used for any purpose. It must be put in water. And it shall be unclean until the evening; then it shall be clean. Every clay vessel into which any of these falls, everything in it shall be unclean, and you shall break it. Any food in it that may be eaten on which water is poured shall be unclean, and any drink that may be drunk in every such vessel shall be unclean. Everything on which any part of their carcass falls shall be unclean; whether it is an oven or stove, it shall be broken to pieces. They are unclean and shall be unclean to you. Nevertheless a fountain or cistern where there is plenty of water shall be clean, but whoever touches their carcass shall be unclean. If any part of their carcass falls on any grain seed that is to be sown, it shall be clean. But if any water is put on the seed, and any part of their carcass fall on it, it shall be unclean to you.

If any animal from which you may eat dies, whoever touches the carcass shall be unclean until the evening. And the person who eats of the carcass shall wash his clothes and be unclean until the evening. The person who carries the carcass shall wash his clothes and be unclean until the evening.

Every crawling thing that moves on the ground shall be detestable. It shall not be eaten. Whatever goes on its belly, and whatever goes on all fours, or whatever has many feet from any crawling things that move on the earth, you shall not eat them for they are detestable. You shall not make yourselves detestable with any crawling thing that moves, nor shall you make yourselves unclean with them, that you should thereby be defiled by them. For I am the LORD your God. You shall therefore sanctify yourselves, and you shall be holy, for I am holy. Neither shall you defile yourselves with any manner of crawling thing that moves on the ground. For I am the LORD who brings you up out of the land of Egypt to be your God. Therefore you shall be holy, for I am holy.

This is the law for the animals, and the fowls, and every living creature that moves in the waters, and every creature that crawls on the ground, to differentiate between the unclean and the clean, and between the animal that may be eaten and the animal that may not be eaten.

Tazria

She bears seed

(Leviticus 12:1–13:59)

T hen the LORD spoke to Moses, saying: Speak to the children of Israel, saying: If a woman has conceived and bears a male child, then she shall be unclean seven days, as in the days of her *monthly* menstruation she shall be unclean. On the eighth day the flesh of his foreskin shall be circumcised. And she shall then continue in the blood of her purifying for thirty-three days. She shall not touch anything holy, nor come into the sanctuary until the days of her purifying are fulfilled. But if she gives birth to a female child, then she shall be unclean for two weeks as in her monthly menstruation, and she shall continue in the blood of her purifying for sixty-six days.

When the days of her purifying are fulfilled, whether for a son or for a daughter, she shall bring a year-old lamb for a burnt offering, and a young pigeon or a turtledove for a sin offering, to the priest at the entrance of the tent of meeting, who shall offer it before the LORD and make atonement for her. Then she shall be cleansed from the issue of her blood.

This is the law for the woman who has given birth to a male or a female child. If she cannot afford a lamb, then she shall bring two turtledoves or two pigeons, one for the burnt offering and the other for a sin offering, and the priest shall make atonement for her, and she shall be clean.

And the LORD spoke to Moses and Aaron, saying: When a man has on the skin of his body a swelling, a scab, or spot, and it turns on the skin of his body like a mark of a leprous sore, then he shall be brought to Aaron the priest or to one of his sons the priests. And the priest shall examine the mark on the skin of the body, and when the hair on the diseased area is white, and the mark appears to be deeper than the skin of his body, then it is a leprous sore. So the priest shall look on him and pronounce him unclean. If the spot is white on the skin of his body, and it appears to be no deeper than the skin, and the hair is not white, then the priest shall isolate the person who has the mark for seven days. Then the priest shall examine him on the seventh day, and if the mark is still visible, and the mark has not spread into the skin, then the priest shall isolate him for seven days more. And the priest shall examine him again on the seventh day, and if the mark has faded and not spread into the skin, then the priest shall pronounce him clean; it is only a scab, and he shall wash his clothes and be clean. But if the scab spreads in the skin after he has been seen by the priest for his cleansing, he shall be seen by the priest again. And if the priest sees that the scab has spread in the skin, then the priest shall pronounce him unclean. It is leprosy.

When a person has leprosy, then it shall be reported to the priest. And the priest shall examine him, and if there is a white swelling in the skin, and it has turned the hair white, and there is raw flesh in the swelling, it is a recurring leprosy in the skin of his body, and the priest shall pronounce him unclean, but he shall not isolate him, for he is unclean.

If the leprosy breaks out all over the skin, and the disease covers all the skin of the person who has the disease from his head to his feet, wherever the priest looks, then the priest shall examine, and if the leprosy has covered all his body, he shall pronounce him clean from the disease. It has all turned white, and he is clean. But when raw flesh appears on him, he shall be unclean. The priest shall see the raw flesh and pronounce him to be unclean, for the raw flesh is unclean. It is leprosy. Or if the raw flesh turns again, and it is changed to white, then he shall come to the priest. And the priest shall see him, and if the disease is changed to white, then the priest shall pronounce him clean who has the disease. He is clean.

And when the skin has a boil, and it is healed, and in the place of the boil there is a white swelling or a reddish-white spot, then it will be shown to the priest. And if the priest sees it, and it is deeper than the skin, and the hair has turned white, then the priest shall pronounce him unclean. It is a leprous sore that has broken out in the boil. But if the priest looks at it, and there are no white hairs in it, and if it is not deeper than the skin but has faded, then the priest shall isolate the person for seven days. If it spreads around the skin, then the priest shall pronounce him unclean. It is a leprous sore. But if the spot stays in its place and does not spread, then it is the scar of a boil, and the priest shall pronounce him clean.

Or if there is some of the skin on the body where there is a burn, and the raw flesh that has a burn becomes a reddish or white spot, then the priest shall examine it, and if the hair in the spot has turned white, and it is deeper than the skin, then it is a leprous disease broken out from the burn. Therefore the priest shall pronounce him unclean. It is a leprous sore. But if the priest looks at it, and there is no white hair in the spot, and it is no deeper than the other skin and is faded, then the priest shall isolate him for seven days. And the priest shall examine him on the seventh day, and if it has spread around the skin, then the priest shall pronounce him unclean. It is a leprous sore. If the spot stays in its place and it does not spread in the skin, but is faded, then it is a swelling from the burn, and the priest shall pronounce him clean, for it is a scar from the burn.

If a man or woman has a sore on the head or in the beard, then the priest shall examine the sore, and if it is deeper than the skin and there is in it a yellow thin hair, then the priest shall pronounce him unclean. It is a scaly leprosy of the head or beard. If the priest examines the scaly sore, and it is no deeper than the skin, and there is no black hair in it, then the priest shall isolate the person with the scale for seven days. And on the seventh day the priest shall examine the sore, and if the scale has not spread, and there is no yellow hair in it, and the scale is not deeper than the skin, then he shall shave, but the scale he shall not shave, and the priest shall isolate the person with the scale another seven days. And on the seventh day the priest shall examine the scale. If the scale has not spread in the skin and is no deeper than the skin, the priest shall pronounce him clean. He shall wash his clothes and be clean. But if the scale spreads over the skin after his cleansing, then the priest shall examine him. If the scale has spread over the skin, the priest shall not look for yellow hair. He is unclean. But if the scale appears not to have changed and there is black hair growing in it, then the scale is healed. He is clean and the priest shall pronounce him clean.

If a man or a woman has spots on the skin of the body, even white bright spots, then the priest shall examine, and if the bright spots on the skin of the body are a faded white, then it is just a rash that has broken out on the skin. He is clean.

When a man has lost hair from his head, then he is bald. He is still clean. And when a man has lost hair from his forehead, then he is bald on the forehead. He is still clean. But if there is on the bald head or bald forehead a reddish-white sore, it is a leprous disease breaking out on his bald head or his bald forehead. Then the priest shall examine it. If the diseased swelling is reddish-white on his bald head or on his bald forehead, resembling a leprous disease in the skin of the body, he is leprous. He is unclean. The priest shall pronounce him unclean. His disease is on his head.

The man who has the leprous disease shall have torn clothes and disheveled hair; and he shall cover his mustache and shall cry, "Unclean, unclean." All the days that he has the disease, he shall be defiled. He is unclean. He shall dwell alone, and he shall live outside the camp.

If a garment has a leprous disease, whether it is a wool or a linen garment, whether it is in the warp or woof of the linen or wool fabric, or in the leather or anything made of leather, and if the disease is greenish or reddish in the garment, or in the leather, or in the warp or woof, or in anything made of leather, it is a leprous disease and shall be shown to the priest. And the priest shall examine the disease, and isolate the infected article for seven days. And he shall examine the disease on the seventh day. If the disease has spread in the garment, either in the warp or in the woof, or in the leather, or in any work that is made of leather, this is a spreading leprous disease. It is unclean. He shall therefore burn that garment, whether warp or woof, wool or linen, or anything of leather that has the disease, for it is a spreading leprous disease. It shall be burned in the fire.

If the priest examines *it*, and the disease has not spread in the garment, either in the warp or the woof, or in anything of leather, then the priest shall command that they wash the article in which the disease appears, and he shall isolate it for seven days more. The priest shall examine the infected article after it has been washed. If the infected spot has not changed its color, even if the disease has not spread, it is unclean. You shall burn it in the fire, whether the leprous spot is on the inside or on the outside of the article. If the priest examines and the disease has faded after washing it, he shall tear the spot out of the garment, or out of the leather, or out of the warp or the woof. If it still appears in the garment, either in the warp or in the woof, or in anything of leather, it is spreading. You shall burn in the fire that in which the disease appears. The garment that you have washed, either in the warp or woof, or anything of leather, if the disease is gone from it, then it shall be washed a second time and shall be clean.

This is the law of the leprous disease in a garment of wool or linen, either in the warp or woof, or anything of leather to determine if it is clean or unclean.

Metzora

Infected one

(Leviticus 14:1–15:33)

The LORD spoke to Moses, saying: This shall be the law of the leper in the day of his cleansing: It shall be reported to the priest, and the priest shall go out of the camp, and the priest shall examine him and see if the disease is healed in the leprous person. Then the priest shall command that two live clean birds and cedar wood and scarlet fabric and hyssop be brought for him who is to be cleansed. The priest shall command that one of the birds be slaughtered in a clay vessel over running water. As for the living bird, he shall take it, the cedar wood, the scarlet, and the hyssop, and shall dip them and the living bird in the blood of the bird that was killed over the running water. Then he shall sprinkle *it* seven times on him who is to be cleansed from leprosy, and he shall pronounce him clean and shall let the living bird loose into the open field.

He that is to be cleansed shall wash his clothes, and shave off all his hair, and wash himself in water, so that he may be clean. After that he shall come into the camp and shall stay outside of his tent seven days. But it shall be on the seventh day that he shall shave all his hair off his head and his beard and his eyebrows, all his hair he shall shave off, and he shall wash his clothes. Also he shall wash his body in water, and he shall be clean.

On the eighth day he shall take two male lambs without blemish, and one ewe lamb one year old without blemish, and three-tenths of an *ephah* of wheat flour mixed with oil for a grain offering, and one log of oil. The priest who makes him clean shall present the man who is to be made clean and those things before the LORD at the entrance of the tent of meeting.

Then the priest shall take one male lamb and offer it for a guilt offering, along with the log of oil, and wave them for a wave offering before the LORD. Then he shall slaughter the lamb in the place where they kill the sin offering and the burnt offering in the holy sanctuary. For as the sin offering is the priest's, so is the guilt offering. It is most holy. And the priest shall take some of the blood of the guilt offering, and the priest shall put it on the tip of the right ear of him who is to be cleansed, and on the thumb of his right hand, and on the big toe of his right foot. And the priest shall take some of the log of oil and pour it into the palm of his own left hand. Then the priest shall dip his right finger in the oil that is in his left hand, and shall sprinkle from the oil with his finger seven times before the LORD. And some of the rest of the oil that is in his hand the priest shall put on the tip of the right ear of him who is to be cleansed, and on the thumb of his right hand, and on the big toe of his right foot, and on the blood of the guilt offering. And the rest of the oil that is in the priest's hand he shall pour upon the head of him who is to be cleansed, and the priest shall make atonement for him before the LORD.

The priest shall offer the sin offering, and make atonement for him who is to be cleansed from his *ceremonial* uncleanness, and afterward he shall kill the burnt offering. Then the priest shall offer the burnt offering and the grain offering on the altar, and the priest shall make atonement for him, and he shall be clean.

But if he is poor and cannot afford so much, then he shall take one male lamb for a guilt offering to be waved to make atonement for him, and one-tenth of an *ephah* of wheat flour mixed with oil for a grain offering, and a log of oil, and two turtledoves or two pigeons, such as he is able to afford. The one shall be a sin offering and the other a burnt offering.

He shall bring them on the eighth day for his cleansing to the priest at the entrance of the tent of meeting before the LORD. The priest shall take the lamb of the guilt offering, along with the log of oil, and the priest shall wave them for a wave offering before the LORD. Then he shall kill the lamb of the guilt offering; and the priest shall take some of the blood of the guilt offering and put it on the tip of the right ear of him who is to be cleansed and on the thumb of his right hand and on the big toe of his right foot. Next the priest shall pour some of the oil into the palm of his own left hand, and the priest shall sprinkle with his right finger some of the oil that is in his left hand seven times before the LORD. Then the priest shall put some of the oil that is in his hand on the tip of the right ear of him who is to be cleansed, and on the thumb of his right hand, and on the big toe of his right foot on the place of the blood of the guilt offering. The rest of the oil that is in the priest's hand he shall pour on the head of him who is to be cleansed to make atonement for him before the LORD. He shall offer one of the turtledoves or the pigeons, such as he can afford, even such as he is able to get, one for a sin offering and the other for a burnt offering, along with the grain offering, and the priest shall make atonement for him who is to be cleansed before the LORD.

This is the law for a person who has a leprous sore who cannot afford the offerings for his cleansing.

The LORD spoke to Moses and to Aaron, saying: When you have come into the land of Canaan, which I am giving to you for a possession, and I put a leprous disease in a house of the land of your possession, then he who owns the house shall come and tell the priest, "It seems to me there is some disease in the house." Then the priest shall command that they empty the house before the priest goes into it to examine the disease, so that all that is in the house is not made unclean. Afterwards, the priest shall go in to examine the house. He shall examine the disease and see if the disease is in the walls of the house with greenish or reddish spots, which appear to go deeper than the wall. Then the priest shall go out to the door of the house and close off the house seven days. The priest shall return on the seventh day and shall examine and see if the disease has spread in the walls of the house. Then the priest shall command that they take away the stones in which the disease appears and throw them into an unclean place outside the city. And he shall cause the house to be scraped all around, and they shall pour out the plaster that they scrape off outside the city into an unclean place. And they shall take other stones and put them in the place of those stones, and he shall take other plaster and shall plaster the house.

If the disease comes again and breaks out in the house after he has taken away the stones and after he has scraped the house and after it is plastered, then the priest shall come and examine and see if the disease has spread in the house. If the disease has spread in the house, it is a persistent leprosy in the house; it is unclean. He shall break down the house, the stones and the timber, and all the plaster of the house, and he shall carry them out of the city into an unclean place.

Moreover, he who goes into the house while it is closed off shall be unclean until the evening. And he who sleeps in the house shall wash his clothes, and he who eats in the house shall wash his clothes.

If the priest comes in and examines it and sees the disease has not spread in the house after the house was plastered, then the priest shall pronounce the house clean, because the disease is healed. He shall take two birds, and cedar wood, and scarlet, and hyssop to cleanse the house. Then he shall kill one of the birds in a clay vessel over running water. He shall take the cedar wood, and the hyssop, and the scarlet, and the living bird, and dip them in the blood of the slain bird, and in the running water, and sprinkle the house seven times. Then he shall cleanse the house with the blood of the bird, and with the running water, and with the living bird, and with the cedar wood, and with the hyssop, and with the scarlet. But he shall let the living bird loose outside the city into the open fields and make atonement for the house, and it shall be clean.

This is the law for all manner of leprous sore and scale, and for the disease of a garment, or of a house, and for a swelling, or for a scab, or for a spot, to discern when it is unclean and when it is clean.

This is the law of leprosy.

Then the Lord spoke to Moses and to Aaron, saying: Speak to the children of Israel, and say to them: When any man has a discharge out of his body, his discharge is unclean. This is the instruction for his uncleanness in his discharge, whether the discharge from his body flows or his body is stopped up by his discharge, it is his uncleanness.

Every bed on which the man with the discharge lies shall be unclean, and everything on which he sits shall be unclean. Whoever touches the bed shall wash his clothes, and bathe himself in water, and be unclean until the evening. And whoever sits on anything where the man sat who has the discharge shall wash his clothes, and bathe himself in water, and be unclean until the evening.

And whoever touches the body of him who has the discharge shall wash his clothes, and bathe himself in water, and be unclean until the evening.

If the man with the discharge spits on someone who is clean, then he shall wash his clothes, and bathe himself in water, and be unclean until the evening.

Any saddle on which the man with a discharge rides shall be unclean. Whoever touches anything that was under him shall be unclean until the evening, and he who carries any of those things shall wash his clothes, and bathe himself in water, and be unclean until the evening.

Whomever he who has the discharge touches, and has not rinsed his hands in water, he shall wash his clothes and bathe in water, and be unclean until evening.

The earthen vessel that he who has the discharge touches shall be broken, and every vessel of wood shall be rinsed in water.

When he who has a discharge is cleansed of his issue, then he shall count to himself seven days for his cleansing, and wash his clothes, and bathe his body in running water, and shall be clean. On the eighth day he shall take two turtledoves or two pigeons and come before the LORD at the entrance of the tent of meeting and give them to the priest. And the priest shall offer them, one for a sin offering and the other for a burnt offering, and the priest shall make atonement for him before the LORD for his discharge.

If any man has a seminal emission, then he shall wash all his body in water and be unclean until the evening. Every garment and all leather on which there is seminal emission shall be washed with water and be unclean until the evening. If a man lies with a woman, and there is an emission of semen, they shall both bathe themselves in water and be unclean until the evening.

If a woman has a discharge, and the discharge from her body is blood, she shall be set apart for seven days; and whoever touches her shall be unclean until the evening.

Everything that she lies on in her menstrual impurity shall be unclean. Also, everything that she sits on shall be unclean. Whoever touches her bed shall wash his clothes and bathe himself in water, and be unclean until the evening. Whoever touches anything on which she sits shall wash his clothes and bathe himself in water, and be unclean until the evening. Whether it is the bed or anything on which she sits, when he touches it he shall be unclean until the evening.

If any man lies with her, and her menstrual impurity is on him, he shall be unclean seven days, and every bed where he lies shall be unclean.

If a woman has a discharge of blood for many days, not at the time of her menstrual impurity, or if she has a discharge beyond the time of her impurity, all the days of the discharge she shall be in uncleanness, as in the days of her impurity. She shall be unclean. Every bed that she lies on all the days of her discharge shall be for impurity, and whatever she sits on shall be unclean, as the uncleanness of her menstrual impurity. Whoever touches those things shall be unclean and shall wash his clothes and bathe himself in water and be unclean until the evening.

But if she is cleansed of her discharge, then she shall count to herself seven days, and after that she shall be clean. On the eighth day she shall take two turtledoves or two pigeons and bring them to the priest at the entrance of the tent of meeting. The priest shall offer one for a sin offering and the other for a burnt offering, and the priest shall make atonement for her before the LORD for her unclean discharge.

Thus you shall separate the children of Israel from their uncleanness, so that they do not die in their uncleanness by defiling My tabernacle that is among them.

This is the law for him who has a discharge and for him who has a seminal emission and thus becomes unclean, and for her who is sick from her menstruation, and for him who has a discharge, for anyone male or female, and for the man who lies with a woman who is unclean.

Achrei Mot

After the death

(Leviticus 16:1–18:30)

The LORD spoke to Moses after the death of the two sons of Aaron, when they drew near to the LORD and died. The LORD said to Moses: Speak to Aaron your brother so that he does not come at any time into the Holy Place within the veil before the mercy seat, which is on the ark, so that he will not die, for I will appear in the cloud on the mercy seat.

Thus Aaron shall come into the Holy Place with a young bull for a sin offering and a ram for a burnt offering. He shall put on the holy linen tunic, and he shall have the linen undergarment on his body, and shall be girded with a linen sash, and shall be wearing the linen turban. These are holy garments. Therefore he shall wash his body in water and then put them on. He shall take from the congregation of the children of Israel two male goats for a sin offering and one ram for a burnt offering.

Aaron shall offer his bull for the sin offering, which is for himself, and make atonement for himself and for his house. Then he shall take the two goats and present them before the LORD at the entrance of the tent of meeting. Aaron shall cast lots for the two goats: one lot for the LORD and the other lot for the scapegoat. Aaron shall bring the goat on which the lot of the LORD falls and offer him for a sin offering. But the goat on which the lot falls to be the scapegoat shall be presented alive before the LORD to make atonement with it, that it may be sent away as a scapegoat into the wilderness.

Aaron shall bring the bull of the sin offering, which is for himself, and shall make atonement for himself, and for his house, and shall kill the bull of the sin offering for himself. And he shall take a censer full of burning coals of fire from the altar before the LORD, and two handfuls of sweet incense beaten small, and bring it within the veil. And he shall put the incense on the fire before the LORD, that the cloud of the incense may cover the mercy seat that is over the testimony, so that he does not die. And he shall take of the blood of the bull, and sprinkle it with his finger on the mercy seat on the eastern side, and before the mercy seat he shall sprinkle from the blood with his finger seven times.

Then he shall kill the goat of the sin offering, which is for the people, and bring its blood within the veil, and do with that blood as he did with the blood of the bull, and sprinkle it over and in front of the mercy seat. And he shall make atonement for the Holy Place, because of the uncleanness of the children of Israel and because of their transgressions in all their sins, and so he shall do for the tent of meeting that remains among them in the midst of their uncleanness. There shall be no man in the tent of meeting when he goes in to make atonement in the Holy Place, until he comes out and has made atonement for himself, and for his household, and for all the congregation of Israel.

Then he shall go out to the altar that is before the LORD and make atonement for it, and he shall take some of the blood of the bull and some of the blood of the goat, and put it on the horns of the altar all around. He shall sprinkle from the blood on it with his finger seven times, and cleanse it, and consecrate it from the uncleanness of the children of Israel.

When he has made an end of atonement for the Holy Place, and the tent of meeting, and the altar, then he shall bring the live goat. And Aaron shall lay both his hands on the head of the live goat, and confess over it all the iniquities of the children of Israel, and all their transgressions in all their sins, putting them on the head of the goat, and shall send it away by the hand of a designated man into the wilderness. And the goat shall bear on it all their iniquities to a desolate land, and he shall let the goat go free in the wilderness.

Then Aaron shall come into the tent of meeting, and shall take off the linen garments which he put on when he went into the Holy Place, and shall leave them there. And he shall wash his body with water in a holy place, and put on his garments, and come out, and offer his burnt offering, and the burnt offering of the people, and make atonement for himself and for the people. The fat of the sin offering he shall burn on the altar.

He who releases the goat as the scapegoat shall wash his clothes, and bathe his body in water, and afterward come into the camp. The bull for the sin offering and the goat for the sin offering, whose blood was brought in to make atonement in the Holy Place, shall be carried outside the camp. They shall burn in the fire their hides, their flesh, and their refuse. He who burns them shall wash his clothes, and bathe his body in water, and afterward he shall come into the camp.

This shall be a perpetual statute for you so that in the seventh month, on the tenth day of the month, you shall humble yourselves, and do no work of any kind, whether it is the native citizen or the stranger who sojourns among you. For on that day the priest shall make atonement for you to cleanse you, so that you may be clean from all your sins before the LORD. It shall be a sabbath, a solemn rest for you, and you shall humble yourselves. It is a perpetual statute. The priest, who is anointed and consecrated to minister as a priest in the place of his father, shall make atonement, and shall put on the linen garments, the holy garments. And he shall make atonement for the Holy Sanctuary, for the tent of meeting, and for the altar, and he shall make atonement for the priests, and for all the people of the congregation.

This shall be a perpetual statute for you to make atonement for the children of Israel for all their sins once a year.

And Moses did as the LORD commanded him.

And the LORD spoke to Moses, saying: Speak to Aaron, and to his sons, and to all the children of Israel, and say to them: This is the thing which the LORD has commanded, saying: If anyone of the house of Israel *ritually* slaughters an ox, a lamb, or goat in the camp, or slaughters it outside of the camp, and does not bring it to the entrance of the tent of meeting to offer it as a gift to the LORD before the tabernacle of the LORD, then blood guilt shall be accounted to that man. He has shed blood, and that man shall be cut off from among his people. This is so that the children of Israel may bring their sacrifices which they offer in the open field, even that they may bring them to the LORD at the entrance of the tent of meeting, to the priest, and offer them for peace offerings to the LORD. The priest shall sprinkle the blood on the altar of the LORD at the entrance of the tent of meeting, and burn the fat for a pleasing aroma to the LORD. They shall no more offer their sacrifices to goat demons, after whom they have acted like whores. This shall be a perpetual statute for them throughout their generations.

You shall say to them: Any man from the house of Israel, or from the foreigners who sojourn among you, who offers a burnt offering or sacrifice, and does not bring it to the entrance of the tent of meeting to offer it to the LORD, even that man shall be cut off from among his people.

Whoever from the house of Israel, or from the strangers who sojourn among you, who eats any manner of blood, I will set My face against that person who eats blood, and will cut him off from among his people. For the life of the flesh is in the blood, and I have given it to you on the altar to make atonement for your lives; for it is the blood that makes atonement for the soul. Therefore I said to the children of Israel: No person among you shall eat blood, nor shall any stranger who sojourns among you eat blood.

Whoever from the children of Israel, or from the foreigners who sojourn among you, who hunts and catches any wild animal or fowl that may be eaten, he shall even pour out the blood and cover it with dirt. For the life of every creature is its blood; in its blood is its life. Therefore I said to the children of Israel: You shall not eat the blood of any creature, for the life of every creature is its blood. Whoever eats it shall be cut off.

Every person who eats that which died of itself, or that which was torn by animals, whether he is a native citizen or a foreigner, he shall both wash his clothes and bathe himself in water, and be unclean until the evening. Then he shall be clean. But if he does not wash them or bathe his body, then he shall bear his iniquity.

The L<small>ORD</small> spoke to Moses, saying: Speak to the children of Israel, and say to them: I am the L<small>ORD</small> your God. After the practices of the land of Egypt, from where you lived, you shall not follow, and after the practices of the land of Canaan, to where I will bring you, you shall not follow; nor shall you walk in their ordinances. You shall follow My decrees and keep My ordinances to walk in them: I am the L<small>ORD</small> your God. You shall therefore keep My statutes and My judgments, which if a man does them, then he shall live by them: I am the L<small>ORD</small>.

None of you shall approach any of his near relatives to have relations: I am the L<small>ORD</small>.

You shall not have relations with your father or have relations with your mother. She is your mother. You shall not have relations with her.

You shall not have relations with your father's wife, for this exposes your father's nakedness.

You shall not have relations with your sister, whether your father's or mother's daughter, whether raised in the family or another home.

You shall not have relations with your son's daughter or your daughter's daughter, for this exposes your own nakedness.

You shall not have relations with your father's wife's daughter who is raised in your father's family, for she is your sister.

You shall not have relations with your father's sister, for she is your father's relative.

You shall not have relations with your mother's sister, for she is your mother's relative.

You shall not expose the nakedness of your father's brother. You shall not approach his wife for relations; she is your aunt.

You shall not have relations with your daughter-in-law, for she is your son's wife—you shall not have relations with her.

You shall not have relations with your brother's wife, for this exposes your brother's nakedness.

You shall not have relations with a woman and her daughter, nor shall you have her son's daughter or her daughter's daughter, for this exposes the woman's nakedness. They are all near relatives. It is depravity.

And you shall not have a woman as a rival wife, who is the sister of your other wife, for this is to expose her nakedness while her sister, your other wife, is still alive.

Also you shall not approach a woman to have relations as long as she is in her menstrual uncleanness.

Moreover, you shall not have relations with your neighbor's wife to defile yourself with her.

You shall not let any of your children be offered through the fire to Molech, and so profane the name of your God: I am the L<small>ORD</small>.

You shall not lie with a man as one does with a woman. It is an abomination.

You shall not lie with an animal to defile yourself, nor shall any woman lie with an animal. It is a perversion.

Do not defile yourselves in any of these ways, for in these practices the nations I am casting out before you have defiled themselves. And the land has become defiled; therefore I have punished its iniquity, and the land has vomited out her inhabitants. But you shall therefore keep My statutes and My decrees, and you shall not commit any of these abominations, either the native citizen or any foreigner who sojourns among you (for the people of the land, who were before you, committed all of these abominations, and the land became defiled), lest the land vomit you out also when you defile it, as it vomited out the nations that were before you.

For whoever shall commit any of these abominations, those persons who commit them shall be cut off from among their people. Therefore you shall keep My ordinances, that you do not commit any one of these abominable customs which were committed before you, so that you do not defile yourselves by them: I am the LORD your God.

Kedoshim

Holy ones

(Leviticus 19:1–20:27)

A nd the LORD spoke to Moses, saying: Speak to all the congregation of the children of Israel, and say to them: You shall be holy, for I the LORD your God am holy.

Every one of you shall revere his mother and his father, and you will keep My Sabbaths: I am the LORD your God.

Do not turn to idols, nor make for yourselves cast metal gods: I am the LORD your God.

When you offer a sacrifice of peace offerings to the LORD, you shall offer it so that you might be accepted. It shall be eaten the same day you offer it or on the next day, and if any remains until the third day, it shall be burned in the fire. If it is eaten at all on the third day, then it is contaminated. It shall not be accepted. Therefore everyone who eats it shall bear his iniquity, because he has defiled what is holy of the LORD, and that person shall be cut off from among his people.

When you reap the harvest of your land, you shall not reap up to the edge of your field, nor shall you gather the gleanings of your harvest. You shall not glean bare your vineyard, nor shall you gather every fallen grape of your vineyard. You shall leave them for the poor and stranger: I am the LORD your God.

You shall not steal, nor deal falsely, nor lie to one another.

You shall not swear falsely by My name, and so defile the name of your God: I am the LORD.

You shall not defraud your neighbor or rob him. The wages of him who is hired shall not stay with you all night until the morning.

You shall not curse the deaf, nor put a stumbling block before the blind, but you shall fear your God: I am the LORD.

You shall do no unrighteousness in a court. You shall not be partial to the poor, nor honor the person who is great, but in righteousness you shall judge your neighbor.

You shall not go around as a slanderer among your people, nor shall you stand by while the life of your neighbor is in danger: I am the LORD.

You shall not hate your brother in your heart. You shall surely reason honestly with your neighbor, and not suffer sin because of him.

You shall not take vengeance, nor bear any grudge against the children of your people, but you shall love your neighbor as yourself: I am the LORD.

You shall keep My statutes.

You shall not let your livestock breed with a different kind.

You shall not sow your field with mixed seed, nor shall your garment be mixed from two types of fabric.

Whoever lies with a slave woman who is betrothed to another man and not yet ransomed or given freedom, compensation will be made. They shall not be put to death, because she was not free. He shall bring his guilt offering to the LORD at the entrance of the tent of meeting, a ram for a guilt offering. The priest shall make atonement for him with the ram of the guilt offering before the LORD for his sin which he has done, and he will be forgiven for the sin that he has committed.

When you come into the land and plant any kind of tree for food, then you shall count the fruit as forbidden. Three years it shall be forbidden to you. It shall not be eaten. But in the fourth year all the fruit shall be holy and an offering of praise to the LORD. And in the fifth year you shall eat of the fruit that it may yield an increase to you: I am the LORD your God.

You shall not eat anything with the blood in it, nor shall you practice divination or fortune-telling.

You shall not round the corners of the hair on your head, nor shall you mar the edges of your beard.

You shall not make any cuttings in your flesh for the dead nor make any tattoo marks on yourselves: I am the LORD.

Do not prostitute your daughter and cause her to be defiled, lest the land fall into whoredom and become full of wickedness.

You shall keep My Sabbaths and revere My sanctuary: I am the LORD.

Do not turn to spirits through mediums or necromancers. Do not seek after them to be defiled by them: I am the LORD your God.

You shall rise up before a gray head, and honor the face of an old man, and fear your God: I am the LORD.

When a foreigner sojourns with you in your land, you shall not do him wrong. The foreigner who dwells with you shall be to you as one born among you, and you shall love him as yourself for you were foreigners in the land of Egypt: I am the LORD your God.

You shall do no unrighteousness in judgment regarding measures in length, weight, or quantity. You shall have honest balances, honest weights, an honest ephah, and an honest hin: I am the LORD your God, who brought you out of the land of Egypt.

Therefore you shall observe all My statutes and all My judgments and do them: I am the LORD.

Then the LORD spoke to Moses, saying: Again, you shall say to the children of Israel: Whoever from the children of Israel or from the foreigners who sojourn in Israel who gives any of his children to Molech, he shall surely be put to death. The people of the land shall stone him. I will set My face against that man and will cut him off from among his people, because he has given some of his descendants to Molech to defile My sanctuary and to defile My holy name. If the people of the land in any way hide their eyes from the man when he gives of his children to Molech and do not put him to death, then I will set My face against that man and against his family; and I will cut them off from their people, both him and those who follow after him as whores after Molech.

The person who turns to spirits through mediums and necromancers in order to whore after them, I will even set My face against that person and will cut him off from among his people.

Consecrate yourselves therefore, and be holy, for I am the LORD your God. You shall keep My statutes, and do them; I am the LORD who sanctifies you.

For anyone who curses his father or his mother shall be surely put to death. He has cursed his father or his mother, and his blood guilt shall be upon him.

If a man commits adultery with another man's wife, even he who commits adultery with his neighbor's wife, the adulterer and the adulteress shall surely be put to death.

If a man lies with his father's wife, he has exposed his father's nakedness. Both of them shall surely be put to death. Their blood guilt shall be upon them.

If a man lies with his daughter-in-law, both of them shall surely be put to death. They have committed a perversion. Their blood guilt shall be upon them.

If a man lies with another man as with a woman, both of them have committed an abomination. They shall surely be put to death. Their blood guilt shall be upon them.

If a man lies with a woman and also her mother, it is wickedness. Both he and they shall be burned with fire, so that there is no wickedness among you.

If a man lies with an animal, he shall surely be put to death, and you shall kill the animal.

If a woman approaches an animal and lies with it, you shall kill the woman and the animal. They shall surely be put to death. Their blood guilt shall be upon them.

If a man lies with his sister, whether the daughter of his father or mother, they have exposed each other's nakedness; it is a wicked thing and they shall be cut off from the sight of their people. He has exposed his sister's nakedness, and he shall bear his iniquity.

If a man lies with a woman during her menstrual period and exposes her nakedness, her fountain of blood is then exposed. Both of them shall be cut off from among their people.

You shall not have relations with your mother's sister or your father's sister, for this is to expose the nakedness of one's relative. They shall bear their iniquity.

If a man lies with his uncle's wife, he has exposed his uncle's nakedness. They shall bear their sin. They shall die childless.

If a man lies with his brother's wife, it is impurity. He has exposed his brother's nakedness. They shall be childless.

You shall therefore keep all My statutes and all My decrees and do them, so that the land to where I am bringing you will not vomit you out. You shall not walk in the customs of the nation that I am driving out before you, for they committed all these things, and therefore I abhorred them. But I have said to you: You shall inherit their land, and I will give it to you to possess it, a land that flows with milk and honey. I am the LORD your God, who has separated you from other peoples.

You shall therefore make distinction between the clean animal from the unclean, and the unclean fowl from the clean, and you shall not make yourselves detestable by animal, or by fowl, or by any manner of living thing that crawls on the ground, which I have separated from you as unclean. You shall be holy unto Me; for I the LORD am holy and have separated you from other peoples, that you should be Mine.

A man or woman who speaks to spirits as a medium or necromancer shall surely be put to death. They shall stone them. Their blood guilt shall be upon them.

Emor

Say gently

(Leviticus 21:1–24:23)

Then the LORD said to Moses: Speak to the priests, the sons of Aaron, and say to them: None shall make himself unclean for the dead among his people, but for his closest relatives, that is, for his mother, his father, his son, his daughter, his brother, and his virgin sister (who is near him because she has not had a husband), for her he may be made unclean. And he shall not make himself unclean as a husband among his people *because of the dead* and so defile himself.

They shall not make bald areas on their heads, nor shall they shave off the edges of their beards, nor make any cuts in their flesh. They shall be holy unto their God, and not profane the name of their God; for they offer the offerings of the LORD made by fire, and the food of their God. Therefore they shall be holy.

They shall not take a wife who is a whore or has been defiled, nor shall they take a woman divorced from her husband, for he is holy unto his God. You shall sanctify him, for he offers the food of your God. He shall be holy to you, for I the LORD, who sanctifies you, am holy.

The daughter of any priest, if she defiles herself by being a whore, she also defiles her father. She shall be burned with fire.

He who is the high priest among his brothers, on whose head the anointing oil was poured and who is consecrated to wear the garments, shall not dishevel his hair, nor tear his clothes; nor shall he approach any dead body, nor make himself unclean, even for his father or his mother; nor shall he go out of the sanctuary, so as not to defile the sanctuary of his God, for the consecration of the anointing oil of his God is upon him: I am the LORD.

He shall take a wife in her virginity. A widow, or a divorced woman, or a defiled woman, or a prostitute, these he shall not marry. But he shall take for a wife a virgin of his own people, so that he does not defile his offspring among his people, for I am the LORD who sanctifies him.

The LORD spoke to Moses, saying: Speak to Aaron, saying: None of your offspring in their generations who has any blemish may approach to offer the food of his God. For whoever has a blemish, he shall not approach, whether a blind or lame man, or one who has a physical flaw on his face or a limb that is too long, or a man who has a broken foot or broken hand, or a hunchback, or a dwarf, or who has a defect in his eye, or eczema or scabs, or is a eunuch. No man who has a blemish from the offspring of Aaron the priest shall come near to offer the food offerings of the LORD made by fire. He has a blemish; he shall not come near to offer the bread of his God. He shall eat the food of his God, both of the most holy and of the holy. Only he shall not go in through the veil or come to the altar, because he has a blemish, so that he does not defile My sanctuaries, for I am the LORD who sanctifies them.

Moses spoke this to Aaron, and to his sons, and to all the children of Israel.

And the LORD spoke to Moses, saying: Speak to Aaron and to his sons that they should be very respectful with the holy things of the children of Israel, and that they do not defile My holy name with those things which the people have consecrated to Me: I am the LORD.

Say to them: Whoever from your offspring through your generations approaches the holy things, which the children of Israel have dedicated to the LORD, while he has uncleanness, that person shall be cut off from My presence: I am the LORD.

If a man of the offspring of Aaron is a leper or has a discharge, he shall not eat of the holy offerings until he is clean. And whoever touches anything that is unclean by contact with the dead or a man who had an emission of semen, or whoever touches any crawling thing whereby he may be made unclean, or a man from whom he may receive uncleanness, whatever uncleanness he has, the person who has touched any such thing shall be unclean until evening, and shall not eat of the holy things unless he washes his body with water. When the sun goes down, he shall be clean, and afterward he shall eat of the holy things, because it is his food. That which dies of itself or is torn by animals he shall not eat, becoming unclean by it: I am the LORD.

They shall therefore keep My ordinance, lest they bear sin from it and therefore die if they defile it: I am the LORD who sanctifies them.

There shall be no outsider who eats of a holy thing, whether a foreign guest of the priest or a hired servant, he shall not eat of a holy offering. But if a priest buys a person with his money, the person acquired shall eat of it, and he that is born in his house shall eat of his food. If the priest's daughter marries an outsider, she may not eat of an offering of the holy things. But if the priest's daughter is a widow or divorced, and has no child and has returned to her father's house as in her youth, she may eat of her father's food; but no outsider may eat of it.

If a man eats the holy thing unwittingly, then he shall add one-fifth of the value to it and shall give the holy thing to the priest. They shall not defile the holy things of the children of Israel, which they offer to the LORD, and cause them to suffer and to bear the iniquity of guilt when they eat their holy things, for I am the LORD who sanctifies them.

The LORD spoke to Moses, saying: Speak to Aaron, and to his sons, and to all the children of Israel, and say to them: Whoever from the house of Israel or from the foreigners in Israel who offers his burnt offering for any vows or freewill offerings that he offers to the LORD, then if it is to be accepted for you, the offering shall be a male without blemish, a bull, sheep, or goat. But whatever has a blemish you shall not offer, for it shall not be acceptable for you. Whoever offers a sacrifice of peace offerings to the LORD to fulfill his vow or a freewill offering, whether from the herd or flock, to be accepted it shall be perfect, with no blemish on it. Blind, or disabled, or maimed, or having an ulcer or eczema or scabs, you shall not offer these to the LORD, nor make a food offering by fire on the altar to the LORD. A herd animal or a flock animal that has a limb that is too long or short you may offer for a freewill offering, but for a vow it shall not be accepted. You shall not offer to the LORD an animal that is bruised or crushed or torn or cut; nor shall you make any offering of them in your land. Nor from a foreigner shall you offer an animal as the food of your God, because a blemish is in them from their mutilation. They shall not be accepted for you.

The LORD spoke to Moses, saying: When an ox, or a sheep, or a goat is born, then it shall be seven days with its mother, and from the eighth day and thereafter it shall be accepted for a food offering made by fire to the LORD. But you shall not slaughter on the same day an ox or a sheep and her young.

When you offer a sacrifice of thanksgiving to the LORD, offer it so that it may be accepted. On the same day it shall be eaten. You shall leave none of it until the next day: I am the LORD.

Therefore you shall keep My commandments and do them: I am the LORD. You shall not defile My holy name, but I will be sanctified among the children of Israel: I am the LORD who sanctifies you, who brought you out of the land of Egypt, to be your God: I am the LORD.

And the LORD spoke to Moses, saying: Speak to the children of Israel, and say to them: Concerning the feasts of the LORD that you shall proclaim to be holy convocations, these are My appointed feasts.

For six days work shall be done, but the seventh day is the Sabbath of complete rest, a holy convocation. You shall do no work. It is the Sabbath of the LORD in all your dwellings.

These are the appointed feasts of the LORD, holy convocations which you shall proclaim in their appointed times. On the fourteenth day of the first month at evening is the LORD's Passover. On the fifteenth day of the same month is the Feast of Unleavened Bread to the LORD. For seven days you must eat unleavened bread. On the first day you shall have a holy convocation. You shall do no regular work. But you shall offer a food offering made by fire to the LORD for seven days. On the seventh day is a holy convocation. You shall do no regular work.

The LORD spoke to Moses, saying: Speak to the children of Israel, and say to them: When you have come into the land that I am giving to you and reap its harvest, then you shall bring a sheaf bundle of the first fruits of your harvest to the priest. And he shall wave the sheaf before the LORD so that you may be accepted. On the day after the Sabbath the priest shall wave it. You shall offer that day when you wave the sheaf a year-old male lamb without blemish for a burnt offering to the LORD. The grain offering shall be two-tenths of an ephah of wheat flour mixed with oil, a food offering made by fire to the LORD for a pleasing aroma; its drink offering shall be of wine, one-fourth of a hin. You shall eat neither bread nor grain, parched or fresh, until the same day that you have brought an offering to your God. It shall be a perpetual statute throughout your generations in all your dwellings.

You shall count seven full weeks from the next day after the Sabbath, from the day that you brought the sheaf bundle of the wave offering. You shall count fifty days to the day after the seventh Sabbath; then you shall offer a new grain offering to the LORD. You shall bring out of your habitations two wave loaves of two-tenths of an ephah. They shall be of wheat flour, baked with leaven. They are the first fruits to the LORD. You shall offer with the bread seven lambs without blemish of the first year, one bull, and two rams. They shall be for a burnt offering to the LORD, with their grain offering and their drink offerings, that is, a food offering made by fire, of a pleasing aroma to the LORD. Then you shall sacrifice one male goat for a sin offering, and two lambs of the first year for a sacrifice of peace offerings. The priest shall wave them with the bread of the first fruits for a wave offering before the LORD with the two lambs. They shall be holy to the LORD for the priest. You shall make a proclamation on the same day and shall hold a holy convocation. You shall do no regular work. It shall be a perpetual statute in all your dwellings throughout your generations.

When you reap the harvest of your land, you shall not reap your field up to the edge, nor shall you gather any gleaning of your harvest. You shall leave them to the poor and to the foreigner: I am the LORD your God.

The LORD spoke to Moses, saying: Speak to the children of Israel, saying: In the seventh month, on the first day of the month, you shall have a sabbath, a memorial with the blowing of trumpets, a holy convocation. You shall do no regular work, and you shall offer a food offering made by fire to the LORD.

The LORD spoke to Moses, saying: Also on the tenth day of this seventh month there shall be the Day of Atonement. It shall be a holy convocation to you, and you shall humble yourselves, and offer a food offering made by fire to the LORD. You shall do no work on that same day, for it is the Day of Atonement to make atonement for you before the LORD your God. For whoever is not humbled on that same day, he shall be cut off from among his people. And whoever does any work in that same day, that person I will destroy from among his people. You shall do no manner of work. It shall be a perpetual statute throughout your generations in all your dwellings. It shall be to you a sabbath of complete rest, and you shall afflict your souls. On the ninth day of the month starting at the evening, from evening to evening, you shall celebrate your sabbath.

The LORD spoke to Moses, saying: Speak to the children of Israel, saying: The fifteenth day of this seventh month shall be the Feast of Tabernacles for seven days to the LORD. On the first day shall be a holy convocation. You shall do no regular work. For seven days you shall offer food offerings made by fire to the LORD. On the eighth day it shall be a holy convocation to you, and you shall offer a food offering made by fire to the LORD. It is a solemn assembly, and you shall do no regular work.

These are the appointed feasts of the LORD, which you shall proclaim to be holy convocations, to offer a food offering made by fire to the LORD, burnt offerings and grain offerings, sacrifices and drink offerings, each on its proper day, besides the Sabbaths of the LORD, besides your gifts, besides all your vows, and besides all your freewill offerings which you give to the LORD.

On the fifteenth day of the seventh month, when you have gathered in the produce of the land, you shall keep a feast to the LORD for seven days. On the first day shall be a sabbath, and on the eighth day shall be a sabbath. You shall take on the first day the branches of majestic trees—branches of palm trees, branches of leafy trees, and willows from a brook, and you shall rejoice before the LORD your God for seven days. You shall keep it as a feast to the LORD for seven days in the year. It shall be a perpetual statute in your generations. You shall celebrate it in the seventh month. You shall dwell in booths for seven days. All who are native children of Israel shall dwell in booths, that your generations may know that I made the children of Israel dwell in booths when I brought them out of the land of Egypt: I am the LORD your God.

Moses declared to the children of Israel the feasts of the LORD.

And the LORD spoke to Moses, saying: Command the children of Israel that they bring to you pure olive oil beaten for the lamp, to cause the lamps to burn continually. Outside the veil of the sanctuary, in the tent of meeting, Aaron shall arrange it continually, from the evening until the morning before the LORD. It shall be a perpetual statute in your generations. He shall arrange the lamps continually on the pure *gold* lampstand before the LORD.

You shall take wheat flour and bake twelve cakes. Two-tenths of an ephah shall be in each cake. You shall set them in two rows, six in a row, on the pure *gold* table before the LORD. You shall put pure frankincense on each row, so that it may be on the bread for a memorial, a food offering made by fire to the LORD. Every Sabbath he shall set it in order continually before the LORD, with the portion taken from the children of Israel by a perpetual covenant. It shall be for Aaron and his sons, and they shall eat it in a holy place, for it is most holy to him of the food offerings of the LORD made by fire by a perpetual statute.

The son of an Israelite woman, whose father was an Egyptian, went out among the children of Israel, and this son of the Israelite woman and a man of Israel fought together in the camp. And the Israelite woman's son blasphemed the name of the LORD and cursed. And they brought him to Moses. (His mother's name was Shelomith, the daughter of Dibri, of the tribe of Dan.) And they put him in custody, so that the words of the LORD might be shown to them.

The LORD spoke to Moses, saying: Bring outside the camp him who has cursed, and let all who heard him lay their hands on his head, and let the entire congregation stone him. You shall speak to the children of Israel, saying: Whoever curses his God shall bear his sin. Whoever blasphemes the name of the LORD, he shall surely be put to death, and the entire congregation shall certainly stone him. The foreigner as well as the native in the land, when he blasphemes the name, then he shall be put to death.

Whoever kills any man shall surely be put to death. Whoever kills an animal shall make restitution, animal for animal. If anyone causes injury to his neighbor, as he has done, so shall it be done to him, fracture for fracture, eye for eye, tooth for tooth; as he has caused an injury to another, so shall it be done to him. Whoever kills an animal shall make restitution. And whoever kills a man shall be put to death. You shall have one manner of law for the foreigner as for the native, for I am the LORD your God.

So Moses spoke to the children of Israel, and they brought outside the camp him who had cursed, and stoned him. And the children of Israel did as the LORD commanded Moses.

Behar

On the Mountain

(Leviticus 25:1–26:2)

Then the LORD spoke to Moses on Mount Sinai, saying: Speak to the children of Israel, and say to them: When you come into the land that I give you, the land shall keep a sabbath to the LORD. For six years you shall sow your field, and six years you shall prune your vineyard and gather in its fruit, but in the seventh year there shall be a sabbath of complete rest for the land, a sabbath for the LORD. You shall neither sow your field nor prune your vineyard. That which grows by itself from your harvest you shall not reap, nor gather the grapes of your unpruned vines, for it is a year of complete rest for the land. The sabbath produce of the land shall be food for you: for you, and for your male and female servants, and for your hired servant, and for your stranger who sojourns with you, and for your livestock, and for the wild animals in your land, shall all its increase be food.

You shall count seven *sabbath* weeks of years, seven times seven years, and the time of the seven sabbaths of years shall be to you forty-nine years. Then you shall sound the horn blasts on the tenth day of the seventh month. On the Day of Atonement you shall make the sound of the horn throughout all your land. You shall consecrate the fiftieth year, and proclaim liberty throughout all the land to all the inhabitants. It shall be a Jubilee to you, and each of you shall return to his possession, and every person shall return to his family. That fiftieth year will be a Jubilee for you. You shall neither sow nor reap that which grows by itself, nor gather the grapes of your unpruned vines. For it is the Jubilee. It shall be holy to you. You shall eat the produce of the field.

In the Year of Jubilee you shall return to your property.

If you sell anything to your neighbor or buy anything from your neighbor, you shall not oppress one another. According to the number of years after the Jubilee you shall pay your neighbor, and according to the number of years of the crops he shall sell to you. According to the increase of years you shall increase the price, and according to the decrease of years you shall diminish the price of it. For he shall sell to you according to the number of years of crops. You shall not therefore oppress one another, but you shall fear your God. For I am the LORD your God.

Therefore you shall do My statutes, and keep My decrees, and do them, and you shall dwell securely in the land. The land shall yield its fruit, and you shall eat your fill and live securely in it. If you shall say, "What shall we eat in the seventh year, if we shall not sow nor gather in our crop?" then I will command My blessing upon you in the sixth year, and it shall bring forth produce for three years. You shall sow in the eighth year, and eat yet of old crops until the ninth year until its crops come in for you.

The land shall not be permanently sold, for the land is Mine. For you are foreigners and sojourners with Me. In all the land of your possession you shall grant a redemption for the land.

If your brother becomes poor and has sold some of his possession, then his nearest redeemer will come to redeem it, and buy back that which his brother sold. If the man has none to redeem it, but he himself is able to redeem it, then let him count the years since the sale and pay back the balance to the man to whom he sold it, so that he may return to his property. But if he is not able to restore it to himself, then that which he sold shall remain in the hand of him who has bought it until the Year of Jubilee, and in the Jubilee it shall be released, and he shall return to his possession.

If a man sells a house in a walled city, then he may redeem it within a year after it is sold, within a full year he may have the right to buy it back. If it is not redeemed within the time of a full year, then the house that is in the walled city shall be given permanently to him who bought it throughout his generations. It shall not be returned in the Jubilee. But the houses of the villages that have no wall around them shall be counted as the fields of the land. They may be redeemed, and they shall be returned in the Jubilee.

For the cities of the Levites, they may redeem at any time the houses in the cities that they possess. If a Levite purchases back the house that was sold in the city of his possession, then it shall be returned in the Jubilee. For the houses of the cities of the Levites are their possession among the children of Israel. But the fields of the land of their cities may not be sold, for they are their perpetual possession.

If your brother becomes poor and cannot maintain himself with you, then you shall support him as if he were a foreigner or a sojourner, so that he may live with you. Take no usury or interest from him; but fear your God, so that your brother may live with you. You shall not lend him your money at interest, nor lend him your food for profit. I am the LORD your God, who brought you out of the land of Egypt, to give you the land of Canaan and to be your God.

If your brother who dwells near you becomes poor and sells himself to you, you shall not compel him to serve as a bondservant. But as a hired servant and as a sojourner he shall be with you. He shall serve you until the Year of Jubilee. And then he shall depart from you, both he and his children with him, and he shall return to his own family and to the possession of his fathers. For they are My servants, whom I brought out of the land of Egypt. They shall not be sold as slaves. You shall not rule over him with harshness, but you shall fear your God.

Both your male and female slaves, whom you may have, they shall be bought from the nations that are around you. Moreover of the foreigners who sojourn among you and of their families who are with you, who were born in your land, you may also buy from them, and they may be your possession. You may take them as an inheritance for your children after you, for their possession. They shall be your slaves forever. But over your brothers, the children of Israel, you shall not rule over one another with rigor.

If a sojourner or foreigner becomes rich by you, and your brother who dwells beside him becomes poor and sells himself to the foreigner or sojourner with you, or to a member of the stranger's family, then after he is sold he may be redeemed again. One of his brothers may redeem him, or either his uncle or his cousin may redeem him, or any who is near of kin to him of his family may redeem him. Or if he is able, he may redeem himself. He shall calculate with him who bought him from the year that he was sold to the Year of Jubilee, and the price of his sale shall be according to the number of years, according to the time of a hired servant. If there are still many years left *until the Jubilee*, he shall pay the price proportionately for his redemption as some of the price that he was bought for. If there remain but a few years until the Year of Jubilee, then he shall calculate and pay the price proportionately for his redemption according to his years of service. As a yearly hired servant he shall be treated, and the other shall not rule harshly over him in your sight.

If he is not redeemed in these years, then he shall go out in the Year of Jubilee, both he and his children with him. For to Me the children of Israel are servants. They are My servants whom I brought out of the land of Egypt: I am the LORD your God.

You shall not make for yourselves idols; neither set up a carved image nor a standing stone, nor shall you set up any sculpted stone in your land to bow down to it, for I am the LORD your God.

You shall keep My Sabbaths and reverence My sanctuary: I am the LORD.

Bechukotai

In My statutes

(Leviticus 26:3–27:34)

I f you walk in My statutes and keep My commandments and do them, then I will give you rain in due season, and the land shall yield its increase, and the trees of the field shall yield their fruit. Your threshing shall last till the grape harvest, and the grape harvest shall last till the time for sowing, and you shall eat your bread till you are full and dwell in your land safely.

I will give peace in the land, and you shall lie down *for sleep*, and none shall make you afraid; I will remove harmful beasts from the land, and the sword shall not go through your land. You shall chase your enemies, and they shall fall before you by the sword. Five of you shall chase one hundred, and one hundred of you shall put ten thousand to flight, and your enemies shall fall before you by the sword.

I will turn toward you and make you fruitful and multiply you, and I will confirm My covenant with you. You shall eat the old harvest long stored, and clear out the old to make way for the new. I will set My tabernacle among you, and I shall not abhor you. I will walk among you, and I will be your God, and you shall be My people. I am the LORD your God, who brought you out of the land of Egypt, that you should not be their slaves, and I have broken the bars of your yoke and made you walk upright.

But if you will not listen to Me, and will not do all these commandments, if you despise My statutes, or if you abhor My judgments, so that you will not do all My commandments, but you break My covenant, then I will do this to you: I will visit you with terror, with wasting disease, and with a fever that shall consume the eyes and cause sorrow of heart, and you shall sow your seed in vain, for your enemies shall eat it. I will set My face against you, and you shall be slain before your enemies. They that hate you shall reign over you, and you shall flee when none pursues you.

If you will not yet listen to Me after all this, then I will punish you seven times more for your sins. I will break the pride of your power, and I will make your heaven as iron and your land as bronze. Your strength shall be spent in vain, for your land shall not yield her increase, nor shall the trees of the land yield their fruits.

If you continue to walk contrary to Me and will not listen to Me, I will bring seven times more plagues upon you according to your sins. I will also send wild beasts among you, which shall rob you of your children, destroy your livestock, and make you few in number. And your roads shall be desolate.

And if by these things you are not turned to Me, but walk contrary to Me, then I will also walk contrary to you and will punish you yet seven times for your sins. I will bring a sword upon you that shall extract vengeance for My covenant. And when you are gathered together within your cities, I will send pestilence among you, and you shall be delivered into the hand of the enemy. When I have broken the supply of your bread, ten women shall bake your bread in one oven, and they shall ration your bread again by weight, and you shall eat and not be satisfied.

If you will not listen to Me for all this, but walk contrary to Me, then I will walk contrary to you also in fury, and I Myself will chastise you seven times for your sins. You shall eat the flesh of your sons and the flesh of your daughters. I will destroy your high places, and cut down your images, and cast your funeral offerings on the lifeless forms of your idols, and I shall abhor you. I will make your cities a waste and bring your sanctuaries to desolation, and I will not smell the aroma of your fragrant offerings. I will bring the land into desolation, and your enemies that dwell there shall be astonished at it. I will scatter you among the nations and I will draw out a sword after you. And your land shall be desolate and your cities a waste. Then the land shall enjoy its sabbaths as long as it lies desolate, while you are in your enemies' land; then the land shall rest and enjoy its sabbaths. As long as it lies desolate it shall rest because it did not rest during your sabbaths when you lived upon it.

And on those who are left alive of you I will send faintness into their hearts in the lands of their enemies; and the sound of a shaken leaf shall make them flee, and they shall flee as from a sword, and they shall fall when no one pursues. They shall fall one upon one another, as to escape before the sword, though no one pursues, and you shall have no power to stand before your enemies. You shall perish among the nations, and the land of your enemies shall consume you. And those who are left of you shall rot away in their iniquity in your enemies' lands, and also because of the iniquities of their fathers, they shall rot away with them.

But if they confess their iniquity, and the iniquity of their fathers, with their treachery that they committed against Me, and also that they have walked contrary to Me, and that I also have walked contrary to them and have brought them into the land of their enemies; if then their uncircumcised hearts are humbled, and they then accept the punishment of their iniquity, then will I remember My covenant with Jacob, and also My covenant with Isaac, and also My covenant with Abraham, and I will remember the land. But the land shall be abandoned by them, and enjoy its sabbaths while it lies desolate without them. They shall make amends for their iniquity, because they despised My judgments and because they abhorred My statutes. Yet for all that, when they are in the land of their enemies, I will not cast them away, nor will I abhor them to destroy them utterly and to break My covenant with them, for I am the LORD their God. But for their sake I will remember the covenant with their fathers, whom I brought out of the land of Egypt in the sight of the nations, that I might be their God: I am the LORD.

These are the statutes and judgments and laws that the LORD made between Himself and the children of Israel on Mount Sinai by the hand of Moses.

And the LORD spoke to Moses, saying: Speak to the children of Israel, and say to them: When a man makes a special vow to the LORD based on the equivalent value of persons, then the equivalent value of a male from twenty to sixty years old shall be fifty shekels of silver, according to the sanctuary shekel. If the person is a female, then the equivalent value shall be thirty shekels. If the person is five to twenty years old, then the equivalent value shall be twenty shekels for a male and ten shekels for a female. If the person is one month to five years old, then the equivalent value shall be five shekels for a male and three shekels of silver for a female. If the person is sixty years old or older, then the equivalent value shall be fifteen shekels for a male and ten shekels for a female. But if he is too poor *to afford* the equivalent value, then he shall present himself before the priest and the priest shall set his value. According to what the person making the vow can afford, so the priest shall set his value.

And if it be an animal, of which men bring an offering to the LORD, all that any man gives of such to the LORD shall be holy. He shall not exchange it nor substitute it, good for bad or bad for good. If he in fact substitutes an animal for another, then both it and its substitute shall be holy. If it is any sort of unclean animal that is not permitted as an offering to the LORD, then he shall present the animal before the priest. And the priest shall set its value, whether good or bad; according to the equivalent value set by the priest, so shall it be. But if he plans on redeeming it, then he shall add one-fifth to the equivalent value.

When a man consecrates his house as holy to the LORD, then the priest shall set its value, whether good or bad, according to the equivalent value set by the priest, so shall it be established. If he who consecrates the house should redeem it, then he shall add one-fifth to its equivalent value, and it shall be his.

If a man shall consecrate to the LORD some of his land, then the equivalent value shall be according to the seed *needed to sow it*: fifty shekels of silver per homer of barley seed. If he consecrates his field from the Year of Jubilee, the equivalent value shall stay fixed, but if he consecrates his field

after the Jubilee, then the priest shall calculate for him the price according
to the years that remain until the *next* Year of Jubilee, and the equivalent value shall be reduced. And if he who consecrated the field plans on
redeeming it, then he shall add one-fifth to the equivalent value, and it will
be established as his. If he does not redeem the field, but rather sells the
field to another man, it may not be redeemed again. But when the field
is released in the Jubilee, it shall be holy to the Lord as a devoted field; it
shall become the possession of the priest.

If a man consecrates to the Lord a field that he purchased, which is not
part of his land property, then the priest shall calculate for him the amount
of the valuation, up to the Year of Jubilee, and he shall give your valuation
on that day as a holy thing to the Lord. In the Year of Jubilee the field shall
return to the one from whom it was bought, to him to whom the property
of land belongs. All your estimations shall be according to the shekel of the
sanctuary: Twenty gerahs shall be one shekel.

A firstborn of animals, which as firstborn belongs to the Lord, no man
may consecrate; whether ox or sheep, it is the Lord's. If it is among the
unclean animals, then he shall ransom it at the equivalent value and shall
add one-fifth to it, but if it is not redeemed, then it shall be sold at the
equivalent value.

Anything that a man shall devote to the Lord from all that he has, whether
human, animal, or land, shall not be sold or redeemed. Every devoted thing
is most holy to the Lord.

No one devoted of men, who shall be doomed to death, shall be
redeemed; he shall surely be put to death.

Any tithe of the land, whether seed of the land or fruit of the trees,
belongs to the Lord. It is holy to the Lord. If a man plans on redeeming
some of his tithe, he shall add one-fifth to it. Any tithe of herd or flock, all
that passes under the *counting* staff, the tenth one shall be holy to the Lord.
A person shall not differentiate between good or bad, nor shall he make a
substitute for it, but if he does, then both it and its substitute shall be holy.
It shall not be redeemed.

These are the commandments that the Lord commanded Moses for the
children of Israel on Mount Sinai.

Bamidbar

In the wilderness

(Numbers 1:1–4:20)

A nd the LORD spoke to Moses in the Wilderness of Sinai in the tent of meeting on the first day of the second month in the second year after they went out from the land of Egypt, saying: Take the sum of all the congregation of the children of Israel, after their families, by the house of their fathers, with the number of their names, every male by their polls, from twenty years old and upward, all who are able to go out to war in Israel. You and Aaron will number them by their armies. With you there will be a man of every tribe, each one the head of his father's house. These are the names of the men who will stand with you:

of the tribe of Reuben, Elizur the son of Shedeur;
of Simeon, Shelumiel the son of Zurishaddai;
of Judah, Nahshon the son of Amminadab;
of Issachar, Nethanel the son of Zuar;
of Zebulun, Eliab the son of Helon;
of the children of Joseph:
    of Ephraim, Elishama the son of Ammihud;
    of Manasseh, Gamaliel the son of Pedahzur;
of Benjamin, Abidan the son of Gideoni;
of Dan, Ahiezer the son of Ammishaddai;
of Asher, Pagiel the son of Okran;
of Gad, Eliasaph the son of Deuel;
of Naphtali, Ahira the son of Enan.

These were the renowned of the congregation, leaders of the tribes of their fathers, heads of thousands in Israel.

Moses and Aaron took these men who had been mentioned by name, and they assembled all the congregation on the first day of the second month, and they declared their pedigrees according to their families, by the house of their fathers, according to the number of the names, from twenty years old and upward, by their polls. As the LORD commanded Moses, so he numbered them in the Wilderness of Sinai.

The children of Reuben, the oldest son of Israel,
   by their generations, after their families, by the house of their fathers,
   according to the number of the names, by their polls, every male from
   twenty years old and upward, all who were able to go out to war, those
   who were numbered of them, even of the tribe of Reuben, were forty-six
   thousand five hundred.

Of the children of Simeon,
   by their generations, after their families, by the house of their fathers,
   those who were numbered of them, according to the number of the
   names, by their polls, every male from twenty years old and upward, all
   who were able to go out to war, those who were numbered of them,
   even of the tribe of Simeon, were fifty-nine thousand three hundred.

Of the children of Gad,
   by their generations, after their families, by the house of their fathers,
   according to the number of the names, from twenty years old and upward,
   all who were able to go out to war, those who were numbered of them,
   even of the tribe of Gad, were forty-five thousand six hundred fifty.

Of the children of Judah,
   by their generations, after their families, by the house of their fathers,
   according to the number of the names, from twenty years old and upward,
   all who were able to go out to war, those who were numbered of them,
   even of the tribe of Judah, were seventy-four thousand six hundred.

Of the children of Issachar,
   by their generations, after their families, by the house of their fathers,
   according to the number of the names, from twenty years old and upward,
   all who were able to go out to war, those who were numbered of them,
   even of the tribe of Issachar, were fifty-four thousand four hundred.

Of the children of Zebulun,
   by their generations, after their families, by the house of their fathers,
   according to the number of the names, from twenty years old and
   upward, all who were able to go out to war, those who were numbered
   of them, even of the tribe of Zebulun, were fifty-seven thousand four
   hundred.

Of the children of Joseph,
namely, of the children of Ephraim,
   by their generations, after their families, by the house of their fathers,
   according to the number of the names, from twenty years old and

upward, all who were able to go out to war, those who were numbered
of them, even of the tribe of Ephraim, were forty thousand five hundred.
Of the children of Manasseh,
by their generations, after their families, by the house of their fathers,
according to the number of the names, from twenty years old and
upward, all who were able to go out to war, those who were numbered
of them, even of the tribe of Manasseh, were thirty-two thousand two
hundred.

Of the children of Benjamin,
by their generations, after their families, by the house of their fathers,
according to the number of the names, from twenty years old and upward,
all who were able to go out to war, those who were numbered of them,
even of the tribe of Benjamin, were thirty-five thousand four hundred.

Of the children of Dan,
by their generations, after their families, by the house of their fathers,
according to the number of the names, from twenty years old and
upward, all who were able to go out to war, those who were numbered of
them, even of the tribe of Dan, were sixty-two thousand seven hundred.

Of the children of Asher,
by their generations, after their families, by the house of their fathers,
according to the number of the names, from twenty years old and
upward, all who were able to go out to war, those who were numbered of
them, even of the tribe of Asher, were forty-one thousand five hundred.

Of the children of Naphtali,
by their generations, after their families, by the house of their fathers,
according to the number of the names, from twenty years old and upward,
all who were able to go out to war, those who were numbered of them,
even of the tribe of Naphtali, were fifty-three thousand four hundred.

These are those who were numbered, which Moses and Aaron numbered, and the leaders of Israel, being twelve men. Each one was for the
house of his fathers. So were all those who were numbered of the children
of Israel, by the house of their fathers, from twenty years old and upward,
all who were able to go out to war in Israel. Even all they who were numbered were six hundred three thousand five hundred fifty.

But the Levites after the tribe of their fathers were not numbered among
them. For the LORD had spoken to Moses, saying: Only you will not number
the tribe of Levi, nor take the census of them among the children of Israel,
but you will appoint the Levites over the tent of the testimony, and over all

its vessels, and over all things that belong to it. They will carry the tabernacle, and all its vessels, and they will minister to it, and will camp around
the tabernacle. When the tabernacle sets out, the Levites will take it down,
and when the tabernacle is to be set up, the Levites will set it up, and the
foreigner that approaches will be put to death. The children of Israel will
pitch their tents, every man by his own camp, and every man by his own
standard, throughout their armies. But the Levites will camp around the
tabernacle of the testimony, so there will be no wrath on the congregation
of the children of Israel. And the Levites will keep the charge of the tabernacle of the testimony.

Thus the children of Israel did according to all that the LORD commanded
Moses.

And the LORD spoke to Moses and to Aaron, saying: Every man of the
children of Israel will camp by his own standard, with the ensign of his
father's house. Facing the tent of meeting they will camp.

On the east side toward the rising of the sun the standard of the camp of
Judah will camp throughout their armies, and Nahshon the son of Amminadab will be captain of the children of Judah. His host, and those who were
numbered of them, were seventy-four thousand six hundred.

Those who camp next to him will be the tribe of Issachar, and Nethanel
the son of Zuar will be captain of the children of Issachar. His host, and
those who were numbered of them, were fifty-four thousand four hundred.

Then comes the tribe of Zebulun, and Eliab the son of Helon will be
captain of the children of Zebulun. His host, and those who were numbered
of them, were fifty-seven thousand four hundred.

All who were numbered throughout the armies in the camp of Judah were
one hundred eighty-six thousand four hundred. They will march out first.

On the south side will be the standard of the camp of Reuben according
to their armies, and the captain of the children of Reuben will be Elizur the
son of Shedeur. His host, and those who were numbered of them, were
forty-six thousand five hundred.

Those who camp by him will be the tribe of Simeon, and the captain of
the children of Simeon will be Shelumiel the son of Zurishaddai. His host,
and those who were numbered of them, were fifty-nine thousand three
hundred.

Then comes the tribe of Gad, and the captain of the sons of Gad will be
Eliasaph the son of Reuel. His host, and those who were numbered of them,
were forty-five thousand six hundred fifty.

All who were numbered in the camp of Reuben were one hundred fifty-
one thousand four hundred fifty, throughout their armies. And they will set
out in the second rank.

Then the tent of meeting will set out with the camp of the Levites in the middle of the camp. As they camp, so they will set out, every man in his place by their standards.

On the west side will be the standard of the camp of Ephraim according to their armies, and the captain of the sons of Ephraim will be Elishama the son of Ammihud. His host, and those who were numbered of them, were forty thousand five hundred.

By him will be the tribe of Manasseh, and the captain of the children of Manasseh will be Gamaliel the son of Pedahzur. His host, and those who were numbered of them, were thirty-two thousand two hundred.

Then comes the tribe of Benjamin, and the captain of the sons of Benjamin will be Abidan the son of Gideoni. His host, and those who were numbered of them, were thirty-five thousand four hundred.

All who were numbered of the camp of Ephraim were one hundred eight thousand one hundred, throughout their armies. And they will go out in the third rank.

The standard of the camp of Dan will be on the north side by their armies, and the captain of the children of Dan will be Ahiezer the son of Ammishaddai. His host, and those who were numbered of them, were sixty-two thousand seven hundred.

Those who camp by him will be the tribe of Asher, and the captain of the children of Asher will be Pagiel the son of Okran. His host, and those who were numbered of them, were forty-one thousand five hundred.

Then the tribe of Naphtali, and the captain of the children of Naphtali will be Ahira the son of Enan. His host, and those who were numbered of them, were fifty-three thousand four hundred.

All they who were numbered in the camp of Dan were one hundred fifty-seven thousand six hundred. They will set out in the back with their standards.

These are those who were numbered of the children of Israel by the house of their fathers. All those who were numbered of the camps throughout their hosts were six hundred three thousand five hundred fifty. But the Levites were not numbered among the children of Israel, as the LORD commanded Moses.

The children of Israel did according to all that the LORD commanded Moses. So they camped by their standards, and so they set out, each one after his family, according to their fathers' houses.

These also are the generations of Aaron and Moses in the day that the LORD spoke with Moses in Mount Sinai.

These are the names of the sons of Aaron: Nadab the firstborn, and Abihu, Eleazar, and Ithamar. These are the names of the sons of Aaron, the priests who were anointed, whom he consecrated to minister as priests. Nadab and Abihu died before the LORD when they brought strange fire before the LORD in the Wilderness of Sinai, and they had no children, and Eleazar and Ithamar ministered as priests in the sight of Aaron their father.

The LORD spoke to Moses, saying: Bring the tribe of Levi near, and present them before Aaron the priest, and they will minister to him. They will keep his directives, and serve the whole congregation before the tent of meeting, to do the service of the tabernacle. They will keep all the instruments of the tent of meeting, and attend to the needs of the children of Israel, to do the service of the tabernacle. You will give the Levites to Aaron and to his sons. They are wholly given to him from the children of Israel. You will appoint Aaron and his sons, and they will attend to their priesthood, and the foreigner that approaches will be put to death.

The LORD spoke to Moses, saying: I Myself have taken the Levites from among the children of Israel instead of all the firstborn that open the womb among the children of Israel. Therefore the Levites will be Mine because all the firstborn are Mine, for on the day that I struck all the firstborn in the land of Egypt I set apart to Me all the firstborn in Israel, both man and beast. They will be Mine. I am the LORD.

The LORD spoke to Moses in the Wilderness of Sinai, saying: Number the children of Levi after the house of their fathers, by their families. You will number every male from one month old and older. Moses numbered them according to the word of the LORD, as he was commanded.

These were the sons of Levi by their names:

Gershon, and Kohath, and Merari.

These are the names of the sons of Gershon by their families:

Libni and Shimei;

the sons of Kohath by their families:

Amram, and Izhar, Hebron, and Uzziel;

the sons of Merari by their families:

Mahli and Mushi.

These are the families of the Levites according to the house of their fathers.

From Gershon was the family of the Libnites and the family of the Shimeites. These are the families of the Gershonites. Those who were numbered of them, according to the number of all the males, from one month old and older, those who were numbered of them were seven thousand five hundred. The families of the Gershonites were to camp behind the west side of the tabernacle. The chief of the house of the father of the Gershonites was Eliasaph the son of Lael. The charge of the sons of Gershon in the tent of meeting *included* the tabernacle, and the tent, its covering, and the hanging for the door of the tent of meeting, the hangings of the court, the curtain for the opening of the court that is around the tabernacle and the altar, and its cords—all the service pertaining to these.

Of Kohath was the family of the Amramites, and the family of the Izharites, and the family of the Hebronites, and the family of the Uzzielites. These are the families of the Kohathites. The number of all the males, from one month old and older, were eight thousand six hundred, keeping the guard of the sanctuary. The families of the sons of Kohath were to camp on the south side of the tabernacle. The chief of the house of the father of the families of the Kohathites was Elizaphan the son of Uzziel. Their duty included the ark, and the table, and the lampstand, and the altars, and the vessels of the sanctuary they minister with, and the hanging, and all its service. Eleazar the son of Aaron the priest was to be chief over the leaders of the Levites and to have the oversight of those who kept the guard of the sanctuary.

Of Merari was the family of the Mahlites and the family of the Mushites. These are the families of Merari. Those who were numbered of them, according to the number of all the males from one month old and older, were six thousand two hundred. The chief of the house of the father of the families of Merari was Zuriel the son of Abihail. These were to camp on the north side of the tabernacle. Under the oversight and guard of the sons of Merari were the frames of the tabernacle, the bars, the pillars, the sockets, all their accessories, all the service pertaining to these, and the pillars of the court all around, with their sockets, and pins, and cords.

But those who were to camp before the tabernacle toward the east, even before the tent of meeting on the east side, were Moses, and Aaron and his sons, keeping the guard of the sanctuary for the guard of the children of Israel, and the foreigner who approached was to be put to death.

All who were numbered of the Levites, which Moses and Aaron numbered at the commandment of the LORD, throughout their families, all the males from one month old and older, were twenty-two thousand.

The LORD said to Moses: Number all the firstborn of the males of the children of Israel from one month old and older and take the number of their names. You will take the Levites for Me (I am the LORD) instead of all the firstborn among the children of Israel, and the livestock of the Levites instead of all the firstborn among the livestock of the children of Israel.

Moses numbered, as the LORD commanded him, all the firstborn among the children of Israel. All the firstborn males, by the number of names, from one month old and upward, of those who were numbered of them, were twenty-two thousand two hundred seventy-three.

The LORD spoke to Moses, saying: Take the Levites instead of all the first-born among the children of Israel, and the livestock of the Levites instead of their livestock, and the Levites will be Mine. I am the LORD. For those who are to be redeemed of the two hundred seventy-three of the firstborn of the children of Israel, which are more than the Levites, you will take five shekels apiece by the poll; according to the shekel of the sanctuary you will take them (the shekel is twenty gerahs). And you will give the money, by which the number of them is to be redeemed, to Aaron and to his sons.

Moses took the redemption money of those who were over and above those who were redeemed by the Levites. Of the firstborn of the children of Israel he took the money, one thousand three hundred sixty-five shekels, after the shekel of the sanctuary. And Moses gave the money of those who were redeemed to Aaron and to his sons, according to the word of the LORD, as the LORD commanded Moses.

And the LORD spoke to Moses and to Aaron, saying: Take the sum of the sons of Kohath from among the sons of Levi, after their families, by the house of their fathers, from thirty years old and older, even to fifty years old, all that enter into the host, to do the work in the tent of meeting.

This will be the service of the sons of Kohath in the tent of meeting, concerning the holiest things. And when the camp sets out, Aaron will come, and his sons, and they will take down the covering curtain, and cover the ark of the testimony with it, and will put on it the covering of porpoise skins, and will spread over it a cloth completely of blue, and will put in its poles.

Upon the table of showbread they will spread a cloth of blue, and put the dishes on it, and the spoons, and the bowls, and covers to cover it, and the showbread will be on it. And they will spread on them a cloth of scarlet, and cover the same with a covering of porpoise skins, and will put in its poles.

They will take a cloth of blue, and cover the lampstand of the light, and its lamps, and its tongs, and its snuff dishes, and all its oil vessels, with which they minister to it. And they will put it and all its vessels within a covering of porpoise skins and will put it on a carrying pole.

Upon the golden altar they will spread a cloth of blue, and cover it with a covering of porpoise skins, and will put in its poles.

And they will take all the instruments of ministry, with which they minister in the sanctuary, and put them in a cloth of blue, and cover them with a covering of porpoise skins, and will put them on a carrying pole.

And they will take away the ashes from the altar and spread a purple cloth on it. They shall put on it all the instruments with which they minister there, the censers, the flesh hooks, the shovels, the basins, all the utensils of the altar. And they will spread on it a covering of porpoise skins and insert its poles.

When Aaron and his sons have finished covering the sanctuary, and all the instruments of the sanctuary, as the camp is to set out, after that, the sons of Kohath will come to carry it. But they will not touch any holy thing, lest they die. These things are the burden of the sons of Kohath in the tent of meeting.

To the office of Eleazar, Aaron the priest's son, pertains the oil for the light, and the sweet incense, and the daily grain offering, and the anointing oil, and the oversight of all the tabernacle, and of all that is in it, in the sanctuary, and in the instruments thereof.

The LORD spoke to Moses and to Aaron, saying: Do not cut the tribe of the families of the Kohathites from among the Levites. But do this to them, that they may live and not die, when they approach the most holy things. Aaron and his sons will go in, and appoint each one to his service and to his burden. But they will not go in to see when the holy things are covered, lest they die.

Nasso

Elevate!

(Numbers 4:21–7:89)

The LORD spoke to Moses, saying: Take also the sum of the sons of Gershon, throughout the houses of their fathers, by their families. From thirty years old and older to fifty years old you will number them, all that enter in to perform the service, to do the work in the tent of meeting.

This is the service of the families of the Gershonites, to serve, and to work. And they will carry the curtains of the tabernacle, and the tent of meeting, its covering, and the covering of the porpoise skins that is on it, and the hanging for the door of the tent of meeting, and the hangings of the courtyard, and the hanging for the opening of the gate of the courtyard, which is by the tabernacle and by the altar all around, and their cords, and all the instruments of their service, and all that is made for them. So they will serve. At the appointment of Aaron and his sons will be all the service of the sons of the Gershonites, in all their burdens, and in all their service. And you shall assign to them all their tasks as their duty. This is the service of the families of the sons of Gershon in the tent of meeting. And their charge will be under the hand of Ithamar the son of Aaron the priest.

As for the sons of Merari, you will number them by their families, by the house of their fathers. From thirty years old and older, even to fifty years old, you will number them, everyone who enters into the service, to do the work of the tent of meeting. This is the charge of their burden, according to all their service in the tent of meeting. The boards of the tabernacle, and its bars thereof, and its pillars, and its sockets, and the pillars of the court round about, and their sockets, and their pins, and their cords, with all their instruments, and with all their service, and by name you will list the instruments of the charge of their burden. This is the service of the families of the sons of Merari, according to all their service, in the tent of meeting, under the hand of Ithamar the son of Aaron the priest.

Moses, Aaron, and the leaders of the congregation numbered the sons of the Kohathites by their families, and by the house of their fathers, from thirty years old and older to fifty years old, everyone who entered into the service, for the work in the tent of meeting. And those who were numbered by their families were two thousand seven hundred fifty. These were the ones listed of the families of the Kohathites, all who might do service in the tent of meeting, which Moses and Aaron numbered according to the commandment of the LORD by the hand of Moses.

Those who were numbered of the sons of Gershon, throughout their families, and by the house of their fathers, from thirty years old and older to fifty years old, everyone who entered into the service, for the work in the tent of meeting, even those who were numbered of them, throughout their families, by the house of their fathers, were two thousand six hundred thirty. These were the ones listed by the families of the sons of Gershon, of all who might do service in the tent of meeting, whom Moses and Aaron numbered according to the commandment of the LORD.

Those who were numbered of the families of the sons of Merari, throughout their families, by the house of their fathers, from thirty years old and older to fifty years old, everyone who entered into the service, for the work in the tent of meeting, even those who were numbered by their families, were three thousand two hundred. These were the ones listed of the families of the sons of Merari, whom Moses and Aaron numbered according to the word of the LORD by the hand of Moses.

All those who were numbered of the Levites, whom Moses, Aaron, and the leaders of Israel numbered, by their families, and by the house of their fathers, from thirty years old and older to fifty years old, everyone who came to do the service of the ministry, and the service of the work in the tent of meeting, even those who were numbered were eight thousand five hundred eighty. According to the commandment of the LORD they were numbered by the hand of Moses, each according to his service, and according to his burden. Thus they were numbered by him, as the LORD commanded Moses.

And the LORD spoke to Moses, saying: Command the children of Israel that they put out of the camp every leper, and everyone who has a discharge, and whoever is defiled by the dead. Both male and female you will put out. You will put them outside the camp, so they do not defile their camps in the midst of which I dwell. The children of Israel did so, and put them outside the camp. As the LORD spoke to Moses, so the children of Israel did.

The LORD spoke to Moses, saying: Tell the children of Israel: When a man or woman commits any sin against another, acting unfaithfully against the LORD, that person is guilty, and shall confess his sin which he has committed, and he will repay his offense with its principal, and add to it one-fifth, and give it to him who was wronged. But if the man has no relative to repay the offense to, let the offense be repaid to the LORD, even to the priest, beside the ram of the atonement, whereby an atonement will be made for him. Every offering of all the holy things of the children of Israel, which they bring to the priest, will be his. Every man's holy things will be his. Whatever any man gives the priest, it will be his.

The LORD spoke to Moses, saying: Speak to the children of Israel and say to them: If any man's wife goes astray, and acts treacherously against him, and a man lies with her carnally, and it is hidden from the eyes of her husband, and it is concealed though she has defiled herself, and there is no witness against her, nor is she caught in the act, and if the spirit of jealousy comes on him, and he is jealous of his wife who has defiled herself, or if the spirit of jealousy comes on him and he is jealous of his wife, though she has not defiled herself, then the man shall bring his wife to the priest and he shall bring her offering for her, one-tenth of an ephah of barley flour. He shall pour no oil on it nor put frankincense on it, for it is a grain offering of jealousy, a grain offering of remembrance, bringing iniquity to remembrance.

The priest will bring her near, and set her before the LORD. And the priest will take holy water in an earthen vessel, and the priest will take some of the dust that is on the floor of the tabernacle and put it into the water. And the priest will set the woman before the LORD, and uncover the woman's head, and put the memorial offering in her hands, which is the grain offering of jealousy, and the priest will have in his hand the bitter water that causes the curse. And the priest will charge her by an oath, and say to the woman, "If no man has lain with you, and if you have not gone astray to impurity with another instead of your husband, be free from this bitter water that causes the curse. But if you have gone astray to another instead of your husband, and if you are defiled, and a man besides your husband has lain with you"— then the priest will charge the woman with an oath of cursing, and the priest will say to the woman, "The LORD make you a curse and an oath among your people, when the LORD makes your thigh rot and your belly swell. And this water that causes the curse will go into your bowels, to make your belly swell and your thigh rot."

And the woman will say, "Amen, amen."

The priest will write these curses in a book, and he will wash them out with the bitter water. And he will cause the woman to drink the bitter water that causes the curse. And the water that causes the curse will enter into her and become bitter. Then the priest will take the grain offering of jealousy out of the woman's hand and will wave the offering before the LORD and offer it on the altar. And the priest will take a handful of the offering, the memorial portion, and burn it on the altar, and afterward will cause the woman to drink the water. When he has made her to drink the water, then it will be that, if she is defiled and has acted treacherously against her husband, the water that causes the curse will enter into her, and become bitter, and her belly will swell, and her thigh will rot, and the woman will be a curse among her people. If the woman is not defiled, but is clean, then she will be free and will conceive offspring.

This is the law of jealousies, when a wife goes astray to another instead of her husband, and is defiled, or when the spirit of jealousy comes on him, and he is jealous over his wife, and will set the woman before the LORD, and the priest will perform on her all this law. Then the man will be guiltless from iniquity, and this woman will bear her iniquity.

And the LORD spoke to Moses, saying: Speak to the children of Israel and say to them: When either a man or woman will make a hard vow, the vow of a Nazirite, to separate themselves to the LORD, he will separate himself from wine and strong drink and will drink no vinegar of wine, or vinegar of strong drink. Neither shall he drink any juice of grapes, nor eat fresh or dry grapes. All the days of his separation he will eat nothing that is made of the grapevine, from the seed to the skin.

All the days of the vow of his separation no razor will come on his head until the days are fulfilled in which he separates himself to the LORD. He will be holy and will let the locks of the hair of his head grow. All the days that he separates himself to the LORD he will not approach a dead body. He will not defile himself for his father or for his mother, for his brother or for his sister if they die because the separation of his God is on his head. All the days of his separation he is holy to the LORD.

If any man dies very suddenly beside him, and he has defiled his conse-crated head, then he will shave his head in the day of his cleansing, on the seventh day will he shave it. On the eighth day he will bring two turtledoves or two young pigeons to the priest, to the door of the tent of meeting. And the priest will offer one as a sin offering and the other as a burnt offering and make an atonement for him, since he sinned because of the dead, and will sanctify his head that same day. He will consecrate to the LORD the days of his separation and bring a male lamb in its first year as a guilt offering. But the previous days will be lost because his separation was defiled.

This is the law of the Nazirite. When the days of his separation are ful-filled, he will be brought to the door of the tent of meeting. And he will offer his offering to the LORD, one male lamb one year old without blemish as a burnt offering, one ewe lamb one year old without blemish as a sin offer-ing, one ram without blemish as a peace offering, a basket of unleavened bread, loaves of fine flour mixed with oil, unleavened wafers anointed with oil, and their grain offering with their drink offerings.

The priest will bring them before the LORD and will offer his sin offering and his burnt offering. And he will offer the ram as a sacrifice of a peace offering to the LORD with the basket of unleavened bread. The priest will offer also his grain offering and his drink offering.

The Nazirite will shave his consecrated head at the door of the tent of meeting, and will take the hair from his consecrated head and put it in the fire which is under the sacrifice of the peace offerings.

The priest will take the cooked shoulder of the ram, and one unleavened cake out of the basket, and one unleavened wafer and will put them on the hands of the Nazirite, after he has shaved his consecrated hair. And the priest will wave them as a wave offering before the LORD. This is holy for the priest, with the breast waved and the shoulder offered. And after that the Nazirite may drink wine.

This is the law of the Nazirite who has vowed to the LORD, his offering for his separation, besides whatever else his hand is able to provide. According to the vow which he spoke, so he must do, according to the law of his separation.

The LORD spoke to Moses, saying: Speak to Aaron and to his sons, saying, This is how you will bless the children of Israel, saying to them,

The LORD bless you
and keep you;
the LORD make His face to shine upon you,
and be gracious unto you;
the LORD lift His countenance upon you,
and give you peace.

They will put My name upon the children of Israel, and I will bless them. And it was on the day that Moses had fully set up the tabernacle and anointed it and sanctified it and all its instruments, both the altar and all its vessels, and anointed them, and sanctified them, that the leaders of Israel, heads of their fathers' houses, who were the leaders of the tribes, and were over them who were counted, made an offering. And they brought their offering before the LORD, six covered wagons, and twelve oxen, a wagon for two of the leaders, and for each one an ox. And they brought them before the tabernacle.

The LORD spoke to Moses, saying: Accept these things from them, that they may be used in the service of the tent of meeting. Give them to the Levites, to each man according to his service.

Moses took the wagons and the oxen and gave them to the Levites. Two wagons and four oxen he gave to the sons of Gershon, according to their service. And four wagons and eight oxen he gave to the sons of Merari, according to their service, under the hand of Ithamar the son of Aaron the priest. But to the sons of Kohath he gave none because the service of the sanctuary belonging to them was that they should carry on their shoulders.

The leaders brought their dedication offerings when the altar was anointed, and offered their offerings before the altar. The LORD said to Moses: They will offer their offering, each leader on his day, for the dedicating of the altar.

He that offered his offering the first day was Nahshon the son of Amminadab, of the tribe of Judah.

And his offering was one silver charger, the weight of which was one hundred thirty shekels, one silver bowl of seventy shekels, after the shekel of the sanctuary, both of them full of fine flour mixed with oil as a grain offering; one spoon of ten shekels of gold, full of incense; one young bull, one ram, and one male lamb in its first year as a burnt offering; one goat kid as a sin offering; and as a sacrifice of peace offerings, two oxen, five rams, five male goats, and five male lambs in their first year. This was the offering of Nahshon the son of Amminadab.

On the second day Nethanel the son of Zuar, leader of Issachar, presented an offering.

He offered as his offering one silver charger, the weight of which was one hundred thirty shekels, one silver bowl of seventy shekels, after the shekel of the sanctuary, both of them full of fine flour mingled with oil as a grain offering; one spoon of ten shekels of gold, full of incense; one young bull, one ram, and one male lamb in its first year as a burnt offering; one goat kid as a sin offering; and as a sacrifice of peace offerings, two oxen, five rams, five male goats, and five male lambs in their first year. This was the offering of Nethanel the son of Zuar.

On the third day Eliab the son of Helon, leader of the children of Zebulun, presented an offering.

And his offering was one silver charger, the weight of which was one hundred thirty shekels, one silver bowl of seventy shekels, after the shekel of the sanctuary, both of them full of fine flour mixed with oil as a grain offering; one spoon of ten shekels of gold, full of incense; one young bull, one ram, one male lamb in its first year as a burnt offering; one goat kid as a sin offering; and as a sacrifice of peace offerings, two oxen, five rams, five male goats, five male lambs in their first year. This was the offering of Eliab the son of Helon.

On the fourth day Elizur the son of Shedeur, leader of the children of Reuben, presented an offering.

And his offering was one silver charger, the weight of which was one hundred thirty shekels, one silver bowl of seventy shekels, after the shekel of the sanctuary, both of them full of fine flour mixed with oil as a grain offering; one spoon of ten shekels of gold, full of incense; one young bull, one ram, one male lamb in its first year as a burnt offering; one goat kid as a sin offering; and as a sacrifice of peace offerings, two oxen, five rams, five male goats, five male lambs in their first year. This was the offering of Elizur the son of Shedeur.

On the fifth day Shelumiel the son of Zurishaddai, leader of the children of Simeon, presented an offering.

And his offering was one silver charger, the weight of which was one hundred thirty shekels, one silver bowl of seventy shekels, after the shekel of the sanctuary, both of them full of fine flour mixed with oil as a grain offering; one spoon of ten shekels of gold, full of incense; one young bull, one ram, one male lamb in its first year, as a burnt offering: one goat kid as a sin offering; and as a sacrifice of peace offerings, two oxen, five rams, five male goats, five male lambs in their first year. This was the offering of Shelumiel the son of Zurishaddai.

On the sixth day Eliasaph the son of Deuel, leader of the children of Gad, presented an offering.

And his offering was one silver charger, the weight of which was one hundred thirty shekels, one silver bowl of seventy shekels, after the shekel of the sanctuary, both of them full of fine flour mixed with oil as a grain offering; one spoon of ten shekels of gold, full of incense; one young bull, one ram, one male lamb in its first year as a burnt offering; one goat kid as a sin offering; and as a sacrifice of peace offerings, two oxen, five rams, five male goats, five male lambs in their first year. This was the offering of Eliasaph the son of Deuel.

On the seventh day Elishama the son of Ammihud, leader of the children of Ephraim, presented an offering.

And his offering was one silver charger, the weight of which was one hundred thirty shekels, one silver bowl of seventy shekels, after the shekel of the sanctuary, both of them full of fine flour mixed with oil as a grain offering; one spoon of ten shekels of gold, full of incense; one young bull, one ram, one male lamb in its first year as a burnt offering; one goat kid as a sin offering; and as a sacrifice of peace offerings, two oxen, five rams, five male goats, five male lambs in their first year. This was the offering of Elishama the son of Ammihud.

On the eighth day Gamaliel the son of Pedahzur, leader of the children of Manasseh, presented an offering.

And his offering was one silver charger, the weight of which was one hundred thirty shekels, one silver bowl of seventy shekels, after the shekel of the sanctuary, both of them full of fine flour mixed with oil as a grain offering; one spoon of ten shekels of gold, full of incense; one young bull, one ram, and one male lamb in its first year as a burnt offering; one goat kid as a sin offering; and as a sacrifice of peace offerings, two oxen, five rams, five male goats, five male lambs in their first year. This was the offering of Gamaliel the son of Pedahzur.

On the ninth day Abidan the son of Gideoni, leader of the children of Benjamin, presented an offering.

And his offering was one silver charger, the weight of which was one hundred thirty shekels, one silver bowl of seventy shekels, after the shekel of the sanctuary, both of them full of fine flour mixed with oil as a grain offering; one spoon of ten shekels of gold, full of incense; one young bull, one ram, and one male lamb in its first year as a burnt offering; one goat kid as a sin offering; and as a sacrifice of peace offerings, two oxen, five rams, five male goats, and five male lambs in their first year. This was the offering of Abidan the son of Gideoni.

On the tenth day Ahiezer the son of Ammishaddai, leader of the children of Dan, presented an offering.

And his offering was one silver charger, the weight of which was one hundred thirty shekels, one silver bowl of seventy shekels, after the shekel of the sanctuary, both of them full of fine flour mixed with oil as a grain offering; one spoon of ten shekels of gold, full of incense; one young bull, one ram, and one male lamb in its first year as a burnt offering; one goat kid as a sin offering; and as a sacrifice of peace offerings, two oxen, five rams, five male goats, and five male lambs in their first year. This was the offering of Ahiezer the son of Ammishaddai.

On the eleventh day Pagiel the son of Okran, leader of the children of Asher, presented an offering.

And his offering was one silver charger, the weight of which was one hundred thirty shekels, one silver bowl of seventy shekels, after the shekel of the sanctuary, both of them full of fine flour mixed with oil as a grain offering; one spoon of ten shekels of gold, full of incense; one young bull, one ram, and one male lamb in its first year as a burnt offering; one goat kid as a sin offering; and as a sacrifice of peace offerings, two oxen, five rams, five male goats, and five male lambs in their first year. This was the offering of Pagiel the son of Okran.

On the twelfth day Ahira the son of Enan, leader of the children of Naphtali, presented an offering.

And his offering was one silver charger, the weight of which was one hundred thirty shekels, one silver bowl of seventy shekels, after the shekel of the sanctuary, both of them full of fine flour mixed with oil as a grain offering; one spoon of ten shekels of gold, full of incense; one young bull, one ram, and one male lamb in its first year as a burnt offering; one goat kid as a sin offering; and as a sacrifice of peace offerings, two oxen, five rams, five male goats, and five male lambs in their first year. This was the offering of Ahira the son of Enan.

This was the dedication of the altar, in the day when it was anointed, by the leaders of Israel: twelve silver plates, twelve silver bowls, and twelve gold spoons, each silver plate weighing one hundred thirty shekels, each bowl seventy. All the silver vessels weighed two thousand four hundred shekels, according to the shekel of the sanctuary. The gold spoons were twelve, full of incense, weighing ten shekels apiece, according to the shekel of the sanctuary. All the gold of the spoons was one hundred twenty shekels. All the oxen for the burnt offering were twelve bulls, twelve rams, twelve male lambs in their first year, with their grain offering, and twelve goat kids for a sin offering. And all the oxen for the sacrifice of the peace offerings were twenty-four bulls, the rams sixty, the goats sixty, the one-year-old lambs sixty. This was the dedication of the altar after it was anointed.

And then Moses went into the tent of meeting to speak with Him, and he heard the voice of One speaking to him from the mercy seat that was on the ark of the testimony, from between the two cherubim, and He spoke to him.

Beha'alotcha

In your uplifting

(Numbers 8:1–12:16)

And the Lord spoke to Moses, saying: Speak to Aaron and say to him: When you set up the lamps, the seven lamps will give light before the lampstand.

Aaron did so. He lit the lamps before the lampstand, as the Lord commanded Moses. And this was the work of the lampstand: hammered gold, to its shaft, to its flowers was beaten work. According to the pattern which the Lord had shown Moses, so he made the lampstand.

The Lord spoke to Moses, saying: Take the Levites from among the children of Israel and cleanse them. Thus you will do to them to cleanse them: Splash purifying water on them, and let them shave their whole body, and let them wash their clothes, and so make themselves clean. Then let them take a young bull with its grain offering, also fine flour mixed with oil, and you will take another young bull as a sin offering. You will bring the Levites before the tent of meeting. And you will gather the whole assembly of the children of Israel together. And you will bring the Levites before the Lord. And the children of Israel will put their hands on the Levites. And Aaron will offer the Levites before the Lord as a wave offering of the children of Israel, that they may do the service of the Lord.

The Levites will lay their hands on the heads of the bulls, and you will offer one as a sin offering and the other as a burnt offering to the Lord, to make an atonement for the Levites. You will set the Levites before Aaron and before his sons, and offer them as a wave offering to the Lord. Thus will you separate the Levites from among the children of Israel, and the Levites will be Mine.

And afterwards the Levites will go in to do the service of the tent of meeting, and you will cleanse them and offer them as a wave offering. For they are completely set aside for Me by the children of Israel. Instead of all who open the womb, instead of the firstborn of all the children of Israel, I have taken them for Myself. For all the firstborn of the children of Israel are Mine, both man and animal. On the day that I struck every firstborn in the land of Egypt I sanctified them for Myself. I have taken the Levites instead of all the firstborn of the children of Israel. I have given the Levites as a gift to

Aaron and to his sons from among the children of Israel, to serve the service of the children of Israel in the tent of meeting and to make an atonement for the children of Israel, so there will be no plague among the children of Israel when the children of Israel approach the sanctuary.

Moses and Aaron and all the congregation of the children of Israel did to the Levites; according to all that the LORD commanded Moses concerning the Levites, so the children of Israel did to them. The Levites cleansed themselves from sin, and they washed their clothes, and Aaron offered them as a wave offering before the LORD, and Aaron made an atonement for them to cleanse them. And after that the Levites went in to do their service in the tent of meeting before Aaron and before his sons. As the LORD had commanded Moses concerning the Levites, so they did to them.

The LORD spoke to Moses, saying: This is what belongs to the Levites: From twenty-five years old and older they will go in to do their duty concerning the service of the tent of meeting. And from the age of fifty years they will cease doing their duty concerning its service and will serve no more. But *they* will minister with their brothers in the tent of meeting, to attend to their needs, but will not do the work. Thus you will do to the Levites concerning their duties.

And the LORD spoke to Moses in the Wilderness of Sinai, in the first month of the second year after they came out of the land of Egypt, saying: Let the children of Israel also keep the Passover at its appointed time. On the fourteenth day of this month, at evening, you will keep it at its appointed time. According to all its rites and according to all its ceremonies, you will keep it.

Moses spoke to the children of Israel, that they should keep the Passover. They kept the Passover on the fourteenth day of the first month at evening in the Wilderness of Sinai. According to all that the LORD commanded Moses, so the children of Israel did.

There were men who were unclean by the dead body of a man, so they could not keep the Passover on that day, and they came before Moses and before Aaron on that day. And those men said to him, "We are defiled by the dead body of a man. Why are we kept back, that we may not offer an offering of the LORD at its appointed time among the children of Israel?"

And Moses said to them, "Stand still, and I will hear what the LORD will command concerning you."

The LORD spoke to Moses, saying: Speak to the children of Israel, saying: If any man of you or of your posterity is unclean because of a dead body, or is far off on a journey, he will still keep the Passover to the LORD. The fourteenth day of the second month at evening they will keep it, and eat it with unleavened bread and bitter herbs. They will leave none of it until the morning, nor break any of its bones. According to all the ordinances of the Passover they will keep it. But the man who is ceremonially clean, and is not on a journey, and fails to keep the Passover, even the same person will be cut off from his people. Because he did not bring the offering of the LORD at its appointed time, that man will bear his sin.

If a stranger will sojourn among you and will keep the Passover to the LORD, according to the ordinance of the Passover, and according to the manner of it, so he will do. You will have one ordinance both for the resident foreigner and for the natural born citizen of the land.

And on the day that the tabernacle was erected, the cloud covered the tabernacle, the tent of the testimony, and at evening there was over the tabernacle the appearance of fire until the morning. So it was always. The cloud covered it by day, and the appearance of fire by night. When the cloud was lifted up from over the tabernacle, then after it the children of Israel journeyed, and in the place where the cloud settled, there the children of Israel camped. At the commandment of the LORD the children of Israel journeyed, and at the commandment of the LORD they camped. As long as the cloud dwelt over the tabernacle they camped. When the cloud remained many days over the tabernacle, then the children of Israel kept the charge of the LORD and did not journey. When the cloud remained a few days over the tabernacle, according to the commandment of the LORD they dwelt in their tents, and according to the commandment of the LORD they journeyed. When the cloud dwelt from evening until morning and the cloud was lifted up in the morning, then they journeyed. Whether it was by day or by night that the cloud was lifted up, they journeyed. Whether it was two days, or one month, or a long time that the cloud dwelt over the tabernacle, the children of Israel dwelt in their tents and did not journey. But when it was lifted up they journeyed. At the command of the LORD they camped, and at the command of the LORD they journeyed. They kept the charge of the LORD at the command of the LORD by the hand of Moses.

And the LORD spoke to Moses, saying: Make for yourself two silver trumpets. Of a hammered work you will make them, and you will use them for summoning of the assembly and directing the breaking up of the camps. When they blow both of them, all the assembly will assemble themselves to you at the door of the tent of meeting. If they blow only one, then the leaders, who are heads of the thousands of Israel, will gather themselves to you. When you blow an alarm, then the camps that lie on the east will set out. When you blow an alarm the second time, then the camps that lie on the south will set out. They will blow an alarm for their setting out. But when the assembly is to be gathered together, you will blow, but you will not sound an alarm.

The sons of Aaron, the priests, will blow the trumpets, and they will be to you as an ordinance forever throughout your generations. And if you go to war in your land against the enemy that oppresses you, then you will blow an alarm with the trumpets, and you will be remembered before the

LORD your God, and you will be saved from your enemies. Also in the day of your gladness, and at your appointed days, and in the beginnings of your months, you shall blow the trumpets over your burnt offerings, and over the sacrifices of your peace offerings that they may be a memorial for you before your God. I am the LORD your God.

And it was on the twentieth day of the second month, in the second year, that the cloud was lifted up from over the tabernacle of the testimony. The children of Israel set out from the Wilderness of Sinai. And the cloud dwelt in the Wilderness of Paran. And they set out for the first time at the command of the LORD by the hand of Moses.

And the standard of the camp of the sons of Judah set out first by their armies, and over his armies was Nahshon the son of Amminadab. Over the armies of the tribe of the children of Issachar was Nethanel the son of Zuar. Over the armies of the tribe of the children of Zebulun was Eliab the son of Helon. The tabernacle was taken down, and the sons of Gershon and the sons of Merari set out, carrying the tabernacle.

The standard of the camp of Reuben set out by their armies, and over his armies was Elizur the son of Shedeur. Over the armies of the tribe of the children of Simeon was Shelumiel the son of Zurishaddai. Over the armies of the tribe of the children of Gad was Eliasaph the son of Deuel. The Kohathites set out, carrying the sanctuary, and they set up the tabernacle before they came.

The standard of the camp of the children of Ephraim set out by their armies, and over his armies was Elishama the son of Ammihud. Over the armies of the tribe of the children of Manasseh was Gamaliel the son of Pedahzur. Over the armies of the tribe of the children of Benjamin was Abidan the son of Gideoni.

Then the standard of the camp of the children of Dan set out, which was the rear guard of all the camps by their armies, and over his armies was Ahiezer the son of Ammishaddai. Over the armies of the tribe of the children of Asher was Pagiel the son of Okran. Over the armies of the tribe of the children of Naphtali was Ahira the son of Enan. This was the order of march of the children of Israel, company by company, when they set out.

Moses said to Hobab, the son of Reuel the Midianite, Moses' father-in-law, "We are setting out to the place of which the LORD said, 'I will give it to you.' Come with us, and we will do good to you because the LORD has spoken good concerning Israel."

Hobab said to him, "I will not go. But I will depart to my own land, and to my kindred."

So Moses said, "Please do not leave us, because you know where to camp in the wilderness, and you may be our eyes. Moreover, if you go with us, then it will be that whatever good the LORD will do for us, we will likewise do for you."

They set out three days from the mountain of the LORD, and the ark of the covenant of the LORD went before them the three days' journey, to find a resting place for them. And the cloud of the LORD was over them by day when they set out from of the camp.

And it was, when the ark set out, that Moses said,

"Rise up, O LORD,
  and let Your enemies be scattered,
  and let them that hate You flee before You."

And when it rested, he said,

"Return, O LORD,
  to the multitude of thousands of Israel."

Now when the people complained openly before the LORD, the LORD heard, and His anger burned. Then the fire of the LORD burned among them and consumed the outskirts of the camp. And the people cried out to Moses, and Moses prayed to the LORD, and the fire was quenched. He called the name of the place Taberah because the fire of the LORD burned among them.

The mixed multitude that was among them lusted, and the children of Israel wept again and said, "Who will give us meat to eat? We remember the fish, which we ate in Egypt for free, the cucumbers, and the melons, and the leeks, and the onions, and the garlic. But now our life is dried up. There is nothing at all except this manna before our eyes."

The manna was as coriander seed, and it looked like bdellium. The people went about and gathered it, and ground it in mills or beat it in a mortar, and boiled it in pots, and made cakes of it, and the taste of it was like the taste of cakes baked in oil. When the dew fell on the camp at night, the manna fell on it.

Then Moses heard the people weep throughout their families, every man in the opening of his tent, and the anger of the LORD burned greatly. Moses was also displeased. Moses said to the LORD, "Why have You hurt Your servant? And why have I not found favor in Your eyes, that You lay the burden of all this people on me? Have I conceived all this people? Have I given them birth, that You should say to me, 'Carry them in your bosom, as a nurse bears the nursing child,' to the land which You swore to their fathers? Where am I to get meat to give to all these people? For they weep to me, saying, 'Give us meat, that we may eat.' I am not able to bear all these people alone, because the burden is too heavy for me. If You do this to me, please kill me at once, if I have found favor in Your eyes, and do not let me see my misery."

Then the LORD said to Moses, "Gather to Me seventy men of the elders of Israel, whom you know to be the elders of the people, and officers over them, and bring them to the tent of meeting, that they may take a stand there with you. And I will come down, and I will speak with you there, and I will take of the Spirit which is on you and will put it on them, and they will bear the burden of the people with you, and you will not bear it by yourself.

"And say to the people: Consecrate yourselves for tomorrow, and you shall eat meat, for you have wept in the hearing of the LORD, saying, 'Who will give us meat to eat? For it was better for us in Egypt.' Therefore the LORD will give you meat, and you shall eat. You shall eat, not one day, or two days, or five days, or ten days, or twenty days, but a whole month, until it comes out at your nostrils, and it will be nauseating to you because you rejected the LORD who is among you and have wept before Him, saying, 'Why did we come out of Egypt?'"

And Moses said, "The people I am with number six hundred thousand foot soldiers, and You have said, 'I will give them meat that they may eat a whole month.' Will the flocks and the herds be slaughtered for them, to satisfy them? Or will all the fish of the sea be gathered together for them, to satisfy them?"

And the LORD said to Moses, "Is the hand of the LORD shortened? Now you will see if My word will happen to you or not."

Moses went out, and he spoke to the people the words of the LORD and gathered the seventy men of the elders of the people and set them around the tabernacle. And the LORD came down in a cloud, and spoke to him, and took of the Spirit that was on him, and gave it to the seventy elders, and when the Spirit rested on them, they prophesied, but did not do it again.

But two men remained in the camp. The name of one was Eldad, and the name of the other, Medad. And the Spirit rested on them. They were among those listed, but they had not gone out to the tent, and so they prophesied in the camp. And a young man ran and told Moses and said, "Eldad and Medad prophesy in the camp."

Then Joshua the son of Nun, the assistant of Moses from his youth, answered and said, "My lord Moses, forbid them."

Moses said to him, "Are you jealous for my sake? Oh, that all the people of the LORD were prophets, and that the LORD would put His Spirit upon them!" And Moses returned to the camp, he and the elders of Israel.

Now a wind from the LORD started up, and it swept quail from the sea and let them fall beside the camp, about a day's journey on this side and a day's journey on the other side, around the camp, and about two cubits above the ground. And the people stayed up all that day, all night, and all the next day, and gathered the quail. Those who gathered least gathered ten homers. And they spread them out for themselves all around the camp. While the meat was between their teeth, before it was chewed, the anger of the LORD burned against the people, and the LORD struck the people with a very great slaughter. And he called the name of that place Kibroth Hattaavah because there they buried the people who had the craving.

The people journeyed from Kibroth Hattaavah to Hazeroth, and they camped at Hazeroth.

And Miriam and Aaron spoke against Moses because of the Cushite woman whom he married, for he had married a Cushite woman. They said, "Has the LORD spoken only by Moses? Has He not spoken also by us?" And the LORD heard it.

(Now the man Moses was very humble, more than all the men on the face of the earth.)

And the LORD spoke at once to Moses and to Aaron and to Miriam, "Come out, you three, to the tent of meeting." And those three came out. The LORD came down in a pillar of cloud, and stood in the opening of the tabernacle, and called Aaron and Miriam, and they both came forward. He said, "Hear now My word.

If there is a prophet among you,
   I the LORD will make Myself known to him in a vision,
   and I will speak to him in a dream.
Not so with My servant Moses;
   he is entrusted with all My house.
Face to face I speak with him clearly,
   and not in riddles,
   and the likeness of the LORD will he behold.
Then why were you not afraid
   to speak against My servant, against Moses?"

And the anger of the LORD burned against them, and He set out.

When the cloud went away from over the tabernacle, Miriam became leprous as snow, and Aaron turned toward Miriam and saw that she was leprous. Aaron said to Moses, "Alas, my lord, do not lay the sin on us, which we have done foolishly, and which we have sinned. Do not let her be as dead, who when he goes out of his mother's womb half his flesh is eaten."

And Moses cried out to the LORD, saying, "O God, heal her, I pray!"

But the LORD said to Moses, "If her father had but spit in her face, would she not be ashamed seven days? Let her be shut out of the camp seven days, and afterward she may be received again." Miriam was shut out from the camp seven days, and the people did not set out until Miriam was brought in again.

Afterward the people set out from Hazeroth and camped in the Wilderness of Paran.

Sh'lach

Send

(Numbers 13:1–15:41)

A nd the LORD spoke to Moses, saying, "Send men that they may explore the land of Canaan, which I am giving to the children of Israel. Of every tribe of their fathers you will send a man, each one a chief among them."

And Moses sent them from the Wilderness of Paran according to the LORD. All those men were heads of the children of Israel. These were their names:

of the tribe of Reuben, Shammua the son of Zakkur;
of the tribe of Simeon, Shaphat the son of Hori;
of the tribe of Judah, Caleb the son of Jephunneh;
of the tribe of Issachar, Igal the son of Joseph;
of the tribe of Ephraim, Hoshea the son of Nun;
of the tribe of Benjamin, Palti the son of Raphu;
of the tribe of Zebulun, Gaddiel the son of Sodi;
of the tribe of Joseph, namely, of the tribe of Manasseh, Gaddi the son of Susi;
of the tribe of Dan, Ammiel the son of Gemalli;
of the tribe of Asher, Sethur the son of Michael;
of the tribe of Naphtali, Nahbi the son of Vophsi;
of the tribe of Gad, Geuel the son of Maki.

These are the names of the men whom Moses sent to explore the land. And Moses called Hoshea the son of Nun Joshua.

Moses sent them to explore the land of Canaan and said to them, "Go up to this southland, and go up into the mountain. And see what the land is, and the people that dwell in it, whether they are strong or weak, few or many; and what the land is that they dwell in, whether it is good or bad, and what cities are that they dwell in, whether in tents, or in fortifications; and what the land is, whether it is fat or lean, whether there is wood in it or not. And you be courageous and bring some of the fruit of the land." Now the time was the time of the first ripe grapes.

So they went up and explored the land from the Wilderness of Zin to Rehob, near Lebo Hamath. They went up by the Negev and came to Hebron where Ahiman, Sheshai, and Talmai, the children of Anak, were (now Hebron was built seven years before Zoan in Egypt). And they came to the Valley of Eshkol, and cut down from there a branch with one cluster of grapes, and they carried it on a pole between two of them, and they brought some of the pomegranates and of the figs. The place was called the Valley of Eshkol because of the cluster of grapes which the children of Israel cut down from there. They returned from exploring the land after forty days.

And they returned and came to Moses and to Aaron and to all the assembly of the children of Israel, to the Wilderness of Paran, to Kadesh, and brought back word to them and to the entire assembly and showed them the fruit of the land. They reported to him and said, "We came to the land where you sent us, and surely it flows with milk and honey, and this is the fruit of it. However, the people are strong that dwell in the land, and the cities are fortified and very great, and also we saw the children of Anak there. The Amalekites dwell in the land of the Negev, and the Hittites, and the Jebusites, and the Amorites dwell in the mountains, and the Canaanites dwell by the sea and by the edge of the Jordan."

Caleb silenced the people before Moses and said, "Let us go up at once and possess it, for we are able to overcome it."

But the men that went up with him said, "We are not able to go up against the people because they are stronger than we." They gave the children of Israel a bad report of the land which they had spied out, saying, "The land through which we have gone as spies is a land that devours its inhabitants, and all the people whom we saw in it are men of great stature. And there we saw the giants, the sons of Anak, which come from the giants, and in our eyes we were like grasshoppers, and so we were in their eyes."

And the whole assembly lifted up their voices and cried, and the people wept that night. All the children of Israel grumbled against Moses and against Aaron, and the whole assembly said to them, "O that we had died in the land of Egypt! Or that we had died in this wilderness! And why has the LORD brought us to this land to fall by the sword, that our wives and our children should become prey? Is it not better for us to return to Egypt?" And they said one to another, "Let us select a leader, and let us return to Egypt."

Then Moses and Aaron fell on their faces before all the congregation of the assembly of the children of Israel. Joshua the son of Nun, and Caleb the son of Jephunneh, from the ones who explored the land, tore their clothes. And they spoke to all the assembly of the children of Israel, saying, "The land which we passed through to explore it is a very, very good land. If the LORD delights in us, then He will bring us into this land and give it to us, a land which flows with milk and honey. Only do not rebel against the LORD, nor fear the people of the land because they are bread for us. Their defense is gone from them, and the LORD is with us. Do not fear them."

But all the assembly said, "Stone them with stones." And the glory of the LORD appeared at the tent of meeting before all the children of Israel. The LORD said to Moses, "How long will this people disgrace Me? And how long will they not believe Me, in spite of all the signs which I have done among them? I will strike them with the pestilence, and disinherit them, and will make from you a nation greater and mightier than they."

Moses said to the LORD, "Then the Egyptians will hear of it, for by Your power You brought this people up from among them, and they will say to the inhabitants of this land that they heard that You, LORD, are among this people, that You, LORD, are seen face to face, and Your cloud stands over them, and in the pillar of cloud You go before them by day and by a pillar of fire at night. Now if You kill all this people as one man, then the nations which have heard the fame of You will speak, saying, 'The LORD was not able to bring this people into the land which He swore to them, so He slaughtered them in the wilderness.'

"So now, I pray, let the power of my Lord be great, just as You have spoken, saying, 'The LORD is slow to anger and abounding in mercy, forgiving iniquity and transgression; but He will by no means clear the guilty, visiting the iniquity of the fathers upon the children to the third and fourth generation.' Pardon the iniquity of this people, I pray, according to the greatness of Your grace, just as You have pardoned this people, from Egypt even until now."

The LORD said, "I have forgiven according to your word. But truly as I live, all the earth will be filled with the glory of the LORD. Because all those men seeing My glory and My signs which I did in Egypt and in the wilderness, and have tempted Me now these ten times, and have not listened to My voice, surely they will not see the land which I swore to their fathers, nor will any of them who disgraced Me see it. But My servant Caleb, because he had a different spirit with him and followed Me fully, I will bring him into the land where he went, and his seed will possess it. Now the Amalekites and the Canaanites lived in the valley. Tomorrow you will turn, and you will set out for the wilderness by the way of the Red Sea."

The LORD spoke to Moses and to Aaron, saying: How long will this evil assembly be murmuring against Me? I have heard the murmurings of the children of Israel which they murmur against Me. Say to them, "As I live," says the LORD, "just as you have spoken in My ears, so I will do to you. In this wilderness your corpses will fall, and all who were numbered of you, according to your whole number, from twenty years old and upward, who have murmured against Me, you will not go into the land which I swore by My hand to cause you to dwell in it, except Caleb the son of Jephunneh and Joshua the son of Nun. But your children, whom you said would be a prey, I will bring them in and they will know the land, which you rejected. But as for you, your corpses will fall in this wilderness. Your children will be shepherds in the wilderness forty years, and they will suffer for your fornications, until your corpses are in the wilderness. According to the number of the days in which you spied out the land, forty days, a year for each day you will bear your iniquity, forty years, and you will know My displeasure." I the LORD have spoken. I will surely do this to all this evil assembly gathered against Me. In this wilderness they will be finished, and there they will die.

The men whom Moses sent to explore the land, who returned and made all the assembly murmur against him by bringing up an evil report about the land, the men who brought an evil report about the land, died by the pestilence before the LORD. But Joshua the son of Nun and Caleb the son of Jephunneh, from the men that went to explore the land, lived.

Moses spoke these words to all the children of Israel, and the people mourned greatly. They rose up early in the morning, and they went up to the top of the mountain, saying, "Here we are. We will go up to the place which the LORD has promised, for we have sinned."

Moses said, "Why do you now transgress the commandment of the LORD? This will not prosper. Do not go up, for the LORD is not among you; do not let yourselves be defeated by your enemies. For the Amalekites and the Canaanites are there before you, and you will fall by the sword because you are turned from the LORD, and the LORD will not be with you."

But they presumed to go up to the top of the mountain. But the ark of the covenant of the LORD and Moses did not depart from the midst of the camp. Then the Amalekites and the Canaanites who dwelt on that mountain went down and defeated them, pursuing them as far as Hormah.

And the LORD spoke to Moses, saying: Speak to the children of Israel, and say to them: When you come into the land of your dwelling, which I am giving to you, when you make an offering by fire to the LORD, a burnt offering, or a sacrifice in performing a vow, or as a freewill offering, or in your appointed feasts, to make a pleasing aroma to the LORD, of the herd or of the flock, then he who brings his offering to the LORD will bring a grain offering of one-tenth of an ephah of flour mixed with one-fourth of a hin of oil. One-fourth of a hin of wine as a drink offering you will prepare with the burnt offering or sacrifice, for each lamb.

Or for a ram, you will make a grain offering of two-tenths of an ephah of flour mixed with one-third of a hin of oil. As a drink offering you will offer one-third of a hin of wine, as a pleasing aroma to the LORD.

When you prepare a bull as a burnt offering, or as a sacrifice in performing a vow, or as a peace offering to the LORD, then shall be brought with the bull a grain offering of three-tenths of an ephah of flour mixed with one-half a hin of oil. You will bring as a drink offering one-half a hin of wine, as a fire offering, as a pleasing aroma to the LORD. Thus it will be done for one herd animal, or for one ram, or for a flock animal, whether from the sheep or from the goats. According to the number that you will make, so you will do for every one according to their number.

Every native Israelite will do these things in this manner, in offering a fire offering as a pleasing aroma to the LORD. A foreigner who lives with you, or who resides among you throughout your generations, and would present a fire offering, a pleasing aroma to the LORD, shall do as you do. One ordinance will be for you of the assembly and for the foreigner who lives with you, an ordinance forever throughout your generations. As you are, so will the foreigner be before the LORD. One law and one justice will be for you and for the foreigner who lives with you.

The LORD spoke to Moses, saying: Speak to the children of Israel, and say to them: When you come into the land where I bring you, then it will be, when you eat of the bread of the land you will offer up an offering to the LORD. From the first of your dough you will offer a cake as an offering. As you make the offering of the threshing floor, so will you offer it. Of the first of your dough you will give to the LORD an offering throughout your generations.

If you have erred and not observed all these commandments which the LORD has spoken to Moses, even all that the LORD has commanded you by the hand of Moses, from the day that the LORD commanded Moses and onward through your generations, then it will be, if it is committed by ignorance without the knowledge of the assembly, that all the assembly will offer one young bull as a burnt offering, as a pleasing aroma to the LORD, with its grain offering and its drink offering, according to the rule, and one kid of the goats as a sin offering. The priest will make atonement for all the assembly of the children of Israel, and it will be forgiven them because it is ignorance, and they will bring their offering, a sacrifice made by fire to the LORD, and their sin offering before the LORD, for their ignorance. And it will be forgiven all the assembly of the children of Israel and the foreigner who lives among them, because all the people were in ignorance.

If a person sins unintentionally, then he will bring a year-old female goat as a sin offering. The priest will make an atonement for the person who sins unintentionally, when he sins by ignorance before the LORD, to make an atonement for him; and it will be forgiven him. You shall have one law for the person who acts through ignorance, for the natural-born citizen among the children of Israel and foreigner who lives in your midst.

But the person who acts by a high hand, the natural-born citizen or the foreigner, the same reviles the LORD, and that person will be cut off from among his people. Because he has despised the word of the LORD and has broken His commandment, that person will be totally cut off. His iniquity will be on him.

While the children of Israel were in the wilderness, they found a man who gathered sticks on the Sabbath day. The ones who found him gathering sticks brought him to Moses and Aaron and to all the assembly. They put him in confinement because it was not declared what should be done to him. The LORD said to Moses, "The man will surely die. All the assembly will stone him with stones outside the camp." All the assembly brought him outside the camp and stoned him with stones, and he died as the LORD commanded Moses.

The LORD spoke to Moses, saying: Speak to the children of Israel, and tell them to make for themselves tassels on the corners of their garments throughout the generations to come, and they will put a ribbon of blue on the corners of their garments. And it will be for you a tassel, and you will see it, and you will remember all the commandments of the LORD, and you will do them, and you will not follow the lust of your own heart and your own eyes. So shall you remember and do all My commandments, and be holy to your God. I am the LORD your God who brought you out of the land of Egypt, to be your God: I am the LORD your God.

Korach

Korach

(Numbers 16:1–18:32)

Now Korah the son of Izhar, the son of Kohath, the son of Levi, and Dathan and Abiram the sons of Eliab, and On the son of Peleth, sons of Reuben, took men, and they rose up before Moses and men of the children of Israel, two hundred fifty chiefs of the assembly, famous in the assembly, well-known men. They assembled against Moses and against Aaron, and said to them, "You take too much upon yourselves, seeing all the congregation are holy, every one of them, and the Lord is among them. So why do you exalt yourselves above the assembly of the Lord?"

And when Moses heard it, he fell on his face, and he spoke to Korah and to all his company, saying, "In the morning the Lord will show who is His and who is holy, and He will bring him to come near to Him. Whom He has chosen He will bring near to Him. Do this: Take censers, Korah and all his company; put fire in them, and put incense in them before the Lord tomorrow, and it will be that the man whom the Lord chooses, he will be holy. You take too much upon yourselves, sons of Levi."

Moses said to Korah, "Listen, please, sons of Levi. Does it seem a small thing to you that the God of Israel has separated you from the assembly of Israel to bring you near to Himself to do the service of the tabernacle of the Lord, and to stand before the assembly to minister to them? And He has brought you near to Him, and all your brothers, the sons of Levi, with you, and you also seek the priesthood? Therefore both you and all your company are gathered together against the Lord, and who is Aaron that you murmur against him?"

And Moses sent for Dathan and Abiram the sons of Eliab, who said, "We will not come up. Is it a small thing that you have brought us up out of a land that flows with milk and honey to kill us in the wilderness because you make yourself a prince over us? Moreover you have not brought us into a land that flows with milk and honey nor given us inheritance of fields and vineyards. Will you put out the eyes of these men? We will not come up."

Moses was very angry and said to the Lord, "Do not respect their offering. I have not taken one donkey from them, nor have I hurt one of them."

Moses said to Korah, "You and all your company be before the LORD, you and them and Aaron, tomorrow. Let each man take his censer and put incense in it, and each of you bring his censer before the LORD, two hundred fifty censers. Also you and Aaron shall each bring his censer." Every man took his censer and put fire in it, and laid incense on it, and stood at the door of the tent of meeting with Moses and Aaron. Korah gathered all the assembly against them to the door of the tent of meeting, and the glory of the LORD appeared to all the assembly. The LORD spoke to Moses and to Aaron, saying: Separate yourselves from among this assembly, that I may consume them in a moment.

They fell on their faces and said, "O God, the God of the spirits of all flesh, will one man sin and You will be angry with all the assembly?"

And the LORD spoke to Moses, saying: Speak to the assembly, saying: Get up from around the tents of Korah, Dathan, and Abiram.

Moses rose up and went to Dathan and Abiram, and the elders of Israel followed him. He spoke to the assembly, saying, "Depart now from the tents of these wicked men, and touch nothing of theirs, lest you be swept away for all their sins." So they got up from the tents of Korah, Dathan, and Abiram, on every side, and Dathan and Abiram came out and stood in the opening of their tents, and their wives, and their sons, and their children.

Moses said, "By this you will know that the LORD has sent me to do all these works, because I have not done them of my own mind. If these men die the common death of all men, or if they are visited after the visitation of all men, then the LORD has not sent me. But if the LORD makes a new thing, and the earth opens its mouth and swallows them with all that belongs to them, and they go down alive into the pit, then you will know that these men have despised the LORD."

So it was, when he finished speaking all these words, that the ground that was under them split open. And the earth opened its mouth and swallowed them, and their houses, and all the men that belonged to Korah, and all their goods. And they and all that belonged to them went down alive into the pit, and the earth closed on them, and they perished from among the assembly. All Israel that was around them fled at their cry because they said, "The earth will swallow us also."

A fire went out from the LORD and consumed the two hundred fifty men that offered incense.

The LORD spoke to Moses, saying: Tell Eleazar the son of Aaron the priest to take up the censers out of the blaze, for they are holy. Then scatter the fire far and wide. As for the censers of these men who have sinned at the cost of their own lives, make them into hammered plates as a covering for the altar, for they presented them before the LORD and they are holy. They shall be a sign to the children of Israel.

So Eleazar the priest took the bronze censers, which those who were burned had offered, and they were hammered out as a covering on the altar, to be a memorial to the children of Israel, that no outsider, who is not of the descendants of Aaron, shall approach to offer incense before the LORD, that he might not become like Korah and his company, as the LORD has said to him through Moses.

But the next day all the assembly of the children of Israel murmured against Moses and against Aaron, saying, "You have killed the people of the LORD."

When the assembly was gathered against Moses and Aaron, they looked toward the tent of meeting. The cloud covered it, and the glory of the LORD appeared. Moses and Aaron went before the tent of meeting. And the LORD spoke to Moses, saying, "Get up from among this assembly, that I may destroy them in a moment." And they fell on their faces.

Moses said to Aaron, "Take a censer and put fire in it from off the altar, and put in incense, and go quickly to the assembly, and make an atonement for them, because wrath has gone out from the LORD. The plague has begun." Aaron took it as Moses commanded and ran into the midst of the assembly, where the plague had begun among the people. He put in incense and made an atonement for the people. He stood between the dead and the living, and the plague was stopped. Now those who died in the plague were fourteen thousand seven hundred, besides those that died concerning the thing of Korah. Aaron returned to Moses, to the door of the tent of meeting, and the plague was stopped.

And the LORD spoke to Moses, saying: Speak to the children of Israel, and take from them a rod, a rod for the house of their fathers, from all their leaders according to the house of their fathers, twelve rods. Write each man's name on his rod. You will write the name of Aaron on the rod of Levi, because one rod will be for each father's house. You will lay them in the tent of meeting before the testimony, where I will meet with you. It will be that the rod of the man whom I choose will bud. Thus I will rid myself of the complaints of the children of Israel, that they have been making against you.

Moses spoke to the children of Israel, and each one of their leaders gave him a rod, one for each leader, according to their fathers' houses, even twelve rods, and the rod of Aaron was among their rods. Moses laid the rods before the LORD in the tent of witness.

When Moses went into the tent of witness the next day, the rod of Aaron, for the house of Levi, had sprouted. It brought forth buds, produced blossoms, and yielded almonds. Moses brought out all the rods from before the LORD to all the children of Israel, and they looked, and each man took his rod.

The LORD said to Moses, "Return the rod of Aaron before the testimony, to be kept for a warning to rebels, that you may put an end to their complaints before Me, or else they will die." Moses did so. As the LORD commanded him, so he did.

The children of Israel spoke to Moses, saying, "Behold, we expire, we perish, we all perish. Anyone approaching the tabernacle of the LORD will die. Are we all to perish?"

And the LORD said to Aaron: You and your sons and your father's house with you will bear the iniquity of the sanctuary, and you and your sons with you will bear the iniquity of your priesthood. Your brothers also of the tribe of Levi, the tribe of your father, bring with you, and let them be joined with you, and minister to you. But you and your sons with you will minister before the tent of witness. They will perform duties for you and for the whole tent; but they will not come near the vessels of the sanctuary or the altar, so that neither they nor you die. They will be joined to you and perform the duties of the tent of meeting, for all the service of the tent; no foreigner will come near you.

You yourselves will perform the duties of the sanctuary and the duties of the altar, so that wrath may never come upon the children of Israel again. I Myself have taken your brothers, the Levites, from among the children of Israel; they are given to you as a gift from the LORD to perform the service of the tent of meeting. And you and your sons with you will attend to your priesthood for everything at the altar, and within the veil, and you will serve. I have given your priesthood to you as a gift service, and the foreigner that comes near will be put to death.

The LORD spoke to Aaron: I have certainly given you the charge of the offerings made to Me, all the sanctified gifts of the children of Israel. To you and to your sons have I given them as a portion, as an ordinance forever. This will be yours of the most holy things, reserved from the fire: All of their offerings, all of their grain offerings and all of their sin offerings, and all of their guilt offerings, which they render to Me, will be most holy for you and for your sons. In a most holy place shall you eat it; every male shall eat it. It shall be holy to you.

This is yours: the offering of their gift, with all the wave offerings of the children of Israel. I have given them to you and to your sons and to your daughters with you, as an eternal statute. Everyone who is clean in your house will eat of it.

All the best of the oil, and all the best of the wine, and of the wheat, the first fruits of what they will offer to the LORD, those have I given to you. The first ripe fruit of all which is in their land, which they will bring to the LORD, will be yours. Everyone who is clean in your house will eat of it.

Everything devoted in Israel will be yours. Everything that opens the womb of all flesh, which they bring to the LORD, whether it is of men or animals, will be yours. However, you will surely redeem the firstborn of man, and the firstborn of unclean beasts you will redeem. Their redemption price, reckoned from one month of age, is five shekels, after the shekel of the sanctuary, which is twenty gerahs.

But the firstborn of a herd animal, or the firstborn of a sheep, or the firstborn of a goat, you will not redeem. They are holy. You will splash their blood on the altar and will burn their fat as a fire offering, as a pleasing aroma to the LORD. Their flesh will be yours, as the wave breast and as the right shoulder are yours. All the offerings of the holy things which the children of Israel offer to the LORD I have given to you, and to your sons and your daughters with you, as an eternal statute. It is a covenant of salt forever before the LORD, to you and to your seed with you.

The LORD said to Aaron: You will not have an inheritance in their land, nor will you have any territory among them. I am your territory and your inheritance among the children of Israel.

I have given the children of Levi all the tithes in Israel for an inheritance, for their service, which they serve, even the service of the tent of meeting. Hereafter, the children of Israel shall not come near the tent of meeting, lest they bear sin and die. But the Levites will do the service of the tent of meeting, and they will bear their iniquity. It will be an eternal statute throughout your generations, that among the children of Israel they have no inheritance. But the tithes of the children of Israel, which they offer as an offering to the LORD, I have given to the Levites to inherit. Therefore I have said to them, among the children of Israel they will have no inheritance.

The LORD spoke to Moses, saying: You will speak to the Levites, and say to them: When you take from the children of Israel the tithes that I have given you from them for your inheritance, then you will offer up an offering of it to the LORD, even one-tenth of the tithe. And this offering will be counted to you, as though it was the grain of the threshing floor, and as the fullness of the winepress. Thus you also will set apart an offering to the LORD from all the tithes which you receive from the children of Israel. Out of them you will give the offering of the LORD to Aaron the priest. Out of all your gifts you shall present every offering due to the LORD, from all the best of them, the consecrated part of them.

You will say to them: When you have offered the best from it, then it will be counted to the Levites as the increase of the threshing floor, and as the increase of the winepress. You will eat it in every place, you and your households, because it is your reward for your service in the tent of meeting. You will bear no sin because of it, when you have offered the best of it. The holy things of the children of Israel you will not pollute, and you will not die.

Chukat

Law

(Numbers 19:1–22:1)

A nd the Lord spoke to Moses and to Aaron, saying: This is the statute of the law which the Lord has commanded, saying: Tell the children of Israel that they will bring you a healthy red heifer, which has no blemish, and on which a yoke has never gone, and you will give it to Eleazar the priest, and he will bring it outside the camp, and it will be slaughtered before him. And Eleazar the priest will take from its blood with his finger and sprinkle some of its blood directly before the tent of meeting seven times. Then it will be burned in his sight. Its hide and its flesh and its blood, with her dung, will be burned. And the priest will take cedar wood, and hyssop, and scarlet and throw it into the midst of the burning of the heifer. Then the priest will wash his clothes, and he will bathe his body in water, and afterward he will come into the camp, and the priest will be unclean until evening. He who burns it will wash his clothes in water, and bathe his body in water, and will be unclean until evening.

A man who is clean will gather the ashes of the heifer and deposit them outside the camp in a clean place, and it will be guarded for the assembly of the children of Israel for water of purification. It is for purifying from sin. He that gathers the ashes of the heifer will wash his clothes and be unclean until evening, and it will be for the children of Israel and for the foreigner that lives among them, for an eternal statute.

He that touches the dead body of any man will be unclean seven days. He will make himself clean on the third day, and on the seventh day he will be clean. But if he does not make himself clean on the third day, then the seventh day he will not be clean. Whoever touches the body of any man that is dead and does not purify himself defiles the tabernacle of the Lord, and that person will be cut off from Israel. Because the water of purification was not sprinkled on him, he will be unclean. His uncleanness is still on him.

This is the law, when a man dies in a tent. Each person who comes into the tent and all that is in the tent will be unclean seven days. Every open vessel which has no covering fastened on it is unclean.

Whoever in the field touches one that is slain with a sword, or a dead body, or a bone of a man, or a grave will be unclean seven days.

For an unclean person they will take from the ashes of the burnt sin offering, and running water will be on it in a vessel. A clean person will take hyssop, and dip it in the water, and splash it on the tent, and on all the vessels, and on the people who were there, and on him that touched a bone, or one slain, or one dead, or a grave. The clean person will splash on the unclean person on the third day and on the seventh day. And on the seventh day he shall purify himself, wash his clothes, and bathe in water; and he will be clean at evening. But the man who is unclean and does not purify himself, that person will be cut off from among the assembly because he has defiled the sanctuary of the Lord. The water of purification has not been sprinkled on him. He is unclean. It will be an eternal statute to them.

He that sprinkles the water of purification will wash his clothes, and he that touches the water of purification will be unclean until evening. Whatever the unclean person touches will be unclean, and the person that touches it will be unclean until evening.

Then the children of Israel, the whole assembly, came to the Wilderness of Zin in the first month, and the people dwelt in Kadesh, and Miriam died there and was buried there.

And there was no water for the assembly, and they gathered themselves together against Moses and against Aaron. The people argued with Moses, and spoke, saying, "O that we had died when our brothers died before the Lord! And why have you brought up the assembly of the Lord into this wilderness, that we and our livestock should die here? And why have you brought us up from Egypt, to bring us into this evil place? It is no place of seed, or of figs, or of vines, or of pomegranates. Nor is there any water to drink."

Moses and Aaron went from the presence of the assembly to the door of the tent of meeting, and they fell on their faces, and the glory of the Lord appeared to them. The Lord spoke to Moses, saying: Take the rod, and gather the assembly together, you and Aaron your brother, and speak to the rock before their eyes, and it will give its water, and you will bring out to them water from the rock; so you will give the assembly and their livestock drink.

So Moses took the rod from before the Lord, as He commanded him. Moses and Aaron gathered the assembly before the rock, and he said to them, "Hear now, you rebels. Will we bring out water from this rock for you?" And Moses lifted up his hand, and he struck the rock twice with his rod, and plenty of water came out, and the assembly drank, and their livestock.

The Lord spoke to Moses and Aaron, "Because you did not believe in Me, to sanctify Me in the eyes of the children of Israel, therefore you will not bring this assembly into the land which I have given them."

This is the water of Meribah because the children of Israel argued with the Lord, and He was sanctified among them.

Moses sent messengers from Kadesh to the king of Edom,

> "Thus says your brother Israel: You know all the hardship that has found us, how our fathers went down into Egypt, and we lived in Egypt a long time, and the Egyptians distressed us and our fathers. And when we cried out to the Lord, He heard our voice and sent an angel and brought us out of Egypt.
>
> "And here we are in Kadesh, a city on the edge of your territory. Please let us pass through your land. We will not pass through the fields or the vineyards, or drink of the water of the wells. We will travel the king's highway. We will not turn to the right hand nor the left, until we have passed through your territory."

Edom said to him,

> "You will not pass through me, lest with the sword I come out against you."

The children of Israel said to him,

> "We will travel the highway, and if we and our livestock drink of your water, then we will pay for it. I will only go through on my feet without doing anything else."

He said,

> "You will not go through."

And Edom came out against them with many people and with a strong hand. Edom refused to give Israel passage through his territory, so Israel turned away from him.

They journeyed from Kadesh, and the children of Israel, even the whole assembly, came to Mount Hor. The Lord spoke to Moses and Aaron in Mount Hor, by the border of the land of Edom, saying, "Aaron will be gathered to his people because he will not enter into the land which I have given to the children of Israel because you rebelled against Me at the water of Meribah. Take Aaron and Eleazar his son, and bring them up to Mount Hor, and strip Aaron of his garments, and put them on Eleazar his son, and Aaron will be gathered to his people, and he will die there."

Moses did as the Lord commanded, and they went up onto Mount Hor in the sight of all the assembly. Moses stripped Aaron of his garments and put them on Eleazar his son. And Aaron died there on the top of the mountain, and Moses and Eleazar came down from the mountain. When all the assembly saw that Aaron was dead, they wept for Aaron thirty days, all the house of Israel.

When King Arad the Canaanite, who lived in the Negev, heard that Israel came by the way of Atharim, he fought against Israel and took some of them captive. Israel vowed a vow to the LORD and said, "If You will indeed deliver this people into my hand, then I will utterly destroy their cities." The LORD listened to the voice of Israel and delivered up the Canaanites, and they utterly destroyed them and their cities, and he called the name of the place Hormah.

They journeyed from Mount Hor by the way of the Red Sea, to go around the land of Edom, and the soul of the people was very discouraged because of the way. The people spoke against God and against Moses, "Why have you brought us up from Egypt to die in the wilderness? For there is no bread or water, and our soul loathes this worthless manna."

So the LORD sent poisonous serpents among the people, and they bit the people, and many children of Israel died. So the people came to Moses and said, "We have sinned for we have spoken against the LORD and against you. Pray to the LORD, and He will take away the serpents from us." And Moses prayed for the people.

The LORD said to Moses, "Make a poisonous serpent, and put it on a pole, and it will be, that everyone who is bitten, when he looks at it, will live." Moses made a bronze serpent and put it on a pole, and if a serpent had bitten any man, when he looked at the bronze serpent he lived.

The children of Israel set out and camped in Oboth. They journeyed from Oboth and camped at Iye Abarim in the wilderness, which is before Moab toward the sunrise. From there they journeyed and camped in the Valley of Zered. From there they journeyed and camped on the other side of Arnon, which is in the wilderness that comes out of the borders of the Amorites, for Arnon is the border of Moab, between Moab and the Amorites. Therefore it is said in the Book of the Wars of the LORD:

> "Zahab in Suphah, and in the brooks
>   of Arnon, and at the stream of the brooks
> that goes down to the dwelling of Ar,
>   and lies on the border of Moab."

From there they went to Beer. That is the well of which the LORD spoke to Moses, "Gather the people together, and I will give them water."

Then Israel sang this song:

> "Spring up, O well!
>   sing to it—

the leaders dug the well;
   the nobles of the people dug,
   by the lawgiver, with their staffs."

And from the wilderness they went to Mattanah, and from Mattanah to Nahaliel, and from Nahaliel to Bamoth, and from Bamoth in the valley that is in the country of Moab to the top of Pisgah, which looks toward Jeshimon.

Israel sent messengers to Sihon king of the Amorites, saying,

"Let me pass through your land. We will not turn into the fields nor into the vineyards. We will not drink of the waters of the well. But we will go along by the king's highway until we are past your borders."

Sihon would not allow Israel to pass through his border. But Sihon gathered all his people together and went out against Israel into the wilderness, and he came to Jahaz and fought against Israel. Israel defeated him with the edge of the sword and possessed his land from Arnon to Jabbok, all the way to the children of Ammon, because the border of the children of Ammon was strong. Israel took all these cities, and Israel lived in all the cities of the Amorites, in Heshbon, and in all its villages. Because Heshbon was the city of Sihon the king of the Amorites, who had fought against the former king of Moab and taken all his land out of his hand, to Arnon.

Therefore they that speak in proverbs say:

"Come into Heshbon; let it be built,
   and let the city of Sihon be established,
because a fire went out of Heshbon,
   a flame from the city of Sihon;
it has devoured Ar of Moab
   and the masters of the high places of Arnon.
Woe to you, Moab!
   You have perished, O people of Chemosh!
He has made his sons fugitives,
   and his daughters captives,
   to Sihon king of the Amorites.

"We have overthrown them;
   Heshbon is perished to Dibon,
and we have desolated them to Nophah,
   which reaches to Medeba."

Thus Israel lived in the land of the Amorites.

Moses sent to spy out Jazer, and they took its villages and drove out the Amorites who were there. They turned and went up by the way of Bashan, and Og the king of Bashan went out against them, he and all his people, to the battle at Edrei.

The Lord said to Moses, "Do not fear him because into your hand I have given him, and all his people, and his land, and you will do to him as you did to Sihon king of the Amorites, who dwelt at Heshbon."

So they killed him, and his sons, and all his people, until there was not a survivor left to him alive, and they possessed his land.

Then the children of Israel set out and camped in the plains of Moab on the other side of the Jordan from Jericho.

Balak

Balak

(Numbers 22:2–25:9)

Balak the son of Zippor saw all that Israel had done to the Amorites. Moab was very afraid of the people because they were many, and Moab was distressed because of the children of Israel.

Moab said to the elders of Midian, "Now this company will lick up all that are around us, as the ox licks up the grass of the field."

And Balak the son of Zippor was king of the Moabites at that time. He sent messengers to Balaam the son of Beor at Pethor, which is by the Euphrates in the land of the sons of his people, to call him, saying,

"A people went out from Egypt. They cover the face of the earth, and they dwell next to me. And now, please come curse this people for me because they are too mighty for me. Perhaps I will prevail, and we will defeat them, and I will drive them out of the land because I know that he whom you bless is blessed, and he whom you curse is cursed."

The elders of Moab and the elders of Midian went with the divination payments in their hand, and they came to Balaam and spoke to him the words of Balak.

He said to them, "Lodge here tonight, and I will bring you word again, as the Lord will speak to me." And the leaders of Moab dwelt with Balaam.

God came to Balaam and said, "Who are these men with you?"

And Balaam said to God, "Balak the son of Zippor, king of Moab, has sent word to me, saying, 'A people went out of Egypt who covers the face of the earth. Now come, curse them for me. Perhaps I will be able to battle them and drive them out.'"

God said to Balaam, "You will not go with them. You will not curse the people because they are blessed."

So Balaam rose up in the morning and said to the princes of Balak, "Go to your land because the Lord refuses to let me to go with you."

The princes of Moab rose up, and they went to Balak and said, "Balaam refuses to come with us."

Again Balak sent officials, more numerous and more honorable than they. They came to Balaam and said to him,

> "Thus says Balak the son of Zippor, 'Please, let nothing hold you back from coming to me, because I will promote you to very great honor, and anything you say to me I will do. Come please, curse this people for me.' "

Balaam answered the servants of Balak, "If Balak gave me his house full of silver and gold, I am not able to go beyond the command of the LORD my God, to do less or more. Now please remain here tonight, that I may know what more the LORD will say to me."

God came to Balaam at night and said to him, "If the men come to call you, rise up and go with them. But surely the word which I will say to you, that will you do."

Balaam rose up in the morning, and saddled his donkey, and went with the princes of Moab. The anger of God was inflamed because he went, and the angel of the LORD stood in the way as an adversary against him. Now he was riding on his donkey, and his two servants were with him. The donkey saw the angel of the LORD standing in the way, and His sword was drawn in His hand, so the donkey turned out of the way and went into the field. Balaam struck the donkey to turn her onto the road.

But the angel of the LORD stood in a narrow path of the vineyards, a wall on this side and a wall on that side. When the donkey saw the angel of the LORD, she threw herself into the wall and crushed the foot of Balaam against the wall, and he struck her again.

The angel of the LORD went further and stood in a narrow place where there was no way to turn either to the right hand or to the left. When the donkey saw the angel of the LORD, she fell down under Balaam, and the anger of Balaam was inflamed, and he struck the donkey with a staff. Then the LORD opened the mouth of the donkey, and she said to Balaam, "What have I done to you, that you have struck me these three times?"

And Balaam said to the donkey, "You have mocked me. O that there was a sword in my hand, for now I would kill you."

The donkey said to Balaam, "Am I not your donkey, whom you have ridden since I became yours, to this day? Do I normally do this to you?"

And he said, "No."

Then the LORD opened the eyes of Balaam, and he saw the angel of the LORD standing in the way, and His sword was drawn in His hand, and he bowed his head and fell flat on his face.

The angel of the LORD said to him, "Why have you struck your donkey these three times? I have come out to oppose you, because your way is perverse before Me. And the donkey saw Me and turned from Me these three times. If she had not turned from Me, surely by now I would have slain you and saved her alive."

Balaam said to the angel of the LORD, "I have sinned because I did not know that You stood in the way against me. Now therefore, if it displeases You, I will return."

The angel of the LORD said to Balaam, "Go with the men. But only speak the word that I tell you to speak." So Balaam went with the leaders of Balak.

When Balak heard that Balaam had come, he went out to meet him in a city of Moab which is on the border of Arnon, which is at the furthest end of the border. Balak said to Balaam, "Did I not earnestly send to summon you? Why did you not come to me? Indeed am I not able to honor you?"

And Balaam said to Balak, "I have come to you now. But am I able to speak just anything? The word God puts in my mouth is what I will speak."

Balaam went with Balak, and they came to Kiriath Huzoth. Balak offered oxen and sheep and sent them to Balaam and to the officials who were with him.

It came to pass on the next day that Balak took Balaam and brought him up to Bamoth Baal, and from there he saw the extent of the people.

And Balaam said to Balak, "Build for me seven altars, and prepare for me seven oxen and seven rams." Balak did as Balaam had spoken, and Balak and Balaam offered on every altar a bull and a ram.

Balaam said to Balak, "Stand by your burnt offering, and I will go. Perhaps the LORD will come to meet me, and whatever He shows me I will tell you." And he went to a high place.

God met Balaam, and he said to Him, "I have prepared seven altars, and I have offered on every altar a bull and a ram."

The LORD put a word in the mouth of Balaam and said, "Return to Balak, and thus you will speak."

So he returned to Balak, who was standing by his burnt offering with all the princes of Moab. Then Balaam uttered his oracle, saying:

"Balak has brought me from Aram,
    the king of Moab from the mountains of the east,
saying, 'Come, curse Jacob for me,
    and come, defy Israel!'
How will I curse
    whom God has not cursed?
Or how will I defy
    whom the LORD has not defied?
For from the top of the rocks I see him,
    and from the hills I behold him;
there, the people will dwell alone
    and will not be counted among the nations.

Who can count the dust of Jacob
    and the number of one-fourth of Israel?
Let me die the death of the righteous,
    and let my last end be like his!"

And Balak said to Balaam, "What have you done to me? I brought you to curse my enemies, but now you have certainly blessed them."

He answered and said, "Must I not take heed to speak what the LORD puts in my mouth?"

And Balak said to him, "Please come with me to another place from where you may see them. You will see part of them, but will not see them all. Curse them for me from there." He brought him into the field of Zophim, to the top of Pisgah, and built seven altars and offered a bull and a ram on each altar.

He said to Balak, "Stand here by your burnt offerings while I meet the LORD over there."

The LORD met Balaam and put a word in his mouth and said, "Go again to Balak, and thus you will speak."

When he came to him, he was standing by his burnt offerings with the princes of Moab. And Balak said to him, "What has the LORD spoken?"

And he took up his parable and said:

"Rise up, Balak, and hear!
    Listen to me, you son of Zippor!
God is not a man, that He should lie,
    nor a son of man, that He should repent.
Has He spoken, and will He not do it?
    Or has He spoken, and will He not make it good?
See, I have received a commandment to bless,
    and He has blessed, and I cannot reverse it.

"He has not beheld iniquity in Jacob,
    nor has He seen perverseness in Israel.
The LORD his God is with him,
    and the shout of a king is among them.
God, who brings them out of Egypt,
    has strength like a wild ox.
Surely there is no enchantment against Jacob,
    nor is there any divination against Israel.
For this time it will be said of Jacob and of Israel,
    'See what God has done!'
A people rises up as a great lion,
    and lifts itself up like a lion;

it shall not lie down until it eats the prey
and drinks the blood of the slain."

Balak said to Balaam, "Do not curse them at all, nor bless them at all."
But Balaam answered and said to Balak, "Did I not tell you, saying, 'All
that the LORD speaks, I must do'?"
And Balak said to Balaam, "Please come. I will bring you to another place.
Perhaps it will please God that you may curse them for me from there."
Balak brought Balaam to the top of Peor, which looks toward Jeshimon.
Balaam said to Balak, "Build for me seven altars, and prepare for me
seven bulls and seven rams." Balak did as Balaam said and offered a bull and
a ram on each altar.

And when Balaam saw that it pleased the LORD to bless Israel, he did not go
as other times to seek for enchantments, but he set his face toward the wilderness. Balaam lifted up his eyes, and he saw Israel dwelling in their tents by their
tribes, and the Spirit of God came on him. He took up his proverb and said:

"Balaam the son of Beor has said,
and the man whose eyes are open has said,
he has said, who heard the words of God,
who saw the vision of the Almighty,
falling into a trance, but having his eyes open:

"How lovely are your tents, O Jacob,
and your tabernacles, O Israel!

"Like palm trees are they spread out,
like gardens by the river's side,
like the aloe plant, which the LORD has planted,
and like cedar trees beside the waters.
He will pour the water out of his buckets,
and his seed will be in many waters.

"His king will be higher than Agag,
and his kingdom will be exalted.

"God brings him out of Egypt;
he has the horns of a wild ox;
he will eat up the nations, his enemies,
and will break their bones,
and pierce them through with his arrows.
He crouches, he lies down as a lion, and as a lion,
who will stir him up?

"Blessed is he who blesses you,
and cursed is he who curses you."

The anger of Balak was inflamed against Balaam, and he struck his hands together. And Balak said to Balaam, "I called you to curse my enemies, and indeed, you have certainly blessed them these three times. Now flee to your own place. I thought to promote you to great honor. But certainly, the LORD has kept you back from honor."

Balaam said to Balak, "Did I not speak to your messengers which you sent to me, saying, 'If Balak would give me his house full of silver and gold, I cannot go beyond the mouth of the LORD, to do either good or bad of my own mind. But what the LORD speaks, I will speak'? And now, I am going to my people. Come, I will advise you what this people will do to your people in the latter days."

He took up his parable and said:

"The oracle of Balaam the son of Beor,
and the oracle of the man whose eyes are open;
the oracle of the one hearing the words of God,
and knowing the knowledge of the Most High,
who sees the vision of the Almighty,
falling into a trance, but having his eyes open:

"I will see him, but not now;
I will behold him, but not near;
a star will come out of Jacob,
and a scepter will rise out of Israel,
and will crush the borderlands of Moab,
and destroy all the children of Sheth.
Edom will be a possession,
and Seir, a possession of its enemies,
while Israel does valiantly.
One out of Jacob shall have dominion,
and destroy the survivors of the city."

Then he looked on Amalek; he took up his proverb and said:

"Amalek was the first of the nations,
but his end will be that he perishes forever."

He looked on the Kenites and took up his proverb and said:

"Strong is your dwelling place,
and you put your nest in a rock;

nevertheless the Kenite will be wasted.
How long until Ashur carries you away captive?"

He took up his proverb and said:

"Alas, who will live when God does this?
And ships will come from the coasts of Cyprus
and will afflict Ashur and will afflict Eber,
and he also will perish forever."

Balaam rose up and went and returned to his place, and Balak also went his way.

While Israel dwelt in Shittim, the people began to commit harlotry with the women of Moab. They called the people to the sacrifices of their gods, and the people ate and bowed down to their gods. Israel joined himself to the Baal of Peor, and the anger of the LORD was inflamed against Israel.

The LORD said to Moses, "Take all the chiefs of the people and hang them before the LORD in the sun, that the fierce anger of the LORD turn from Israel."

Moses said to the judges of Israel, "Kill each of the men who have aligned themselves with the Baal of Peor."

Behold, one of the children of Israel came and brought to his brothers a Midianite woman in the sight of Moses and in the sight of all the assembly of the children of Israel, who were weeping before the door of the tent of meeting. When Phinehas the son of Eleazar, the son of Aaron the priest, saw it, he rose up from among the assembly and took a spear in his hand, and he went after the man of Israel into the tent, and thrust both of them through, the man of Israel and the woman through her belly. So the plague was stopped from the children of Israel. Those that died in the plague were twenty-four thousand.

Pinchas

Phinehas

(Numbers 25:10–29:40)

The LORD spoke to Moses, saying, "Phinehas the son of Eleazar, the son of Aaron the priest, has turned My wrath away from the children of Israel, because he was zealous for My sake among them, so I did not exterminate the children of Israel in My zeal. Therefore say, 'I hereby grant him My covenant of peace. And it will be for him and his seed after him, even the covenant of an everlasting priesthood, because he was zealous for his God and made an atonement for the children of Israel.' "

Now the name of the slain Israelite who was slain with the Midianite woman was Zimri the son of Salu, a leader of a chief house among the Simeonites. The name of the Midianite woman that was slain was Kozbi the daughter of Zur. He was chief over a people and of a father's house in Midian.

The LORD spoke to Moses, saying, "Be hostile to the Midianites, and defeat them, because they have been hostile to you with their wiles, with which they have deceived you in the matter of Peor and in the matter of Kozbi the daughter of a leader of Midian, their sister, who was slain on the day of the plague because of Peor."

After the plague, the LORD spoke to Moses and to Eleazar the son of Aaron the priest, saying, "Take the count of all the assembly of the children of Israel from twenty years old and older, throughout their fathers' houses, all that are able to go to war in Israel." Moses and Eleazar the priest spoke with them in the plains of Moab by Jordan near Jericho, saying, "Take the count of the people from twenty years old and older," as the LORD commanded Moses.

The children of Israel, who went out of the land of Egypt, were these:

Reuben, the oldest son of Israel. The children of Reuben:
    of Hanok, from whom comes the family of the Hanokites;
    of Pallu, the family of the Palluites;
    of Hezron, the family of the Hezronites;
    of Karmi, the family of the Karmites.

These are the families of the Reubenites: those who were counted were forty-three thousand seven hundred thirty.

The son of Pallu was Eliab. The sons of Eliab were Nemuel, and Dathan, and Abiram. This is that Dathan and Abiram, called out from the assembly, who argued against Moses and against Aaron in the company of Korah when they argued against the LORD. And the earth opened its mouth and swallowed them with Korah when that company died, when the fire devoured two hundred fifty men, and they became a sign. But the children of Korah did not die.

The sons of Simeon by their families were:
    of Nemuel, the family of the Nemuelites;
    of Jamin, the family of the Jaminites;
    of Jakin, the family of the Jakinites;
    of Zerah, the family of the Zerahites;
    of Shaul, the family of the Shaulites.
These are the families of the Simeonites: twenty-two thousand two hundred.

The children of Gad by their families were:
    of Zephon, the family of the Zephonites;
    of Haggi, the family of the Haggites;
    of Shuni, the family of the Shunites;
    of Ozni, the family of the Oznites;
    of Eri, the family of the Erites;
    of Arodi, the family of the Arodites;
    of Areli, the family of the Arelites.
These are the families of the children of Gad according to those by their count: forty thousand five hundred.

The sons of Judah were Er and Onan, and Er and Onan died in the land of Canaan.
The sons of Judah after their families were:
    of Shelah, the family of the Shelanites;
    of Perez, the family of the Perezites;
    of Zerah, the family of the Zerahites.
        The sons of Perez were:
        of Hezron, the family of the Hezronites;
        of Hamul, the family of the Hamulites.
These are the families of Judah by their count: seventy-six thousand five hundred.

The sons of Issachar by their families were:
    of Tola, the family of the Tolaites;

of Puah, the family of the Puites;
of Jashub, the family of the Jashubites;
of Shimron, the family of the Shimronites.
These are the families of Issachar by their count: sixty-four thousand three
hundred.

The sons of Zebulun by their families were:
of Sered, the family of the Seredites;
of Elon, the family of the Elonites;
of Jahleel, the family of the Jahleelites.
These are the families of the Zebulunites by their count: sixty thousand
five hundred.

The sons of Joseph according to their families, by Manasseh and Ephraim,
were:

The sons of Manasseh:
of Makir, the family of the Makirites, and Makir begot Gilead;
of Gilead, the family of the Gileadites.
These are the sons of Gilead:
of Iezer, the family of the Iezerites;
of Helek, the family of the Helekites;
and of Asriel, the family of the Asrielites;
and of Shechem, the family of the Shechemites;
and of Shemida, the family of the Shemidaites;
and of Hepher, the family of the Hepherites.
Zelophehad the son of Hepher had no sons, but daughters, and the
names of the daughters of Zelophehad were Mahlah, Noah, Hoglah,
Milkah, and Tirzah.
These are the families of Manasseh, and those who were numbered of them
were fifty-two thousand seven hundred.

These are the sons of Ephraim according to their families:
of Shuthelah, the family of the Shuthelahites;
of Beker, the family of the Bekerites;
of Tahan, the family of the Tahanites.
These are the sons of Shuthelah:
of Eran, the family of the Eranites.
These are the families of the sons of Ephraim by their count: thirty-two
thousand five hundred.

These are the sons of Joseph by their families.

The sons of Benjamin by their families were:
    of Bela, the family of the Belaites;
    of Ashbel, the family of the Ashbelites;
    of Ahiram, the family of the Ahiramites;
    of Shupham, the family of the Shuphamites;
    of Hupham, the family of the Huphamites.
    The sons of Bela were Ard and Naaman:
        of Ard, the family of the Ardites;
        and of Naaman, the family of the Naamites.
These are the sons of Benjamin by their families, and by their count: forty-
five thousand six hundred.

These are the sons of Dan according to their families:
    of Shuham, the family of the Shuhamites.
These are the families of Dan after their families. All the families of the
Shuhamites, by their count, were sixty-four thousand four hundred.

The sons of Asher by their families were:
    of Imnah, the family of the Imnites;
    of Ishvi, the family of the Ishvites;
    of Beriah, the family of the Beriites.
        Of the sons of Beriah were:
        of Heber, the family of the Heberites;
        of Malkiel, the family of the Malkielites.
    The name of the daughter of Asher was Serah.
These are the families of the sons of Asher by their count: fifty-three thousand four hundred.

Of the sons of Naphtali by their families were:
    of Jahzeel, the family of the Jahzeelites;
    of Guni, the family of the Gunites;
    of Jezer, the family of the Jezerites;
    of Shillem, the family of the Shillemites.
These are the families of Naphtali according to their families; those who
were numbered of them were forty-five thousand four hundred.

These were the counted of the children of Israel: six hundred one thousand
seven hundred thirty.

The LORD spoke to Moses, saying: To these the land will be divided for
an inheritance by the number of names. To a large tribe you shall give a
large inheritance, and to a small tribe you shall give a small inheritance.
To each one his inheritance will be given according to those who were

numbered of him. But the land will be divided by lot. By the names of the tribes of their fathers they will inherit. According to the lot his possession will be divided between large and small.

These are those counted of the Levites by their families:
of Gershon, the family of the Gershonites;
of Kohath, the family of the Kohathites;
of Merari, the family of the Merarites.
These are the families of the Levites:
the family of the Libnites,
the family of the Hebronites,
the family of the Mahlites,
the family of the Mushites,
the family of the Korahites.
And Kohath begot Amram. And the name of the wife of Amram was Jochebed, the daughter of Levi, whom her mother bore to Levi in Egypt, and she bore to Amram Aaron and Moses and Miriam their sister. To Aaron was born Nadab, and Abihu, Eleazar, and Ithamar. Nadab and Abihu died when they offered foreign fire before the LORD.

Those who were numbered of them were twenty-three thousand, each male from one month old and older; for they were not counted among the children of Israel, because there was no inheritance given them among the children of Israel.

These were counted by Moses and Eleazar the priest, who counted the children of Israel in the plains of Moab by Jordan near Jericho. But among these there was not a man counted by Moses and Aaron the priest when they counted the children of Israel in the Wilderness of Sinai because the LORD had said of them, "They will surely die in the wilderness." And there was not a man left of them, except Caleb the son of Jephunneh and Joshua the son of Nun.

Then came near the daughters of Zelophehad, the son of Hepher, the son of Gilead, the son of Makir, the son of Manasseh, of the families of Manasseh the son of Joseph, and these are the names of his daughters: Mahlah, Noah, Hoglah, Milkah, and Tirzah. They stood before Moses, and before Eleazar the priest, and before the leaders and all the assembly by the door of the tent of meeting, saying, "Our father died in the wilderness, and he was not in the company of them that gathered against the LORD, in the company of Korah, but died in his own sin and had no sons. Why should the name of our father diminish from among his family, because he has no son? Give to us a possession among the brothers of our father."

Moses brought their case before the LORD. The LORD spoke to Moses, saying: The daughters of Zelophehad speak right. You will certainly give them an inheritance among their father's brothers, and you will cause the inheritance of their father to pass on to them.

You will speak to the children of Israel, saying, "If a man dies, and has no son, then you will cause his inheritance to pass on to his daughter. If he has no daughter, then you will give his inheritance to his brothers. If he has no brothers, then you will give his inheritance to his father's brothers. If his father has no brothers, then you will give his inheritance to his closest kinsman in his family, and he will possess it. And it will be for the children of Israel a statute of judgment, as the LORD commanded Moses."

The LORD said to Moses, "Go up into this mountain of Abarim, and see the land which I have given to the children of Israel. When you have seen it, you also will be gathered to your people as Aaron your brother was gathered. For you rebelled against My commandment in the Wilderness of Zin when the congregation argued against Me. You did not show My holiness at the waters before their eyes." (These are the waters of Meribah in Kadesh in the Wilderness of Zin.)

Moses spoke to the LORD, saying, "Let the LORD, the God of the spirits of all flesh, appoint a man over the assembly who will go out before them, and who will go in before them, and who will lead them out, and who will bring them in, so the assembly of the LORD will not be like sheep who do not have a shepherd."

The LORD said to Moses, "Take Joshua the son of Nun, a man in whom is the Spirit, and lay your hand on him, and cause him to stand before Eleazar the priest and before all the assembly, and command in their sight. You will put some of your majesty on him, in order that all the assembly of the children of Israel will listen. He will stand before Eleazar the priest, who will ask for him about the judgment of the Urim before the LORD. At his word will they go out, and at his word they will come in, both he and all the children of Israel with him, even all the assembly."

Moses did as the LORD commanded him, and he took Joshua, and he caused him to stand before Eleazar the priest and before all the assembly. And he laid his hands on him and commanded him as the LORD spoke by the hand of Moses.

And the LORD spoke to Moses, saying: Command the children of Israel and say to them: My offering, My bread for My sacrifices made by fire, as a pleasing aroma to Me, you will guard to offer to Me at their time. You will say to them: This is the fire offering which you will bring near to the LORD: two male lambs in their first year, without blemish, day by day, as a regular burnt offering. The one lamb you will offer in the morning, and the other lamb you will offer at evening, and one-tenth of an ephah of flour as a grain offering, mingled with one-fourth of a hin of beaten oil. It is a regular burnt offering, which was ordained at Mount Sinai as a pleasing aroma, a sacrifice made by fire to the LORD. Its drink offering will be one-fourth of a hin for the one lamb. In a holy place you will pour the strong wine to the LORD as a drink offering. The other lamb you will offer at evening. As the morning grain offering and its drink offering, you will offer it as an offering made by fire, a pleasing aroma to the LORD.

On the Sabbath day two lambs in their first year, without blemish, and two-tenths of an ephah of flour as a grain offering, mixed with oil, and its drink offering— this is the burnt offering of every Sabbath, in addition to the regular burnt offering and its drink offering.

At the beginnings of your months you will offer a burnt offering to the LORD: two young bulls, one ram, seven lambs in their first year, without blemish; three-tenths of an ephah of flour as a grain offering, mixed with oil, for one bull; and two-tenths of an ephah of flour as a grain offering, mixed with oil, for one ram; and one-tenth of an ephah of flour mixed with oil as a grain offering for one lamb; as a burnt offering of a pleasing aroma, a sacrifice made by fire to the LORD. Their drink offerings will be one-half a hin of wine for a bull, and one-third of a hin for a ram, and one-fourth of a hin for a lamb. This is the burnt offering of each month throughout the months of the year. Also one male goat as a sin offering to the LORD shall be offered, besides the regular burnt offering and its drink offering.

On the fourteenth day of the first month is the Passover of the LORD. On the fifteenth day of this month is the feast. Unleavened bread will be eaten for seven days. On the first day there will be a holy convocation. You will not do any ordinary work, but you will offer a sacrifice made by fire as a burnt offering to the LORD: two young bulls, and one ram, and seven lambs in their first year. Be sure they are without blemish. And their grain offering will be of flour mixed with oil. Three-tenths of an ephah you will offer for a bull, and two-tenths of an ephah for a ram. One-tenth of an ephah you will offer for each of the seven lambs, and one goat as a sin offering, to make an atonement for you. You will offer these in addition to the burnt offering in the morning, which is for a regular burnt offering. The same way you will offer daily, throughout the seven days, the food of the sacrifice made by fire, as a pleasing aroma to the LORD. It will be offered in addition to the regular burnt offering and its drink offering. And on the seventh day you will have a holy assembly. You will not do any ordinary work.

And on the day of the first fruits, when you bring a new grain offering to the LORD at your Feast of Weeks, you will have a holy assembly. You will do no ordinary work. But you will offer the burnt offering as a pleasing aroma to the LORD: two young bulls, one ram, and seven lambs in their first year; and their grain offering of flour mixed with oil, three-tenths of an ephah for one bull, two-tenths of an ephah for one ram, one-tenth of an ephah for each of the seven lambs; and one goat, to make an atonement for you. Make sure they are without blemish. You will offer them with their drink offerings, besides the regular burnt offering and its grain offering.

In the seventh month, on the first day of the month, you will have a holy assembly. You will do no ordinary work. It is a day of blowing the trumpets for you. You will offer a burnt offering as a pleasing aroma to the LORD: one young bull, one ram, and seven lambs in their first year, without blemish; their grain offering will be of flour mixed with oil, three-tenths of an ephah for a bull, and two-tenths of an ephah for a ram, and one-tenth of an ephah for one lamb, for the seven lambs; also one goat as a sin offering, to make an atonement for you; besides the burnt offering of the month and its grain offering, and the daily burnt offering and its grain offering, and their drink offerings, according to their rule, as a pleasing aroma, a sacrifice made by fire to the LORD.

You will have a holy assembly on the tenth day of this seventh month, and you will afflict yourselves. You will not do any work on it. But you will offer a burnt offering to the LORD as a pleasing aroma: one young bull, one ram, and seven lambs in their first year. Be sure they are without blemish. Their grain offering will be of flour mixed with oil, three-tenths of an ephah for the bull, and two-tenths of an ephah for one ram, and one-tenth of an ephah for each of the seven lambs; also one goat as a sin offering in addition to the sin offering of atonement, and the regular burnt offering, and its grain offering, and their drink offerings.

On the fifteenth day of the seventh month you will have a holy convocation. You will do no ordinary work, and you will keep a feast to the LORD seven days. And you will offer a burnt offering, a sacrifice made by fire, as a pleasing aroma to the LORD: thirteen young bulls, two rams, and fourteen lambs in their first year, without blemish. And their grain offering will be of flour mixed with oil, three-tenths of an ephah to a bull, and two-tenths of an ephah to each ram of the two rams, and one-tenth to each lamb of the fourteen lambs; and one goat as a sin offering in addition to the regular burnt offering, its grain offering, and its drink offering.

On the second day present twelve young bulls, two rams, fourteen lambs in their first year without blemish, and their grain offering and their drink offerings, for the bulls, for the rams, and for the lambs, by their number according to the ordinance; also one goat as a sin offering, besides the regular burnt offering, and its grain offering, and their drink offerings.

On the third day present eleven bulls, two rams, fourteen lambs in their first year without blemish, and their grain offering and their drink offerings, for the bulls, for the rams, and for the lambs, by their number according to the ordinance; also one goat as a sin offering, besides the regular burnt offering, and its grain offering, and its drink offering.

On the fourth day present ten bulls, two rams, and fourteen lambs in their first year without blemish, and their grain offering and their drink offerings, for the bulls, for the rams, and for the lambs, by their number according to the ordinance; also one goat as a sin offering in addition to the regular burnt offering, its grain offering, and its drink offering.

On the fifth day present nine bulls, two rams, and fourteen lambs in their first year without blemish, and their grain offering and their drink offerings, for the bulls, for the rams, and for the lambs, by their number according to the ordinance; also one goat as a sin offering in addition to the regular burnt offering, and its grain offering, and its drink offering.

On the sixth day present eight bulls, two rams, and fourteen lambs in their first year without blemish, and their grain offering and their drink offerings, for the bulls, for the rams, and for the lambs, by their number according to the ordinance; also one goat as a sin offering in addition to the regular burnt offering, its grain offering, and its drink offering.

On the seventh day present seven bulls, two rams, and fourteen lambs in their first year without blemish, and their grain offering and their drink offerings, for the bulls, for the rams, and for the lambs, by their number according to the ordinance; also one goat as a sin offering in addition to the regular burnt offering, its grain offering, and its drink offering.

On the eighth day you will have a solemn assembly. You will do no ordinary work on it. But you will offer a burnt offering, a sacrifice made by fire as a pleasing aroma to the LORD: one bull, one ram, seven lambs in their first year, without blemish. Their grain offering and their drink offerings, for the bull, for the ram, and for the lambs, will be according to their number, according to the rule; also one goat as a sin offering in addition to the regular burnt offering, and its grain offering, and its drink offering.

These things you will do to the LORD in your set feasts in addition to your vows and your freewill offerings, as your burnt offerings, and as your grain offerings, and as your drink offerings, and as your peace offerings.

Moses told the children of Israel everything, according to all that the LORD commanded Moses.

Matot

Tribes

(Numbers 30:1–32:42)

And Moses spoke to the heads of the tribes of the children of Israel, saying: This is the thing that the LORD has commanded. If a man vows a vow to the LORD, or swears an oath to bind himself with a bond, he will not break his word. He will do according to all that proceeds out of his mouth.

If a woman makes a vow to the LORD, and binds herself by a bond, while in her father's house in her youth, and her father hears her vow and her bond with which she has bound herself, and her father is silent to her, then all her vows will stand, and every bond with which she has bound herself will stand. But if her father restrains her in the day he hears, none of her vows or her bonds with which she has bound herself will stand, and the LORD will forgive her, because her father restrained her.

If she had a husband when she vowed, or uttered anything out of her lips with which she bound herself, and her husband heard it and was silent to her in the day that he heard it, then her vows will stand, and her bonds with which she bound herself will stand. But if her husband restrains her on the day that he heard it, then he will make her vow which she vowed and that which she uttered with her lips, with which she bound herself, of no effect, and the LORD will forgive her.

But every vow of a widow and of her that is divorced, with which she has bound herself, will stand against her.

If she vowed in her husband's house, or bound herself by a bond with an oath, and her husband heard it and was silent to her and did not restrain her, then all her vows will stand, and every bond with which she bound herself will stand. But if her husband has clearly voided them on the day he heard them, then whatever proceeded out of her lips concerning her vows, or concerning the bond of herself, will not stand. Her husband has voided them, and the LORD will forgive her. Every vow, and every binding oath to afflict her soul, her husband may establish, or her husband may nullify. But if her husband says nothing to her from day to day, then he confirms all her vows, or all her pledges, which bind her. He confirms them because he said nothing to her on the day that he heard them. But if he clearly makes them void after he has heard them, then he will bear her iniquity.

These are the statutes which the LORD commanded Moses, between a man and his wife, and between the father and his daughter, while she is still young and in her father's house.

And the LORD spoke to Moses, saying, "Avenge the children of Israel on the Midianites. Afterward you will be gathered to your people."

Moses spoke to the people, saying, "Arm some of your men for war, and let them go against the Midianites to give the vengeance of the LORD against Midian. One thousand from each tribe, throughout all the tribes of Israel, you will send to the war." So there were delivered from the thousands of Israel one thousand of each tribe, twelve thousand armed for war. Moses sent them to the war, one thousand from each tribe, with Phinehas the son of Eleazar the priest, with the holy vessels and the trumpets to sound the alarm in his hand.

They waged war against the Midianites, as the LORD commanded Moses, and they killed every male. They killed the kings of Midian, in addition to the rest of those who were killed: Evi, and Rekem, and Zur, and Hur, and Reba, five kings of Midian. Balaam the son of Beor they also killed with the sword. The children of Israel returned with the women of Midian and their children and took their livestock, and all their flocks, and all their wealth for plunder. They burned with fire all their cities in which they lived and all their camps. They took all the plunder and all the prey of men and of beasts. They brought the captives, the prey, and the plunder to Moses, to Eleazar the priest, to the assembly of the children of Israel, and to the camp on the plains of Moab, which are by Jordan across from Jericho.

Moses and Eleazar the priest and all the leaders of the assembly went to meet them outside the camp. Moses was angry with the officers of the army, with the captains over thousands, and captains over hundreds, who came from the battle.

Moses said to them, "Have you saved all the women alive? These caused the children of Israel, through the word of Balaam, to act unfaithfully against the LORD concerning the thing of Peor, and there was a plague among the assembly of the LORD. So now kill every male among the little ones, and kill every woman who has known a man by lying with him. But keep alive for yourselves all the young girls who have not known a man by lying with him.

"And you stay outside the camp seven days. Whoever has killed any person and whoever has touched any slain, purify both yourselves and your captives on the third day and on the seventh day. Purify all your clothes, and all that is made of skins, and all work of goats' hair, and all things made of wood."

Eleazar the priest said to the fighting men of Israel who went to the battle, "This is the ordinance of the law which the LORD commanded Moses: Only the gold, and the silver, the bronze, the iron, the tin, and the lead, everything that can go through the fire, you will make it go through the fire, and it will be clean, but some of it will be purified with the water of purification, and all that cannot pass through the fire you will make go through the water. You will wash your clothes on the seventh day, and you will be clean, and afterward you will come into the camp."

The LORD spoke to Moses, saying, "Take the count of the plunder that was taken, of man and of beast, you and Eleazar the priest, and the chief of the fathers of the assembly. And divide the prey into two parts between those that took the war on themselves, who went out to battle, and between all the assembly. And levy a tribute to the LORD from the fighting men of Israel who went out to battle: one person out of five hundred, of the people and of the oxen, and of the donkeys, and of the sheep; take it from their half, and give it to Eleazar the priest as an offering to the LORD. Of the half of the children of Israel, you will take one portion of fifty, of the people, of the oxen, of the donkeys, and of the flocks, of all manner of beasts, and give them to the Levites, who keep the guard of the tabernacle of the LORD." Moses and Eleazar the priest did as the LORD commanded Moses.

The plunder, being the rest of the prey, which the fighting men of Israel had caught, was six hundred seventy-five thousand sheep, seventy-two thousand oxen, and sixty-one thousand donkeys, and thirty-two thousand people in all, of women who had not known a man by lying with him.

The half, which was the portion of those that went out to war, was three hundred thirty-seven thousand five hundred sheep.

And the LORD's tribute of the sheep was six hundred seventy-five.

The oxen were thirty-six thousand, of which the LORD's tribute was seventy-two.

The donkeys were thirty thousand five hundred, of which the LORD's tribute was sixty-one.

The people were sixteen thousand, of which the LORD's tribute was thirty-two people.

Moses gave the tribute which was the LORD's offering to Eleazar the priest, as the LORD commanded Moses.

Of the half of the children of Israel, which Moses divided from the men who fought, the half belonging to the assembly was three hundred thirty-seven thousand five hundred sheep, thirty-six thousand oxen, thirty thousand five hundred donkeys, and sixteen thousand people. From the half of the children of Israel Moses took one out of fifty, of man and of beast, and gave them to the Levites, who kept the guard of the tabernacle of the LORD, as the LORD commanded Moses.

The officers who were over thousands of the army, the captains of thousands, and captains of hundreds, came near to Moses, and they said to Moses, "Your servants have taken the count of the fighting men of Israel who are in our hand, and not a man of us is missing. We have brought an offering for the LORD, what every man has gotten of jewels of gold, chains, and bracelets, rings, earrings, and pendants, to make an atonement for ourselves before the LORD."

Moses and Eleazar the priest took the gold from them, all in the form of fashioned articles. All the gold of the offering that they offered up to the LORD, of the captains of thousands and of the captains of hundreds, was sixteen thousand seven hundred fifty shekels. The fighting men of Israel had taken plunder, each man for himself. And Moses and Eleazar the priest took the gold of the captains of thousands and of hundreds and brought it into the tent of meeting as a memorial for the children of Israel before the LORD.

Now the children of Reuben and the children of Gad had a very great number of livestock, and when they saw the land of Jazer and the land of Gilead was a place for livestock, the children of Gad and the children of Reuben came and spoke to Moses, and to Eleazar the priest, and to the leaders of the assembly, saying, "Ataroth, and Dibon, and Jazer, and Nimrah, and Heshbon, and Elealeh, and Sebam, and Nebo, and Beon, the land which the LORD defeated before the assembly of Israel is a land for livestock, and your servants have livestock." And they said, "If we have found mercy in your sight, let this land be given to your servants for a possession, and do not take us over the Jordan."

Moses said to the children of Gad and to the children of Reuben, "Will your brothers go to war, and you will dwell here? And why would you discourage the hearts of the children of Israel from going over into the land which the LORD has given to them? Thus your fathers did, when I sent them from Kadesh Barnea to see the land. When they went up to the Valley of Eshkol and saw the land, they discouraged the hearts of the children of Israel so they would not go into the land which the LORD had given them. And the anger of the LORD was inflamed on that day, and He swore, saying, 'Surely none of the men who came up out of Egypt, from twenty years old and older, will see the ground which I swore to Abraham, to Isaac, and to Jacob, because they did not completely follow Me, except Caleb the son of Jephunneh the Kenizzite, and Joshua the son of Nun, because they completely followed the LORD.' The anger of the LORD was inflamed against Israel, and He made them wander in the wilderness forty years, until all the generation that did evil in the eyes of the LORD was finished.

"Behold, you have risen up in your fathers' place, an increase of sinful men, to increase more the burning anger of the LORD toward Israel. If you turn away from following Him, He will again abandon them in the wilderness, and you will destroy all this people."

They approached him and said, "We will build sheepfolds here for our livestock and cities for our children. But we ourselves will be armed, ready before the children of Israel, until we have brought them to their place. Our little ones will dwell in the fortified cities because of the inhabitants of the land. We will not return to our houses until all the children of Israel have inherited their inheritance. We will not inherit with them on the other side of the Jordan or beyond, because our inheritance fell to us on this side of the Jordan to the east."

Moses said to them, "If you will do this thing, if you will be armed before the LORD for war, and all of you, each armed, will go over the Jordan before the LORD until He has driven out His enemies from before Him and the land is subdued before the LORD, then after that you will return and be exempt before the LORD and before Israel, and this land will be your possession before the LORD.

"But if you will not do so, you have sinned against the LORD, and be sure your sin will find you out. Build for yourselves cities for your children and folds for your sheep, and do that which has proceeded out of your mouth."

The children of Gad and the children of Reuben spoke to Moses, saying, "Your servants will do as my lord commands. Our children, our wives, our flocks, and all our livestock will be there in the cities of Gilead, but your servants will cross over, each man armed for war, before the LORD to battle, as my lord says."

So Moses commanded Eleazar the priest, and Joshua the son of Nun, and the chief fathers of the tribes of the children of Israel. And Moses said to them, "If the children of Gad and the children of Reuben will cross over the Jordan with you, each man armed for battle before the LORD, and the land will be subdued before you, you are to give them the land of Gilead as a possession. But if they do not cross over with you armed, they will have possessions among you in the land of Canaan."

The children of Gad and the children of Reuben answered, saying, "As the LORD has said to your servants, so we will do. We will cross over, armed before the LORD into the land of Canaan, so the possession of our inheritance on this side of the Jordan may be ours."

Moses gave to the children of Gad, to the children of Reuben, and to half the tribe of Manasseh the son of Joseph, the kingdom of Sihon king of the Amorites and the kingdom of Og king of Bashan, the land with the cities within the borders, the cities of the surrounding land.

The children of Gad built Dibon and Ataroth and Aroer, Atroth Shophan and Jazer and Jogbehah, Beth Nimrah and Beth Haran, fortified cities, and folds for sheep. And the children of Reuben built Heshbon and Elealeh and Kiriathaim, Nebo and Baal Meon (their names being changed) and Sibmah; and they named the other cities which they built.

The children of Makir the son of Manasseh went to Gilead and captured it and drove out the Amorites who were in it. Moses gave Gilead to Makir the son of Manasseh, and he lived in it. Jair the son of Manasseh went and captured its small towns and called them Havvoth Jair. Nobah went and captured Kenath and its villages and called it Nobah, after his own name.

Masei

Journeys of

(Numbers 33:1–36:13)

These are the journeys of the children of Israel, who went out of the land of Egypt with their armies under the hand of Moses and Aaron. Moses recorded the starting points of their journeys at the command of the LORD. These are their journeys according to their starting points.

They set out from Rameses in the first month, on the fifteenth day of the first month. On the day after the Passover the children of Israel went out with a high hand in the sight of all the Egyptians, because the Egyptians buried all their firstborn, whom the LORD had killed among them. Upon their gods the LORD executed judgments.

The children of Israel set out from Rameses and camped in Sukkoth.

They set out from Sukkoth and camped in Etham, which is on the edge of the wilderness.

They set out from Etham and turned to Pi Hahiroth, which is before Baal Zephon, and they camped before Migdol.

They set out from before Pi Hahiroth, and passed through the midst of the sea into the wilderness, and went three days' journey in the Wilderness of Etham, and camped in Marah.

They set out from Marah, and came to Elim, and in Elim were twelve fountains of water and seventy palm trees, and they camped there.

They set out from Elim and camped by the Red Sea.

They set out from the Red Sea and camped in the Wilderness of Sin.

They set out from the Wilderness of Sin and camped in Dophkah.

They set out from Dophkah and camped in Alush.

They set out from Alush and camped at Rephidim, where there was no water for the people to drink.

They set out from Rephidim and camped in the Wilderness of Sinai.

They set out from the Wilderness of Sinai and camped at Kibroth Hattaavah.

They set out from Kibroth Hattaavah and camped at Hazeroth.

They set out from Hazeroth and camped in Rithmah.

They set out from Rithmah and camped at Rimmon Perez.

They set out from Rimmon Perez and camped in Libnah.

They set out from Libnah and camped at Rissah.

They set out from Rissah and camped in Kehelathah.

They set out from Kehelathah and camped at Mount Shepher.

They set out from Mount Shepher and camped in Haradah.

They set out from Haradah and camped in Makheloth.

They set out from Makheloth and camped at Tahath.

They set out from Tahath and camped at Terah.

They set out from Terah and camped in Mithkah.

They went from Mithkah and camped in Hashmonah.

They set out from Hashmonah and camped at Moseroth.

They set out from Moseroth and camped in Bene Jaakan.

They set out from Bene Jaakan and camped at Hor Haggidgad.

They set out from Hor Haggidgad and camped in Jotbathah.

They set out from Jotbathah and camped at Abronah.

They set out from Abronah and camped at Ezion Geber.

They set out from Ezion Geber and camped in the Wilderness of Zin, which is Kadesh.

They set out from Kadesh and camped at Mount Hor, at the edge of the land of Edom. Aaron the priest went up onto Mount Hor at the word of the LORD and died there in the fortieth year after the children of Israel came out of the land of Egypt, in the first day of the fifth month. Aaron was one hundred twenty-three years old when he died on Mount Hor.

King Arad the Canaanite, who lived in the south in the land of Canaan, heard of the coming of the children of Israel.

They set out from Mount Hor and camped in Zalmonah.

They set out from Zalmonah and camped in Punon.

They set out from Punon and camped in Oboth.

They set out from Oboth and camped in Iye Abarim, on the border of Moab.

They set out from Iye Abarim and camped in Dibon Gad.

They set out from Dibon Gad and camped in Almon Diblathaim.

They set out from Almon Diblathaim and camped in the mountains of Abarim, before Nebo.

They set out from the mountains of Abarim and camped in the plains of Moab near Jordan of Jericho. They camped by Jordan, from Beth Jeshimoth to Abel Shittim in the plains of Moab.

The LORD spoke to Moses in the plains of Moab by Jordan near Jericho, saying: Speak to the children of Israel, and say to them: When you are crossing over Jordan into the land of Canaan, then you will drive out all the inhabitants of the land from before you, and destroy all their carved images, and destroy all their molded images, and destroy all their high places, and you will drive out the inhabitants of the land and dwell in it, because I have given you the land to inherit it. You will possess the land by lot for an inheritance among your families, and to the larger you will give the larger inheritance, and to the smaller you will give the smaller inheritance. Every man's inheritance will be in the place where his lot falls. By the tribes of your fathers you will inherit.

But if you do not drive out the inhabitants of the land from before you, then those whom you let remain will be like thorns in your eyes and thorns in your sides. They will show hostility to you in the land in which you live. And what I had planned to do to them, I will do to you.

And the LORD spoke to Moses, saying: Command the children of Israel, and say to them: When you are going into the land of Canaan, this is the land that will fall to you for an inheritance, the land of Canaan with its borders.

Then your south side will be from the Wilderness of Zin along by the border of Edom, and your south border will be the end of the Dead Sea to the east. And your border will turn from the south to the Ascent of Akrabbim, and continue to Zin, and the end of it will be from the south to Kadesh Barnea. Then it will continue to Hazar Addar, and pass on to Azmon. And the border will circle around from Azmon to the Brook of Egypt, and the end of it will be at the *Mediterranean* Sea.

For the western border, you will have the *Mediterranean* Sea and its coastline. This will be your western border.

This will be your northern border: From the *Mediterranean* Sea you will mark a line to Mount Hor; from Mount Hor you will mark a line of your border to Lebo Hamath, and the limits of the border will be to Zedad. And the border will go on to Ziphron, and the limits of it will be at Hazar Enan. This will be your northern border.

You will mark a line for your eastern border from Hazar Enan to Shepham. And the border will go down from Shepham to Riblah, on the east side of Ain, and the border will go down and will reach the side of the Sea of Kinnereth to the east. And the border will go down to the Jordan, and the limits of it will be at the Dead Sea.

This will be your land with its borders all around.

Moses commanded the children of Israel, saying: This is the land which you will possess by lot, which the LORD commanded to give to the nine tribes, and to the half-tribe because the tribe of the children of Reuben by the house of their fathers and the tribe of the children of Gad by the house of their fathers have received their inheritance, and half the tribe of Manasseh has received their inheritance. The two tribes and the half-tribe have received their inheritance on this side of the Jordan near Jericho to the east, toward the sunrise.

The LORD spoke to Moses, saying: These are the names of the men who will divide the land for you: Eleazar the priest and Joshua the son of Nun. You will take one leader of each tribe to divide the land by inheritance. These are the names of the men:

of the tribe of Judah,
    Caleb the son of Jephunneh;
of the tribe of the children of Simeon,
    Shemuel the son of Ammihud;
of the tribe of Benjamin,
    Elidad the son of Kislon;
the leader of the tribe of the children of Dan,
    Bukki the son of Jogli;
the leader of the children of Joseph, for the tribe of the children of Manasseh,
    Hanniel the son of Ephod;
the leader of the tribe of the children of Ephraim,
    Kemuel the son of Shiphtan;
the leader of the tribe of the children of Zebulun,
    Elizaphan the son of Parnak;
the leader of the tribe of the children of Issachar,
    Paltiel the son of Azzan;
the leader of the tribe of the children of Asher,
    Ahihud the son of Shelomi;
the leader of the tribe of the children of Naphtali,
    Pedahel the son of Ammihud.

These are the ones whom the LORD commanded to divide the inheritance among the children of Israel in the land of Canaan.

And the LORD spoke to Moses in the plains of Moab by Jordan near Jericho, saying: Command the children of Israel, and they will give to the Levites of the inheritance of their possession cities to dwell in, and you will give the Levites pasturelands around the city. The cities will be for them to dwell in, and their pasturelands will be for their livestock, and for their property, and for all their animals.

The pasturelands of the cities, which you will give to the Levites, will reach from the wall of the city and beyond one thousand cubits all around. You will measure from without the city on the east side two thousand cubits, and on the south side two thousand cubits, and on the west side two thousand cubits, and on the north side two thousand cubits, and the city will be in the middle. This will be for them the pasturelands of the cities.

Among the cities which you will give to the Levites there will be six cities of refuge, which you will appoint for the manslayer, that he may flee there, and to them you will add forty-two cities. So all the cities which you will give to the Levites will be forty-eight cities. You will give them with their pasturelands. The cities which you shall give shall be from the possession of the children of Israel. From the larger tribes you shall give many, and from the smaller tribes you shall give few. Each tribe, in proportion to the inheritance that it receives, shall give of its cities to the Levites.

The LORD spoke to Moses, saying: Speak to the children of Israel and say to them: When you are crossing over the Jordan into the land of Canaan, then you shall designate cities as your cities of refuge, so that a manslayer who unintentionally kills a person may flee there. The cities will be for you a refuge from the avenger, so that the manslayer does not die until he stands trial before the assembly. The cities which you designate shall be your six cities of refuge. You will give three cities across the Jordan, and three cities you will give in the land of Canaan, which will be cities of refuge. For the children of Israel, and for the stranger, and for the foreign sojourner among them will be six cities. These will be for a refuge. Everyone that unintentionally kills any person may flee there.

If he strikes him with an instrument of iron, so that he dies, he is a murderer. The murderer shall surely be put to death. If he strikes him with a stone in hand, by which he could die, and he dies, he is a murderer. The murderer shall surely be put to death. Or if he strikes him with a weapon of wood in hand, by which he could die, and he dies, he is a murderer. The murderer shall surely be put to death. The avenger of blood himself will slay the murderer. When he meets him, he will slay him. But if he pushed him out of hatred, or threw something at him, lying in wait, so he dies, or in hatred struck him with his hand, so he died, he that struck him shall surely be put to death, because he is a murderer. The avenger of blood will slay the murderer when he meets him.

But if he pushed him suddenly without hatred, or threw anything at him without lying in wait, or used a stone that may cause death, unintentionally throwing it at him, resulting in death, though they were not enemies, and was not trying to harm him, then the assembly will judge between the manslayer and the avenger of blood according to these judgments. And the assembly will deliver the manslayer out of the hand of the avenger of blood, and the assembly will restore him to the city of his refuge where he fled, and he will dwell in it until the death of the high priest, who was anointed with the holy oil.

But if the manslayer will go out at any time beyond the border of the city of his refuge where he fled, and the avenger of blood finds him outside the borders of the city of his refuge, and the avenger of blood kills the manslayer, he will not be guilty of blood, because the manslayer should have remained in the city of his refuge until the death of the high priest. But after the death of the high priest the manslayer may return to the land of his possession.

So these things will be for a statute of judgment to you throughout your generations in all your dwelling places.

Whoever kills a person, the murderer will be put to death by the testimony of witnesses, but one witness will not testify against a person for death.

And you will not take a ransom for the life of a murderer who is guilty of death, but he will surely be put to death.

You will not take a ransom for him who fled to the city of his refuge, that he should come out again to dwell in the land, until the death of the priest.

So you will not defile the land which you are in, because blood defiles the land, and the land cannot be cleansed of the blood that is shed in it, except by the blood of him that shed it. So do not defile the land which you are dwelling in, where I am residing, because I the LORD am residing among the children of Israel.

And the chief fathers of the families of the children of Gilead the son of Makir, the son of Manasseh, of the families of the sons of Joseph, came near, and spoke before Moses and before the leaders, the chief fathers of the children of Israel. And they said, "The LORD commanded my lord to give the land for an inheritance by lot to the children of Israel, and my lord was commanded by the LORD to give the inheritance of Zelophehad our brother to his daughters. If they are married to any of the sons of the other tribes of the children of Israel, then their inheritance will be taken from the inheritance of our fathers and will be added to the inheritance of the tribe to which they are married, so will it be taken from the lot of our inheritance. When the jubilee of the children of Israel happens, then their inheritance will be added to the inheritance of the tribe to which they are married, so their inheritance will be taken away from the inheritance of the tribe of our fathers."

Moses commanded the children of Israel according to the word of the LORD, saying: "The tribe of the sons of Joseph has spoken right. This is the thing which the LORD commands concerning the daughters of Zelophehad, saying, 'Let them marry whom they think best. But they may marry only within a clan of their father's tribe. So the inheritance of the children of Israel will not turn from tribe to tribe, because every one of the children of Israel will keep the inheritance of the tribe of his fathers. Every daughter that possesses an inheritance in any tribe of the children of Israel will be wife to one of the families of the tribe of her father, so every man of the children of Israel may enjoy the inheritance of his fathers. Thus no inheritance will turn from one tribe to another tribe, but every tribe of the children of Israel will keep its own inheritance.'"

Just as the LORD commanded Moses, thus the daughters of Zelophehad did, for Mahlah, Tirzah, Hoglah, Milkah, and Noah, the daughters of Zelophehad, were married to their uncles' sons. And they were married into the families of the sons of Manasseh the son of Joseph, and their inheritance remained in the tribe of the family of their father.

These are the commandments and the judgments which the LORD commanded by the hand of Moses to the children of Israel in the plains of Moab by Jordan near Jericho.

Devarim

Words

(Deuteronomy 1:1–3:22)

These are the words which Moses spoke to all Israel on the other side of the Jordan in the wilderness, in the plain opposite Suph, between Paran and Tophel and Laban and Hazeroth and Dizahab. (It is an eleven-day *journey* from Horeb by the way of Mount Seir to Kadesh Barnea.)

In the fortieth year, in the eleventh month, on the first day of the month, Moses spoke to the children of Israel, according to all that the LORD had commanded him *to give* to them. *It was* after he had slain Sihon the king of the Amorites, who lived in Heshbon, and Og the king of Bashan, who lived at Ashtaroth in Edrei.

Across the Jordan, in the land of Moab, Moses began to declare this law, saying: The LORD our God spoke to us in Horeb, saying, "You have dwelt long enough at this mountain. Turn, and take your journey, and go to the mountains of the Amorites, and to all their neighbors, in the plain, in the mountains and in the lowland, in the Negev and by the seacoast, to the land of the Canaanites and to Lebanon, as far as the great river, the Euphrates River. See, I have set the land before you. Go in and possess the land which the LORD swore to your fathers, Abraham, Isaac, and Jacob, to give to them and to their descendants after them."

I spoke to you at that time, saying, "I am not able to bear you by myself. The LORD your God has multiplied you, and surely you are this day as numerous as the stars of heaven. May the LORD, the God of your fathers, make you one thousand times more numerous and bless you, just as He has promised you! How can I myself bear your load and your burden and your strife? Choose wise, discerning, and knowing men, among your tribes, and I will appoint them as leaders over you."

You answered me, and said, "The thing which you have said is good for us to do."

So I took the leaders of your tribes, wise and well-known men, and appointed them as leaders over you, leaders over thousands, and leaders over hundreds, and leaders over fifties, and leaders over tens, and officers among your tribes. I charged your judges at that time, saying, "Hear the issues between your countrymen, and judge righteously between every man and his fellow countryman, and the foreigner that is with him. You shall not show partiality in judgment, but you shall hear the small as well as the great. You shall not be afraid in any man's presence, for the judgment is God's. The case that is too hard for you, you shall bring it to me, and I will hear it." At that time, I commanded you all the things you should do.

When we departed from Horeb, we went through all that great and terrible wilderness, which you saw by the way of the mountain of the Amorites, as the LORD our God commanded us, and we came to Kadesh Barnea. I said to you, "You have come to the mountains of the Amorites, which the LORD our God is giving to us. See, the LORD your God has set the land before you. Go up and possess it, just as the LORD, the God of your fathers, spoke to you. Do not fear or be discouraged."

So all of you came near to me and said, "Let us send men before us, so that they shall scout out the land, and bring back to us word concerning what way we should go up and into what cities we shall come."

The thing pleased me, and I took twelve men from you, one out of each tribe. They turned and went up into the hill country and came to the Valley of Eshkol and scouted it out. They took the fruit of the land in their hands, and brought it down to us, and brought us word again, and said, "It is a good land which the LORD our God is giving us."

Yet you were not willing to go up, but rebelled against the commandment of the LORD your God. You murmured in your tents, and said, "Because the LORD hates us, He has brought us out of the land of Egypt to deliver us into the hand of the Amorites to destroy us. Where shall we go up? Our brothers have discouraged our hearts, saying, 'The people are greater and taller than we. The cities are great and walled up to heaven. And moreover, we have seen the sons of the Anakites there.'"

Then I said to you, "Do not be terrified, or afraid of them. The LORD your God who goes before you, He shall fight for you, just as all that He did for you in Egypt before your eyes, and in the wilderness, where you saw how the LORD your God carried you, as a man carries his son, in all the way that you went, until you came to this place."

Yet in this thing you did not believe the LORD your God, who went in the way before you, to find you a place to pitch your tents, in fire by night and in a cloud by day, to show you by what way you should go.

The LORD heard the sound of your words, and was angry, and vowed, saying, "Not one of these men of this evil generation will see the good land which I swore to give to your fathers. The exception will be Caleb the son of Jephunneh. He shall see it, and to him I will give the land upon which he has walked, and to his children, because he has wholly followed the LORD."

Also the LORD was angry with me on your account, saying, "You also shall not go in. But Joshua the son of Nun, who stands before you, he shall go in. Encourage him, for he will cause Israel to inherit it. Moreover, your little ones, who you said would be a prey, and your children, who in that day had no knowledge between good and evil, they shall go in, and to them will I give it, and they shall possess it. But as for you, turn around, and take your journey into the wilderness by the way of the Red Sea."

Then you answered and said to me, "We have sinned against the LORD. We will go up and fight, just as the LORD our God commanded us." So each of you girded on his weapons of war and you thought it easy to go up into the hill country.

Then the LORD said to me, "Tell them, 'Do not go up nor fight, for I am not among you; lest you be defeated before your enemies.'"

So I spoke to you, but you would not listen. Instead, you rebelled against the commandment of the LORD and went presumptuously up into the hill country. The Amorites, who lived in the hill country, came out against you, and chased you as bees do, and destroyed you in Seir as far as Hormah. Then you returned and wept before the LORD, but the LORD would neither listen to your voice nor give ear to you. So you dwelt in Kadesh many days, according to the days you dwelt there.

Then we turned, and set out toward the wilderness by the way of the Red Sea, as the LORD spoke to me, and we circled Mount Seir for many days.

Then the LORD spoke to me, saying, "You have circled this mountain long enough. Now turn north. Command the people, saying: You are to pass through the territory of your brothers the children of Esau, who dwell in Seir, and they shall be afraid of you. So carefully watch yourselves. Do not provoke them, for I will not give you any of their land, no, not so much as a footprint, because I have given Mount Seir to Esau for a possession. You may buy food from them with money so that you may eat, and you may also buy water from them with money so that you may drink.

"For the LORD your God has blessed you in all the works of your hands. He knows your wanderings through this great wilderness. These forty years the LORD your God has been with you. You have lacked nothing."

So we passed by our brothers, the children of Esau, who lived in Seir, through the way of the plain from Elath and from Ezion Geber, and we turned and passed by the way of the Wilderness of Moab.

The LORD said to me, "Do not harass the Moabites, nor contend with them in battle, for I will not give you any of their land for a possession, because I have given Ar to the children of Lot as a possession."

(The Emites lived there in times past, a people as great and as many and as tall as the Anakites. These people, as well as the Anakites, also were regarded as giants, but the Moabites call them Emites. The Horites also formerly lived in Seir, but the children of Esau dispossessed and destroyed them, and settled there in their place, just as Israel did to the land of its possession, which the LORD gave to them.)

"Cross over the Zered Valley." So we went over the Zered Valley.

Now the length of time it took for us to come to Kadesh Barnea until we crossed over the brook Zered was thirty-eight years, until all the generation of the men of war perished from among the army, just as the LORD swore to them. For indeed the hand of the LORD was against them, to destroy them from among their midst, until they were gone.

So it came to pass, when all the men of war were gone and dead from among the people, then the LORD spoke to me, saying, "Today, you are to pass over through Ar, the border of Moab. When you come close to the Ammonites, do not harass them or provoke them, for I will not give you any of the land of the Ammonites as a possession, because I have given it to the children of Lot for a possession."

(That also is considered the land of giants. Giants formerly lived there, but the Ammonites call them Zamzummites. They were a great people, as numerous and tall as the Anakites. But the LORD destroyed them before *the Ammonites*. Then they dispossessed them and lived in their place, just as He had done *for* the children of Esau, who lived in Seir, when He destroyed the Horites from before them, and they dispossessed them, and lived in their place even to this day. And the Avvites, who lived in villages as far as Gaza, the Caphtorites, who came out of Caphtor, destroyed them, and lived in their place.)

"Arise, set out, and cross the River Arnon. See, I have given Sihon the Amorite, king of Heshbon, and his land into your hand. Begin to possess it and contend with him in battle. This day I will begin to put the dread of you and the fear of you on the nations that are under the whole heaven, who shall hear the report of you, and shall tremble, and be in anguish because of you."

I sent messengers out of the Wilderness of Kedemoth to Sihon, king of Heshbon, with words of peace, saying, "Let me pass through your land. I will only go on the main road. I will not turn aside to the right or the left. You shall sell me food for money so that I may eat, and give me water for money so that I may drink, only allow me to pass through on foot, just as the children of Esau who dwell in Seir and the Moabites who dwell in Ar did for me, until I pass over the Jordan into the land which the LORD our God is giving us." But Sihon, king of Heshbon, would not let us pass by him, for the LORD your God hardened his spirit and made his heart obstinate, so that He might deliver him into your hand as he is to this day.

The LORD said to me, "See, I have begun to give Sihon and his land to you. Begin to possess *it*, so that you may inherit his land."

Then Sihon came out against us, he and all his people, to fight at Jahaz. Then the LORD our God delivered him over to us, and we struck him down with his sons and all his people. We took all his cities at that time and utterly destroyed the men, the women, and the children of every city. We left no survivors. We took only the livestock for plunder and the spoils of the cities which we took. From Aroer, which is on the bank of the River Arnon, and from the city that is in the valley, all the way to Gilead, there was not one city too strong for us. The LORD our God delivered all to us. Only you did not come near the land of the Ammonites, nor to any place on the River Jabbok, nor to the cities in the hill country, nor to any place the LORD our God had forbidden us.

Then we turned and went up the way to Bashan, and Og, the king of Bashan, came out against us, he and all his people, to battle at Edrei. Then the LORD said to me, "Do not fear him, for I will deliver him and all his people and his land into your hand; and you shall do to him as you did to Sihon, king of the Amorites, who lived at Heshbon."

So the LORD our God delivered Og, the king of Bashan, with all his people, into our hands also, and we struck him down until there was no survivor remaining. We took all his cities at that time. There was not a city which we did not take from them: sixty cities, all the region of Argob, the kingdom of Og in Bashan. All these cities were fortified with high walls, gates, and bars, besides a great many rural towns. We utterly destroyed them, as we did to Sihon, king of Heshbon, utterly destroying the men, women, and children of every city. But we took all the livestock and the spoil of the cities as plunder for ourselves.

So at that time we took from the hand of the two kings of the Amorites the land that was across the Jordan, from the River Arnon to Mount Hermon (the Sidonians call Hermon Sirion, and the Amorites call it Senir), all the cities of the plain, and all Gilead, and all Bashan, as far as Salekah and Edrei, cities of the kingdom of Og in Bashan. For only Og, king of Bashan, remained of the remnant of the giants. (Notably, his bedstead was a bedstead of iron. Is it not in Rabbah of the children of Ammon? It is nine cubits long and four cubits wide, according to the cubit of a man.)

This is the land which we possessed at that time from Aroer, which is by the River Arnon, and half the hill country of Gilead and its cities I gave to the Reubenites and to the Gadites. The rest of Gilead, and all Bashan, the kingdom of Og, I gave to the half-tribe of Manasseh. (All the region of Argob, with all Bashan, was called the land of giants. Jair, the son of Manasseh, took all the region of Argob, that is, Bashan, as far as the border of the Geshurites and the Maakathites, and called the villages after his own name, Havvoth Jair, as it is to this day.) I gave Gilead to Makir. To the Reubenites and to the Gadites I gave *the territory* from Gilead even as far as the stream bed of the River Arnon, half the valley as the border to the River Jabbok, which is the border of the Ammonites; the plain also, with the Jordan as the border, from Kinnereth as far as the east side of the Sea of the Arabah (that is, the Dead Sea), below the slopes of Pisgah.

Then I commanded you at that time, saying, "The LORD your God has given you this land to possess it. All you men of valor shall pass over armed before your brothers, the children of Israel. But your wives and your little ones, and your livestock (for I know that you have much livestock) shall remain in your cities which I have given you until the LORD has given rest to your brothers, as well as to you, and until they also possess the land which the LORD your God has given them beyond the Jordan. Then each of you shall return to his possession which I have given you."

I commanded Joshua at that time, saying, "Your eyes have seen all that the LORD your God has done to these two kings. So shall the LORD do to all the kingdoms where you pass. Do not fear them, for the LORD your God, He shall fight for you."

Vaetchanan

Pleaded

(Deuteronomy 3:23–7:11)

I pleaded with the LORD at that time, saying, "O LORD God, You have begun to show Your servant Your greatness, and Your mighty hand, for what god is there in heaven or in earth that can do according to Your works and according to Your might? Let me, I pray, go over and see the good land that is beyond the Jordan, that good hill country, and Lebanon."

But the LORD was angry with me because of you and would not listen to me, and the LORD said to me, "Enough of that! Speak to Me no more of this matter. Get up to the top of Pisgah and lift up your eyes to the west and north and south and east, and see it with your eyes, for you shall not cross over this Jordan. But charge Joshua and encourage him and strengthen him, for he shall cross over before this people, and he shall cause them to inherit the land which you will see." So we remained in the valley over against Beth Peor.

Now therefore, listen, O Israel, to the statutes and to the judgments which I am teaching you to do, so that you may live; and go in and possess the land which the LORD, the God of your fathers, is giving you. You shall not add to the word which I am commanding you, nor shall you take anything from it, so that you may keep the commandments of the LORD your God which I command you.

Your eyes have seen what the LORD did at Baal Peor; for the LORD your God has destroyed from among you all the men who followed Baal of Peor. But you who held fast to the LORD your God are alive to this day, every one of you.

See, I have taught you statutes and judgments, just as the LORD my God commanded me, that you should do so in the land where you are entering to possess it. Therefore, keep and do *them,* for this is your wisdom and your understanding in the sight of the nations which shall hear all these statutes, and say, "Surely this great nation is a wise and understanding people." For what nation is there so great, who has a god so near to it as the LORD our God is in all things whenever we call on Him? And what nation is there so great that has statutes and judgments so righteous as all this law, which I am setting before you today?

Only give heed to yourself and keep your soul diligently, lest you forget the things which your eyes have seen and lest they depart from your heart all the days of your life; but teach them to your sons, and your grandsons. Especially concerning the day you stood before the LORD your God at Horeb, when the LORD said to me, "Gather the people together to Me, so that I will let them hear My words so that they may learn to fear Me all the days they shall live on the earth, and so that they may teach their children." Then you came near and stood at the foot of the mountain, and the mountain burned with fire up to the midst of heaven, with darkness, a cloud, a thick cloud. Then the LORD spoke to you out of the midst of the fire. You heard the sound of the words but saw no form—only a voice was heard. He declared to you His covenant, which He commanded you to perform, even the Ten Commandments, and He wrote them on two tablets of stone. The LORD commanded me at that time to teach you statutes and judgments, so that you might do them in the land which you are crossing over to possess.

Give good care to yourselves, for you saw no form on the day that the LORD spoke to you in Horeb from the midst of the fire, lest you corrupt yourselves and make a graven image for yourselves in the form of any figure, the likeness of male or female, the likeness of any beast that is on the earth, the likeness of any winged fowl that flies in the air, the likeness of anything that creeps on the ground, the likeness of any fish that is in the waters beneath the earth. And *beware*, lest you lift up your eyes to heaven, and when you see the sun, and the moon, and the stars, even all the host of heaven, you are led astray and worship them, and serve them, that which the LORD your God has allotted to all nations under the whole heaven. But the LORD has taken you and brought you out of the iron furnace, from Egypt, to be to Him a people of inheritance, as you are today.

Furthermore, the LORD was angry with me because of you and swore that I should not cross over the Jordan, and that I would not go into that good land which the LORD your God is giving you for an inheritance. So I must die in this land. I shall not cross over the Jordan, but you shall go over and possess that good land. Watch yourselves, so that you do not forget the covenant of the LORD your God, which He made with you, and make yourself a graven image or the likeness of anything as the LORD your God has forbidden you. For the LORD your God is a consuming fire. He is a jealous God.

When you produce children and grandchildren and you have remained a long time in the land, and you corrupt yourselves and make a graven image, or the likeness of anything, and do evil in the sight of the LORD your God, to provoke Him to anger, I call heaven and earth to witness against you today, that you will surely and suddenly perish from off the land that you are going across the Jordan to possess. You will not prolong your days on it, but shall be completely destroyed. The LORD shall scatter you among the peoples, and you shall be left few in number among the nations where the LORD shall lead you. There you will serve gods, the work of men's hands, wood and stone, which neither see nor hear nor eat nor smell. But if from there you will seek the LORD your God, you will find Him, if you seek Him with all your heart and with all your soul. When you are in distress and all these things come upon you, even in the latter days, if you turn to the LORD your God and shall be obedient to His voice (for the LORD your God is a merciful God), He will not abandon you or destroy you or forget the covenant of your fathers which He swore to them.

Indeed, ask about the days that are past, which were before you, since the day that God created man on the earth, and ask from one end of heavens to the other, whether there has ever been any such thing as this great thing, or has *anything* like it ever been heard? Has a people ever heard the voice of God speaking out of the midst of the fire, as you have heard, and lived? Or has God ever tried to take for Himself a nation from the midst of another nation, by trials, by signs, and by wonders, and by war, and by a mighty hand, and by an outstretched arm, and by great terrors, according to all that the LORD your God did for you in Egypt before your eyes?

To you it was shown so that you might know that the LORD, He is God. There is no one else besides Him. Out of heaven He let you hear His voice so that He might instruct you, and on earth He showed you His great fire, and you heard His words out of the midst of the fire. Because He loved your fathers, therefore He chose their descendants after them and personally brought you out of Egypt with His mighty power to drive out nations from before you greater and mightier than you are, to bring you in, to give you their land for an inheritance, as it is today.

Know therefore today, and consider it in your heart, that the LORD, He is God in heaven above and on the earth below. There is no other. Therefore, you shall keep His statutes and His commandments which I command you this day, so that it may go well with you and with your children after you, and so that you may prolong your days in the land, which the LORD your God gives you, forever.

Then Moses set apart three cities across the Jordan, toward the east, that the manslayer might flee there, that is, anyone who killed his neighbor unintentionally without hating him in time past could flee to one of these cities and live: Bezer in the wilderness in the plateau of the Reubenites, and Ramoth in Gilead of the Gadites, and Golan in Bashan of the Manassites.

This is the law which Moses set before the children of Israel. These are the testimonies, and the statutes, and the ordinances which Moses spoke to the children of Israel, after they came out of Egypt, on this side of the Jordan, in the valley over against Beth Peor, in the land of Sihon, king of the Amorites, who lived at Heshbon, whom Moses and the children of Israel struck down, after they had come out of Egypt. They possessed his land, and the land of Og, king of Bashan, the two kings of the Amorites, who were across the Jordan toward the east, from Aroer, which is by the edge of the River Arnon, even as far as Mount Sion (that is, Hermon), with all the Arabah across the Jordan to the east, even to the sea of the Arabah, under the slopes of Pisgah.

Then Moses called all Israel and said to them: Hear, O Israel, the statutes and ordinances which I am speaking in your hearing today, so that you may learn them, and keep, and do them. The LORD our God made a covenant with us in Horeb. The LORD did not make this covenant with our fathers, but with us, we who are living now and here today. The LORD talked with you face to face on the mountain from the midst of the fire. I stood between the LORD and you at that time to declare to you the word of the LORD; for you were afraid because of the fire and would not go up to the mountain. He said:

I am the LORD, your God, who brought you out of the land of Egypt, from the house of bondage.

You shall have no other gods before Me.

You shall not make yourself any graven image, or any likeness of anything that is in heaven above, or that is in the earth beneath, or that is in the waters beneath the earth; you shall not bow down to them, nor serve them. For I, the LORD your God, am a jealous God, visiting the iniquity of the fathers on the children, and on the third and fourth generations of those who hate Me, but showing mercy to thousands of them who love Me and keep My commandments.

You shall not take the name of the LORD your God in vain, for the LORD will not exonerate anyone who takes His name in vain.

Keep the Sabbath day, to keep it holy, just as the LORD your God has commanded you. Six days you shall labor and do all your work, but the seventh day is the Sabbath of the LORD your God. *On it* you shall not do any work: you, nor your son, nor your daughter, nor your male servant, nor your female servant, nor your ox, nor your donkey, nor any of your livestock, nor the foreigner that is within your gates, so that your male servant and your female servant may rest as well as you. Remember that you were a servant in the land of Egypt, and that the LORD your God brought you out from there with a mighty hand and by an outstretched arm; therefore your God commanded you to keep the Sabbath day.

Honor your father and your mother, just as the LORD your God has commanded you, that your days may be prolonged, and that it may go well with you in the land which the LORD your God is giving you.

You shall not murder.

You shall not commit adultery.

You shall not steal.

You shall not bear false witness against your neighbor.

You shall not covet your neighbor's wife, nor shall you covet your neighbor's house, his field, his male servant, his female servant, his ox, his donkey, or anything that belongs to your neighbor.

These are the words the LORD spoke to all your assembly at the mountain out from the midst of the fire, the cloud, and the thick darkness with a great voice, and He added no more. He wrote them on two tablets of stone and gave them to me.

When you heard the voice out of the midst of the darkness, while the mountain did burn with fire, you came near to me, all the heads of your tribes, and your elders. You said, "See, the LORD our God has shown us His glory and His greatness, and we have heard His voice from the midst of the fire. We have seen this day that God speaks with man, yet he lives. Now, therefore, why should we die? For this great fire will consume us. If we hear the voice of the LORD our God any more, then we will die. For who is there of all flesh who has heard the voice of the living God speaking out of the midst of the fire, as we have, and lived? Go near and hear all that the LORD our God will say. Then speak to us all that the LORD our God will speak to you, and we will hear and do it."

The LORD heard the sound of your words when you spoke to me, and the LORD said to me, "I have heard the sound of the words of this people which they have spoken to you. They have done well in all that they have spoken. O that there were such a heart in them that they would fear Me and always keep all My commandments, that it might be well with them and with their children forever!

"Go say to them, 'Return to your tents.' But as for you, stand here by Me, so that I may speak to you all the commandments, and the statutes, and the ordinances which you shall teach them, that they may keep them in the land which I am giving them to possess."

Therefore, be careful to do as the LORD your God has commanded you. You shall not turn aside to the right hand or to the left. You shall walk in all the ways which the LORD your God has commanded you, so that you may live and that it may be well with you, and that you may prolong *your* days in the land which you shall possess.

Now these are the commandments, the statutes, and the ordinances which the LORD your God commanded to teach you, so that you may observe them in the land which you are crossing over to possess, so that you might fear the LORD your God in order to keep all His statutes and His commandments which I command you—you, and your son, and your grandson—all the days of your life, so that your days may be prolonged. Hear therefore, O Israel, and be careful to do it, so that it may be well with you and so that you may multiply greatly, as the LORD the God of your fathers has promised you in the land that flows with milk and honey.

Hear, O Israel: The LORD is our God, the LORD alone! And you shall love the LORD your God with all your heart and with all your soul and with all your might. These words, which I am commanding you today, shall be in your heart. You shall teach them diligently to your children and shall talk of them when you sit in your house, and when you walk by the way, and when you lie down, and when you rise up. You shall bind them as a sign on your hand, and they shall be as frontlets between your eyes. You shall write them on the doorposts of your house and on your gates.

Then it shall be when the LORD your God brings you into the land which He swore to your fathers, to Abraham, Isaac, and Jacob, to give you great and fine cities, which you did not build, and houses full of all good things which you did not fill, and hewn cisterns which you did not dig, vineyards and olive trees which you did not plant, and you eat and are full, then beware lest you forget the LORD who brought you out of the land of Egypt, out of the house of bondage.

You shall fear the LORD your God and serve Him and shall swear by His name. You shall not go after other gods, the gods of the people which surround you (for the LORD your God is a jealous God among you). Otherwise the anger of the LORD your God will be inflamed against you and destroy you from off the face of the earth. You shall not tempt the LORD your God, as you tempted *Him* in Massah. You shall diligently keep the commandments of the LORD your God, and His testimonies and His statutes which He has commanded you. You shall do what is right and good in the sight of the LORD that it may be well with you and that you may go in and possess the good land which the LORD swore to your fathers, to drive out all your enemies before you, just as the LORD has spoken.

When your son asks you in time to come, saying, "What do the testimonies and the statutes and the judgments mean which the LORD our God has commanded you?" then you shall say to your son, "We were slaves of Pharaoh in Egypt, and the LORD brought us out of Egypt with a mighty hand. And the LORD showed great and devastating signs and wonders upon Egypt, upon Pharaoh, and upon all his household before our eyes. He brought us out from there, so that He might bring us in, to give us the land which He swore to our fathers. The LORD commanded us to do all these statutes, to fear the LORD our God, for our good always, that He might preserve us, as He has to this day. It will be our righteousness if we are careful to keep all these commandments before the LORD our God, just as He has commanded us."

When the LORD your God brings you into the land which you are entering to possess and has driven out many nations before you, the Hittites and the Girgashites and the Amorites and the Canaanites and the Perizzites and the Hivites and the Jebusites, seven nations greater and mightier than you, and when the LORD your God delivers them before you and you strike them down, then you must utterly destroy them. You shall make no covenant

with them nor show mercy to them. What is more, you shall not inter-
marry with them. You shall not give your daughters to their sons or take
their daughters for your sons. For they will turn your sons away from following Me to serve other gods. Then the anger of the LORD will be inflamed
against you, and He will quickly destroy you. But this is how you shall deal
with them: You shall destroy their altars and break down their images and
cut down their Asherim and burn their graven images with fire. For you are
a holy people to the LORD your God. The LORD your God has chosen you
to be His special people, treasured above all peoples who are on the face of
the earth.

The LORD did not set His love on you nor choose you because you were
more in number than any of the peoples, for you were the fewest of all the
peoples. But it is because the LORD loved you and because He kept the oath
which He swore to your fathers. The LORD brought you out with a mighty
hand and redeemed you out of the house of slavery, from the hand of Pharaoh, king of Egypt. Know therefore that the LORD your God, He is God,
the faithful God, who keeps covenant and mercy with them who love Him
and keep His commandments to one thousand generations, yet He repays
those who hate Him to their face, to destroy them. He will not be slack
with him who hates Him. He will repay him to his face. Therefore keep the
commandments and the statutes and the judgments which I command you
today, by doing them.

Eikev

As a result

(Deuteronomy 7:12–11:25)

I f you listen to these judgments, keep them, and do them, then the LORD your God shall keep with you the covenant and the mercy which He swore to your fathers. He will love you and bless you and multiply you. He will also bless the fruit of your womb and the fruit of your land, your grain, and your wine, and your oil, the increase of your herd and the young of your flock, in the land which He swore to your fathers to give you. You shall be blessed above all peoples. There will not be male or female barren among you or among your livestock. The LORD will take away from you all sickness, and will afflict you with none of the evil diseases of Egypt, which you know, but will lay them on all those who hate you. You must consume all the peoples whom the LORD your God will deliver to you. Your eye shall have no pity on them, nor shall you serve their gods, for that will be a snare to you.

If you say in your heart, "These nations are greater than I—how can I dispossess them?" you shall not be afraid of them. You must surely remember what the LORD your God did to Pharaoh and to all Egypt, the great trials which your eyes saw, and the signs, and the wonders, and the mighty hand, and the outstretched arm, by which the LORD your God brought you out. So the LORD your God will do to all the peoples of whom you are afraid. Moreover the LORD your God will send the hornet among them, until they who are left and hide themselves from you perish. You must not be frightened of them, for the LORD your God is among you, a great and awesome God. The LORD your God will drive out those nations before you, little by little. You will not be able to destroy them all at once, lest the beasts of the field become too numerous for you. But the LORD your God will deliver them to you and will throw them into a great confusion until they are destroyed. He will deliver their kings into your hand so that you may erase their names from under heaven. No man will be able to stand before you until you have destroyed them. You must burn the graven images of their gods with fire. You must not desire the silver or gold that is on them nor take any of it, lest you be snared by them, for it is an abomination to the LORD your God. You shall not bring an abomination into your house, lest you become cursed like it, but you must absolutely detest and abhor it, for it is a cursed thing.

You must carefully keep all the commandments that I am commanding you today, so that you may live, and multiply, and go in and possess the land which the LORD swore to your fathers. You must remember that the LORD your God led you all the way these forty years in the wilderness, to humble you, and to prove you, to know what was in your heart, whether you would keep His commandments or not. He humbled you and let you suffer hunger, and fed you with manna, which you did not know, nor did your fathers know, that He might make you know that man does not live by bread alone; but man lives by every word that proceeds out of the mouth of the LORD. Your clothing did not wear out on you, nor did your feet swell these forty years. You must also consider in your heart that, as a man disciplines his son, so the LORD your God disciplines you.

Therefore you must keep the commandments of the LORD your God, to walk in His ways and to fear Him. For the LORD your God is bringing you into a good land, a land of brooks of water, of fountains and springs that flow out of valleys and hills, a land of wheat, barley, vines, fig trees, and pomegranates, a land of olive oil and honey, a land where you may eat bread without scarcity, in which you will not lack anything, a land whose stones are iron, and out of whose hills you may dig copper.

When you have eaten and are full, then you shall bless the LORD your God for the good land which He has given you. Beware that you do not forget the LORD your God by not keeping His commandments, and His judgments, and His statutes, which I am commanding you today. Otherwise, when you have eaten and are full and have built and occupied good houses, and when your herds and your flocks multiply, and your silver and your gold multiply, and all that you have multiplies, then your heart will become proud and you will forget the LORD your God who brought you out of the land of Egypt, from the house of slavery, who led you through that great and terrible wilderness, where there were fiery serpents and scorpions and drought, where there was no water, who brought forth for you water out of the rock of flint, who fed you in the wilderness with manna, which your fathers did not know, that He might humble you and that He might prove you, to do good for you in the end. Otherwise, you may say in your heart, "My power and the might of my hand have gained me this wealth." But you must remember the LORD your God, for it is He who gives you the ability to get wealth, so that He may establish His covenant which He swore to your fathers, as it is today.

If you ever forget the LORD your God and go after other gods and serve them and worship them, then I testify against you today that you will surely perish. Just like the nations which the LORD will destroy before you, so shall you perish because you would not be obedient to the voice of the LORD your God.

Hear, O Israel! You are to cross over the Jordan today, to go in to possess nations greater and mightier than you, great cities fortified up to heaven, a great and tall people, the children of the Anakites, whom you know and of whom you have heard *it* said, "Who can stand before the children of Anak?" Understand therefore today that the LORD your God is He who goes over before you as a consuming fire. He shall destroy them and shall bring them down before you, so that you drive them out and destroy them quickly, as the LORD has spoken to you.

Do not say in your heart, after the LORD your God has driven them out before you, "On account of my righteousness the LORD has brought me in to possess this land," but it is because of the wickedness of these nations the LORD is driving them out before you. It is not because of your righteousness or the uprightness of your heart that you enter to possess their land, but because of the wickedness of these nations that the LORD your God drives them out before you, and that He may fulfill the word which the LORD swore to your fathers, Abraham, Isaac, and Jacob. Understand, therefore, that the LORD your God is not giving you this good land to possess on account of your righteousness, for you are a stubborn people.

Remember, and do not forget how you provoked the LORD your God to wrath in the wilderness. From the day that you departed out of the land of Egypt until you came to this place, you have been rebellious against the LORD. Also in Horeb you provoked the LORD to wrath, so that the LORD was angry enough with you to destroy you. When I went up into the mountain to receive the tablets of stone, the tablets of the covenant which the LORD made with you, then I remained on the mountain forty days and forty nights. I did not eat bread or drink water. The LORD delivered to me two tablets of stone, written with the finger of God, and on them was written all the words which the LORD spoke to you at the mountain out of the midst of the fire on the day of the assembly.

At the end of forty days and forty nights, the LORD gave me the two tablets of stone, the tablets of the covenant. Then the LORD said to me, "Arise, go down from here quickly, for your people whom you brought out of Egypt have corrupted themselves. They are quickly turned aside from the way which I commanded them. They have made a molded image for themselves."

Furthermore the LORD spoke to me, saying, "I have seen this people, and indeed, they are a stubborn people. Let Me alone, so that I may destroy them and blot out their name from under heaven, and I will make of you a nation mightier and greater than they."

So I returned and came down from the mount, and the mount burned with fire, and the two tablets of the covenant were in my two hands. I looked, and indeed, you had sinned against the LORD your God and had made yourselves a molded calf. You had quickly turned aside out of the way which the LORD had commanded you. I took the two tablets and threw them out of my two hands and broke them before your eyes.

I fell down before the LORD, as at the first, forty days and forty nights. I did not eat bread or drink water because of all your sins which you committed, doing what was wicked in the sight of the LORD to provoke Him to anger. For I was afraid of the anger and hot displeasure with which the LORD was wrathful against you to destroy you. But the LORD listened to me at that time also. The LORD was angry enough with Aaron to destroy him, so I also prayed for Aaron at the same time. I took your sin, the calf which you had made, and burned it with fire, and crushed it, and ground it very small until it was as small as dust. Then I threw the dust into the brook that descended down from the mountain.

Also at Taberah and at Massah and at Kibroth Hattaavah you provoked the LORD to wrath.

Likewise when the LORD sent you from Kadesh Barnea, saying, "Go up and possess the land which I have given you," then you rebelled against the commandment of the LORD your God, and you did not believe Him or listen to His voice. You have been rebellious against the LORD from the day I knew you.

So I fell down before the LORD forty days and forty nights; I fell down because the LORD had said He would destroy you. I prayed therefore to the LORD, and said, "O Lord GOD, do not destroy Your people, Your inheritance, which You have redeemed through Your greatness, which You have brought out of Egypt with a mighty hand. Remember Your servants, Abraham, Isaac, and Jacob. Do not look at the stubbornness of this people or at their wickedness or their sin. Otherwise, the land from which You brought us may say, 'Because the LORD was not able to bring them into the land which He promised them and because He hated them, He has brought them out to slay them in the wilderness.' Yet they are Your people, Your inheritance, whom You brought out by Your mighty power and by Your outstretched arm."

At that time the LORD said to me, "Cut out for yourself two tablets of stone like the first and come up to Me onto the mountain and make an ark of wood for yourself. I will write on the tablets the words that were on the first tablets which you broke, and you shall put them in the ark."

So I made an ark of acacia wood and cut out two tablets of stone just like the first and went up onto the mountain with the two tablets in my hand. He wrote on the tablets just like the first writing, the Ten Commandments which the LORD spoke to you at the mountain out of the midst of the fire on the day of the assembly, and the LORD gave them to me. I turned around and came down from the mountain and put the tablets in the ark which I had made, and there they are, just as the LORD commanded me.

(The children of Israel set out from Beeroth of the sons of Jaakan to Moserah. There Aaron died and was buried, and his son Eleazar ministered in the priest's office in his place. From there they journeyed to Gudgodah, and from Gudgodah to Jotbathah, a land of rivers of waters. At that time the LORD set apart the tribe of Levi to carry the ark of the covenant of the LORD, to stand before the LORD to minister to Him, and to bless in His name, to this day. Therefore, Levi has no portion or inheritance with his brothers. The LORD is his inheritance, just as the LORD your God promised him.)

As for me, I stayed on the mountain like the first time, forty days and forty nights, and the LORD listened to me at that time also. The LORD was not willing to destroy you. The LORD said to me, "Arise, take your journey before the people, so that they may go in and possess the land which I swore to give to their fathers."

Now, Israel, what does the LORD your God require of you, but to fear the LORD your God, to walk in all His ways, and to love Him, and to serve the LORD your God with all your heart and with all your soul, to keep the commandments of the LORD and His statutes which I am commanding you today for your good?

Indeed, heaven and the highest heavens belong to the LORD your God, also the earth with all that is in it. The LORD delighted only in your fathers, to love them; and He chose their descendants after them, *even* you above all people, as *it* is today. Therefore, circumcise your heart, and do not be stubborn anymore. For the LORD your God is the God of gods and Lord of lords, the great, the mighty, and the fearsome God who is unbiased and takes no bribe. He executes the judgment of the orphan and the widow and loves the foreigner, giving him food and clothing. Therefore, love the foreigner, for you were foreigners in the land of Egypt. You must fear the LORD your God. You must serve Him and cling to Him, and swear by His name. He is your praise, and He is your God, who has done for you these great and fearsome things which your eyes have seen. Your fathers went down into Egypt with seventy people, and now the LORD your God has made you as numerous as the stars of heaven.

You must love the LORD your God and keep His charge, His statutes, His ordinances, and His commandments always. Know this day that I am not speaking with your children who have not known and who have not seen the discipline of the LORD your God, His greatness, His mighty hand, and His outstretched arm, and His signs and His works which He did in the midst of Egypt to Pharaoh, the king of Egypt, and to all his land, and what He did to the army of Egypt, to their horses, and to their chariots, when He made the water of the Red Sea to flow over them as they pursued after you, and how the LORD utterly destroyed them, and what He did to you in the wilderness until you came to this place, and what He did to Dathan and Abiram, the sons of Eliab, the son of Reuben, when the earth opened its mouth and swallowed them up, their households, their tents, and everything that was in their possession, in the midst of all Israel. But your eyes have seen all the great deeds of the LORD which He did.

Therefore you must keep all the commandments which I am commanding you today, so that you may be strong and go in and possess the land which you are going to possess; and that you may prolong your days in the land which the LORD swore to your fathers to give to them and to their descendants, a land flowing with milk and honey. For the land which you are entering to possess is not like the land of Egypt from where you came, where you sowed your seed and watered it with your foot like a vegetable garden, but the land, which you are entering to possess, is a land of hills and valleys and drinks water from the rain of heaven, a land for which the LORD your God cares. The eyes of the LORD your God are always on it, from the beginning of the year even to the end of the year.

It will be, if you will diligently obey My commandments which I am commanding you today, to love the LORD your God, and to serve Him with all your heart and with all your soul, then I will give you the rain of your land in its season, the early rain and the latter rain, that you may gather in your grain and your wine and your oil. I will provide grass in your fields for your livestock, that you may eat and be full.

Take heed to yourselves that your heart be not deceived, and you turn away and serve other gods and worship them. Then the LORD's wrath will be inflamed against you, and He will shut up the heavens so that there will be no rain and the land will not yield its fruit, and you will quickly perish from the good land which the LORD is giving you. Therefore you must fix these words of Mine in your heart and in your soul, and bind them as a sign on your hand, so that they may be as frontlets between your eyes. You shall teach them to your children, speaking of them when you sit in your house and when you walk by the way, when you lie down, and when you rise up. You shall write them on the doorposts of your house and on your gates, so that your days and the days of your children may be multiplied in the land which the LORD swore to your fathers to give them, as long as the days of heaven on the earth.

For if you diligently keep all these commandments which I am commanding you to do—to love the LORD your God, to walk in all His ways, and to hold fast to Him— then the LORD will drive out all these nations from before you, and you will dispossess nations greater and mightier than you. Every place where the soles of your feet tread will be yours. Your border will be from the wilderness to Lebanon, from the river, the Euphrates River, as far as the *Mediterranean* Sea. No man will be able to resist you, for the LORD your God shall lay the fear of you and the dread of you on all the land where you shall tread, just as He has spoken to you.

Re'eh

See!

(Deuteronomy 11:26–16:17)

S ee, I am setting before you today a blessing and a curse: the blessing if
you obey the commandments of the LORD your God, which I am commanding you today, and the curse, if you will not obey the commandments of the LORD your God, but turn from the way which I am commanding
you today, to go after other gods which you have not known. Now it shall be,
when the LORD your God has brought you into the land which you are entering to possess, that you shall put the blessing on Mount Gerizim and the curse
on Mount Ebal. Are they not on the other side of the Jordan, west where the
sun goes down, in the land of the Canaanites, who dwell in the plain opposite
Gilgal, beside the oaks of Moreh? For you will cross over the Jordan to go in to
possess the land which the LORD your God is giving you, and you will possess
it, and dwell in it. You must be careful to do all the statutes and judgments
which I am setting before you today.

These are the statutes and judgments which you shall be careful to
observe in the land, which the LORD, the God of your fathers, has given you
to possess, all the days that you live on the earth. You must utterly destroy
all the places where the nations which you will possess served their gods, on
the high mountains, and on the hills, and under every green tree. And you
shall overthrow their altars, and break their pillars, and burn their Asherah
poles with fire, and you shall cut down the engraved images of their gods,
and eliminate their names out of that place.

You shall not act this way toward the LORD your God. But you must
seek only the place which the LORD your God shall choose out of all your
tribes to establish His name, and there you must go. There you shall bring
your burnt offerings, your sacrifices, your tithes, the offerings of your
hand, your vows, your freewill offerings, and the firstborn of your herds
and of your flocks. There you must eat before the LORD your God, and you
shall rejoice in all that you put your hand to, you and your households,
where the LORD your God has blessed you.

You are not to do all the things that we are doing here today, where every
man does whatever is right in his own eyes. For you have not yet come to
the rest and to the inheritance which the LORD your God has given you. But

when you cross the Jordan, and dwell in the land which the LORD your God has given you to inherit, and when He gives you rest from all your enemies round about, so that you dwell in safety, then there will be a place which the LORD your God will choose to cause His name to dwell. There you must bring all that I command you: your burnt offerings, and your sacrifices, your tithes, the offering of your hand, and all your choice vows which you vow to the LORD. You will rejoice before the LORD your God, you, your sons, your daughters, your male servants, your female servants, and the Levite who is within your gates, for he has no portion or inheritance with you. Be careful that you do not offer your burnt offerings in every place that you see. Rather, in the place which the LORD will choose in one of your tribes, there you must offer your burnt offerings, and there you must do all that I command you.

Notwithstanding, you may kill and eat meat within all your gates, whatever your heart desires, according to the blessing of the LORD your God which He has given you. The unclean and the clean may eat of it, of the gazelle and of the deer, only you must not eat the blood. You shall pour it on the ground like water. You may not eat within your gates the tithe of your grain, your wine, your oil, the firstborn of your herds or of your flock, any of your vows which you vow, your freewill offerings, or the offering of your hand. Rather you must eat them before the LORD your God in the place which the LORD your God will choose—you, your son, your daughter, your male servant, your female servant, and the Levite that is within your gates— and you shall rejoice before the LORD your God in all that you undertake to do. Take heed to yourself that you do not forsake the Levite as long as you live on the earth.

When the LORD your God shall enlarge your border as He has promised you, and you say, "I will eat meat," because you desire to eat meat, then you may eat as much meat as your heart desires. If the place which the LORD your God has chosen to put His name is too far from you, then you shall kill of your herd and of your flock, which the LORD has given you, as I have commanded you, and you must eat in your gates whatever your heart desires. Even as the gazelle and the deer are eaten, so you shall eat them. The unclean and the clean shall eat of them alike. Only be sure that you do not eat the blood. For the blood is the life, and you may not eat the life with the meat. You must not eat it. You must pour it on the ground like water. You must not eat it, so that it may go well with you and with your children after you, when you do that which is right in the sight of the LORD.

You shall take only your holy things which you have, along with your vows, and go to the place which the LORD shall choose. You must offer your burnt offerings, the meat and the blood, on the altar of the LORD your God, and the blood of your sacrifices will be poured out on the altar of the LORD your God, and you shall eat the meat. Observe and hear all these words which I command you, so that it may go well with you and with your children after you forever, when you do that which is good and right in the sight of the LORD your God.

When the LORD your God shall cut off the nations from before you, where you go to possess them, and you dispossess them, and dwell in their land, take heed to yourself so that you are not ensnared by following them, after they have been destroyed before you, and that you not inquire after their gods, saying, "How did these nations serve their gods? Even so I will do likewise." You shall not do so to the LORD your God, for every abomination to the LORD, which He hates, they have done to their gods. They have even burned their sons and their daughters in the fire to their gods.

Whatever I command you, be careful to do it. You shall not add to it or take away from it.

If a prophet or a dreamer of dreams arises among you and gives you a sign or a wonder, and the sign or the wonder comes to pass concerning that which he spoke to you, saying, "Let us go after other gods," which you have not known, "and let us serve them," you must not listen to the words of that prophet or that dreamer of dreams, for the LORD your God is testing you, to know whether you love the LORD your God with all your heart and with all your soul. You must follow after the LORD your God, fear Him, and keep His commandments, obey His voice, and you must serve Him, and cling to Him. That prophet or that dreamer of dreams must be put to death because he has spoken in order to turn you away from the LORD your God, who brought you out of the land of Egypt and redeemed you out of the house of bondage, to entice you away from the way in which the LORD your God commanded you to walk. So you must put the evil away from your midst.

If your brother, the son of your mother, or your son, or your daughter, or your beloved wife, or your friend, who is as your own soul, entices you secretly, saying, "Let us go and serve other gods," which you have not known, neither you nor your fathers, namely, of the gods of the people who are all around you, near you or far away from you, from one end of the earth to the other end of the earth, you shall not consent to him or listen to him, neither should your eye pity him, nor shall you spare or conceal him, but you must surely kill him. Your hand must be first upon him to put him to death, and afterwards, the hand of all the people. You shall stone him with stones so that he dies because he has sought to entice you away from the LORD your God who brought you out of the land of Egypt, from the house of bondage. All Israel shall hear and fear and no more do any such wickedness as this among you.

If you hear it said in one of your cities, in which the LORD your God has given you to dwell, saying, "Certain men, the sons of wickedness, are gone out from among you and have seduced the inhabitants of their city, saying, 'Let us go and serve other gods,'" which you have not known, then you shall inquire, search out, and ask diligently. If it be true and certain that such an abomination has been among you, you shall surely put the inhabitants of that city to the sword, utterly destroying it, all that is in it and its livestock—with the edge of the sword. You must gather all the spoils of it into the middle of the street and burn the city with fire along with all the spoils within it for the LORD your God, and it will be a heap forever. It must not be rebuilt. Nothing of the cursed thing there must cling to your hand, so that the LORD may turn from the fierceness of His anger and show you mercy, have compassion on you, and multiply you, just as He swore to your fathers, if you listen to the voice of the LORD your God, to keep all His commandments which I command you today, and do that which is right in the eyes of the LORD your God.

You are the sons of the LORD your God. You shall not cut yourselves or make any baldness between your eyes for the dead. For you are a holy people to the LORD your God, and the LORD has chosen you to be a peculiar people to Himself, treasured above all the nations that are on the earth.

You must not eat any detestable thing. These are the animals which you may eat: the ox, the sheep, and the goat, the deer, the gazelle, the fallow deer, the wild goat, and the ibex, and the antelope, and the mountain sheep. You may eat every animal with divided hooves, with the hoof divided into two parts, and that chews the cud. Nevertheless, you may not eat of these that chew the cud, or of them that divide the hoof: the camel, the rabbit, and the coney. For they chew the cud, but their hoof is not divided, therefore they are unclean to you. The pig is unclean to you because it divides the hoof, yet it does not chew the cud. You must not eat of their flesh or touch their dead carcass.

These you shall eat of all that are in the water: All that have fins and scales you may eat. Whatever does not have fins and scales you may not eat. It is unclean to you.

You may eat of all clean birds. However, these are the ones which you cannot eat: the eagle, the vulture, the buzzard, the red kite, the falcon, and the kite after its kind, every raven after its kind, and the ostrich, the owl, the seagull, and the hawk after its kind, the little owl, and the great owl, and the white owl, the pelican, the carrion vulture, and the cormorant, the stork, and the heron after its kind, and the hoopoe, and the bat.

Every creeping thing that flies is unclean to you. They must not be eaten. You may eat all the clean birds.

You must not eat of anything that dies of itself, but you may give it to the foreigner that is in your gates, so that he may eat it, or you may sell it to a foreigner, for you are a holy people to the LORD your God.

You shall not boil a young goat in its mother's milk.

You must be certain to tithe all the produce of your seed, so that the field produces year by year. You must eat before the LORD your God, in the place in which He shall choose to place His name, the tithe of your grain, of your wine, of your oil, and of the firstborn of your herds and of your flocks so that you may learn to always fear the LORD your God. If the distance is too long for you, so that you are not able to carry it, because the place is too far from you, where the LORD your God shall choose to set His name, when the LORD your God blesses you, then you shall exchange it for money and bind up the money in your hand and go to the place which the LORD your God shall choose. Then you may spend that money for whatever your heart desires, for oxen, or for sheep, or for wine, or for strong drink, or for whatever your heart desires, and you may eat there before the LORD your God, and you shall rejoice, you, and your household, and the Levite that is within your gates. You must not forsake him, for he has no portion or inheritance with you.

At the end of three years you must bring forth all the tithe of your produce the same year and lay it up within your gates. Then the Levite (because he has no portion or inheritance with you), the foreigner, the fatherless, and the widow, who are within your gates, shall come and shall eat and be satisfied, so that the LORD your God may bless you in all the work of your hand which you do.

At the end of every seven years you shall grant a relinquishing *of debts*. This is the manner of the relinquishing: Every creditor that has loaned anything to his neighbor shall relinquish it. He shall not exact it of his neighbor, or of his brother, because it is called the LORD's relinquishment. You may collect it from a foreigner, but that which your brother has that is yours your hand shall release. However, there will be no poor among you, for the LORD will greatly bless you in the land which the LORD your God has given you for an inheritance to possess, if only you carefully obey the voice of the LORD your God, by carefully observing all these commandments which I command you today. For the LORD your God will bless you, just as He promised you, and you will lend to many nations, but you shall not borrow. You will reign over many nations, but they will not reign over you.

If there be among you a poor man, one of your brothers within any of your gates in your land which the LORD your God has given you, you must not harden your heart or shut your hand from your poor brother. But you shall open your hand wide to him and must surely lend him what is sufficient for his need, in that which he lacks. Beware lest there be a wicked thought in your heart, saying, "The seventh year, the year of release, is at hand," and your eye be evil against your poor brother and you give him nothing, and he cry out to the LORD against you, and it become sin in you. You must surely give to him, and your heart shall not be grieved when you give to him, because in this thing the LORD your God will bless you in all your works, and in all that you put your hand to do. For the poor will never cease from being in the land. Therefore, I command you, saying, "You shall open your hand wide to your brother, to your poor and needy in your land."

If your brother, a Hebrew man, or a Hebrew woman, is sold to you and serves you six years, then in the seventh year you must let him go free from you. When you send him out free from you, you must not let him go away empty-handed. You shall supply him liberally out of your flock, out of your floor, and out of your winepress. From that with which the LORD your God has blessed you, you shall give to him. You shall remember that you were a slave in the land of Egypt and the LORD your God redeemed you. Therefore, I command this to you today.

It shall be, if he says to you, "I will not go away from you," because he loves you and your house, because he is well off with you, then you must take an awl and pierce it through his ear into the door, and he shall be your servant forever. And you shall also do likewise to your female servant.

It will not seem difficult for you when you send him away free from you, for he has been worth a double hired servant in serving you six years. Then the LORD your God will bless you in all that you do.

You must sanctify all the firstborn males that come out of your herd and flock to the LORD your God. You must do no work with the firstborn of your bulls or shear the firstborn of your sheep. You shall eat it before the LORD your God year by year in the place where the LORD shall choose, you and your household. If there is any defect in it, if it is lame or blind or has a serious defect, you shall not sacrifice it to the LORD your God. You shall eat it within your gates. The unclean and the clean person alike shall eat it, as if it were a gazelle or a deer. Only you must not eat its blood. You shall pour it on the ground like water.

Observe the month of Aviv and keep the Passover to the LORD your God, for in the month of Aviv the LORD your God brought you out of Egypt by night. Therefore, you must sacrifice the Passover to the LORD your God, from the flock or the herd, in the place where the LORD shall choose to place His name. You must not eat leavened bread with it. For seven days you must eat unleavened bread, the bread of affliction, for you came out of the land of Egypt in a hurry, so that you may remember all the days of your life the day when you came out of the land of Egypt. There must not be any leavened bread seen with you within all your borders for seven days, nor may any of the meat which you sacrificed in the evening on the first day remain overnight until morning.

You may not sacrifice the Passover within any of your gates that the LORD your God has given you. But at the place where the LORD your God chooses to place His name, there you shall sacrifice the Passover in the evening at sunset, at the time that you came out of Egypt. You shall roast and eat it in the place where the LORD your God will choose, and you must return in the morning, and go to your tents. For six days you must eat unleavened bread, and on the seventh day there shall be a solemn assembly to the LORD your God. You must do no work *on that day.*

You must count seven weeks for yourself. Begin counting the seven weeks from the time you begin to put the sickle to the standing grain. You must keep the Feast of Weeks to the LORD your God with a tribute of a free-will offering from your hand, which you must give to the LORD your God, in proportion to how much the LORD your God has blessed you. You shall rejoice before the LORD your God—you, your son, your daughter, your male servant, your female servant, the Levite who is within your gates, the foreigner, the orphan, and the widow who are among you—in the place where the LORD your God has chosen to place His name. You must remember that you were a slave in Egypt, and you must be careful to observe these statutes.

You shall observe the Feast of Tabernacles seven days after you have gathered in your threshing floor and your winepress, and you shall rejoice in your feast, you, your son, your daughter, your male servant, your female servant, the Levite, the foreigner, the orphan, and the widow who are within your gates. You are to celebrate the festival for seven days to the LORD your God in the place where the LORD will choose, because the LORD your God will bless you in all your produce, and in all the works of your hands. Therefore, you will indeed rejoice.

Three times a year all your males must appear before the LORD your God in the place where He will choose: at the Feast of Unleavened Bread, at the Feast of Weeks, and at the Feast of Tabernacles, and they must not appear before the LORD empty. Every man must give as he is able, in proportion to the blessing of the LORD your God, which He has given you.

Shoftim

Judges

(Deuteronomy 16:18–21:9)

Y ou must appoint judges and officers in all your gates, which the LORD
your God gives you, throughout your tribes, and they shall judge the
people with righteous judgment. You must not pervert judgment
nor show partiality. You must not accept a bribe, for a bribe blinds the eyes
of the wise and perverts the words of the righteous. You must follow that
which is altogether just, so that you may live and inherit the land which the
LORD your God is giving you.

You must not plant for yourself an Asherah of any trees near the altar of
the LORD your God, which you make for yourself. You shall not set up for
yourself any image, which the LORD your God hates.

You must not sacrifice to the LORD your God any bull or sheep that has a
blemish or any defect, for that is detestable to the LORD your God.

If there be found among you, within any of your gates which the LORD your
God gives you, man or woman, who has acted wickedly in the sight of the LORD
your God, by transgressing His covenant, and has gone and served other gods
and worshipped them, either the sun, or moon, or any of the host of heaven,
which I have not commanded, and if it is told to you, and you have heard of it,
and investigated diligently, and it is true, and the matter is certain that such a
detestable thing has happened in Israel, then you must bring forth that man
or that woman who has committed that wicked thing to your gates, that very
man or woman, and stone them with stones until they die. On the testimony
of two or three witnesses he that is to die must be put to death, but on the testimony of one witness he cannot be put to death. The hands of the witnesses
shall be first against him to put him to death, and afterward the hands of all the
people. So you shall purge the evil from among you.

If there arises a matter too difficult for you in judgment, between one
kind of bloodshed and another, between one kind of lawsuit and another,
and between one kind of assault and another, matters of controversy
within your gates, then you must arise and go up to the place where
the LORD your God shall choose. You must go to the Levitical priests
or to the judge in *office* those days, and inquire, and they will show you
the verdict of judgment. You shall do according to the verdict which they

declare to you from the place where the LORD will choose to show you, and you must be careful to do all that they instruct you to do. You must do according to the terms of the law which they instruct you and according to the verdict which they tell you. You must not deviate from the sentence which they show you, to the right or to the left. The man who acts presumptuously and does not listen to the priest who stands to minister before the LORD your God, or to the judge—that man must die, and you must purge the evil from Israel. Then all the people will hear, and fear, and not act presumptuously again.

When you have come into the land which the LORD your God gives you and possess it and dwell there and then say, "I will set a king over me just like all the nations that are around me," you must set a king over you whom the LORD your God will choose. You must select a king over you who is from among your brothers. You may not select a foreigner over you who is not your countryman. What is more, he shall not accumulate horses for himself or cause the people to return to Egypt in order that he accumulate horses, for as the LORD has said to you, "You must not go back that way ever again." He shall not acquire many wives for himself, lest his heart turn away; nor shall he acquire for himself excess silver and gold.

It must be, when he sits on the throne of his kingdom, that he shall write a copy of this law for himself on a scroll before the priests, the Levites. It must be with him, and he must read it all the days of his life so that he may learn to fear the LORD his God, and carefully observe all the words of this law and these statutes, and do them, that his heart will not be lifted up above his brothers and so that he may not turn aside from the commandment, to the right or to the left, to the end, so that he may prolong his days in his kingdom, he and his children, in the midst of Israel.

The Levitical priests and all the tribe of Levi will not have any portion or inheritance with Israel. They must eat the offerings of the LORD made by fire and His portion. They will have no inheritance among their brothers. The LORD is their inheritance, just as He has said to them.

This shall be the priest's due from the people, from them that offer a sacrifice, whether it be an ox or sheep: they shall give to the priest the shoulder, the two cheeks, and the stomach. You must give him the first fruit of your grain, of your wine, and of your oil, and the first of the fleece of your sheep also. For the LORD your God has chosen him out of all your tribes to stand to minister in the name of the LORD, him and his sons forever.

If a Levite comes from any of your gates out of all Israel, where he lives, and comes with all the desire of his mind to the place where the LORD shall choose, then he shall minister in the name of the LORD his God, as all his brothers the Levites do, who stand there before the LORD. They must have the same portions to eat, besides any profits he may receive from the sale of his father's inheritance.

When you enter into the land which the LORD your God gives you, you must not learn to practice the abominations of those nations. There must not be found among you anyone who makes his son or his daughter pass through the fire, or who uses divination, or uses witchcraft, or an interpreter of omens, or a sorcerer, or one who casts spells, or a spiritualist, or an occultist, or a necromancer. For all that do these things are an abomination to the LORD, and because of these abominations the LORD your God will drive them out from before you. You must be blameless before the LORD your God.

For these nations, which you shall possess, listened to soothsayers and to diviners, but as for you, the LORD your God has not permitted you to do so. The LORD your God will raise up for you a prophet from the midst of you, of your brothers, like me. You must listen to him. This is according to all that you desired of the LORD your God in Horeb on the day of the assembly, saying, "Let me not hear again the voice of the LORD my God, nor let me see this great fire anymore, so that I do not die."

The LORD said to me, "They have done well in what they have said. I will raise up a prophet from among their brothers, like you, and will put My words in his mouth, and he will speak to them all that I command him. It will be that whoever will not listen to My words which he will speak in My name, I will require it of him. But the prophet, who presumes to speak a word in my name, which I have not commanded him to speak, or who shall speak in the name of other gods—that prophet shall die."

And you may say in your heart, "How can we know the word which the LORD has not spoken?" When a prophet speaks in the name of the LORD, if the thing does not occur or come to pass, that is the thing which the LORD has not spoken; the prophet has spoken it presumptuously. You shall not be afraid of him.

When the LORD your God has cut off the nations, whose land the LORD your God is giving you, and you dispossess them, and dwell in their cities, and in their houses, you shall set apart three cities for yourselves in the midst of your land, which the LORD your God is giving you to possess. You shall prepare a roadway for yourself, and divide the territory of your land into three parts, which the LORD your God is giving you to inherit, so that every manslayer may flee there.

This is the word concerning the manslayer who will flee there, so that he may live: Whoever kills his neighbor unintentionally, whom he did not hate previously, like when a man goes into the forest with his neighbor to cut wood, and his hand raises the axe to cut down the tree, and the axe head slips from the handle and lands on his neighbor causing him to die, then he may flee to one of those cities, and live. Otherwise the avenger of blood might, while he is angry, pursue the manslayer and overtake him (because the way is long) and kill him, even though he was not worthy of death (since he did not hate him previously). Therefore, I command you, saying, "You shall set apart three cities for yourselves."

If the LORD your God enlarges your borders as He promised your fathers, and gives you all the land which He promised to give to your fathers, and if you will carefully keep all these commandments, which I command you today, to love the LORD your God, and to always walk in His ways, then you must add three cities more for yourself, besides these three. Then innocent blood will not be shed in your land, which the LORD your God is giving you for an inheritance, and blood guiltiness be on you.

But if any man hates his neighbor, and lies in wait for him, and rises up against him, and mortally strikes him, causing him to die, and flees to one of these cities, then the elders of his city must send and fetch him from there, and deliver him to the hand of the avenger of blood, so that he may die. Your eye must not pity him, but you must remove the guilt of innocent blood from Israel, so that it may go well with you.

You shall not remove your neighbor's landmark, which they of old time have set in your inheritance, which you shall inherit in the land that the LORD your God is giving you to possess.

A single witness must not rise up against a man on account of any iniquity or any sin that he sins. At the testimony of two witnesses or at the testimony of three witnesses shall the matter be established.

If a false witness rises up against any man to testify against him to accuse him of doing wrong, then both the men between whom the controversy is must stand before the LORD, before the priests and the judges, who are in *office* those days. The judges will thoroughly investigate, and if the witness is a false witness and has testified falsely against his brother, then you must do to him as he conspired to have done to his brother. In this way you must remove the evil from among you. Those who remain will hear and fear, and will never again commit any such evil among you. You must not show pity. But life will be for life, eye for eye, tooth for tooth, hand for hand, foot for foot.

When you go out to battle against your enemies, and see horses, and chariots, and a people that outnumber you, do not be afraid of them, for the LORD your God is with you, who brought you up out of the land of Egypt. It will be, when you approach the battle, that the priest will approach and speak to the people, and he shall say to them, "Hear, O Israel, you approach today to do battle against your enemies. Do not be fainthearted. Do not fear, and do not tremble or be terrified because of them. For the LORD your God is He that goes with you, to fight for you against your enemies, to save you."

The officers will speak to the people, saying, "What man is there who has built a new house and has not dedicated it? Let him go and return to his house, lest he die in the battle, and another man dedicate it. What man is there who has planted a vineyard, and has not yet eaten of it? Let him also go and return to his house, lest he die in the battle, and another man eat of it. What man is there who is engaged to a woman but has not married her? Let him go and return to his house, lest he die in the battle, and another man take her." The officers are to speak further to the people, and they shall say, "What man is there that is fearful and fainthearted? Let him go and return to his house, lest his brother's heart faint as well as his heart." It will be, when the officers have made an end of speaking to the people, that they must make captains of the armies to lead the people.

When you come near to a city to fight against it, then proclaim peace to it. It shall be, if it gives you a reply of peace and opens to you, then it must be that all the people that are found within shall become slaves to you and they shall serve you. If it will not make peace with you but makes war against you, then you are to besiege it. And when the Lord your God has delivered it into your hands, you are to slay every male there with the edge of the sword. But the women, and the little ones, and the livestock, and all that is in the city, all the spoil within, you are to take to yourself, and you will eat the spoil of your enemies, which the Lord your God has given you. Thus you are to do to all the cities which are far away, which are not the cities of these nearby nations.

But of the cities of these people, which the Lord your God is giving you for an inheritance, you must not leave alive anything that breathes. But you shall completely destroy them: namely, the Hittites, and the Amorites, the Canaanites, and the Perizzites, the Hivites, and the Jebusites, just as the Lord your God has commanded you, so that they do not teach you to participate in all their abominations, which they have done to their gods, causing you to sin against the Lord your God.

When you lay siege to a city for a long time, in making war against it in order to take it, you shall not destroy the trees there by chopping them down with an axe, for you may eat from them, and you shall not cut them down. For the tree of the field is not a man in which to lay siege. However, you may destroy and cut down only the trees which you know are not fruit trees, so that you may build siege engines against the city that makes war with you until it falls.

If someone is found slain in the land which the Lord your God is giving you to possess, lying in the field, and it is not known who has slain him, then your elders and your judges are to come forth, and they must measure *how far* it is to the cities which are around him who was slain. And it must be, that the city which is closest to the slain man, that is, the elders of that city shall take a heifer which has not been worked, that has never pulled in yoke, and the elders of that city must bring down the heifer to a valley with flowing water, which is neither plowed nor sown, and shall break the heifer's neck there in the valley. Then the priests, the sons of Levi, must come near, for the Lord your God has chosen them to minister to Him, and to bless in the name of the LORD, and by their word every controversy and every assault will be settled. And all the elders of that city, which is nearest to the slain man, shall wash their hands over the heifer whose neck was broken in the valley. Then they must answer and say, "Our hands have not shed this blood, and our eyes have not seen it. Be merciful, O LORD, to Your people Israel, whom You have redeemed, and lay not innocent blood in the midst of Your people Israel." And the blood guilt will be forgiven them. In this way you are to remove the guilt of innocent blood from among you when you do that which is right in the eyes of the LORD.

Ki Teitzei

When you go out

(Deuteronomy 21:10–25:19)

When you go forth to war against your enemies, and the Lord your God has delivered them into your hands, and you have taken them captive, and you see among the captives a beautiful woman, and have a desire for her to have her as your wife, then you are to bring her home to your house, and she is to shave her head and trim her nails. She must also discard the clothing of her captivity and shall remain in your house, and mourn her father and her mother for a full month. After that you may have relations with her, and be her husband, and she will be your wife. It will be, if you are not pleased with her, then you must let her go wherever she pleases, but you may not sell her at all for money, nor are you to make merchandise of her, because you have humbled her.

If a man has two wives, one beloved and another unloved, and both have borne him children, both the loved one and the unloved one, and if the firstborn son is hers that is unloved, then it must be, when he gives his sons the inheritance which he has, that he may not make the firstborn son of the loved come before the son of the unloved, who was indeed the firstborn. On the contrary, he must acknowledge the son of the unloved for the firstborn, by giving him a double portion of all that he has, for he is the beginning of his strength. The right of the firstborn is his.

If a man has a stubborn and rebellious son, who will not obey the voice of his father or the voice of his mother, and who, when they have disciplined him, will not listen to them, then his father and his mother are to lay hold of him and bring him out to the elders of his city, to the gate of his city. They shall say to the elders of his city, "This son of ours is stubborn and rebellious. He will not listen to us. He is a glutton and a drunkard." Then all the men of his city must stone him with stones, until he dies. In this way you are to remove the evil from among you, and all Israel shall hear and fear.

If a man has committed a sin worthy of death and is executed, and you hang him on a tree, then his body must not remain all night on the tree, but you must bury him that day (for he that is hanged is accursed of God) so that your land may not be defiled, which the Lord your God is giving you for an inheritance.

You must not see your brother's ox or his sheep go astray and hide your-self from them. You must certainly bring them back to your brother. If your brother is not near you or if you do not know him, then you are to bring it to your own house, and it will be with you until your brother seeks after it. Then you must return it to him. In the same way, you must do so with his donkey, with his clothing, and with anything lost by your brother which he has lost and you have found. You must not hide yourself *from him*.

You are not to see your brother's donkey or his ox fall down by the way and hide yourself from them. You certainly must help him to lift them up.

A woman must not wear man's clothing, nor is a man to put on a wom-an's clothing. For all that do so are abominations to the LORD your God.

If you happen to notice a bird's nest along the way, in any tree or on the ground, whether they be young ones or eggs, and the mother is sitting on the young or on the eggs, you are not to take the mother from the young. You must certainly let the mother go, but you may take the young for your-self, so that it may be well with you, and that you may prolong your days.

When you build a new house, you must make a guard rail for your roof so that you bring no blood guilt on your house, should anyone fall from there.

You must not sow your vineyard with two kinds of seeds, or the fruit of your seed which you have sown and the fruit of your vineyard will be defiled.

You must not plow with an ox and a donkey together.

You must not wear clothing made of a material of wool and linen together.

You must make tassels on the four quarters of your clothing with which you cover yourself.

If any man takes a wife and has sexual relations with her and then rejects her, and accuses her of impropriety and publicly defames her, saying, "I married this woman, but when I had sexual relations with her, I found her not to be a virgin," then the father and mother of the girl must produce *evidence* of the girl's virginity to the elders of the city at the gate. The girl's father must say to the elders, "I gave my daughter to this man to wife, and he has rejected her. What is more, he has accused her of impropriety, saying, 'I did not find your daughter to be a virgin.' However, this is the evidence of my daughter's virginity." And they shall spread the cloth before the elders of the city. The elders of that city must take that man and punish him, and they must fine him one hundred *shekels* of silver and give them to the father of the girl, because he has publicly humiliated a virgin of Israel. Then she is to remain his wife. He may not divorce her all his days.

But if the accusation is true, and the evidence of virginity does not exist for the girl, then they shall bring the girl out to the door of her father's house, and the men of her city shall stone her with stones until she dies, because she has brought disgrace into Israel, to act like a whore in her father's house. In this way you may purge the evil from among you.

If a man is discovered lying with a married woman, then both of them must die, both the man that lay with the woman, and the woman. In this way you may purge the evil from Israel.

If a girl who is a virgin is engaged to a man, and *another* man finds her in the city and has sexual relations with her, then you must bring them both out to the gate of that city and you must stone them with stones until they die, the girl because she did not cry out even though in the city, and the man because he has violated his neighbor's wife. In this way you may purge the evil from among you.

But if a man finds an engaged girl in the field, and the man forces her and rapes her, then only the man that raped her shall die. However, you are to do nothing to the girl. There is no sin worthy of death in the girl, for just as when a man rises against his neighbor and murders him, so is this matter. For he found her in the field, the engaged girl cried out, but there was no one to save her.

If a man finds a girl who is a virgin who is not engaged and seizes her and lies with her and they are discovered, then the man who lay with her must give fifty shekels of silver to the girl's father, and she shall be his wife because he has violated her. He may not divorce her all his days.

A man must not marry his father's wife and in this way dishonor his father.

No one who is emasculated or has his male organ cut off may enter the assembly of the LORD.

No one of illegitimate birth may enter the assembly of the LORD. Even to his tenth generation no one *related to him* may enter the assembly of the LORD.

No Ammonite or Moabite may enter the assembly of the LORD. Even to their tenth generation they may not enter the assembly of the LORD forever, because they refused you bread and water on the way, when you came from out of Egypt and because they hired Balaam, the son of Beor of Pethor of Mesopotamia, against you to curse you. Nevertheless, the LORD your God would not listen to Balaam. Instead the LORD your God turned the curse into a blessing on you because the LORD your God loves you. You are not ever to seek their peace nor their prosperity all your days.

You are not to abhor an Edomite, for he is your brother. You shall not abhor an Egyptian, because you were a foreigner in his land. The children who are born of them may enter the assembly of the LORD in their third generation.

When the army goes out against your enemies, then keep yourself from every wicked thing. If there be among you any man who is not clean because of a nocturnal emission, then he must leave the camp. He may not re-enter the camp. And it must be that when evening comes, he must wash himself with water, and at sunset he may re-enter the camp.

You must also have a place outside the camp where one may go outside. You must have a spade among your equipment, and it must be, when you relieve yourself outside, you must dig there and turn and cover up your excrement. For the LORD your God walks in the midst of your camp, to deliver you, and to defeat your enemies before you. Therefore, your camp must be holy, so that He does not see any indecent thing among you, and turn away from you.

You must not deliver *back* to his master a slave who has escaped from his master to you. He is to dwell with you, even among you, in a place which he shall choose in one of your towns, where he prefers. You must not oppress him.

There must never be a cult prostitute among the daughters of Israel nor a cult prostitute among the sons of Israel. You must never bring the wage of a prostitute or the wage of a dog into the house of the LORD your God for any vow, for both of these are abominations to the LORD your God.

You must not charge interest on a loan to your brother: interest on money, interest on food, or on anything that may be lent with interest. You may charge interest to a foreigner, but to your brother you may not lend with interest so that the LORD your God may bless you in all to which you set your hand in the land which you are entering to possess.

When you make a vow to the LORD your God, you must not be slow to pay it, for the LORD your God will surely require it of you, and it would be a sin to you. But if you refrain from making a vow, it will not be a sin to you. That which goes out of your lips you must keep and do, even a free-will offering, just as you have vowed to the LORD your God, what you have promised with your mouth.

When you go into your neighbor's vineyard, you may eat grapes to your fill at your own pleasure, but you may not put any in your basket. When you enter into the standing grain of your neighbor, you may pluck the ears with your hand, but you may not use a sickle on your neighbor's standing grain.

When a man takes a wife and marries her, and it happens that she finds no favor in his eyes because he has found some indecency in her, then let him write her a bill of divorce and put it in her hand and send her out of his house. When she departs out of his house, she may go and be another man's wife. If the second husband rejects her and writes her a bill of divorce and puts it in her hand and sends her out of his house, or if the second husband who took her to be his wife dies, her first husband, who sent her away, may not take her again to be his wife, since she is defiled, for that is abomination before the LORD, and you must not bring sin on the land, which the LORD your God is giving you for an inheritance.

When a man has taken a new wife, he shall not go out to war or be charged with any business; he is to be free at home one year, and must bring joy to his wife which he has taken.

No man shall take a lower or upper millstone as a pledge, for he would be taking a man's life as a pledge.

If a man is found kidnapping any of his brothers of the children of Israel, and makes property of him or sells him, then that kidnapper must die, and you must remove the evil from among you.

Be careful with an outbreak of leprosy, that you diligently observe and do according to all that the Levitical priests instruct you. As I have commanded them, so you must carefully do. Remember what the LORD your God did to Miriam on the way, after you came out of Egypt.

When you do lend your brother anything, you may not go into his house to take his pledge. You must stand outside, and the man to whom you lend must bring the pledge outside to you. If the man is poor, you may not sleep with his pledge. In any case, you must return the pledge to him when the sun goes down, so that he may sleep in his own cloak and bless you, and it will be righteousness to you before the LORD your God.

You may not oppress a hired servant that is poor and needy, whether he is one of your brothers or one of your foreigners who are in your land within your towns. You must give him his wages on that very day before the sun sets, for he is poor, and sets his heart on it, lest he cry against you to the LORD, and it be a sin to you.

Fathers may not be put to death for the sons, nor shall sons be put to death for their fathers. Every man shall be put to death for his own sin.

You must not pervert the justice of the foreigner or of the fatherless, nor take a widow's cloak as a pledge. On the contrary, you must remember that you were a slave in Egypt and the LORD your God redeemed you there. Therefore, I command you to do this.

Whenever you reap your harvest in your field and have forgotten a sheaf in the field, you may not go back to get it. It will be for the foreigner, for the fatherless, and for the widow, so that the LORD your God may bless you in all the work of your hands. When you beat your olive tree, you may not go over the boughs again. It will be for the foreigner, for the fatherless, and for the widow. When you gather the grapes of your vineyard, you shall not glean it again. It will be for the foreigner, for the fatherless, and for the widow. You must remember that you were a slave in the land of Egypt. Therefore I command you to do this thing.

If there is a controversy between men, they are to go to court for judgment, so that the judges may judge them. Then they shall justify the righteous and condemn the wicked. It must be, if the wicked man is worthy to be beaten, then the judge must make him lie down and be beaten in his presence, with the number of strikes his guilt deserves. He may give him forty stripes, but no more, lest, if he should exceed and beat him more with numerous stripes, then your brother may appear contemptible to you.

You must not muzzle the ox when he treads out the grain.

If brothers dwell together, and one of them dies without having had a child, the wife of the deceased may not marry outside *the family* to a stranger. Her husband's brother must go to her and take her to himself as a wife and perform the duty of a husband's brother to her. It shall be, that the firstborn whom she bears shall continue in the name of his brother who is deceased, so that his name will not be blotted out of Israel.

If the man does not want to take his brother's wife, then let his brother's wife go up to the gate to the elders and say, "My husband's brother refuses to raise up his brother's name in Israel. He will not perform the duty of my husband's brother." Then the elders of his city shall call him, and speak to him, and if he persists and says, "I do not want to take her," then his brother's wife must come to him in the presence of the elders and remove his sandal from his foot, and spit in his face, and answer and say, "So shall it be done to that man who will not build up his brother's house." His name will be called in Israel, "The house of him who has his sandal removed."

When a man and his brother fight one another, and the wife of the one draws near in order to deliver her husband out of the hand of him who fights him, and reaches out her hand and seizes him by the private parts, then you must cut off her hand. You must not pity her.

You must not have in your bag different weights, a large and a small. You must not have in your house differing measures, a large and a small. But you must have a perfect and just weight—a perfect and just measure you must have, so that your days may be lengthened in the land which the LORD your God is giving you. For all who do such things and all who act unjustly are an abomination to the LORD your God.

Remember what Amalek did to you by the road when you were coming out of Egypt, how he met you by the way and attacked at your rear all that were stragglers behind you, when you were exhausted and weary. He did not fear God. Therefore it shall be, when the LORD your God has given you rest from all your surrounding enemies, in the land which the LORD your God is giving you for an inheritance to possess, that you must blot out the remembrance of Amalek from under heaven. You must not forget it.

Ki Tavo

When you enter in

(Deuteronomy 26:1–29:9)

A nd it must be, when you come into the land which the LORD your God is giving you for an inheritance, and you possess it, and dwell in it, that you shall take from the first of all the produce of the ground which you shall bring from your land that the LORD your God is giving you, and put it in a basket and go to the place where the LORD your God chooses to make His name abide. You shall go to the priest in office at that time and say to him, "I profess this day to the LORD your God that I have come into the land which the LORD promised to our fathers to give us." The priest will take the basket out of your hand and set it down before the altar of the LORD your God. Then you must answer and say before the LORD your God, "A wandering Aramean was my father, and he went down into Egypt, and sojourned there *with only* a few in number, but there he became a great, mighty, and populous nation. However, the Egyptians mistreated and afflicted us, and laid upon us harsh labor. And when we cried to the LORD God of our fathers, the LORD heard our voice, and looked on our affliction, our labor, and our oppression. And the LORD brought us forth out of Egypt with a mighty hand and with an outstretched arm and with great terror, and with signs and wonders. Then He brought us into this place, and has given us this land, a land that flows with milk and honey. Now, indeed, I have brought the first fruits of the land, which You, O LORD, have given me." Then you must set it before the LORD your God and worship before the LORD your God. You must rejoice in every good thing which the LORD your God has given to you and your house, you, and the Levite, as well as the foreigner who is among you.

When you have finished tithing all the tithes of your income the third year, which is the year of tithing, and have given it to the Levite, the foreigner, the orphan, and the widow, that they may eat within your towns and be satisfied, then you shall say before the LORD your God, "I have removed the sacred things out of my house and also have given them to the Levite, and to the foreigner, to the orphan, and to the widow, according to all Your commandments which You have commanded me. I have not transgressed Your commandments or forgotten them. I have not eaten anything when in mourning, nor have I removed anything while unclean, nor offered anything to the dead. I have listened to the voice of the LORD my God and have done according to all that You have commanded me. Look down from Your holy habitation, from heaven, and bless Your people Israel and the land which You have given us, as You swore to our fathers, a land flowing with milk and honey."

Today the LORD your God has commanded you to do these statutes and judgments. You must therefore keep and do them with all your heart and with all your soul. You have affirmed today that the LORD is your God and vowed to walk in His ways, and to keep His statutes, and His commandments, and His judgments, and to listen to His voice. And the LORD has affirmed today that you are His special people, just as He has promised you, and that you should keep all His commandments. He will exalt you above all nations which He has made, in praise, and in name, and in honor; and that you may be a holy people to the LORD your God, just as He has spoken.

Then Moses and the elders of Israel commanded the people, saying: Keep all the commandments which I am commanding you today. On the day when you cross over the Jordan into the land which the LORD your God is giving you, you must set up for yourself great stones, and cover them with plaster. Then you must write all the words of this law on them, when you cross over, so that you may enter into the land which the LORD your God is giving you, a land flowing with milk and honey, just as the LORD God of your fathers promised you. Therefore, when you cross over the Jordan, you shall set up these stones, which I am commanding you today, on Mount Ebal, and you shall cover them with plaster. There you must build an altar to the LORD your God, an altar of stones. You must not use any iron tool on them. You must build the altar of the LORD your God with whole stones, and you must offer burnt offerings on it to the LORD your God. You must offer peace offerings and eat there, and rejoice before the LORD your God. You must write all the words of this law very clearly on the stones.

Moses and the Levitical priests spoke to all Israel, saying: Be silent and listen, O Israel. Today you have become the people of the LORD your God. Therefore, you must obey the voice of the LORD your God and do His commandments and His statutes, which I am commanding you today.

Moses commanded the people the same day, saying:

These shall stand on Mount Gerizim to bless the people when you cross over the Jordan: Simeon, Levi, Judah, Issachar, Joseph, and Benjamin. And these must stand on Mount Ebal for the curse: Reuben, Gad, Asher, Zebulun, Dan, and Naphtali.

The Levites will answer and say to all the men of Israel with a loud voice:

"Cursed is the man who makes any graven or molded image, an abomination to the LORD, the work of the hands of the craftsman, and puts it in a secret place." And all the people shall answer and say, "Amen."

"Cursed is he who disrespects his father or his mother." And all the people shall say, "Amen."

"Cursed is he who removes his neighbor's landmark." And all the people shall say, "Amen."

"Cursed is he who misleads the blind man on the road." And all the people shall say, "Amen."

"Cursed is he who perverts justice for the foreigner, orphan, and widow." And all the people shall say, "Amen."

"Cursed is he who lies with his father's wife, for he dishonors his father." And all the people shall say, "Amen."

"Cursed is he who lies with any kind of beast." And all the people shall say, "Amen."

"Cursed is he who lies with his sister, the daughter of his father, or the daughter of his mother." And all the people shall say, "Amen."

"Cursed is he who lies with his mother-in-law." And all the people shall say, "Amen."

"Cursed is he who strikes down his neighbor secretly." And all the people shall say, "Amen."

"Cursed is he who receives pay to slay an innocent person." And all the people shall say, "Amen."

"Cursed is he who does not confirm all the words of this law by doing them." And all the people shall say, "Amen."

Now it will be, if you will diligently obey the voice of the LORD your God, being careful to do all His commandments which I am commanding you today, then the LORD your God will set you high above all the nations of the earth. And all these blessings will come on you and overtake you if you listen to the voice of the LORD your God.

You will be blessed in the city and blessed in the field.

Your offspring will be blessed, and the produce of your ground, and the offspring of your livestock, the increase of your herd and the flocks of your sheep.

Your basket and your kneading bowl will be blessed.

You will be blessed when you come in and blessed when you go out.

The LORD will cause your enemies who rise up against you to be defeated before you; they will come out against you one way and flee before you seven ways.

The LORD will command the blessing on you in your barns and in all that you set your hand to do, and He will bless you in the land which the LORD your God is giving you.

The LORD will establish you as a holy people to Himself, just as He swore to you, if you will keep the commandments of the LORD your God and walk in His ways. All people of the earth shall see that you are called by the name of the LORD, and they shall be afraid of you. The LORD will make you overflow in prosperity, in the offspring of your body, in the offspring of your livestock, and in the produce of your ground, in the land which the LORD swore to your fathers to give you.

The LORD will open up to you His good treasure, the heavens, to give the rain to your land in its season and to bless all the work of your hand. You will lend to many nations, but you will not borrow. The LORD will make you the head and not the tail; you will only be above and you will not be beneath, if you listen to the commandments of the LORD your God, which I am commanding you today, to observe and to do them. Also, you shall not turn aside from any of the words which I am commanding you today, to the right hand or to the left, to go after other gods to serve them.

But it will happen, if you will not listen to the voice of the LORD your God, by being careful to do all His commandments and His statutes which I am commanding you today, that all these curses will come upon you and overtake you.

You will be cursed in the city and cursed in the field.
Your basket and your kneading bowl will be cursed.
Your offspring will be cursed along with the fruit of your land, the produce of your herd, and the flocks of your sheep.
You will be cursed when you come in and cursed when you go out.

The LORD will send cursing, vexation, and rebuke on you in all that you set your hand to do, until you are destroyed and until you perish quickly because of the wickedness of your doings, by which you have forsaken Me. The LORD will make pestilence cling to you until it has consumed you from the land, which you are going to possess. The LORD will strike you with a wasting disease, with a fever, with an inflammation, with an extreme heat, with the sword, with blight, and with mildew, and they shall pursue you until you perish. The heavens which are over your head will be bronze, and the earth that is under you will be iron. The LORD will make the rain of your land powder and dust. It will come from heaven down on you until you are destroyed.

The LORD will cause you to be defeated before your enemies, and you will go out one way against them and flee seven ways before them, and will become *an object* of terror to all the kingdoms of the earth. Your carcass will be meat for all the fowls of the air and beasts of the earth, and no man will frighten them away. The LORD will strike you with the boils of Egypt and with tumors, eczema, and with the itch, from which you cannot be healed. The LORD will strike you with madness, and blindness, and bewilderment of heart. You will grope at noon, as the blind man gropes in darkness, and you will not prosper in your ways. You will only be oppressed and continually robbed, and no man will save you.

You will be engaged to a woman and another man shall rape her. You will build a house, but you will not dwell in it. You will plant a vineyard, but you will not gather its grapes. Your ox will be killed before your eyes, and you will not eat of it. Your donkey will be violently taken away from before you and will not be returned to you. Your sheep will be given to your enemies, and you will have no one to rescue them. Your sons and your daughters will be given to another people. Your eyes will look and fail with longing for them all day long, but there will be nothing you can do. A nation that you do not know will consume the produce of your land and all your labors, and you will be nothing but oppressed and crushed all the time. You will go insane because of what your eyes will see. The LORD will strike you in the knees and legs with sore boils that cannot be healed, from the sole of your foot to the top of your head.

The LORD will bring you and your king, which you will set over you, to a nation which neither you nor your fathers have known, and there you will serve other gods, wood and stone. You will become a horror, a proverb, and an object of ridicule among all nations where the LORD shall lead you.

You will carry a lot of seed out into the field but will gather but little in, for the locust will consume it. You will plant vineyards and dress them, but will neither drink of the wine nor gather the grapes, for worms will eat them. You will have olive trees throughout all your coasts, but you will not anoint yourself with the oil, for your olive will drop off. You will give birth to sons and daughters, but you will not enjoy them, for they will go into captivity. The locust will consume all of your trees and fruit of your land.

The foreigner who resides with you will get up higher and higher, and you will go down lower and lower. He will lend to you, but you will not lend to him. He will be the head, but you will be the tail.

Moreover, all of these curses will come on you and will pursue you and overtake you, until you are destroyed, because you did not obey the voice of the LORD your God, by keeping His commandments and His statutes which He commanded you. They will be a perpetual sign and wonder in regard to you and your descendants, because you did not serve the LORD your God with joy and with gladness of heart, for the abundance of all things. Therefore, you will serve your enemies whom the LORD will send against you, in hunger, thirst, nakedness, and need of all things, and He will put a yoke of iron on your neck until He has destroyed you.

The LORD will bring a nation against you from far away, from the end of the earth, as swift as the eagle flies, a nation whose language you will not understand, a nation with a fierce countenance, which will not respect the old or show favor to the young. They will eat the offspring of your livestock and the produce of your land, until you are destroyed. They will leave you no grain, wine, or oil, or the offspring of your herd or the offspring of your sheep, until they have destroyed you. He will lay siege on you in all your towns until your high and fortified walls in which you trusted come down throughout all your land, and he will lay siege on you in all your towns throughout all your land which the LORD your God has given you.

You will eat the offspring of your own body, the flesh of your sons and of your daughters, which the LORD your God has given you, during the siege and distress in which your enemies will persecute you. The man who is tender among you, and very delicate, his eye shall be hostile toward his brother and toward his beloved wife and toward the rest of his children who remain, so that he will not give to any of them any of the flesh of his children which he will eat, because he has nothing left to him because of the siege and the distress by which your enemies will persecute you in all your towns. The tender and delicate woman among you, who would not venture to set the sole of her foot on the ground *because of her* delicateness and tenderness, will be hostile toward her beloved husband, and toward her son and her daughter, and toward her afterbirth that comes out from between her legs, and toward her children whom she will bear. For she will secretly eat them because of lack during the siege and distress in which your enemy will persecute you in your towns.

If you are not careful to observe all the words of this law that are written in this book so that you may fear this glorious and fearful name, the LORD your God, then the LORD will bring extraordinary plagues on you and your descendants, even great long-lasting plagues, and severe and long-lasting sicknesses. Moreover, He will bring all the diseases of Egypt upon you, which you were afraid of, and they will cling to you. Also every sickness and every plague which is not written in the Book of the Law will the LORD bring upon you until you are destroyed. You will be left few in number, whereas you were as numerous as the stars of heaven, because you would not obey the voice of the LORD your God. It will be that as the LORD rejoiced over you to do you good and to multiply you, so the LORD will take pleasure over you to destroy you and to bring you to nothing. You will be plucked from off the land which you go to possess.

The LORD will scatter you among all the peoples, from the one end of the earth to the other, and there you will serve other gods, wood and stone, which neither you nor your fathers have known. Among these nations you will find no ease, nor will the sole of your foot have rest. But there the LORD will give you a trembling heart, failing of eyes, and despair of soul. Your life shall hang in doubt before you. You will be in dread day and night and will have no assurance of your life. In the morning you will say, "Would to God it were evening!" And at evening you will say, "Would to God it were morning!" because of the fear of your heart and because of the sights your eyes will see. The LORD will bring you into Egypt again with ships, by the way by which I spoke to you, "You will not see it ever again." And there you will be sold to your enemies as male and female slaves, but no one will buy you.

These are the words of the covenant which the LORD commanded Moses to make with the children of Israel in the land of Moab, besides the covenant which He made with them in Horeb.

Moses proclaimed to all Israel, and said to them:

You have seen all that the LORD did before your eyes in the land of Egypt, to Pharaoh and all his servants and to all his land— the great temptations which your eyes have seen, those signs and great wonders. Yet to this day the LORD has not given you a heart to know, eyes to see, and ears to hear. I have led you forty years in the wilderness. Your clothes have not worn out on you, and your sandal has not worn out on your foot. You have not eaten bread, nor have you drunk wine or strong drink, so that you might know that I am the LORD your God.

When you came to this place, Sihon, the king of Heshbon, and Og, the king of Bashan, came out against us to battle, and we defeated them. We took their land and gave it as an inheritance to the Reubenites, the Gadites, and to half of the tribe of Manasseh.

Therefore, keep the words of this covenant and do them, so that you may prosper in all you do.

Nitzavim

Standing

(Deuteronomy 29:10–30:20)

Today all of you stand before the Lord your God, the heads of your tribes, your elders, and your officers, with all the men of Israel, your little ones, your wives, and your foreigners who are in your camp, from the one who chops your wood to the one who draws your water— so that you should enter into a covenant with the Lord your God, and into His oath, which the Lord your God is making with you today. Today He will establish that you are His people and that He is your God, just as He has said to you and He has sworn to your fathers, to Abraham, to Isaac, and to Jacob. It is not with you alone that I am making this covenant and this oath, but with him who stands here with us today before the Lord our God, and with him who is not here with us today (for you know that we lived in the land of Egypt and how we came through the nations which you passed by, and you have seen their abominations and their idols of wood and stone, of silver and gold, which were among them); lest there be among you a man or woman or family or tribe whose heart turns away today from the Lord our God to go and serve the gods of these nations, and lest there be among you a root bearing poisonous and bitter fruit; and it happens that, when he hears the words of this covenant, he blesses himself in his heart, saying, "I shall have peace, even though I walk in the stubbornness of my heart," thus destroying the watered ground with the dry. The Lord will not spare him; rather the anger of the Lord and His jealousy will smolder against that man. All the curses that are written in this book will rest on him, and the Lord will blot out his name from under heaven. The Lord will single him out for disaster out of all the tribes of Israel, according to all the curses of the covenant that are written in this Book of the Law.

The generation to come, your children who will rise up after you and the foreigner who will come from a far land, when they see the plagues of that land, and the sicknesses which the Lord has laid on it, will say, "The whole land is brimstone and salt, a burning waste, unsown and unproductive, and no grass grows there, like the overthrow of Sodom and Gomorrah, Admah and Zeboyim, which the Lord overthrew in His anger and wrath." All nations will say, "Why has the Lord done such to this land? What does the heatedness of this great anger mean?"

Then men will say, "Because they have forsaken the covenant of the LORD God of their fathers, which He made with them when He brought them out of the land of Egypt. For they went and served other gods, and worshipped them, gods which they did not know and which He had not given to them. The anger of the LORD burned against this land, bringing on it all the curses that are written in this book. The LORD rooted them out of their land in anger and in wrath and in great indignation, and threw them into another land, as it is today."

The secret things belong to the LORD our God, but those things which are revealed belong to us and to our children forever, so that we may keep all the words of this law.

When all these things happen to you, the blessing and the curse, which I have set before you, and you remember them among all the nations, where the LORD your God has driven you, then you must return to the LORD your God and obey His voice according to all that I am commanding you today, you and your children, with all your heart, and with all your soul. Then the LORD your God will overturn your captivity and have compassion on you and will return and gather you from all the nations, where the LORD your God has scattered you. If any of you are driven out to the outmost parts of heaven, from there will the LORD your God gather you, and from there He will get you. The LORD your God will bring you to the land which your fathers possessed, and you shall possess it. He will prosper you and multiply you more than your fathers. The LORD your God will circumcise your heart and the heart of your descendants to love the LORD your God with all your heart and with all your soul, so that you may live. The LORD your God will put all these curses on your enemies, on them who hate you, who persecuted you. You will return and obey the voice of the LORD, and obey all His commandments which I am commanding you today. The LORD your God will make you prosper in every work of your hand, in the offspring of your body, and in the offspring of your livestock, and in the produce of your land, for good. For the LORD will once again rejoice over you for good, just as He rejoiced over your fathers, if you obey the voice of the LORD your God, by keeping His commandments and His statutes which are written in this Book of the Law, and if you return to the LORD your God with all your heart and with all your soul.

This commandment which I am commanding you today is not hidden from you, nor is it far off. It is not in heaven, that you should say, "Who will go up for us to heaven and bring it to us, so that we may hear it and do it?" It is not beyond the sea, so that you should say, "Who shall go over the sea for us and bring it to us, so that we may hear it and do it?" But the word is very near to you, in your mouth, and in your heart, so that you may do it.

See, today I have set before you life and prosperity, and death and disaster. What I am commanding you today is to love the LORD your God, to walk in

His ways, and to keep His commandments and His statutes and His judgments, so that you may live and multiply. Then the LORD your God will bless you in the land which you go to possess.

But if your heart turns away, so that you do not obey, but are drawn away, and worship other gods and serve them, then I declare to you today that you will surely perish and that you will not prolong your days in the land which you are crossing the Jordan to go in and possess.

I call heaven and earth to witness against you this day, that I have set before you life and death, blessing and curse. Therefore choose life, that both you and your descendants may live; that you may love the LORD your God, that you may obey His voice, and that you may cling to Him, for He is your life and the length of your days; and that you may dwell in the land that the LORD swore to your fathers, to Abraham, Isaac, and Jacob, to give them.

Vayeilech

And he went

(Deuteronomy 31:1–30)

Then Moses went and spoke these words to all Israel. He said to them, "I am one hundred twenty years old today. I can no longer come and go. Also, the LORD has said to me, 'You may not cross over the Jordan.' The LORD your God will cross over before you. He will destroy these nations before you, you will possess them, and Joshua will cross over before you, just as the LORD has said. The LORD will do to them as He did to Sihon and to Og, the kings of the Amorites, and to their land, which He destroyed. The LORD will give them up before you, so that you may do to them according to all the commandments which I have commanded you. Be strong and of a good courage. Fear not, nor be afraid of them, for the LORD your God, it is He who goes with you. He will not fail you, nor forsake you."

Moses called to Joshua, and said to him in the sight of all Israel, "Be strong and of good courage, for you must go with this people to the land which the LORD has sworn to their fathers to give them, and you will enable them to inherit it. The LORD, He goes before you. He will be with you. He will not fail you nor forsake you. Do not fear, nor be dismayed."

Moses wrote this law and delivered it to the priests, the sons of Levi who bore the ark of the covenant of the LORD, and to all the elders of Israel. Moses commanded them, saying, "At the end of every seven years, at the time of the year of the cancellation of debts, at the Feast of Tabernacles, when all Israel has come to appear before the LORD your God in the place which He will choose, you must read this law before all Israel in their hearing. Gather the people together, men, women, children, and your foreigner who is within your towns, so that they may hear and learn and fear the LORD your God, and observe to do all the words of this law. Their children, who have not known *it*, may hear and learn to fear the LORD your God, as long as you live in the land which you cross the Jordan to possess."

The LORD said to Moses, "Indeed, your days draw near when you must die. Call Joshua, and present yourselves in the tent of meeting, so that I may commission him." So Moses and Joshua went, and presented themselves in the tent of meeting.

The LORD appeared in the tent in a pillar of cloud, and the pillar of cloud stood over the door of the tent. The LORD said to Moses, "You are about to lie down with your fathers, and this people will rise up and begin to prostitute themselves after the gods of the foreigners of the land, where they are going to be among them, and will forsake Me and break My covenant which I have made with them. Then My anger will burn against them on that day, and I will forsake them, and I will hide My face from them, and they will be devoured, and many disasters and troubles will befall them, so that they will say in that day, 'Have not these disasters come upon us because our God is not among us?' And I will surely hide My face in that day for all the evil things which they shall have done, in that they turned to other gods.

"Now therefore write yourself this song and teach it to the children of Israel. Put it on their mouths, so that this song may be a witness for Me against the children of Israel. For when I have brought them into the land which I swore to their fathers, flowing with milk and honey, and they have eaten, and filled themselves, and become fat, then they will turn to other gods, and serve them, and provoke Me, and break My covenant. Then when many disasters and troubles have fallen on them, this song will testify against them as a witness, for it must not be forgotten from the mouths of their descendants. For I know their intention which they are developing even now, before I have brought them into the land which I promised." Therefore, Moses wrote this song the same day, and taught it to the children of Israel.

He gave Joshua, the son of Nun, an exhortation, and said, "Be strong and of a good courage, for you will bring the children of Israel into the land which I swore to them, and I will be with you."

When Moses had finished writing the words of this law in a book, until they were completed, then Moses commanded the Levites, who bore the ark of the covenant of the LORD, saying, "Take this Book of the Law, and put it beside the ark of the covenant of the LORD your God, so that it may be there for a witness against you. For I know your rebellion and your stiff neck. Even now, while I am yet alive with you today, you have been rebellious against the LORD. How much more after my death? Gather to me all the elders of your tribes, and your officers, so that I may speak these words in their hearing and call heaven and earth to witness against them. For I know that after my death you will utterly corrupt yourselves and turn aside from the way which I have commanded you, and disaster will befall you in the latter days, because you will do evil in the sight of the LORD, to provoke Him to anger through the work of your hands."

Moses spoke the words of this song until they were finished, in the hearing of all the assembly of Israel.

Ha'Azinu

Listen!

(Deuteronomy 32:1–52)

Give ear, O heavens, and I will speak;
hear, O earth, the words of my mouth.
My teaching will drop like the rain,
my sayings will distill as the dew,
as the droplets on the grass,
and as the showers on the herb.

For I will proclaim the name of the LORD:
Ascribe greatness to our God!
He is the rock; His work is perfect;
for all His ways are just.
He is a God of faithfulness and without injustice;
righteous and upright is He.

They have acted corruptly to Him;
they are not His children, but blemished;
they are a perverse and crooked generation.
Is this how you repay the LORD,
you foolish and unwise people?
Is He not your father, who has bought you?
Has He not made you, and established you?

Remember the days of old,
consider the years of previous generations.
Ask your father, and he will show you;
your elders, and they will tell you:
When the Most High gave the nations their inheritance,
when He separated the sons of man,
He set the boundaries of the peoples
according to the number of the children of Israel.
For the LORD's portion is His people;
Jacob is the allotment of His inheritance.

He found him in a desert land
   and in the howling waste of a wilderness;
He led him about, He instructed him,
   He protected him like the pupil of His eye.
Like an eagle stirs up her nest,
   that flutters over her young,
He spread out his wings and took him;
   He lifted him on His pinions;
the Lord alone guided him,
   and there was no foreign god with him.

He made him ride on the high places of the earth,
   and he ate of the produce of the fields;
He made him suck honey out of the rock
   and oil out of the flinty rock,
butter from the herd,
   and milk from the flock,
   along with the fat of lambs,
and rams of the breed from Bashan,
   and goats,
   with the best of the kernels of wheat;
you drank the pure blood of the grape.

But Jeshurun grew fat and kicked;
   you grew fat, you grew thick;
   you are covered with fat.
Then he forsook God who made him,
   and devalued the rock of his salvation.
They made Him jealous with strange gods;
   with abominations they provoked Him to anger.
They sacrificed to demons, not to God,
   to gods whom they knew not,
   to new gods that recently came along,
   whom your fathers did not fear.
You have forgotten the rock who begot you;
   you are unmindful, and have forgotten the God who gave you birth.

When the Lord saw it, He despised them,
   because of the provocation of His sons and daughters.
He said: I will hide My face from them;
   I will see what their end will be,
for they are a very perverse generation,
   children in whom there is no loyalty.

They have made Me jealous with that which is not God;
 they have provoked Me to anger with their empty things.
And I will make them jealous of those who are not a people;
 I will provoke them to anger with a foolish nation.
For a fire has been inflamed by My anger,
 and it will burn to the lowest part of Sheol,
and shall consume the earth and its produce,
 and ignite the foundations of the mountains.

I will heap misfortunes on them;
 I will use My arrows on them.
They will be starved by famine,
 and consumed by plague and bitter destruction;
I will also send the teeth of beasts upon them,
 with the poison of crawling creatures in the dust.
The sword outside and terror within will destroy both the young man
  and the virgin,
 the infant along with the man of gray hair.
I said, "I want to cut them into pieces;
 I will cause the memory of them to disappear from among
  men,"
however, I feared the wrath of the enemy,
 that their adversaries would misunderstand
and say, "Our hand is victorious,
 and the Lord has not done all this."

For they are a nation devoid of counsel;
 there is no understanding in them.
Would that they were wise,
 so that they understood this,
 so that they would comprehend their future!
How should one chase one thousand,
 and two put ten thousand to flight,
unless their rock had sold them,
 and the Lord had given them up?
For their rock is not as our rock;
 even our enemies themselves concede this.
For their vine is from the vine of Sodom
 and from the fields of Gomorrah;
their grapes are grapes of poison;
 their clusters are bitter.
Their wine is the poison of dragons
 and the deadly venom of cobras.

Is not this laid up in store with Me
    and sealed up among My treasures?
Vengeance is Mine, and recompense;
    their foot will slip in due time;
for the day of their calamity is at hand,
    and the things to come hasten upon them.

For the LORD will judge His people,
    and relent in regard to His servants,
when He sees that their power is gone
    and there is no one left, whether restrained or free.
He will say: Where are their gods,
    their rock in whom they trusted,
which ate the fat of their sacrifices
    and drank the wine of their drink offerings?
Let them rise up and help you
    and be your protection.

See now that I, even I, am He,
    and there is no god besides Me;
I kill, and I make alive;
    I wound, and I heal;
    there is no one who can deliver out of My hand.
For I lift up My hand to heaven,
    and say: As I live forever,
if I sharpen My flashing sword
    and My hand takes hold on judgment,
I will render vengeance on My enemies
    and will repay those who hate Me.
I will make My arrows drunk with blood,
    and My sword shall devour flesh,
with the blood of the slain and of the captives,
    from the heads of the leaders of the enemies.

Rejoice, O you nations, with His people;
    for He will avenge the blood of His servants
and will render vengeance on His adversaries
    and will be merciful to His land and people.

Moses came and spoke all the words of this song in the hearing of the
people, he, with Joshua, the son of Nun. When Moses finished speaking all
these words to all Israel, he said to them, "Set your hearts on all the words
which I testify among you today, which you shall command your children

to be careful to observe, all the words of this law. For it is no idle word for you, because it is your life, and by this word you will prolong your days in the land which you cross over the Jordan to possess."

The LORD spoke to Moses that same day, saying, "Go up to this mountain of the Abarim, to Mount Nebo, which is in the land of Moab opposite Jericho, and look at the land of Canaan, which I am giving to the children of Israel for a possession. Die on the mount where you go up, and be gathered to your people, just as Aaron, your brother, died on Mount Hor and was gathered to his people, because you trespassed against Me among the children of Israel at the waters of Meribah Kadesh, in the Wilderness of Zin, because you did not treat Me as holy in the midst of the children of Israel. Nevertheless, you will see the land before you, but you may not go there, to the land which I am giving to the children of Israel."

Vezot Haberakhah

And this the blessing

(Deuteronomy 33:1–34:12)

Now this is the blessing with which Moses, the man of God, blessed the children of Israel before his death. He said:

The LORD came from Sinai and rose up from Seir to them;
   He shone forth from Mount Paran,
and He came with ten thousands of holy ones;
   from His right hand went a fiery law for them.
Surely, He loved the people;
   all His holy ones are in Your hand,
and they sit down at Your feet;
   everyone receives Your words.
Moses decreed to us a law,
   the inheritance of the assembly of Jacob.
He was king over Jeshurun,
   when the heads of the people and the tribes of Israel were gathered
      together.

Let Reuben live, and not die,
   and let not his men be few.

This is the blessing to Judah. He said:

Listen, O LORD, to the voice of Judah,
   and bring him to his people;
may his hands contend for them,
   and may You help him against his enemies.

Of Levi he said:

Let Your Thummim and Your Urim be with Your godly one,
whom You tested at Massah,
   and with whom You contended at the waters of Meribah,

who said to his father and to his mother,
   "I have not seen him,"
and he did not acknowledge his brothers
   or know his own children,
for they have kept Your word
   and guarded Your covenant.
They will teach Jacob Your judgments
   and Israel Your law.
They will put incense before You
   and the whole burnt offerings on your altar.
Bless, O Lord, his substance,
   and accept the work of his hands;
run through the loins of them that rise against him
   and of them that hate him,
     so that they rise never again.

Of Benjamin he said:

The beloved of the Lord
   will dwell in safety by Him,
and the Lord will protect him all day long;
   he will dwell between His shoulders.

Of Joseph he said:

May his land be blessed of the Lord,
   from the harvest of the heavens,
   by the dew,
   and by the deep crouching beneath,
by the precious fruits brought forth by the sun,
   and by the choice things put forth by the moon,
by the finest things of the ancient mountains,
   and by the choice things of the everlasting hills,
by the best things of the earth and its fullness,
   and by the goodwill of Him who dwelt in the bush.
May the blessing rest on the head of Joseph,
   on top of the head of him who was separated from his brothers.
His glory is like the firstborn of his bull,
   and his horns are like the horns of a wild ox;
with them he will push the peoples together to the ends of the
   earth;
they are the ten thousands of Ephraim,
   and they are the thousands of Manasseh.

Of Zebulun he said:

Rejoice, Zebulun, in your going outside,
    and Issachar in your tents.
They will call the peoples to the mountain;
    there they will offer sacrifices of righteousness,
for they will draw out the abundance of the seas
    and the treasures hid in the sand.

Of Gad he said:

Blessed be he who enlarges Gad;
    he dwells as a lion
    and tears an arm and the crown of a head.
He provided the first part for himself,
    because there, in a portion of the ruler, he was
        seated.
He came with the heads of the people.
    He executed the justice of the LORD,
    and His ordinances with Israel.

Of Dan he said:

Dan is a lion's whelp;
    he will leap forth from Bashan.

Of Naphtali he said:

O Naphtali, satisfied with favor
    and full with the blessing of the LORD,
    possess the west and the south.

Of Asher he said:

May Asher be blessed with children;
    may he be acceptable to his brothers,
    and may he dip his foot in oil.
Your sandals will be iron and brass;
    according to your days, so shall be your strength.

There is none like the God of Jeshurun,
    who rides through the heavens to help you,
    and in His majesty through the skies.

The eternal God is your refuge,
  and underneath you are the everlasting arms;
He will drive out the enemy before you,
  and will say, "Destroy them."
Israel dwells in safety;
  the fountain of Jacob will be secluded
in a land of grain and new wine;
  its heavens will rain down dew.
Blessed are you, O Israel!
  Who is like you,
  a people saved by the LORD,
the shield of your help,
  who is the sword of your majesty!
Your enemies will cringe before you,
  and you will tread upon their high places.

Moses went up from the plains of Moab to Mount Nebo, to the top of Pisgah, which is opposite Jericho. Then the LORD showed him all the land—from Gilead to Dan, and all Naphtali and the land of Ephraim and Manasseh, and all the land of Judah, to the *Mediterranean* Sea, and the Negev and the plain of the valley of Jericho, the city of palm trees, as far as Zoar. The LORD said to him, "This is the land which I swore to Abraham, to Isaac, and to Jacob, saying, 'I will give it to your descendants.' I have caused you to see it with your eyes, but you will not cross over there."

So Moses, the servant of the LORD, died there in the land of Moab, according to the word of the LORD. He buried him in a valley in the land of Moab, opposite Beth Peor, but no man knows of his burial place to this day. Moses was one hundred twenty years old when he died. His eye was not dim, nor was his vitality diminished. The children of Israel wept for Moses in the plains of Moab thirty days. Then the days of weeping and mourning for Moses were ended.

Now Joshua, the son of Nun, was full of the spirit of wisdom, for Moses had laid his hands on him. And the children of Israel listened to him and did as the LORD commanded Moses.

Since then there has not arisen a prophet in Israel like Moses, whom the LORD knew face to face, in all the signs and wonders which the LORD sent him to do in the land of Egypt, to Pharaoh, to all his servants, and to all his land, and by all that mighty power and by all the great terror which Moses displayed in the sight of all Israel.

Pesach

Passover

(Exodus 12:21–51; Numbers 28:16–25)

Then Moses called for all the elders of Israel and said to them, "Draw out and take for yourselves a lamb according to your families and kill the Passover *lamb*. You shall take a bunch of hyssop, and dip it in the blood that is in the basin, and apply the lintel and the two side posts with the blood that is in the basin, and none of you shall go out from the door of his house until the morning. For the LORD will pass through to kill the Egyptians. And when He sees the blood upon the lintel and on the two side posts, the LORD will pass over the door and will not permit the destroyer to come to your houses to kill *you*.

"And you shall observe this thing as an ordinance to you and to your sons forever. When you enter the land which the LORD will give you, according as He has promised, that you shall observe this service. And when your children shall say to you, 'What does this service mean to you?' that you shall say, 'It is the sacrifice of the LORD's Passover, who passed over the houses of the children of Israel in Egypt, when He smote the Egyptians, and delivered our households.'" And the people bowed down and worshipped. Then the children of Israel went and did *so*. Just as the LORD had commanded Moses and Aaron, so they did.

At midnight the LORD smote all the firstborn in the land of Egypt, from the firstborn of Pharaoh that sat on his throne to the firstborn of the captive who was in the dungeon and all the firstborn of livestock. Pharaoh rose up in the night, he and all his servants and all the Egyptians, and there was a great cry in Egypt, for there was not a house where there was not someone dead.

Then he called for Moses and Aaron at night and said, "Rise up, and get out from among my people, both you and the children of Israel, and go, serve the LORD, as you have said. Also take your flocks and your herds, as you have said, and be gone, and bless me also."

The Egyptians urged the people, so that they might send them out of the land in haste, for they said, "We all will be dead." So the people took their dough before it was leavened, *with* their kneading troughs being bound up in their clothes on their shoulders. Now the children of Israel did according to the word of Moses, and they requested of the Egyptians articles of silver and articles of gold, and clothing. And the LORD gave the people favor in the sight of the Egyptians, so that they gave them *what they requested*. Thus they plundered the Egyptians.

Then the children of Israel journeyed from Rameses to Sukkoth, about six hundred thousand men on foot, besides children. A mixed multitude also went up with them along with flocks and herds, a large amount of livestock. They baked unleavened cakes of the dough which they brought forth out of Egypt, for it was not leavened because they were driven out of Egypt and could not linger, nor had they prepared for themselves any food.

Now the sojourning of the children of Israel who lived in Egypt was four hundred thirty years. And at the end of the four hundred thirty years, on the very day, all the hosts of the LORD went out from the land of Egypt. It is a night to be observed to the LORD for bringing them out from the land of Egypt. This is that night for the LORD to be observed by all the children of Israel in their generations.

So the LORD said to Moses and Aaron: This is the ordinance of the Passover:

No foreigner may eat of it. But every man's servant bought with money, when you have circumcised him, may eat it. A foreigner or a hired servant shall not eat it.

In one house shall it be eaten. You shall not carry any of the flesh outside of the house, nor shall you break a bone of it. All the congregation of Israel shall keep it.

Now when a stranger sojourns with you and keeps the Passover to the LORD, let all his males be circumcised, and then let him come near and keep it. And he shall be as one that is born in the land. However, no uncircumcised person shall eat of it. The same law shall apply to him that is a native and to the stranger who sojourns among you.

So all the children of Israel did it. They did just as the LORD commanded Moses and Aaron. And that same day the LORD brought the children of Israel out of the land of Egypt by their hosts.

* * *

On the fourteenth day of the first month is the Passover of the LORD. On the fifteenth day of this month is the feast. Unleavened bread will be eaten for seven days. On the first day there will be a holy convocation. You will not do any ordinary work, but you will offer a sacrifice made by fire as a burnt offering to the LORD: two young bulls, and one ram, and seven lambs in their first year. Be sure they are without blemish. And their grain offering will be of flour mixed with oil. Three-tenths of an ephah you will offer for a bull, and two-tenths of an ephah for a ram. One-tenth of an ephah you will offer for each of the seven lambs, and one goat as a sin offering, to make an atonement for you. You will offer these in addition to the burnt offering in the morning, which is for a regular burnt offering. The same way you will offer daily, throughout the seven days, the food of the sacrifice made by fire, as a pleasing aroma to the LORD. It will be offered in addition to the regular burnt offering and its drink offering. And on the seventh day you will have a holy assembly. You will not do any ordinary work.

Shavuot

Weeks

(Deuteronomy 14:22–16:17; Numbers 28:26–31)

Y ou must be certain to tithe all the produce of your seed, so that the field produces year by year. You must eat before the LORD your God, in the place in which He shall choose to place His name, the tithe of your grain, of your wine, of your oil, and of the firstborn of your herds and of your flocks so that you may learn to always fear the LORD your God. If the distance is too long for you, so that you are not able to carry it, because the place is too far from you, where the LORD your God shall choose to set His name, when the LORD your God blesses you, then you shall exchange it for money and bind up the money in your hand and go to the place which the LORD your God shall choose. Then you may spend that money for whatever your heart desires, for oxen, or for sheep, or for wine, or for strong drink, or for whatever your heart desires, and you may eat there before the LORD your God, and you shall rejoice, you, and your household, and the Levite that is within your gates. You must not forsake him, for he has no portion or inheritance with you.

At the end of three years you must bring forth all the tithe of your produce the same year and lay it up within your gates. Then the Levite (because he has no portion or inheritance with you), the foreigner, the fatherless, and the widow, who are within your gates, shall come and shall eat and be satisfied, so that the LORD your God may bless you in all the work of your hand which you do.

At the end of every seven years you shall grant a relinquishing *of debts*. This is the manner of the relinquishing: Every creditor that has loaned anything to his neighbor shall relinquish it. He shall not exact it of his neighbor, or of his brother, because it is called the LORD's relinquishment. You may collect it from a foreigner, but that which your brother has that is yours your hand shall release. However, there will be no poor among you, for the LORD will greatly bless you in the land which the LORD your God has given you for an inheritance to possess, if only you carefully obey the voice of the LORD your God, by carefully observing all these commandments which I command you today. For the LORD your God will bless you, just as He promised you, and you will lend to many nations, but you shall not borrow. You will reign over many nations, but they will not reign over you.

If there be among you a poor man, one of your brothers within any of your gates in your land which the LORD your God has given you, you must not harden your heart or shut your hand from your poor brother. But you shall open your hand wide to him and must surely lend him what is sufficient for his need, in that which he lacks. Beware lest there be a wicked thought in your heart, saying, "The seventh year, the year of release, is at hand," and your eye be evil against your poor brother and you give him nothing, and he cry out to the LORD against you, and it become sin in you. You must surely give to him, and your heart shall not be grieved when you give to him, because in this thing the LORD your God will bless you in all your works, and in all that you put your hand to do. For the poor will never cease from being in the land. Therefore, I command you, saying, "You shall open your hand wide to your brother, to your poor and needy in your land."

If your brother, a Hebrew man, or a Hebrew woman, is sold to you and serves you six years, then in the seventh year you must let him go free from you. When you send him out free from you, you must not let him go away empty-handed. You shall supply him liberally out of your flock, out of your floor, and out of your winepress. From that with which the LORD your God has blessed you, you shall give to him. You shall remember that you were a slave in the land of Egypt and the LORD your God redeemed you. Therefore, I command this to you today.

It shall be, if he says to you, "I will not go away from you," because he loves you and your house, because he is well off with you, then you must take an awl and pierce it through his ear into the door, and he shall be your servant forever. And you shall also do likewise to your female servant.

It will not seem difficult for you when you send him away free from you, for he has been worth a double hired servant in serving you six years. Then the LORD your God will bless you in all that you do.

You must sanctify all the firstborn males that come out of your herd and flock to the LORD your God. You must do no work with the firstborn of your bulls or shear the firstborn of your sheep. You shall eat it before the LORD your God year by year in the place where the LORD shall choose, you and your household. If there is any defect in it, if it is lame or blind or has a serious defect, you shall not sacrifice it to the LORD your God. You shall eat it within your gates. The unclean and the clean person alike shall eat it, as if it were a gazelle or a deer. Only you must not eat its blood. You shall pour it on the ground like water.

Observe the month of Aviv and keep the Passover to the LORD your God, for in the month of Aviv the LORD your God brought you out of Egypt by night. Therefore, you must sacrifice the Passover to the LORD your God, from the flock or the herd, in the place where the LORD shall choose to place His name. You must not eat leavened bread with it. For seven days you must eat unleavened bread, the bread of affliction, for you came out of the land of Egypt in a hurry, so that you may remember all the days of your life the day when you came out of the land of Egypt. There must not be any leavened bread seen with you within all your borders for seven days, nor may any of the meat which you sacrificed in the evening on the first day remain overnight until morning.

You may not sacrifice the Passover within any of your gates that the LORD your God has given you. But at the place where the LORD your God chooses to place His name, there you shall sacrifice the Passover in the evening at sunset, at the time that you came out of Egypt. You shall roast and eat it in the place where the LORD your God will choose, and you must return in the morning, and go to your tents. For six days you must eat unleavened bread, and on the seventh day there shall be a solemn assembly to the LORD your God. You must do no work *on that day*.

You must count seven weeks for yourself. Begin counting the seven weeks from the time you begin to put the sickle to the standing grain. You must keep the Feast of Weeks to the LORD your God with a tribute of a free-will offering from your hand, which you must give to the LORD your God, in proportion to how much the LORD your God has blessed you. You shall rejoice before the LORD your God—you, your son, your daughter, your male servant, your female servant, the Levite who is within your gates, the foreigner, the orphan, and the widow who are among you—in the place where the LORD your God has chosen to place His name. You must remember that you were a slave in Egypt, and you must be careful to observe these statutes.

You shall observe the Feast of Tabernacles seven days after you have gathered in your threshing floor and your winepress, and you shall rejoice in your feast, you, your son, your daughter, your male servant, your female servant, the Levite, the foreigner, the orphan, and the widow who are within your gates. You are to celebrate the festival for seven days to the LORD your God in the place where the LORD will choose, because the LORD your God will bless you in all your produce, and in all the works of your hands. Therefore, you will indeed rejoice.

Three times a year all your males must appear before the LORD your God in the place where He will choose: at the Feast of Unleavened Bread, at the Feast of Weeks, and at the Feast of Tabernacles, and they must not appear before the LORD empty. E very man must give as he is able, in proportion to the blessing of the LORD your God, which He has given you.

* * *

And on the day of the first fruits, when you bring a new grain offering to the LORD at your Feast of Weeks, you will have a holy assembly. You will do no ordinary work. But you will offer the burnt offering as a pleasing aroma to the LORD: two young bulls, one ram, and seven lambs in their first year; and their grain offering of flour mixed with oil, three-tenths of an ephah for one bull, two-tenths of an ephah for one ram, one-tenth of an ephah for each of the seven lambs; and one goat, to make an atonement for you. Make sure they are without blemish. You will offer them with their drink offerings, besides the regular burnt offering and its grain offering.

Rosh Hashanah

New Year

(Genesis 22:1–19; Deuteronomy 29:10–15)

After these things God tested Abraham and said to him, "Abraham!" And he said, "Here I am."

Then He said, "Take your son, your only son Isaac, whom you love, and go to the land of Moriah, and offer him there as a burnt offering on one of the mountains of which I will tell you."

So Abraham rose up early in the morning and saddled his donkey, and took two of his young men with him and Isaac his son; and he split the wood for the burnt offering, and arose and went to the place that God had told him. Then on the third day Abraham lifted up his eyes and saw the place from a distance. Abraham said to his young men, "Stay here with the donkey. The boy and I will go over there and worship and then return to you."

So Abraham took the wood of the burnt offering and laid it on Isaac his son; and he took the fire in his hand and the knife. So the two of them walked on together. But Isaac spoke to Abraham his father and said, "My father!"

And he said, "Here I am, my son."

Then he said, "Here is the fire and the wood, but where is the lamb for the burnt offering?"

Abraham said, "My son, God will provide for Himself the lamb for a burnt offering." So the two of them went together.

Then they came to the place that God had told him. So Abraham built an altar there and arranged the wood; and he bound Isaac his son and laid him on the altar, on the wood. Then Abraham stretched out his hand and took the knife to slay his son. But the angel of the LORD called to him out of heaven and said, "Abraham, Abraham!"

And he said, "Here I am."

Then He said, "Do not lay your hands on the boy or do anything to him, because now I know that you fear God, seeing you have not withheld your only son from Me."

Then Abraham lifted up his eyes and looked, and behind him was a ram caught in a thicket by his horns. So Abraham went and took the ram and offered him up as a burnt offering in the place of his son. Abraham called the name of that place The LORD Will Provide, as it is said to this day, "In the mount of the LORD it will be provided."

Then the angel of the LORD called to Abraham out of heaven a second time, and said, "By Myself I have sworn, says the LORD, because you have done this thing, and have not withheld your son, your only son, I will indeed bless you and I will indeed multiply your descendants as the stars of the heavens and as the sand that is on the seashore. Your descendants will possess the gate of their enemies. Through your offspring all the nations of the earth will be blessed, because you have obeyed My voice."

So Abraham returned to his young men, and they arose and went together to Beersheba. Then Abraham lived at Beersheba.

*   *   *

Today all of you stand before the LORD your God, the heads of your tribes, your elders, and your officers, with all the men of Israel, your little ones, your wives, and your foreigners who are in your camp, from the one who chops your wood to the one who draws your water— so that you should enter into a covenant with the LORD your God, and into His oath, which the LORD your God is making with you today. Today He will establish that you are His people and that He is your God, just as He has said to you and He has sworn to your fathers, to Abraham, to Isaac, and to Jacob. It is not with you alone that I am making this covenant and this oath, but with him who stands here with us today before the LORD our God, and with him who is not here with us today.

Yom Kippur

Day of Atonement

(Leviticus 16:1–34; Numbers 29:7–11)

The Lord spoke to Moses after the death of the two sons of Aaron, when they drew near to the Lord and died. The Lord said to Moses: Speak to Aaron your brother so that he does not come at any time into the Holy Place within the veil before the mercy seat, which is on the ark, so that he will not die, for I will appear in the cloud on the mercy seat.

Thus Aaron shall come into the Holy Place with a young bull for a sin offering and a ram for a burnt offering. He shall put on the holy linen tunic, and he shall have the linen undergarment on his body, and shall be girded with a linen sash, and shall be wearing the linen turban. These are holy garments. Therefore he shall wash his body in water and then put them on. He shall take from the congregation of the children of Israel two male goats for a sin offering and one ram for a burnt offering.

Aaron shall offer his bull for the sin offering, which is for himself, and make atonement for himself and for his house. Then he shall take the two goats and present them before the Lord at the entrance of the tent of meeting. Aaron shall cast lots for the two goats: one lot for the Lord and the other lot for the scapegoat. Aaron shall bring the goat on which the lot of the Lord falls and offer him for a sin offering. But the goat on which the lot falls to be the scapegoat shall be presented alive before the Lord to make atonement with it, that it may be sent away as a scapegoat into the wilderness.

Aaron shall bring the bull of the sin offering, which is for himself, and shall make atonement for himself, and for his house, and shall kill the bull of the sin offering for himself. And he shall take a censer full of burning coals of fire from the altar before the Lord, and two handfuls of sweet incense beaten small, and bring it within the veil. And he shall put the incense on the fire before the Lord, that the cloud of the incense may cover the mercy seat that is over the testimony, so that he does not die. And he shall take of the blood of the bull, and sprinkle it with his finger on the mercy seat on the eastern side, and before the mercy seat he shall sprinkle from the blood with his finger seven times.

Then he shall kill the goat of the sin offering, which is for the people, and bring its blood within the veil, and do with that blood as he did with the blood of the bull, and sprinkle it over and in front of the mercy seat. And he shall make atonement for the Holy Place, because of the uncleanness of the children of Israel and because of their transgressions in all their sins, and so he shall do for the tent of meeting that remains among them in the midst of their uncleanness. There shall be no man in the tent of meeting when he goes in to make atonement in the Holy Place, until he comes out and has made atonement for himself, and for his household, and for all the congregation of Israel.

Then he shall go out to the altar that is before the LORD and make atonement for it, and he shall take some of the blood of the bull and some of the blood of the goat, and put it on the horns of the altar all around. He shall sprinkle from the blood on it with his finger seven times, and cleanse it, and consecrate it from the uncleanness of the children of Israel.

When he has made an end of atonement for the Holy Place, and the tent of meeting, and the altar, then he shall bring the live goat. And Aaron shall lay both his hands on the head of the live goat, and confess over it all the iniquities of the children of Israel, and all their transgressions in all their sins, putting them on the head of the goat, and shall send it away by the hand of a designated man into the wilderness. And the goat shall bear on it all their iniquities to a desolate land, and he shall let the goat go free in the wilderness.

Then Aaron shall come into the tent of meeting, and shall take off the linen garments which he put on when he went into the Holy Place, and shall leave them there. And he shall wash his body with water in a holy place, and put on his garments, and come out, and offer his burnt offering, and the burnt offering of the people, and make atonement for himself and for the people. The fat of the sin offering he shall burn on the altar.

He who releases the goat as the scapegoat shall wash his clothes, and bathe his body in water, and afterward come into the camp. The bull for the sin offering and the goat for the sin offering, whose blood was brought in to make atonement in the Holy Place, shall be carried outside the camp. They shall burn in the fire their hides, their flesh, and their refuse. He who burns them shall wash his clothes, and bathe his body in water, and afterward he shall come into the camp.

This shall be a perpetual statute for you so that in the seventh month, on the tenth day of the month, you shall humble yourselves, and do no work of any kind, whether it is the native citizen or the stranger who sojourns among you. For on that day the priest shall make atonement for you to cleanse you, so that you may be clean from all your sins before the LORD. It shall be a sabbath, a solemn rest for you, and you shall humble yourselves. It is a perpetual statute. The priest, who is anointed and consecrated to minister as a priest in the place of his father, shall make atonement, and shall put on the linen garments, the holy garments. And he shall make atonement for the Holy Sanctuary, for the tent of meeting, and for the altar, and he shall make atonement for the priests, and for all the people of the congregation.

This shall be a perpetual statute for you to make atonement for the children of Israel for all their sins once a year.

And Moses did as the LORD commanded him.

*   *   *

You will have a holy assembly on the tenth day of this seventh month, and you will afflict yourselves. You will not do any work on it. But you will offer a burnt offering to the LORD as a pleasing aroma: one young bull, one ram, and seven lambs in their first year. Be sure they are without blemish. Their grain offering will be of flour mixed with oil, three-tenths of an ephah for the bull, and two-tenths of an ephah for one ram, and one-tenth of an ephah for each of the seven lambs; also one goat as a sin offering in addition to the sin offering of atonement, and the regular burnt offering, and its grain offering, and their drink offerings.

Sukkot

Booths

(Leviticus 22:26–23:44; Numbers 29:12–16)

The Lord spoke to Moses, saying: When an ox, or a sheep, or a goat is born, then it shall be seven days with its mother, and from the eighth day and thereafter it shall be accepted for a food offering made by fire to the Lord. But you shall not slaughter on the same day an ox or a sheep and her young.

When you offer a sacrifice of thanksgiving to the Lord, offer it so that it may be accepted. On the same day it shall be eaten. You shall leave none of it until the next day: I am the Lord.

Therefore you shall keep My commandments and do them: I am the Lord. You shall not defile My holy name, but I will be sanctified among the children of Israel: I am the Lord who sanctifies you, who brought you out of the land of Egypt, to be your God: I am the Lord.

And the Lord spoke to Moses, saying: Speak to the children of Israel, and say to them: Concerning the feasts of the Lord that you shall proclaim to be holy convocations, these are My appointed feasts.

For six days work shall be done, but the seventh day is the Sabbath of complete rest, a holy convocation. You shall do no work. It is the Sabbath of the Lord in all your dwellings.

These are the appointed feasts of the Lord, holy convocations which you shall proclaim in their appointed times. On the fourteenth day of the first month at evening is the Lord's Passover. On the fifteenth day of the same month is the Feast of Unleavened Bread to the Lord. For seven days you must eat unleavened bread. On the first day you shall have a holy convocation. You shall do no regular work. But you shall offer a food offering made by fire to the Lord for seven days. On the seventh day is a holy convocation. You shall do no regular work.

The Lord spoke to Moses, saying: Speak to the children of Israel, and say to them: When you have come into the land that I am giving to you and reap its harvest, then you shall bring a sheaf bundle of the first fruits of your harvest to the priest. And he shall wave the sheaf before the Lord so that you may be accepted. On the day after the Sabbath the priest shall wave it. You shall offer that day when you wave the sheaf a year-old male lamb without blemish for a burnt offering to the Lord. The grain offering shall be two-tenths of an ephah of wheat flour mixed with oil, a food offering made by fire to the Lord for a pleasing aroma; its drink offering shall be of wine, one-fourth of a hin. You shall eat neither bread nor grain, parched or fresh, until the same day that you have brought an offering to your God. It shall be a perpetual statute throughout your generations in all your dwellings.

You shall count seven full weeks from the next day after the Sabbath, from the day that you brought the sheaf bundle of the wave offering. You shall count fifty days to the day after the seventh Sabbath; then you shall offer a new grain offering to the Lord. You shall bring out of your habitations two wave loaves of two-tenths of an ephah. They shall be of wheat flour, baked with leaven. They are the first fruits to the Lord. You shall offer with the bread seven lambs without blemish of the first year, one bull, and two rams. They shall be for a burnt offering to the Lord, with their grain offering and their drink offerings, that is, a food offering made by fire, of a pleasing aroma to the Lord. Then you shall sacrifice one male goat for a sin offering, and two lambs of the first year for a sacrifice of peace offerings. The priest shall wave them with the bread of the first fruits for a wave offering before the Lord with the two lambs. They shall be holy to the Lord for the priest. You shall make a proclamation on the same day and shall hold a holy convocation. You shall do no regular work. It shall be a perpetual statute in all your dwellings throughout your generations.

When you reap the harvest of your land, you shall not reap your field up to the edge, nor shall you gather any gleaning of your harvest. You shall leave them to the poor and to the foreigner: I am the Lord your God.

The Lord spoke to Moses, saying: Speak to the children of Israel, saying: In the seventh month, on the first day of the month, you shall have a sabbath, a memorial with the blowing of trumpets, a holy convocation. You shall do no regular work, and you shall offer a food offering made by fire to the Lord.

The Lord spoke to Moses, saying: Also on the tenth day of this seventh month there shall be the Day of Atonement. It shall be a holy convocation to you, and you shall humble yourselves, and offer a food offering made by fire to the Lord. You shall do no work on that same day, for it is the Day of Atonement to make atonement for you before the Lord your God. For whoever is not humbled on that same day, he shall be cut off from among his people. And whoever does any work in that same day, that person I will destroy from among his people. You shall do no manner of work. It shall be a perpetual statute throughout your generations in all your dwellings. It shall be to you a sabbath of complete rest, and you shall afflict your souls. On the ninth day of the month starting at the evening, from evening to evening, you shall celebrate your sabbath.

The Lord spoke to Moses, saying: Speak to the children of Israel, saying: The fifteenth day of this seventh month shall be the Feast of Tabernacles for seven days to the LORD. On the first day shall be a holy convocation. You shall do no regular work. For seven days you shall offer food offerings made by fire to the LORD. On the eighth day it shall be a holy convocation to you, and you shall offer a food offering made by fire to the LORD. It is a solemn assembly, and you shall do no regular work.

These are the appointed feasts of the LORD, which you shall proclaim to be holy convocations, to offer a food offering made by fire to the LORD, burnt offerings and grain offerings, sacrifices and drink offerings, each on its proper day, besides the Sabbaths of the LORD, besides your gifts, besides all your vows, and besides all your freewill offerings which you give to the LORD.

On the fifteenth day of the seventh month, when you have gathered in the produce of the land, you shall keep a feast to the LORD for seven days. On the first day shall be a sabbath, and on the eighth day shall be a sabbath. You shall take on the first day the branches of majestic trees—branches of palm trees, branches of leafy trees, and willows from a brook, and you shall rejoice before the LORD your God for seven days. You shall keep it as a feast to the LORD for seven days in the year. It shall be a perpetual statute in your generations. You shall celebrate it in the seventh month. You shall dwell in booths for seven days. All who are native children of Israel shall dwell in booths, that your generations may know that I made the children of Israel dwell in booths when I brought them out of the land of Egypt: I am the LORD your God.

Moses declared to the children of Israel the feasts of the LORD.

*   *   *

On the fifteenth day of the seventh month you will have a holy convocation. You will do no ordinary work, and you will keep a feast to the LORD seven days. And you will offer a burnt offering, a sacrifice made by fire, as a pleasing aroma to the LORD: thirteen young bulls, two rams, and fourteen lambs in their first year, without blemish. And their grain offering will be of flour mixed with oil, three-tenths of an ephah to a bull, and two-tenths of an ephah to each ram of the two rams, and one-tenth to each lamb of the fourteen lambs; and one goat as a sin offering in addition to the regular burnt offering, its grain offering, and its drink offering.

Shmini Atzeret
Eighth day of Assembly
(Deuteronomy 14:22–16:17)

You must be certain to tithe all the produce of your seed, so that the field produces year by year. You must eat before the LORD your God, in the place in which He shall choose to place His name, the tithe of your grain, of your wine, of your oil, and of the firstborn of your herds and of your flocks so that you may learn to always fear the LORD your God. If the distance is too long for you, so that you are not able to carry it, because the place is too far from you, where the LORD your God shall choose to set His name, when the LORD your God blesses you, then you shall exchange it for money and bind up the money in your hand and go to the place which the LORD your God shall choose. Then you may spend that money for whatever your heart desires, for oxen, or for sheep, or for wine, or for strong drink, or for whatever your heart desires, and you may eat there before the LORD your God, and you shall rejoice, you, and your household, and the Levite that is within your gates. You must not forsake him, for he has no portion or inheritance with you.

At the end of three years you must bring forth all the tithe of your produce the same year and lay it up within your gates. Then the Levite (because he has no portion or inheritance with you), the foreigner, the fatherless, and the widow, who are within your gates, shall come and shall eat and be satisfied, so that the LORD your God may bless you in all the work of your hand which you do.

At the end of every seven years you shall grant a relinquishing *of debts.* This is the manner of the relinquishing: Every creditor that has loaned anything to his neighbor shall relinquish it. He shall not exact it of his neighbor, or of his brother, because it is called the LORD's relinquishment. You may collect it from a foreigner, but that which your brother has that is yours your hand shall release. However, there will be no poor among you, for the LORD will greatly bless you in the land which the LORD your God has given you for an inheritance to possess, if only you carefully obey the voice of the LORD your God, by carefully observing all these commandments which I command you today. For the LORD your God will bless you, just as He promised you, and you will lend to many nations, but you shall not borrow. You will reign over many nations, but they will not reign over you.

If there be among you a poor man, one of your brothers within any of your gates in your land which the LORD your God has given you, you must not harden your heart or shut your hand from your poor brother. But you shall open your hand wide to him and must surely lend him what is sufficient for his need, in that which he lacks. Beware lest there be a wicked thought in your heart, saying, "The seventh year, the year of release, is at hand," and your eye be evil against your poor brother and you give him nothing, and he cry out to the LORD against you, and it become sin in you. You must surely give to him, and your heart shall not be grieved when you give to him, because in this thing the LORD your God will bless you in all your works, and in all that you put your hand to do. For the poor will never cease from being in the land. Therefore, I command you, saying, "You shall open your hand wide to your brother, to your poor and needy in your land."

If your brother, a Hebrew man, or a Hebrew woman, is sold to you and serves you six years, then in the seventh year you must let him go free from you. When you send him out free from you, you must not let him go away empty-handed. You shall supply him liberally out of your flock, out of your floor, and out of your winepress. From that with which the LORD your God has blessed you, you shall give to him. You shall remember that you were a slave in the land of Egypt and the LORD your God redeemed you. Therefore, I command this to you today.

It shall be, if he says to you, "I will not go away from you," because he loves you and your house, because he is well off with you, then you must take an awl and pierce it through his ear into the door, and he shall be your servant forever. And you shall also do likewise to your female servant.

It will not seem difficult for you when you send him away free from you, for he has been worth a double hired servant in serving you six years. Then the LORD your God will bless you in all that you do.

You must sanctify all the firstborn males that come out of your herd and flock to the LORD your God. You must do no work with the firstborn of your bulls or shear the firstborn of your sheep. You shall eat it before the LORD your God year by year in the place where the LORD shall choose, you and your household. If there is any defect in it, if it is lame or blind or has a serious defect, you shall not sacrifice it to the LORD your God. You shall eat it within your gates. The unclean and the clean person alike shall eat it, as if it were a gazelle or a deer. Only you must not eat its blood. You shall pour it on the ground like water.

Observe the month of Aviv and keep the Passover to the LORD your God, for in the month of Aviv the LORD your God brought you out of Egypt by night. Therefore, you must sacrifice the Passover to the LORD your God, from the flock or the herd, in the place where the LORD shall choose to place His name. You must not eat leavened bread with it. For seven days you must eat unleavened bread, the bread of affliction, for you came out of the land of Egypt in a hurry, so that you may remember all the days of your life the day when you came out of the land of Egypt. There must not be any leavened bread seen with you within all your borders for seven days, nor may any of the meat which you sacrificed in the evening on the first day remain overnight until morning.

You may not sacrifice the Passover within any of your gates that the LORD your God has given you. But at the place where the LORD your God chooses to place His name, there you shall sacrifice the Passover in the evening at sunset, at the time that you came out of Egypt. You shall roast and eat it in the place where the LORD your God will choose, and you must return in the morning, and go to your tents. For six days you must eat unleavened bread, and on the seventh day there shall be a solemn assembly to the LORD your God. You must do no work *on that day*.

You must count seven weeks for yourself. Begin counting the seven weeks from the time you begin to put the sickle to the standing grain. You must keep the Feast of Weeks to the LORD your God with a tribute of a freewill offering from your hand, which you must give to the LORD your God, in proportion to how much the LORD your God has blessed you. You shall rejoice before the LORD your God—you, your son, your daughter, your male servant, your female servant, the Levite who is within your gates, the foreigner, the orphan, and the widow who are among you—in the place where the LORD your God has chosen to place His name. You must remember that you were a slave in Egypt, and you must be careful to observe these statutes.

You shall observe the Feast of Tabernacles seven days after you have gathered in your threshing floor and your winepress, and you shall rejoice in your feast, you, your son, your daughter, your male servant, your female servant, the Levite, the foreigner, the orphan, and the widow who are within your gates. You are to celebrate the festival for seven days to the LORD your God in the place where the LORD will choose, because the LORD your God will bless you in all your produce, and in all the works of your hands. Therefore, you will indeed rejoice.

Three times a year all your males must appear before the LORD your God in the place where He will choose: at the Feast of Unleavened Bread, at the Feast of Weeks, and at the Feast of Tabernacles, and they must not appear before the LORD empty. Every man must give as he is able, in proportion to the blessing of the LORD your God, which He has given you.

Appendix

2020 Parashas and Haftarahs

Date	Parasha (or Festival) Name	Translation	Torah Passage	Haftarah	Page Number
January 4	Vayigash	And he drew near	Gen. 44:18–47:27	Ezek. 37:15–28	68
January 11	Vayechi	And he lived	Gen. 47:28–50:26	1 Kings 2:1–12	74
January 18	Shemot	Names	Exod. 1:1–6:1	Isa. 27:6–28:13; 29:22–23	80
January 25	Vaera	Appeared	Exod. 6:2–9:35	Ezek. 28:25–29:21	87
February 1	Bo	Come!	Exod. 10:1–13:16	Jer. 46:13–28	94
February 8	Beshalach	When he sent out	Exod. 13:17–17:16	Judg. 4:4–5:31	100
February 15	Yitro	Jethro	Exod. 18:1–20:26	Isa. 6:1–7:6; 9:6–7	108
February 22	Mishpatim	Laws	Exod. 21:1–24:18	Jer. 34:8–22; 33:25–26	112
February 29	Terumah	Offering	Exod. 25:1–27:19	1 Kings 5:12–6:13	118
March 7	Tetzaveh	You shall command	Exod. 27:20–30:10	Ezek. 43:10–27	122
March 14	Ki Tisa	When you elevate	Exod. 30:11–34:35	1 Kings 18:1–39	127
March 21	Vayakhel-Pekudei	And he assembled/ Accountings	Exod. 35:1–38:20/ Exod. 38:21–40:38	1 Kings 7:40–50/1 Kings 7:51–8:21	134

Date	Parasha (or Festival) Name	Translation	Torah Passage	Haftarah	Page Number
March 28	Vayikra	And he called	Lev. 1:1–6:7	Isa. 43:21–44:23	143
April 4	Tzav	Command!	Lev. 6:8–8:36	Jer. 7:21–8:3; 9:23–24	149
April 11	Pesach	Passover	Exod. 12:21–51; Num. 28:16–25	Josh. 5:2–6:1	318
April 18	Shmini	Eighth	Lev. 9:1–11:47	2 Sam. 6:1–7:17	154
April 25	Tazria-Metzora	She bears seed/ Infected one	Lev. 12:1–13:59/Lev. 14:1–15:33	2 Kings 4:42–5:19/2 Kings 7:3–20	159
May 2	Achrei Mot-Kedoshim	After the death/Holy ones	Lev. 16:1–18:30/Lev. 19:1–20:27	Ezek. 22:1–19/ Amos 9:7–9:15	168
May 9	Emor	Say gently	Lev. 21:1–24:23	Ezek. 44:15–44:31	177
May 16	Behar-Bechukotai	On the Mountain/In My statutes	Lev. 25:1–26:2/Lev. 26:3–27:34	Jer. 32:6–27/Jer. 16:19–17:14	183
May 23	Bamidbar	In the wilderness	Num. 1:1–4:20	Hos. 1:10–2:20	190
May 30	Shavuot	Weeks	Deut. 14:22–16:17; Num. 28:26–31	Hab. 3:1–19	321
June 6	Nasso	Elevate!	Num. 4:21–7:89	Judg. 13:2–25	199
June 13	Beha'alotcha	In your uplifting	Num. 8:1–12:16	Zech. 2:14–4:7	208
June 20	Sh'lach	Send	Num. 13:1–15:41	Josh. 2:1–24	215
June 27	Korach	Korach	Num. 16:1–18:32	1 Sam. 11:14–12:22	221

Date	Parasha (or Festival) Name	Translation	Torah Passage	Haftarah	Page Number
July 4	Chukat-Balak	Law/Balak	Num. 19:1–22:1/ Num. 22:2–25:9	Judg. 11:1–33/ Mic. 5:7–6:8	226
July 11	Pinchas	Phinehas	Num. 25:10–29:40	1 Kings 18:46–19:21	239
July 18	Matot-Masei	Tribes/ Journeys of	Num. 30:1–32:42/ Num. 33:1–36:13	Jer. 1:1–2:3/Jer. 2:4–28; 3:4	248
July 25	Devarim	Words	Deut. 1:1–3:22	Isa. 1:1–27	259
August 1	Vaetchanan	Pleaded	Deut. 3:23–7:11	Isa. 40:1–26	265
August 8	Eikev	As a result	Deut. 7:12–11:25	Isa. 49:14–51:3	272
August 15	Re'eh	See!	Deut. 11:26–16:17	Isa. 54:11–55:5	278
August 22	Shoftim	Judges	Deut. 16:18–21:9	Isa. 51:12–52:12	285
August 29	Ki Teitzei	When you go out	Deut. 21:10–25:19	Isa. 54:1–10	291
September 5	Ki Tavo	When you enter in	Deut. 26:1–29:9	Isa. 60:1–22	297
September 12	Nitzavim-Vayeilech	Standing/And he went	Deut. 29:10–30:20/ Deut. 31:1–30	Isa. 61:10–63:9/Isa. 55:6–56:8	304
September 19	Rosh Hashanah	New Year	Gen. 22:1–19; Deut. 29:10–15	1 Sam. 1:1–2:10	324
September 26	Ha'Azinu	Listen!	Deut. 32:1–52	2 Sam. 22:1–51	309
October 3	Sukkot	Booths	Lev. 22:26–23:44; Num. 29:12–16	Zech. 14:1–21	329
October 10	Shmini Atzeret	Eighth day of Assembly	Deut. 14:22–16:17	1 Kings 8:54–66	332

Date	Parasha (or Festival) Name	Translation	Torah Passage	Haftarah	Page Number
October 11 (Simchat Torah)	Vezot Haberakhah	And this the blessing	Deut. 33:1–34:12	Josh. 1:1–18	314
October 17	Bereshit	In the beginning	Gen. 1:1–6:8	Isa. 42:5–43:11	1
October 24	Noach	Noah	Gen. 6:9–11:32	Isa. 54:1–55:5	9
October 31	Lech Lecha	Go forth, yourself!	Gen. 12:1–17:27	Isa. 40:27–41:16	16
November 7	Vayera	And he appeared	Gen. 18:1–22:24	2 Kings 4:1–37	22
November 14	Chayei Sara	Life of Sarah	Gen. 23:1–25:18	1 Kings 1:1–31	29
November 21	Toldot	Generations	Gen. 25:19–28:9	Mal. 1:1–2:7	34
November 28	Vayetzei	And he went out	Gen. 28:10–32:2	Hos. 12:12–14:9	40
December 5	Vayishlach	And he sent	Gen. 32:3–36:43	Hos. 11:7–12:11	47
December 12	Vayeshev	And he settled	Gen. 37:1–40:23	Amos 2:6–3:8	55
December 19	Miketz	At the end of	Gen. 41:1–44:17	1 Kings 3:15–4:1	61
December 26	Vayigash	And he drew near	Gen. 44:18–47:27	Ezek. 37:15–37:28	68

2021 Parashas and Haftarahs

Date	Parasha (or Festival) Name	Translation	Torah Passage	Haftarah	Page Number
January 2	Vayechi	And he lived	Gen. 47:28–50:26	1 Kings 2:1–12	74
January 9	Shemot	Names	Exod. 1:1–6:1	Isa. 27:6–28:13; 29:22–23	80
January 16	Vaera	Appeared	Exod. 6:2–9:35	Ezek. 28:25–29:21	87
January 23	Bo	Come!	Exod. 10:1–13:16	Jer. 46:13–28	94

Date	Parasha (or Festival) Name	Translation	Torah Passage	Haftarah	Page Number
January 30	Beshalach	When he sent out	Exod. 13:17–17:16	Judg. 4:4–5:31	100
February 6	Yitro	Jethro	Exod. 18:1–20:26	Isa. 6:1–7:6; 9:6–7	108
February 13	Mishpatim	Laws	Exod. 21:1–24:18	Jer. 34:8–22; 33:25–26	112
February 20	Terumah	Offering	Exod. 25:1–27:19	1 Kings 5:12–6:13	118
February 27	Tetzaveh	You shall command	Exod. 27:20–30:10	Ezek. 43:10–27	122
March 6	Ki Tisa	When you elevate	Exod. 30:11–34:35	1 Kings 18:1–39	127
March 13	Vayakhel-Pekudei	And he assembled/ Accountings	Exod. 35:1–38:20/ Exod. 38:21–40:38	1 Kings 7:40–50/1 Kings 7:51–8:21	134
March 20	Vayikra	And he called	Lev. 1:1–6:7	Isa. 43:21–44:23	143
March 27	Tzav	Command!	Lev. 6:8–8:36	Jer. 7:21–8:3; 9:23–24	149
April 3	Pesach	Passover	Exod. 12:21–51; Num. 28:16–25	Josh. 5:2–6:1	318
April 10	Shmini	Eighth	Lev. 9:1–11:47	2 Sam. 6:1–7:17	154
April 17	Tazria-Metzora	She bears seed/ Infected one	Lev. 12:1–13:59/Lev. 14:1–15:33	2 Kings 4:42–5:19/2 Kings 7:3–20	159
April 24	Achrei Mot-Kedoshim	After the death/Holy ones	Lev. 16:1–18:30/Lev. 19:1–20:27	Ezek. 22:1–19/ Amos 9:7–9:15	168
May 1	Emor	Say gently	Lev. 21:1–24:23	Ezek. 44:15–44:31	177
May 8	Behar-Bechukotai	On the Mountain/In My statutes	Lev. 25:1–26:2/Lev. 26:3–27:34	Jer. 32:6–27/Jer. 16:19–17:14	183

Date	Parasha (or Festival) Name	Translation	Torah Passage	Haftarah	Page Number
May 15	Bamidbar	In the wilderness	Num. 1:1–4:20	Hos. 1:10–2:20	190
May 22	Nasso	Elevate!	Num. 4:21–7:89	Judg. 13:2–25	199
May 29	Beha'alotcha	In your uplifting	Num. 8:1–12:16	Zech. 2:14–4:7	208
June 5	Sh'lach	Send	Num. 13:1–15:41	Josh. 2:1–24	215
June 12	Korach	Korach	Num. 16:1–18:32	1 Sam. 11:14–12:22	221
June 19	Chukat	Law	Num. 19:1–22:1	Judg. 11:1–33	226
June 26	Balak	Balak	Num. 22:2–25:9	Mic. 5:7–6:8	232
July 3	Pinchas	Phinehas	Num. 25:10–29:40	1 Kings 18:46–19:21	239
July 10	Matot-Masei	Tribes/ Journeys of	Num. 30:1– 32:42/ Num. 33:1–36:13	Jer. 1:1– 2:3/Jer. 2:4–28; 3:4	248
July 17	Devarim	Words	Deut. 1:1–3:22	Isa. 1:1–27	259
July 24	Vaetchanan	Pleaded	Deut. 3:23–7:11	Isa. 40:1–26	265
July 31	Eikev	As a result	Deut. 7:12–11:25	Isa. 49:14–51:3	272
August 7	Re'eh	See!	Deut. 11:26–16:17	Isa. 54:11–55:5	278
August 14	Shoftim	Judges	Deut. 16:18–21:9	Isa. 51:12–52:12	285
August 21	Ki Teitzei	When you go out	Deut. 21:10–25:19	Isa. 54:1–10	291
August 28	Ki Tavo	When you enter in	Deut. 26:1–29:9	Isa. 60:1–22	297
September 4	Nitzavim	Standing	Deut. 29:10–30:20	Isa. 61:10–63:9	304
September 11	Vayeilech	And he went	Deut. 31:1–30	Isa. 55:6–56:8	307

Date	Parasha (or Festival) Name	Translation	Torah Passage	Haftarah	Page Number
September 18	Ha'Azinu	Listen!	Deut. 32:1–52	2 Sam. 22:1–51	309
September 25	Sukkot	Booths	Lev. 22:26–23:44; Num. 29:12–16	Zech. 14:1–21	329
September 29 (Simchat Torah)	Vezot Haberakhah	And this the blessing	Deut. 33:1–34:12	Josh. 1:1–18	314
October 2	Bereshit	In the beginning	Gen. 1:1–6:8	Isa. 42:5–43:11	1
October 9	Noach	Noah	Gen. 6:9–11:32	Isa. 54:1–55:5	9
October 16	Lech Lecha	Go forth, yourself!	Gen. 12:1–17:27	Isa. 40:27–41:16	16
October 23	Vayera	And he appeared	Gen. 18:1–22:24	2 Kings 4:1–37	22
October 30	Chayei Sara	Life of Sarah	Gen. 23:1–25:18	1 Kings 1:1–31	29
November 6	Toldot	Generations	Gen. 25:19–28:9	Mal. 1:1–2:7	34
November 13	Vayetzei	And he went out	Gen. 28:10–32:2	Hos. 12:12–14:9	40
November 20	Vayishlach	And he sent	Gen. 32:3–36:43	Hos. 11:7–12:11	47
November 27	Vayeshev	And he settled	Gen. 37:1–40:23	Amos 2:6–3:8	55
December 4	Miketz	At the end of	Gen. 41:1–44:17	1 Kings 3:15–4:1	61
December 11	Vayigash	And he drew near	Gen. 44:18–47:27	Ezek. 37:15–37:28	68
December 18	Vayechi	And he lived	Gen. 47:28–50:26	1 Kings 2:1–12	74
December 25	Shemot	Names	Exod. 1:1–6:1	Isa. 27:6–28:13; 29:22–23	80

Selected Jewish Festival Sabbath Readings

Festival Name	Translation	Torah Passage	Haftarah	Page Number
Pesach	Passover	Exod. 12:21–51; Num. 28:16–25	Josh. 5:2–6:1	318
Shavuot	Weeks	Deut. 14:22–16:17; Num. 28:26–31	Hab. 3:1–19	321
Rosh Hashanah	New Year	Gen. 22:1–19; Deut. 29:10–15	1 Sam. 1:1–2:10	324
Yom Kippur	Day of Atonement	Lev.16:1–34; Num. 29:7–11	Isa. 57:14–58:14	326
Sukkot	Booths	Lev. 22:26–23:44; Num. 29:12–16	Zech. 14:1–21	329
Shmini Atzeret	Eighth day of Assembly	Deut. 14:22–16:17	1 Kings 8:54–66	332